THE UNCIVIL WAR

Campaigns and Commanders

THE UNCIVIL WAR

IRREGULAR WARFARE IN THE UPPER SOUTH, 1861–1865

Robert R. Mackey

UNIVERSITY OF OKLAHOMA PRESS

Parts of chapters 1 and 2 have been published previously as "Bushwhackers, Provosts, and Tories: The Guerrilla War in Arkansas" in *Guerrillas, Unionists, and Violence on the Confederate Homefront*, edited by Daniel E. Sutherland (Fayetteville, Ark.: University of Arkansas Press, 1999). Special thanks to the editorial staff of the University of Arkansas Press and Dr. Sutherland for permission to republish these sections.

This book is published with the generous assistance of the McCasland Foundation, Duncan, Oklahoma.

The Uncivil War: Irregular Warfare in the Upper South, 1861–1865 is Volume 5 in the Campaigns and Commanders series.

Library of Congress Cataloging-in-Publication Data

Mackey, Robert Russell.
   The uncivil war : irregular warfare in the upper South, 1861–1865   / Robert R. Mackey.
      p.   cm. — (Campaigns and commanders ; 5)
   Includes bibliographical references and index.
   ISBN 0-8061-3624-3 (alk. paper)
      1. United States—History—Civil War, 1861–1865—Underground movements. 2. United States—History—Civil War, 1861–1865—Campaigns. 3. Guerrillas—Southern States—History—19th century.
4. Guerrilla warfare—Southern States—History—19th century. 5. Raids (Military science)—History—19th century. 6. Ambushes and surprises—History—19th century. 7. Confederate States of America. Army—History.
8. United States. Army—History—Civil War, 1861–1865. 9. Counter-insurgency—United States—History—19th century. I. Title II. Series.

E470.45.M13 2004
973.7'3—dc22

                                                                    2004043541

   2   3   4   5   6   7   8   9   10

To the officers and men of the 108th Military Police Company (Air Assault), 503rd Military Police Battalion (Airborne), who served with honor and distinction during Operation Just Cause in Panama and Operation Desert Storm in Iraq, and to the soldiers of the Coalition Forces Land Component Command (CFLCC), especially Bo, Brian, and Paul in C3-IO section, and to Ron and Jerry at U.S. Central Command, Iraq, 2003. As long as such men and women defend the Republic, the sacrifices of the Civil War will not have been in vain.

CONTENTS

Illustrations

MAPS

ACKNOWLEDGMENTS

This work, like many that are published each year, is not the work of an individual but grew over time thanks to the guidance and assistance of others. In my case, that assistance literally covered the globe while I was deployed overseas for Operation Iraqi Freedom. I would first like to thank Dr. Joseph Dawson and Dr. Brian Linn, Texas A&M University, who mentored me and guided the development of this manuscript from a rough idea into a finished work. Without their support and assistance, I would have neither finished my doctorate nor published this work. They are scholars without peer whom I proudly call friends.

I would like to extend a special thanks to the staff and faculty at the Department of History, U.S. Military Academy. I have yet to meet officers as competent as the ones who play such a crucial role in the development of not only the cadets of West Point, but the junior officers under their command. Without the understanding and leadership of Colonel Robert Doughty, Colonel Cole Kingseed, and Colonel James Johnson, I could not have written this book. I will always consider it one of my life's greatest honors to have been a soldier under their command.

In 2001, I had the distinct privilege of attending the U.S. Army's School of Advanced Military Studies, commonly known as "SAMS." While there, I was not only academically challenged, but given the opportunity to grow as both a soldier and a scholar. I would like to acknowledge the assistance that Dr. Bob Epstein extended to me in bringing my manuscript to the attention of Charles Rankin at the University of Oklahoma Press and series editor Greg Urwin. Thanks to Dr. Epstein, this work went from being a 500-page doorstop to a published book.

I would also like to acknowledge several scholars I greatly respect, who were kind enough to review my work and give me advice I sorely needed. Dr. Dan Sutherland, at the University of Arkansas, not only first gave me a chance to publish with an academic press in 1999, but was gentlemanly enough to read and critique my work despite my having gone with a rival university press. I hope one day to be half the scholar that he is. Two scholars with whom I had the distinct pleasure of teaching, Dr. Dennis Showalter and Dr. Carol Reardon, not only helped me to focus my ideas and arguments in the early stages of this work, but were treasure troves of Civil War knowledge. Thank you, Dennis and Carol; your body of work is awe inspiring to both your students and peers. And I promise, Dennis, not to make you walk the entire route of Hood's assault at Gettysburg the next time we are there.

The unsung heroes of academia are the librarians and archivists who guide scholars to those golden nuggets of knowledge. The staffs at the U.S. Military Academy library and archives, the University of Arkansas archives, the Library of Congress, the National Archives, the U.S. Army War College's Military History Institute, Texas A&M University, the Ohio Historical Society, and the state archives of Tennessee, Kentucky, Alabama, and Arkansas, along with the myriad other archives and libraries noted in the bibliography, made possible this work.

Finally, I want to thank Nancy, Connor, and Kirsten for their patience and affection. Without their support, this book would not have been written.

THE UNCIVIL WAR

INTRODUCTION

Civil War Irregular Warfare in Theory and Practice

We now come to the civil war, so called, but although I saw quite a bit of it, I could never see the civil part, but I did see a lot of the uncivil and cruel part.

Thomas Estes, *Early Days and War Times in Northern Arkansas*, 1908

In the closing years of his life, Thomas Estes, a survivor of the brutal irregular war in northern Arkansas and southern Missouri, wrote these simple words that captured the spirit of the American Civil War for many of its participants. Instead of colorful banners, chivalrous gentlemen-officers, and glorious set-piece battles, the war of ambush and raid, isolated blockhouse, and burned home exemplified the Civil War to many people. Since 1865, historians have examined nearly every facet of the Civil War, from biographies of presidents and generals to the daily life of individual soldiers and civilians caught in the maelstrom, yet most have slighted the subject of an unconventional war that existed alongside the conventional war of myth and memory. It is the express goal of this work to analyze and discuss the underexamined irregular war that the Confederacy fought, and lost, during the Civil War.

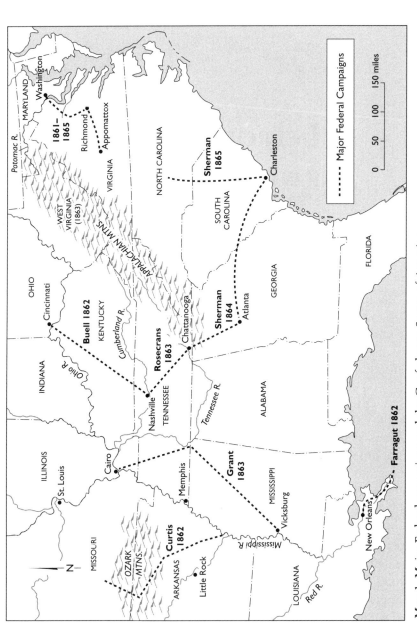

Map 1. Major Federal campaigns and the Confederate States of America.

The Confederacy attempted to fight an irregular conflict in conjunction with the conventional war, doing so within the limits of nineteenth-century concepts of guerrilla, partisan, and raiding warfare. These forms of unconventional warfare, though sharing some traits with guerrilla wars of the twentieth century, were not intended to instigate an insurgent movement behind enemy lines. Instead, the Confederate irregular forces were intended to be an adjunct to the conventional field armies, whether raised in 1862 to slow the Federal invasion of Arkansas or to strike deep behind Union lines in Tennessee and Kentucky. In short, the Confederate vision of irregular warfare was not that of the twentieth century but was well seated in the concepts of warfare developed throughout the early nineteenth century.

As espoused by military theorists of the era and reflected in the actions of Confederate commanders across the battlefields of the Upper South, the triad of irregular warfare—guerrilla, or people's war, partisan warfare, and conventional cavalry used as raiders—developed into a powerful tool for the Confederate war effort. To counter this threat, the Union army developed an extensive counterirregular program wherever it faced Confederate unconventional forces. Federal inventiveness, superior organization and logistical support, and the use of pro-Union Southerners (collectively called "Unionists") as counterguerrilla troops, when combined with Confederate failures to support or control their own irregulars properly, led to the end of the irregular war by early 1865, coinciding with the surrender of the major Rebel field armies in the spring and summer of that year.

This work is shaped by the need for a fresh study of irregular warfare in the Civil War. Although some scholars have examined irregular warfare since 1865, most of their studies have been flawed by inadequate definitions of unconventional warfare and a lack of analysis of the relationships and interactions between guerrilla and conventional military operations during the conflict. Additionally, some historians, in comparing irregular warfare of the American Civil War to guerrilla conflicts in the twentieth century, have done so without considering the facets of nineteenth-century military theory. Later in this introduction I will examine the works of others since 1865, noting how they deal with the issues surrounding what Thomas Estes called the "uncivil" war, and will provide an alternative approach to analyzing irregular warfare in the Civil War era. Chapters 1 through 6 form case studies of unconventional operations in states of the Upper South—

Arkansas, Tennessee, Kentucky, and Virginia—demonstrating how the Confederacy conducted *substantially different* unconventional operations in each, and how the Union dealt with these irregular threats. This does not mean that only one of the three types of irregular warfare took place in those regions; rather, the case studies focus on areas in which the specific type of warfare is most easily seen and evaluated. In truth, all three types of irregular warfare existed simultaneously throughout the Upper South, with a varied amount of impact on the Federal forces. In 1865, when the conventional war ended, the irregular one did as well, despite the desires of some Confederate leaders to turn the war into a wholly guerrilla conflict. In a concluding chapter, I discuss how the irregular war ended, and evaluate its impact on the conduct of the war for both the Confederacy and Union.

To fully appreciate the complexity of unconventional warfare in the era, one must understand the terminology used to define irregulars. Often, scholars do not clearly explain what they mean by "guerrilla," "partisan," "partisan ranger," or other terms used in the war for irregular troops, or they use the terms interchangeably. As a result, confusion reigns over what irregular warfare was in the 1860s and who were its practitioners. Veterans of the conflict, describing the tactics used in the era, often refer to one another as "guerrillas" if the opposing side had fought from ambush or used stealth over direct assault to gain battlefield advantages. Others later called some Confederate irregular leaders, most notably John Hunt Morgan and John S. Mosby, guerrillas to denigrate their actions during the war to a minor supporting role.[1]

In this work, for simplicity and ease of understanding, *irregular warfare* encompasses all forms of conflict—from deep cavalry raids to local bushwhackers—that did *not* involve the main armies of either side. For example, General Nathan Bedford Forrest's operations in Tennessee against the supply lines of the Union army in December 1862 would be considered irregular warfare, but the same officer's tactical reconnaissance or fighting in a major pitched battle (such as Chickamauga) would not.

Guerrilla warfare, a highly misused and misunderstood term in Civil War historiography, will refer to operations that meet the *nineteenth-century* definition of guerrillas. Noted jurist Francis Lieber, in his *Guerrilla Parties Considered with Reference to the Laws and Usages of War* (1862), clearly defined who guerrillas were and what their legal status was. In Lieber's work, which was later issued throughout the Union army as General Orders Number 100 (1863), he defined a *guerrilla* as "*self-constituted* sets of armed men in times of war, who form no integrant part of the organized army, do not stand on the regular pay-roll of the army, or are not paid at all, take up arms and lay them down at intervals, and carry on petty war chiefly by raids, extortion, destruction, and massacre, and who cannot encumber themselves with many prisoners, and will therefore generally give no quarter."[2] Civil War guerrillas closely resemble the soldiers of insurgent movements of the twentieth century, but, in general, lacked the ideological motivation normally associated with the latter.

Partisans, in contrast, refers to small, elite conventional forces given an unconventional role. The most famous of the partisan ranger units raised by the Confederacy was Lieutenant Colonel John S. Mosby's Forty-third Virginia Cavalry Battalion, which operated in northern Virginia during the last two years of the war. Partisan warfare differs from guerrilla warfare in other respects. Partisans were members of organized units, and the best were tightly controlled by their parent field armies. To some extent, partisan ranger units were an outgrowth of the light infantry companies of the French and Indian War and American Revolution, which used the tactics of ambush, raid, and stealth to harass enemy armies.[3] They served as scouts and raiders and set ambushes against conventional enemy forces. Following the experience of warfare in the early and mid–eighteenth century, European nations integrated partisan units into their conventional force structure as light infantry (*trillieurs*) and light cavalry (*hussars* and *dragoons*). These units were not unorganized irregulars, but regular units that often performed irregular functions, such as reconnaissance, raiding, and hunting down enemy irregulars. Johann von Ewald, the commander of a regiment of Hessian *jägers* serving under British command during the Revolution, put his experiences into his influential work *Treatise on Partisan Warfare* (1785).[4] Ewald described the organization of a "Partisan Corps" consisting of over one thousand officers and men and made up of one-third cavalry and two-thirds infantry. He maintained that such a force could not only harass enemy conventional forces but also serve as a counter to the unorganized irregulars (guerrillas, as defined by Lieber) he fought in America. Far from being the basis for guerrilla warfare that some have described the partisans to be, Ewald's partisan corps, as he saw them, were a *counterguerrilla* unit, capable of fighting the enemy on its own terms.[5] Much as guerrillas can be seen as a precursor to twentieth-century insurgents, partisans resemble the conventional special operations forces, such as the British Commandos or U.S. Rangers, that fought in World War II and later formed many of the counterinsurgency units of the second half of the twentieth century.

In the Civil War, units such as Mosby's Forty-third Virginia Cavalry Battalion fell under the definition of partisan forces. Francis Lieber described partisans as soldiers whose "object is to injure the enemy by action separate from that of his own main army; the partisan acts chiefly upon the enemy's lines of connection and communication, and outside of or beyond the lines of operation of his own army, in the rear and on the flanks of the enemy."[6] It must be emphasized that partisans, according to Lieber, were soldiers and not civilians, holding a clearly defined place in the military structure of the warring nation and worthy of consideration as prisoners of war if captured.

Adding to the confusion over terminology, Civil War soldiers coined a wide variety of derogatory names for irregular forces; in some cases, the same word had different meanings for each side. Many Federal soldiers considered all guerrillas to be nothing but brigands, and referred to them as such in their writings. In contrast, the term *guerrilla* was used initially in the South in an almost romantic way. One newspaper editor, waxing poetic about the Southern cause, called guerrillas "a most effective as well as captivating branch of the service," adding that volunteers should "make ready your gun, side-arms and horses for a life of dashing exploits."[7] By the end of the war, the term *guerrilla* came to signify unorganized, undisciplined irregulars who only occasionally recognized the military command structure of the Confederacy. One Confederate cavalry commander, General J. O. Shelby, a notable irregular fighter himself, would call these guerrillas nothing more than "robbers and jayhawkers," and order them shot or hung on the spot if captured.[8]

Hanging on the bottom rung of the ladder was a cast of reprehensible characters. *Bushwhacker*, a term perhaps first used in western Virginia in 1861, came to represent the lowest form of irregular combatant, and labeled someone who occupied a place between criminality and guerrilla warfare. Bushwhackers were considered a minor hindrance to the main armies, easily repulsed when they tried to steal horses or rob a Federal outpost. To the civilian populace, the bushwhackers represented the chaos that followed in the wake of the destructive armies,

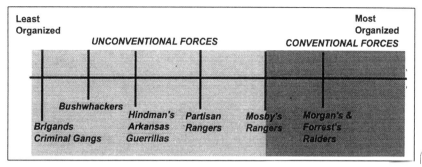

Figure 1. The spectrum of unconventional warfare in the Civil War.

or were gangs of toughs intent on ruling the hinterland of east Tennessee, western Virginia, and northern Arkansas through terror. In the opinion of one Union soldier, serving in Clarksville, West Virginia, the bushwhackers were "composed of a class of men who are noted for their ignorance, duplicity and dishonesty, whose vices and passions fit them for warfare in which they are engaged. He sallies forth with a stealth of a panther and lies in wait for the straggling soldier, courier or citizen and to whom the only warning is the sharp click of the deadly rifle. He kills for the sake of killing and plunders for the sake of gain."[9] For the Confederates, the lowest caste of irregular was often called a *brigand*, or more colorfully, a "greyback," from the slang term for body lice. In his diary, William W. Heartsill, a trooper in Company F, Second Texas Cavalry, wrote that a "greyback . . . is simply a species of the human family, that is lurking in the brush; generally between the opposing armies . . . preying upon whomsoever falls in their way."[10] Union irregulars, especially in the trans-Mississippi West, were often called *jayhawkers*, after the pro-Union settlers of Kansas in the 1850s. Later, many Southerners derogatorily called all Union soldiers "jayhawkers," especially if the soldiers were involved in foraging operations. In effect, a spectrum of irregular warfare existed during the Civil War, one that was recognized by the participants (see figure 1).

As a reflection of military thought in the mid–nineteenth century, Lieber's concept of the legality of irregular warfare had a solid basis in historical example and military theory of the time. Napoleon's experience in Spain, Winfield Scott's in Mexico, and French army operations in Italy and North Africa all reflected the conventional force's low regard for irregular warfare while acknowledging its dangers, and were well known to military leaders of the time. Even Carl von Clausewitz, a central figure in nineteenth- and twentieth-century military theory, specifically addressed irregular warfare in his classic *On War*. He outlined the basic requirements for a successful guerrilla conflict, coining the phrase "people's war" to describe the phenomenon. Clausewitz's list of items included truths that irregulars in the Civil War were intuitively familiar with, such as that "the war is carried on in the heart of the country," "it cannot be decided by a single catastrophe," "the theatre of war embraces a considerable extent of country," "the national character is favorable to the measure," and "the country is of a broken and difficult nature, either from being mountainous, or by reason of woods and marshes, or from the peculiar mode of cultivation in use."[11] Clausewitz's list, as a reflection of general attitudes toward irregular warfare in the post-Napoleonic world, perfectly describes the circumstances and milieu of unconventional warfare in the Civil War.[12]

However, the master theorist fell short in defining the relationship between guerrillas and a popular uprising, which he considered the same, and in clarifying the guerrilla's place within the conventional military command structure. Additionally, Clausewitz differentiated between a *partisan war*, in which small detachments of regular troops are used to harass an invader, and the *people's war*, based on a popular uprising of untrained citizens.[13] For example, he considered the use of Cossack cavalry to harass Napoleon's 1812 invasion of Russia the former, while he considered the resistance in Spain (1809 to 1813) closer to the latter. His analysis of what is required for a successful irregular war is eerily predictive of the uncivil war in the Upper South. Clausewitz warned that "the march of every small body of troops in a mountainous, thickly wooded, or even broken country, becomes a service of a very dangerous character, for at any moment a combat may arise on the march; if in point of fact no armed bodies have even been seen for some time, yet the same peasants already driven off by the head of a column may at any hour make their appearance in its rear."[14] His description of broken, rough terrain perfectly described the states of the Upper South, with the nearly impassable mountain ranges in western Virginia, the virgin forests of Arkansas, and the heavily wooded hills of Tennessee, and the continual threat of partisan and guerrilla activities along the route of march of the invading Federal armies (see map 1).[15]

Clausewitz achieved widespread recognition in the twentieth century, but it was another veteran of the Napoleonic Wars, Baron Antoine

Henri Jomini, who was the preeminent military theorist of the Civil War era. Jomini's theories and conclusions, published in *The Art of War* and his two-volume *Grand Military Operations*, were highly respected by the West Point-trained leadership of both armies, especially Major General Henry W. Halleck and General P. G. T. Beauregard.[16] Jomini's notable book dealt little with the issue of irregular warfare, simply describing the usefulness of partisans (contrasted with guerrillas) as adjuncts to the conventional army. Jomini asserted that "the partisans who are sent to hang around the enemy's lines of operations may [gather intelligence and] doubtless learn something of his movements; but it is almost impossible to communicate with them and receive the information they possess." Sadly for the Confederacy, Jomini's prediction of the difficulties of communication with and control over scattered irregular units by conventional forces would come true and have dire consequences in places such as rural Arkansas and Missouri.[17]

It is Jomini's advocacy of the role of *regular cavalry as raiders* that provides key insights on how Confederate leaders planned and executed their concept of what both Clausewitz and Jomini called "partisan war." While a direct relationship between the writings of these theorists and the actions of Civil War leaders is doubtful at best, as a reflection of general military thought of the era, their works provide a solid contemporary example for evaluating irregular warfare in the 1860s. Given Jomini's focus on the operational level of war, it is natural that he would direct his writings more toward the actual execution of irregular warfare. In his list of seven missions for "detachments" (Jomini's term for organized units dispatched from the main body of the army for independent operations), several serve as examples for the raiding war. Jomini stated that "great moveable and temporary detachments are made for the following reasons":

> To compel your enemy to retreat to cover his line of operations, or else cover your own.
>
> To intercept a corps and prevent its junction with the main body of the enemy, or to facilitate the approach of your own reinforcements.
>
> To observe and hold in position a large portion of the opposing army, while a blow is struck at the remainder.
>
> To carry off a considerable convoy of provisions or munitions, on receiving which depended the continuance of a siege or

the success of any strategic enterprise, or to protect the
march of a convoy of your own.

To make a demonstration to draw the enemy in a direction
where you wish him to go, in order to facilitate the execution of an enterprise in another direction.

To mask, or even invest, one or more fortified places for a certain time, with a view either to attack or to keep the garrison shut up within the ramparts.

To take possession of an important point upon the communications of an enemy already retreating.[18]

Jomini's insights can be applied to the missions conducted by
Confederate regular cavalry and partisan ranger units throughout the
Civil War, especially in Tennessee, Kentucky, and Virginia, because he
separated the specific mission of the guerrilla, the partisan, and the
raider. This distinction is vital in this work, as it forms the basis of how
the Confederacy approached the entire question of irregular warfare.
In Jomini's eyes, and in the eyes of the leaders of the Confederacy,
unconventional operations served the *tactical battlefield*, supporting
a conventional army as it fought an opposing conventional force. Using
examples from the Cossacks against Napoleon in 1812 and 1813, and
the Hungarians in 1742, Jomini emphasized the effectiveness of partisan cavalry in conjunction with conventional forces. He wrote that
"the partisans or irregular corps, which act by their own impulse, able
to move in all directions, escape all pursuits, cut the communications
upon a thousand points without ever being cut off themselves, are as
valuable to those making use of them, as they are disastrous to those
whom they harass."[19] It was not, in any way, a revolutionary army of
national liberation of the twentieth-century model; nor was it a "people's war" warned of by Clausewitz. For the South, the nineteenth-century partisan, a disciplined adjunct to the regular army described by
theorists of the era, was the basis for their official experiment in irregular warfare, the Partisan Ranger Act of 1862, and for their designing
and fielding "partisan cavalry" brigades in the Army of Tennessee in
1863.[20]

Irregular warfare in the Upper South needed little encouragement
from European theorists or the Confederate Congress to thrive. European settlers coming to the New World had used tactics that were
deemed irregular by the soldiers of the Old World; indeed, early conflicts

in the colonies established a pattern of unconventional warfare that exemplified colonial warfare in the Americas. From actions against hostile native tribes, most notably in King Philip's War (1675–76) and the two Tidewater wars in the seventeenth century, to actions against trained European professionals, American settlers had employed small detachments that depended on woodcraft and stealth. The exploits of Rogers' Rangers in the French and Indian War, Revolutionary War patriot guerrillas, such as Colonel Francis Marion, the "Swamp Fox," and partisans cooperating with Nathaniel Greene's 1780–81 campaign in the Carolinas provided a legacy of irregular military experience to American military leaders in the 1860s.

Some European examples may have been influential as well. The Spanish resistance to Napoleon's occupying forces from 1809 to 1813 first introduced the word *guerrilla* into the military lexicon. The French experience in Spain was common knowledge to military leaders of the 1860s and may have served to inspire the widespread partisan conflicts during the war. Other more recent examples, such as the widespread unrest in 1850s Kansas, Florida's Second Seminole War (1835–43), Mexican guerrilla attacks on the U.S. Army during the war with Mexico (1846–48), and battles against the Indians, reinforced the usefulness of irregular warfare in delaying and wearing down an invader. Thus Confederate leaders, in Richmond, Little Rock, and Nashville, possessed a body of common knowledge on the subject, which, while generally unwritten, understood partisan warfare as a viable military tool.[21]

To better evaluate the conventional response to guerrillas and partisans, I will describe Union operations against Confederate irregulars in twentieth-century terms. I do this for several reasons. First, the Union army had no body of doctrine or terminology defining the roles and missions of conventional forces in an irregular war. In essence, the Federals did not differentiate missions during the conflict as irregular or regular. Instead, they expected their forces, especially their cavalry, to perform a variety of roles, to include escorting supply trains or patrolling areas behind the lines searching for deserters and enemy irregulars. Second, using modern terms allows for a clear definition of missions that better suits the actual operations conducted during the Civil War, delineating between operations aimed at destroying the irregulars themselves and those that aimed at separating the irregular from the populace. Some of the key terms used in this work include *antiguerrilla*, *antipartisan*, or *antiraiding* missions, referring to direct combat operations aimed at destroying irregular units, often without regard to the impact on the civilian populace. For example, an antiguerrilla operation could involve the isolation of a guerrilla band in its mountain hideout and ending in its destruction as an effective threat, or the punitive burning of a village in response to local irregular activities. Antiguerrilla operations are not designed to win popular support or pacify a region—they aim at killing guerrillas.

Closely related to antiguerrilla operations are *counterguerrilla operations*. Counterguerrilla operations are passive measures taken by conventional troops to reduce irregular operations, and are exemplified by the series of manned blockhouses guarding critical bridges and tunnels, such as those built on the rail line between Nashville and Chattanooga, and in northwestern Virginia, from 1862 onward. In contrast to antiguerrilla and counterguerrilla operations, *counterinsurgency operations* involve much more than the guerrilla bands themselves. Counterinsurgency focused on reducing the causes of irregular warfare in a region, such as rebuilding the legitimacy of the Federal authority in areas occupied by the Union army. The aspect of counterinsurgency that deals with eliminating the guerrilla's base of support is known as *pacification*. To add to the confusion, many of these operations were conducted simultaneously in a relatively small geographic area, with some Federal units chasing raiders, others attempting to defend key locations against partisans, and still others busying themselves in building local support for the U.S. government.[22]

It is worth emphasizing that most Union and Confederate army officers treated irregulars according to nineteenth-century military norms. Partisans, when captured in gray uniforms, were normally treated as combatants, while guerrillas were not—a clear example of how commanders in the Civil War understood the difference between a partisan and a guerrilla. When General Halleck decreed in March 1862 that since "Maj. Gen. Sterling Price has issued commissions or licenses to certain bandits in this state [Missouri], authorizing them to raise 'guerrilla forces,' for the purpose of plundering and marauding . . . every man who enlists in such an organization forfeits his life and becomes an outlaw," he was defining what professional soldiers of his era understood as the proper relationship between guerrillas and conventional soldiery. For good measure, Halleck, a student of Jomini and Napoleon, added that "all persons are hereby warned that if they join any guerrilla band they will not, if captured, be treated as ordinary prisoners of war, but will be hung as robbers and murderers," continuing the tradition of executing guerrillas behind his lines.[23]

General William T. Sherman, during the 1862–63 Mississippi Campaign, took a similar approach. After his riverboats were fired on by Confederate guerrillas from the Arkansas shore, he passed a letter through the lines to General Hindman, telling the Confederate that "we profess to know what civilized warfare is and has been for hundreds of years, and cannot accept your consideration of it. If, as you threaten [to hang Federal prisoners in retaliation for Union execution of guerrillas], remember we have hundreds of thousands of men bitter and yearning for revenge. Let us but loose these from the restraints of discipline, and no life or property would be safe in the regions where we do hold possession and power." Sherman closed his letter with a prophetic and ominous statement: "You initiate the game, and my word for it your people will regret it long after you pass from earth."[24]

Most works on the irregular conflict during the American Civil War spend little time on defining the terminology or even methodology of partisan and guerrilla warfare that was so important to commanders of the 1860s. The majority of the works dealing with the issue focus on a handful of flamboyant partisan leaders, especially Mosby in Virginia, Morgan in Tennessee and Kentucky, and the semipartisan/semibrigand William Quantrill in the trans-Mississippi. Following the war, former irregulars, such as John Edwards and James Williamson, wrote hero-worshipping biographies. Additionally, many of the participants in irregular warfare, including both Edwards and Williamson plus Mosby and many of his officers, wrote extensively about their actions. These works formed the basis of many later biographies of these leaders, tainting many historians who would see the irregular leader as heroic or villainous, good or evil, and in the process overlook the unconventional warfare in the Civil War.[25] Works written over 130 years after the end of the war continue to show Mosby as both the most successful *guerrilla* in American history and one of the great heroes of the Southern pantheon. From Susan Provost Beller's children's book *Mosby and His Rangers* to Kevin Siepel's *Rebel* and James Ramage's *Gray Ghost*, historians and novelists view the partisan leader as a bold gallant, a chivalrous nineteenth-century swashbuckler who resembled less of a guerrilla fighter than a character from a 1930s Errol Flynn movie. Morgan is portrayed in much the same way, with less emphasis on his individual exploits than on the actions of his Second Kentucky Cavalry.[26]

In contrast, Quantrill, William "Bloody Bill" Anderson, Frank and Jesse James, and other irregulars west of the Mississippi, thanks to numerous appearances in romance novels, motion pictures, and television programs, are known less for their successful operations against the Union troops than for attacks on civilians or their postwar criminal careers. Consequently, biographers of the western guerrillas, such as Albert Castel in *William Clarke Quantrill* and Thomas Goodrich in *Bloody Dawn*, ensure that they are treated as an aberration in the Civil War. It is interesting to note how authors, from 1865 onward, have idolized the aristocratic and flamboyant Mosby and Morgan but stigmatized Quantrill as a criminal.[27]

Richard S. Brownlee's 1958 classic, *Gray Ghosts of the Confederacy*, the first scholarly account of Civil War guerrilla warfare, focuses on Missouri and Kansas, providing one of the best analyses of irregular warfare during the conflict. Brownlee's recognition of the role that the partisans played in the West represented a major change in the study of Civil War guerrilla warfare, as he demonstrates the differences between Confederate guerrilla, partisan, and conventional cavalry operations against the Union army. Following Brownlee's example, Thomas Goodrich's 1995 *Black Flag* and Michael Fellman's 1989 *Inside War* analyze the bloody conflict that tore apart Missouri. Goodrich emphasizes the actions of Confederate guerrillas and their leaders, while Fellman focuses on the impact of Union counterinsurgency operations and occupation policy on Missouri's populace. Both works exemplify a trend of professional scholarship on irregular warfare that developed in the last decades of the twentieth century.[28]

In the first half of the twentieth century, few historians except biographers dealt with the issue of irregular warfare in the Civil War. One notable exception was the work of Ethelbert Barksdale, grandson of the Confederate general killed at Gettysburg. Barksdale sought better definitions for "regular, semi-regular, and irregular" warfare, basing his work on study of the *Official Records* and drawing parallels to the guerrilla war in 1930s China. Although flawed in its comparisons, Barksdale's work stood alone for over thirty years as the only holistic approach to irregular warfare in the Civil War.[29]

Beginning in the 1970s, evidently influenced by the Vietnam War, a new wave of scholarship began addressing irregular warfare as it related to the Civil War. In 1974, Albert Castel devoted an entire issue of *Civil War Times Illustrated* to an examination of the irregular war.

His insightful statement that Confederate partisans such as Mosby "were more like regular cavalry permanently stationed behind enemy lines than guerrillas in the traditional sense of the word," went counter to the growing wave of post-Vietnam analysis of irregular warfare as "people's war." Disdaining hero-worship, Castel's evaluation of the uncivil war encouraged many scholars to again look at the subject and to include the irregular conflict in overall examinations of the war.[30]

In 1995, Mark Grimsley's *The Hard Hand of War* addressed Union occupation policy and the role of the Confederate irregular in shaping that policy. He maintains that the Union's failure to pacify conquered areas of the Confederacy was partly due to Rebel guerrillas keeping alive the flame of rebellion. Calling the Mississippi Delta (eastern Arkansas and Louisiana and western Mississippi) the "Cradle of Hard War," Grimsley establishes that region as the birthplace of Sherman's total war strategy. *The Hard Hand of War* emphasizes the effect of the Union's policy of retaliation for guerrilla attacks, arguing that it "lay the groundwork for the greater hard war measures to come."[31]

Other important works in the late 1980s and early 1990s on irregular warfare include Carl Beamer's "Gray Ghostbusters: Eastern Theater Union Counter-Guerrilla Operations in the Civil War, 1861–1865." Beamer examines how the Federal military reacted to Mosby and other irregulars in western and northwestern Virginia during the war, and how Rebel partisans and guerrillas affected the Union army's conventional operations. John M. Gates's essay "Indians and Insurrectos: The U.S. Army's Experience with Insurgency" and Andrew J. Birtle's *U.S. Army Counterinsurgency and Contingency Operations Doctrine: 1860–1941* both assert that the Union army, far from being a monolithic conventional force, possessed powerful counterinsurgency units and an unwritten doctrine to back them up. In effect, they contend that aggressive counterinsurgency operations by Federal forces took the guerrilla option away from the Rebel leadership.[32]

Outside of the works already mentioned, few biographers and historians have noted the existence, much less the influence, of irregular warfare during the American Civil War. This pattern has continued since the nineteenth century. Colonel C. E. Callwell, a British army officer and veteran of numerous British imperial counterguerrilla operations, wrote the work that became the unconventional warfare field manual for Anglo-American military professionals in the early twentieth century. His *Small Wars: Their Principles and Practice* (1899) was recognized as the definitive work on irregular warfare, yet he entirely neglected the American Civil War. Callwell's approach, focusing on the British experience in the Boer War and, in later editions, the American counterguerrilla war in the Philippines, dominated the study of nineteenth-century guerrilla warfare until the 1950s. Despite the efforts of Brownlee and others, guerrilla warfare historians continued to ignore the American Civil War, implying that true guerrilla warfare in the form of Maoist wars of national liberation did not emerge until the twentieth century. Works such as James Cross's *Conflict in the Shadows* and Lewis Gann's *Guerrillas in History* disregard any major American forms of insurgency and counterinsurgency up to the Cold War. Even historians who recognize the existence of irregular warfare in the Civil War often acknowledge only the more flamboyant of the Confederate partisan leaders and units. One such work was Robert Asprey's two-volume *War in the Shadows: The Guerrilla in History*, which reduces guerrilla warfare in the American Civil War to a few sparse paragraphs on regular Confederate partisan units, like Mosby's and Morgan's, while completely ignoring the bulk of the irregular fighting during the conflict. As a result, few general secondary works exist on Civil War guerrilla warfare, and those that do exist ignore the conflict in Arkansas and Tennessee, focusing on the partisan operations in Virginia alone.[33]

Beginning in the mid-1980s, historians began to look at the causes and conduct of the Civil War from other than purely military perspectives, incorporating irregular warfare's distinct political and ideological aspects into their analysis. From their research, two major questions concerning guerrilla warfare arose. First, why did the Confederacy not adopt a widespread guerrilla strategy from the beginning of the war? Second, why didn't the Confederates turn to irregular warfare after Appomattox? Some historians, such as Robert L. Kerby, lambaste the Confederate leadership for not adopting guerrilla warfare from the start, claiming Southern political and social conservatism prevented a war of national liberation from becoming a reality.[34] This argument, along with the argument that a successful guerrilla war could have been waged after April 1865, forms one of the themes of *Why the South Lost the Civil War*, in which some contributors conclude that a Southern guerrilla war would have stood a good chance of success either during the conflict or after it.[35]

Gary Gallagher and Reid Mitchell take a different approach toward the feasibility of Confederate irregular warfare, yet both fall short of recognizing the depth of the unconventional war. In *The Confederate War*, Gallagher boldly states that "[a general] guerrilla war was not a viable option within the Confederate context and thus should not be put forward in retrospect as the most desirable national strategy for the South." Basing his conclusions largely on twentieth-century examples, he cites the lack of ideology and a unifying nationalism necessary for successful guerrilla warfare. Gallagher fails to recognize that a substantially different model of irregular conflicts existed in the 1860s.[36] Mitchell reinforces Gallagher's view, stating that the Confederacy "did not choose to fight a [general] guerrilla war—because, in large part, it did not seem possible to fight a guerrilla war and keep slavery intact." Like Gallagher, Mitchell also ignores the nineteenth-century concept of partisan/irregular warfare, preferring to shape his argument against a Confederate guerrilla war with twentieth-century examples.[37]

Daniel Sutherland's 1999 compilation of essays, *Guerrillas, Unionists, and Violence on the Confederate Homefront*, deals with the issues facing the civilians living at home during the war, including guerrilla warfare. A book of the "new social history," it also encompasses approaches from traditional military and political history. Several of the state-focused essays focus directly on irregular warfare, internal dissension, and the rise of pro-Union factions within the Confederacy. While not dwelling on irregular warfare alone, the essays in Sutherland's book recognize that, to many Southerners, the guerrilla war was the Civil War.[38] Sutherland's book attempts to bridge the gap between military and social history of the conflict, including irregular warfare. This is a change from much of the existing literature on Civil War guerrilla warfare, which is lacking in several areas. No works, for example, attempt to view irregular warfare in the context of military theory of the time, separating the subject entirely from discussions of the influence of Jomini and other theorists on warfare in the era. Instead, in traditional Civil War histories, guerrilla warfare is treated as an aberration, or ignored entirely. While most scholars acknowledge the devastation of the irregular war along the Missouri/Kansas border and, to a lesser extent, eastern Tennessee, areas outside of these are rarely mentioned. The Union army's methods and actions to counter the irregular threat, even in the major theaters of the war, such as central Tennessee and northern Virginia, are marginalized in favor of traditional battle histories and campaign narratives. It is the intent of this work to focus both on regions that have been ignored in many histories (Arkansas) and on the theaters that garner the bulk of the scholarly study of the war (Tennessee, Kentucky, and Virginia). By focusing on these four states, the three types of Confederate irregular warfare in the Civil War (guerrilla, partisan, and raiding), and the Union army's response to such operations, are seen in the context of both unconventional and conventional operations.[39]

The states of Arkansas, Tennessee, Kentucky, and the western counties of Virginia (admitted to the Union in 1863 as the state of West Virginia) afford a unique environment for evaluating the irregular conflict during the Civil War. First, conventional and unconventional forces of both sides throughout the war campaigned in or occupied all four states. Second, large pro-Union populations (collectively called "Unionists") lived in the states and provided the backbone of the Federal counterguerrilla forces in their respective regions. Third, the rough and underdeveloped terrain of the three states provided safe havens for irregulars while lacking a transportation network capable of supporting large armies. In areas such as Tennessee, the protection of these supply lines dictated the pace of war even more than success or failure on the battlefield and provided the Confederacy with a conducive environment for irregular warfare.[40]

The selection of the Upper South for this study is also based on the fact that the major campaigns of the Civil War, especially before 1864, took place in this region. Just as conventional battles sprang from these invasions of the Confederacy, so did Rebel-supported guerrilla and partisan warfare. Arkansas, while seemingly on the periphery of the Confederacy and lacking industry, actually had more strategic importance than may appear at first glance. The state, as long as it was under Confederate control, prevented Federal control of the Mississippi River and was a constant threat to the U.S. territories west of the river. If the Confederates had controlled the western bank of the Mississippi from the Arkansas side, Major General U. S. Grant's 1862–63 Vicksburg campaign would have been substantially different. Even so, the Federal army never fully occupied the state and allowed Confederate resistance to continue there until the end of the war.[41]

Tennessee and Kentucky saw fighting from the beginning of the war until its end. Numerous major battles occurred in the region, from Perryville, Shiloh, and Stones River in 1862 to Nashville in 1864. Carnage previously unequaled in American history scarred the region, and much as with Arkansas, the Union forces never wholly conquered the area. As late as 1865, Federal troops held only the key cities and lines of communication in Tennessee and were continually vulnerable to Confederate cavalry raids and attacks by pro-Rebel guerrillas. The region, according to some historians, was the *key* battlefield of the war. Without Federal victories there, the Ohio River line would have never been secure. Without Grant's victories at Shiloh in 1862 and Chattanooga in 1863, Vicksburg and Atlanta would have never fallen, nor would the future Federal supreme commander have risen to prominence.[42]

Virginia, and the region of that state that became West Virginia in 1863, was continually fought over from April 1861 to April 1865. For four years, the state would be the center of the conflict, defining for participants on both sides what would be victory in the war. From the Union cry of "On to Richmond!" in 1861 to the Confederacy's political and military focus on the Army of Northern Virginia, the fate of Virginia, in the view of many scholars, decided victory or defeat. Gary Gallagher summarizes that Virginia, and Lee's army, held such an important place in the survival of the Confederacy that the fall of Richmond and "the death of the Army of Northern Virginia removed the Confederate people's cherished rallying point and effectively marked the demise of their nation."[43]

The factors of divided loyalties to the Union and Confederacy, economic differences based on geographical considerations, and the continual presence of large field armies from both sides make Arkansas, Tennessee, and Virginia suitable for case studies evaluating irregular warfare in the American Civil War. This work will focus on one main point and several supplementary issues that deal with the Confederacy and irregular warfare. Contrary to many historians, I argue that the Confederacy overtly organized and fought an irregular conflict but lost. And in contrast to previous scholars, I argue that this unconventional war existed not as a separate conflict from the conventional conflict but as an integral but subordinate part of the overall Confederate conduct of the war. The Confederates lost the unconventional war as they lost the conventional conflict; by 1865, their irregular forces had been defeated along with the regular armies. The Rebel leadership, to their credit, attempted every type of irregular warfare known in the nineteenth century—guerrilla, or "people's" war, partisan warfare, and raiding warfare. Scholars and historians easily confuse these three types of conflict, which together form a cohesive strategy of irregular warfare that the Confederate government attempted to use to gain independence from the United States.

Despite its attempts to fight an unconventional conflict as an adjunct to the conventional war, the Confederacy lost the "uncivil" war. The most important reason, and the least appreciated, is that the Union army was able to adapt to irregular warfare faster than the Confederacy expected. While their counterguerrilla doctrine was never codified into formal written form, Federal commanders instituted changes from the regimental to army levels that limited, and ultimately eliminated, the irregular threat. In addition, the Confederates' failure to properly organize and control irregular units, including not only the scattered bushwhacker bands of the trans-Mississippi but partisan ranger and conventional cavalry as well, had much to do with their inability to win the irregular conflict. Raiding cavalry was often misused by Rebel leaders and wasted on headline-grabbing raids, and poorly organized guerrilla companies often degenerated into little more than brigands by 1865. General Robert E. Lee wrote that "it is impossible . . . to prevent [guerrillas] from becoming an injury instead of a benefit to the service."[44] He referred to the damage the Confederate irregulars were doing both to the organization of the Rebel armies and to the weak nationalism of the Confederacy. As gangs of ostensibly Confederate irregulars preyed on the citizenry to survive, they eroded support for the Rebel cause. Finally, the Confederate leadership adhered to theories of irregular warfare based on Napoleonic and eighteenth-century "partisan war" concepts that focused on assisting the conventional field army in gaining a victory, not a "people's war" aimed at mobilizing the populace, both ideologically and militarily, for prolonged warfare. It was the constraints of nineteenth-century military doctrine (not twentieth-century views) that shaped their conduct of unconventional warfare.

This explanation of the Confederate defeat demonstrates the need for historians to separate the theoretical concepts of irregular war as they existed in the nineteenth century and the twentieth century. If, as the historian Charles Beard surmises, the Civil War was a "Second American Revolution," it was an extremely conservative one. Unlike many of the revolutionary conflicts of the twentieth century, the Confederates' war was not aimed at overthrowing the status quo; rather, it aimed at preventing any disruption to their fragile social system.

When the Rebels sent their irregulars to war, they did so not under a proto-Maoist model of a war of national liberation, but instead followed a tradition of partisan warfare based on the examples of guerrilla (popular) warfare known to the French in Spain and Winfield Scott in Mexico. Throughout the war, the most publicized irregular units, such as Mosby's Rangers or Morgan's Raiders, were led by men who formed the upper crust of antebellum society. These leaders were not members of the proletariat, but wealthy slave owners, professional men, and leaders of their community. A war of national liberation, as fought by Mao in China or Ho Chi Minh in Vietnam, would have been an alien thought to the Confederate leadership in 1861, dangerous to Southern society. For this reason alone, any attempt to draw meaningful parallels between the guerrilla war fought by the Confederates from 1861 to 1865 and conflicts in the twentieth century is based on a false theoretical model, a case of presentism taking precedence over historical occurrence.

The first case study, concerning Arkansas from 1862 to 1865, will outline the closest that the Confederacy came to a guerrilla war of the "people's war" model. The Arkansas guerrilla war, when compared with the organized partisan war in Virginia and the raiding war in Tennessee and Kentucky, provides an illuminating example of the differences between guerrilla and partisan, brigand and soldier. The consequences of guerrilla war in Arkansas, including the breakdown of antebellum society and widespread brigandage, also demonstrate many of the reasons that the Confederate leadership so desperately attempted to avoid an all-out irregular war. For the Confederates, and the people of Arkansas, their guerrilla war became a self-inflicted wound that ultimately led to Union victory.

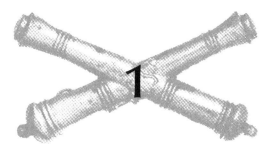

THE CONFEDERACY'S SELF-INFLICTED WOUND

The Guerrilla War in Arkansas, 1862–1865

> The people of Arkansas are united and prepared for any sacrifice necessary to establish Confederate nationality.
>
> Governor Henry M. Rector of Arkansas to
> Governor W. F. Pickens of South Carolina, April 11, 1862

Carl von Clausewitz wrote in *On War* that guerrilla warfare in the nineteenth century was "a broadening and intensification of the fermentation process known as war." Clausewitz, a member of the Prussian nobility, explained that the rise of popular guerrilla warfare, which he called "people's war" and contrasted with organized partisan warfare, led to the "breaking down of barriers." The social, political, and military bulwarks that had held the world of the Enlightenment crumbled in the revolutionary age, as the lower classes were called to arms. Unlike many of his contemporaries, Clausewitz saw a guerrilla war as a method to mobilize the complete resources of a nation to victory. "Any nation who uses it *intelligently* will, as a rule, gain some superiority over those who disdain its use," he surmised, adding, "the question only remains whether mankind at large will gain by this further expansion of the element of war." Clausewitz the theorist would have had his question answered in Arkansas in 1865, as a

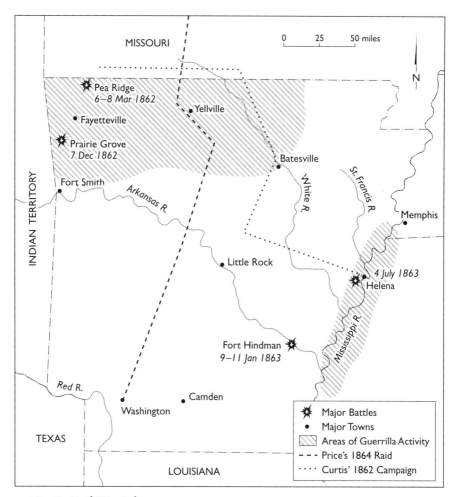

Map 2. Civil War Arkansas.

brutal people's war left Arkansas in ruins, made many of its citizens
homeless, and led others to welcome the invading army (see map 2).[1]

Arkansas, despite its location on the periphery of the Confederacy,
provides an excellent example of a people's war as described by Clausewitz and Jomini.[2] This frontier state, with its rich alluvial bottomland,
nearly impenetrable hill country, and politically divided population,
was the scene of the Confederate government's only planned and executed guerrilla conflict. Following the example of the Spanish guerrillas fighting the French army from 1808 to 1813, the Rebel leadership
hoped to slow or inhibit the Federal invasion of Arkansas. Despite the

efforts of Confederate military and civilian leaders, and the irregulars themselves, the attempt at a guerrilla war was an abject failure. The Rebels lacked a cohesive strategy to employ their guerrilla companies, denied them needed logistical support, and did not provide the conventional military leadership needed for success. The people's war in Arkansas ultimately failed as the Rebel government abandoned the guerrillas to a steadily improving Federal antiguerrilla campaign.

The evening of March 8, 1862, was the darkest in the short history of Confederate Arkansas. The scattered remains of the once-vaunted Army of the West, under the command of General Earl Van Dorn, unsuccessfully attempted to fight a delaying action against the Union Army of the Southwest, led by Major General Samuel R. Curtis. Van Dorn's army, consisting of units from Texas, Louisiana, Missouri, Arkansas, and Native American tribes from the Indian Territory, slowly disintegrated throughout the night. For the Union army, the pursuit was relatively easy, as Federal cavalrymen followed "the trail of the defeated, disorganized army littered with discarded clothing, weapons, cartridge boxes, knives, coffee pots, and even flags," the flotsam and jetsam of a routed enemy.[3]

Van Dorn's defeat at Pea Ridge produced important consequences in the conduct of the Civil War in the trans-Mississippi West. The battle ensured that the Union would control Missouri for the indefinite future and threatened Arkansas with Union occupation. Although it seemed to many leaders in Richmond that Arkansas had few strategic advantages, the state actually possessed a large body of untapped white manpower and a healthy agricultural economy. Geographically, it was situated in an excellent position to menace Federal states and territories throughout the western frontier. The defeat at Pea Ridge also brought Major General Thomas C. Hindman to the command of Confederate forces in Arkansas. An antebellum Arkansas politician and planter, Hindman would change the nature of the conflict in the state by ordering its inhabitants to launch the only organized people's war in the short history of the Confederacy.[4]

For the Rebels, Arkansas was an excellent battleground for guerrilla warfare. First, the state's presence on the periphery of the Confederacy—both politically and geographically—made it acceptable for Rebel leaders to fight that type of conflict. Simply put, the Confederate high command saw Arkansas as expendable, a backward and relatively isolated region that could be sacrificed to buy time for the decisive battles in Tennessee and Virginia. Brutal guerrilla warfare, which could not be fought in places like Richmond, Nashville, or Atlanta without seriously damaging support for the Confederate government, could be conducted in Arkansas with little expectation of political repercussions. A perfect example of the Confederate government's attitude toward Arkansas occurred in March 1862, when Van Dorn withdrew his battered army across the Mississippi River to join General Albert Sidney Johnston's Army of Tennessee. Although Van Dorn arrived too late to help at the Battle of Shiloh on April 6–7, his forces were absorbed into the Army of Tennessee, never to return to Arkansas or the trans-Mississippi. Arkansas's Confederate leadership, especially Governor Henry M. Rector, strongly denounced the Confederate high command's decision. Stripped of most regular troops, Arkansas's leaders resorted to many desperate measures, including guerrilla warfare, to save their state from Union occupation.[5]

Second, the state's terrain supported irregular warfare. The geographic division of the state into highlands, lowlands, and delta, and the concordant economic and political alignment of the region, gave the Confederates a clear delineation of friendly and unfriendly territory. The delta and lowlands regions were relatively guerrilla free (except where Union forces existed) compared with the pro-Union hill country. Lastly, the Confederate defeat at Pea Ridge in March 1862 led the Rebel leadership to turn to irregular warfare to buy time for rebuilding and deploying a new conventional field force. The Battle of Pea Ridge did more than shape the military outcome in the trans-Mississippi Confederacy; it planted the seed of defeat needed to force the Rebel leadership to turn to guerrilla warfare.

Jefferson Davis, faced with the decision to either abandon Arkansas or lose Tennessee, chose to defend the latter and ordered the transfer of Confederate troops and supplies out of Arkansas. After Van Dorn's army departed, Governor Rector demanded a new army and a competent leader to stop the approaching Yankees. Davis responded by attempting to reassure Rector that all possible measures were being taken for the state's defense; however, the Richmond government continued to pull men and munitions out of the state to assist in the defense of Mississippi and Tennessee. Frustrated by Davis's rebuff, the governor turned to the newspapers for action.[6]

In a widely publicized address, Rector castigated Davis: "Arkansas lost, abandoned, subjugated, is not Arkansas as she entered the confederate government." He threatened to make a separate peace with the Union: "nor will she [Arkansas] remain a confederate state, desolated as a wilderness; her children fleeing from the wrath to come, will build them a new ark and launch it on new waters, seeking a haven somewhere, of equality, safety and rest." Calling for all able-bodied men to volunteer for the state's defense, Rector guaranteed they "will not be transferred to confederate service under any circumstances without their consent, *and on no account, unless a confederate force, sufficient to prevent invasion, is sent into the State.*" Governor Rector had issued a challenge that Jefferson Davis could not ignore.[7]

Rector's proclamation infuriated the Confederate president, infamous for his personal vendettas against political opponents. Davis ignored Rector's pleas, writing directly to Van Dorn in May, stating that the "recent proclamation of the Governor of Arkansas . . . which may operate injuriously on our cause" made it "apparent that an impression prevails that the defense of the State of Arkansas . . . has been abandoned by the Confederate government." Davis advised Van Dorn to write to the Arkansas leadership that his army's absence was only temporary and, following the repulse of the Union forces in Mississippi, it would return to the defense of Arkansas. It is revealing to note that Davis himself never wrote directly to Rector, nor were any Confederate forces transferred west to the defense of the trans-Mississippi region. The sole reinforcement for the defense of Arkansas was one man—Major General Thomas C. Hindman.[8]

The defeat at Pea Ridge, the Confederate withdrawal from Arkansas, and Hindman's arrival in May 1862 brought sweeping changes to the state. Recovering from wounds received at Shiloh, he assumed command of the entire Trans-Mississippi District, which covered a huge swath of the southwest, from Missouri to Louisiana north of the Red River. Hindman's mission was staggering in its scope; he was "charged with their [the states of Texas, Louisiana, Missouri, Arkansas, and the Indian Territory] defense, and is fully authorized and empowered to organize their troops."[9]

He arrived to find Little Rock in turmoil. Civilians were fleeing the capital in expectation of the Federal army's arrival, plantation owners were burning their crops, and the handful of Confederate troops in the area were without strong leadership. One of Colonel W. H. Parsons's Texas cavalrymen, halted on their journey to Mississippi by the authorities in Little Rock, said that "most every farm was seen smoking with burning cotton. More than 50,000,000 dollars worth has been burned along the Arkansas and Mississippi rivers during the last month [May 1862]."[10] Van Dorn had done little to defend the city. Considering the capital of Confederate Arkansas untenable, he had ordered troops to evacuate military stores, destroy bridges, and tear down the newly constructed Little Rock–Fort Smith telegraph line, leaving his successor without soldiers, logistical support, or even a working communications system.[11]

Undaunted, Hindman set to work immediately. En route to his new command in Little Rock, he stopped in Memphis and impressed every firearm he could find, and he seized nearly one million dollars in funds from banks to pay his army. When he arrived at his headquarters on May 30, he discovered that the few organized troops that had remained after Van Dorn left for Mississippi had been withdrawn to the Indian Territory under the command of General Albert Pike, a prewar political foe. Hindman gathered a handful of unarmed state militia and Parsons's Texas cavalry and prepared to face Curtis's victorious Army of the Southwest, which was staging in southeast Missouri for the invasion. For Hindman and the Arkansas Confederate government, the future looked bleak indeed.[12]

The military situation in early June 1862 left Hindman several options, few of them promising. He could remove the Confederate government and what little military supplies he had to a safer region of the state, continuing Van Dorn's withdrawal (and violating the implicit agreement between President Davis and Arkansas's political leadership that the state would not be abandoned), or he could fight. Hindman, an avid admirer of Napoleon, planned to make Arkansas a costly conquest for the Union army and chose the latter. He imposed martial law in the state, seizing munitions and supplies wherever possible. He also ordered the rationing of goods and enforced conscription laws in order to raise a new conventional army. Lastly, Hindman ordered the raising of independent guerrilla companies to operate behind enemy lines and to serve as de facto law enforcement officers in the rest of the state. This act, which later became known as the "Bands of Ten" order, put Arkansas on the path toward widespread guerrilla warfare.[13]

When the war erupted, C. C. Danley, editor of the *Arkansas Gazette* and influential state leader, warned "now that the war is upon the country some of the more thoughtless and hot-headed of our citizens seem to be made mad by the very idea of it." He made a plea to the higher motivations of civilized men. "If there were no profit to us in the adoption of such a course [guerrilla warfare]," he continued, "as civilized men we should not lose our civilization and become savages." Ironically, it was to these men that Hindman appealed for a people's war. On June 17, 1862, the headquarters of the newly formed Trans-Mississippi District issued General Orders Number 17 (see appendix B). In this order, Hindman instructed the *people* of Arkansas: "for the more effective annoyance of the enemy upon our rivers and in our mountains and woods, *all citizens* from this district . . . are called upon to organize themselves into independent companies" of ten men, led by an elected "captain," to conduct guerrilla warfare "without waiting for special instructions."[14] Within a single year, Arkansas Confederates went from adherence to the laws of civilized warfare to an unrestrained guerrilla conflict. Hindman's objective was direct and simple—to slow down the Union armies long enough to rebuild a conventional force. The "Bands of Ten" order was not intended to be the beginning of a war of national liberation, as in the twentieth century, but meant to mobilize the populace to resist the invader. It was, in effect, an attempt by Hindman to give the Yankee army a taste of what Napoleon's army experienced in Spain.[15]

Hindman and the Arkansas Confederate leadership realized the problems inherent in controlling an irregular war. From the beginning, commanders feared that the guerrillas would turn to banditry. Just prior to Hindman's assuming command in Arkansas, the departing Van Dorn authorized Brigadier General John S. Roane, whom he left in command of the state in May 1862, to "appoint partisan officers, subject to the approval of the President, and in conferring these appointments he desires you to be careful that none but men of respectable character are appointed."[16]

In light of the concerns over controlling the guerrillas, Hindman issued General Orders Number 18 on June 18, 1862. The order outlined the organization and command relationships of the independent companies authorized by General Orders Number 17. Guerrilla companies were ostensibly placed under the command of county provosts marshal, or military law enforcement officers, and had to submit to inspections and reports by the provosts. However, no evidence exists that these reports were ever filed. Hindman, in the guise of General Orders Number 18, attempted to address command and control issues for the guerrilla units raised in Arkansas. In practice, there was no real organization or control over these units, despite the issuance of the new directive. Unlike General Orders Number 17, General Orders Number 18 did not receive widespread distribution; instead, only parts of it were published, those specifically dealing with martial law and the appointment of provosts marshal to enforce it.[17] Vital sections of this crucial order concerning equipping, supplying, and commanding the guerrillas were omitted from the newspapers. In effect, the Rebels authorized the mobilization of a guerrilla army but without providing for the command and control needed to oversee the independent companies.[18]

In a display of remarkable determination, Hindman managed to raise a force of 18,000 conventional troops and an estimated 5,000 irregular troops by August 1862. In theory, the arrayed forces, both conventional and unconventional, came under his direct command; conventional forces were contained in standard military organizations (battalions, regiments, and divisions), while local provosts marshal controlled the company-size irregular detachments. Seemingly, in the summer of 1862, the system worked, to the pleasure of Hindman and the dismay of the Union army.[19]

The first test of Hindman's guerrillas came during the White River Expedition in June 1862. Curtis's Army of the Southwest, having traveled across Missouri and reentered Arkansas in April, found itself without adequate logistical support to continue the conquest of Arkansas. To overcome the scarcity of supplies, Generals Curtis and Grant (preparing to begin the offensive toward Vicksburg, Mississippi) planned to open the White and Little Red Rivers to Union steamboats. A joint expedition was launched, under the overall command of Colonel Graham N. Fitch. Fitch's small force was accurately estimated by the Confederates as numbering between 1,000 and 1,500 men, supported by the ironclads *St. Louis* and *Mound City*, the wooden gunboats *Lexington* (a veteran of Shiloh) and *Conestoga*, the tug *Tiger*, and three transports. To counter the Union assault, Hindman established a battery of the heaviest guns he possessed, two rifled thirty-two-pounders and four field pieces, on a bluff commanding the river near St. Charles. Additionally, he ordered detachments of Confederate sharpshooters to support the defense of the battery.[20]

Fitch's expedition, despite the crippling of the ironclad *Mound City*, managed to overrun the protective battery at St. Charles. Hindman, in turn, ordered the massing of all his newly formed guerrilla bands along the White River. The residents of Monroe County responded to the call to arms. The guerrillas constantly harassed the Federal force, already demoralized by the loss of half the crew of the *Mound City*. After guerrilla sharpshooters killed several of his men and frustrated by the inability to break through to Curtis's army, Colonel Fitch began to "render rigorous measures" against the local populace. He landed detachments to burn the foliage near Crockett's Bluff, in order to "clear the underbrush opposite this place to deprive the guerrillas of cover." Meanwhile, his men had managed to capture several guerrillas and discovered that the bands had been raised in Monroe County.[21] Fitch's mission appeared to be a failure when he found the White River too low for his flotilla to move further north. The Federal commander balked at the possibility of returning to Memphis without a single victory against the guerrillas and decided to punish the citizens of Monroe County for supporting the irregulars. Accusing them of supporting "guerrilla bands raised in your vicinity" that had "fired from the woods upon the United States gunboats and transports in the White River," Fitch claimed that the locals could stop the guerrilla attacks, and if they did not, would "be held responsible in person and in property." In addition, the Union colonel stated that he would execute any irregular he captured. Although he did not order the burning of Monroe County, Fitch's pronouncement was the first open declaration by Federal authorities that guerrilla attacks would be followed by Federal punitive measures against the civilian populace. Ultimately, this policy would leave the state in ruins by 1865.[22]

As an isolated incident, Fitch's warning to the residents of Monroe County would mean little. However, his directive fit perfectly with later Federal responses to guerrilla attacks. Guerrilla ambushes were followed by the retributive burning of local homes, farms, and entire towns by Federal troops, causing the populace to further resent Union occupation and aiding the recruitment of new Rebel guerrillas. In other areas, Yankee retribution led to local resentment of the guerrillas, who were not necessarily residents of the region. The legality of these Federal antiguerrilla tactics is tied closely to the combatant status of the guerrillas. The Federal army did not consider Hindman's "Bands of Ten" as combatants but as criminals, and tried those captured for "violations of the articles of war," which carried the death penalty. According to the Articles of War and military custom of the time, guerrillas forfeited treatment as prisoners of war by failing to wear uniforms and by attacking from ambush; instead, they were treated as common criminals. Guerrillas were subject to a wide variety of charges—"Violations of the Articles of War," "Being a Guerrilla," and other less esoteric crimes, such as murder, kidnapping, and arson. Under Federal military law, all of these carried a death sentence, and many captured guerrillas in Arkansas ended their careers before a firing squad or a gallows. Such actions only added to the rising level of brutality by both guerrillas and Yankee troops, and the legal status of Hindman's irregulars remained ambiguous until 1864, when a new Union commander initiated a counterinsurgency policy designed to build loyalist support in the state.[23]

The Confederates defended the legality of their guerrilla war. Hindman, on hearing rumors of Fitch's threats to burn towns and summarily execute guerrillas, wrote directly to the Federal officer. In his letter, the Confederate general provided a copy of General Orders Number 17, insisting that the guerrillas "are recognized by me, as the commander of this department, as Confederate troops, and I assert as indisputable the right to dispose and use those troops along the banks of the White River, or wherever else I may deem proper, even should it prove annoying to you in your operations." He closed the letter with, "I respectfully forewarn you that should your threat be executed against any citizens of this district, I shall retaliate, man for man, upon the Federal officers and soldiers who now are, and hereafter may be, in my custody as prisoners of war."[24] After his defeat on the White River, Fitch was in no mood to treat captured guerrillas as soldiers. His response to Hindman was both indignant and prophetic: "You will permit me to suggest that your objections to my proclamation come with ill grace from you when accompanied with your own order above referred to [General Orders Number 17], which order is but an encouragement to rapine and murder upon the part of those in this State, if there be such, so lost to all sense of honor as to avail themselves of your permission to commit such depredations." Fitch warned Hindman that "your captains of ten will soon become little else than highway banditti, more terrible to citizens of your own State than to soldiers and sailors of the United States," a prediction that was fulfilled by 1865.[25]

The Confederate guerrillas in the summer of 1862 infested the entire White River valley, from Batesville to the Mississippi River. Elements of the Ninth Illinois Cavalry, for example, fought a lively skirmish against a guerrilla band known as "Hooker's company" that was estimated at "over three hundred strong." The well-armed Ninth Illinois, which had luckily brought two small howitzers on the foraging expedition, soon put the ill-organized guerrillas to flight. The commander of the force, Colonel Albert G. Brackett, noted that as "I fired two shots [from the howitzers] directly into the enemy . . . four companies of the Ninth Illinois cavalry rode forward with drawn sabers, and made the finest charge I ever witnessed. The enemy was scattered in every direction, being completely routed and broken up." Brackett's troopers gathered thirty-six wagonloads of forage and set fire to the farm of Mr. Waddell in retribution for the attack. Guerrilla losses numbered twenty-eight killed and wounded left on the field; the Federals lost one man captured and twelve wounded. For the Union army in northeast Arkansas during the long summer, foraging would be a full-time occupation owing to the guerrilla menace.[26]

Hindman's decision to adopt guerrilla warfare, although temporarily saving Arkansas for the Confederacy, succeeded in alienating many of the state's residents, who chafed under martial law. The general's political and military rivals, especially General Pike in the Indian Territory, complained to President Davis. Pike specifically disliked Hindman's provost marshal system for controlling the guerrilla bands and for enforcing martial law. Ultimately, Pike's insistence that General Orders Number 17 and the entire provost marshal system was unconstitutional and damaging to Indian-Confederate relations so infuriated Hindman that he sent 250 cavalrymen, under Colonel J. O. Shelby, to arrest Pike. Pike returned to Richmond and pled his case to anyone who would listen. By August, Hindman, despite the military necessity of his actions, had managed to alienate the political leadership of Arkansas and other commanders in the Trans-Mississippi District, and lost the support of the Richmond government.[27] Consequently, he was demoted to divisional command, and the leadership of the Trans-Mississippi District was given to Major General Theophilus Holmes on August 12, 1862.[28]

Despite Hindman's relief, the debate over the legality of the guerrilla bands attacking Union outposts, forage parties, and river traffic continued throughout 1862. The new Federal commander in Memphis, Major General William T. Sherman, held strong opinions about the legal status of captured guerrillas.[29] He was appalled by Hindman's call for a people's war and the guerrilla organization that it had spawned. The general, who some historians consider the father of modern warfare, took a distinctly nineteenth-century view toward guerrillas. In a letter to Hindman (who was still in command of Arkansas, but not the

Trans-Mississippi District) in September 1862, Sherman wrote that "now, whether the guerrillas or partisan rangers, without uniform, without organization except on paper, wandering about the country plundering friend and foe, firing on unarmed boats filled with women and children and on small parties of soldiers, always from ambush, or where they have every advantage, are entitled to the protection and amenities of civilized warfare is a question which I think you would settle very quickly in the abstract." Perhaps more than the Confederate leadership, Sherman recognized the threat to the civilian populace of the South created by unregulated guerrilla bands. Citing that "many gentlemen of the South have beseeched me to protect the people against the acts and inevitable result of this war of ununiformed bands, who, when dispersed, mingle with the people and draw on them the consequences of their individual acts," Sherman demanded that the Confederates either cease unconventional warfare or organize their irregulars as conventional soldiery. If the Confederates did not stop their guerrillas, he threatened to release his own men as irregulars and allow them to plunder the countryside: "You know full well that it is to the interest of the people of the South that we should not disperse our troops as guerrillas; but at that game your guerrillas would meet their equals, and the world would be shocked by the acts of atrocity resulting from such warfare."[30]

Hindman's superior, Major General Holmes, responded to Sherman's threat with one of his own. Citing the prospect of Federals arming freed slaves as the Union's plan for a "war of extermination" against white Southerners, Holmes defended the use of guerrillas who did not wear uniforms: "We cannot be expected to allow our enemies to decide for us whether we shall fight them in masses or individually, in uniform, without uniform, openly or from ambush," he began, continuing that "if you [the Federal high command] go to the extreme which the British threatened [in the American Revolution], of putting our men to death for refusing to conform to your notions [of civilized warfare], we shall be driven, as [General George] Washington avowed that he would be, to retaliate man for man." Holmes closed the letter by coldly stating that "I have at the same time ordered all Federal prisoners in my hands into close confinement to wait your answer to this letter. That answer will decide their fate and fix the character of the war as we are concerned." For both North and South, the guerrilla warfare that began in Arkansas in the summer of 1862 could have easily escalated the conflict into an all-out war, where no quarter was asked or given, and where prisoners would be routinely executed for real and imagined crimes. Added to this explosive mix was the Confederates' racist contention that the Union's black troops were the equivalent of unorganized guerrilla bands. No doubt such actions would have further traumatized the nation's population and undermined the chances of postwar reconciliation.[31]

Sherman, with the backing of his superior, U. S. Grant, continued to capture and try guerrillas as criminals and not as soldiers. In his response to Holmes's threat, Sherman wrote that "if, as you threaten in your letter [to] hang . . . a prisoner in your hands, in retaliation for some act of ours . . . remember that we have hundreds of thousands of men bitter and yearning for revenge. Let us but loose these from the restraints of discipline and no life or property would be safe in the regions where we do hold possession and power." He closed with his own threat to both Holmes and Hindman, stating, "you initiate the game, and my word for it your people will regret it long after you pass from earth." The Confederates responded by executing several captured Federal soldiers. Fortunately, the retributive execution of guerrillas and captured Federals receded as the Rebels themselves began to question the usefulness of the unorganized irregular bands.[32]

From the summer of 1862 to the summer of 1863, the guerrillas reached their peak of military utility, playing an important role in hindering both Curtis's attempt to capture Little Rock in the summer of 1862 and Grant's drive toward Vicksburg in late 1862 and early 1863. The Federal dependence on the Mississippi River for transportation and logistical support made Arkansas an exceptionally advantageous place for irregular warfare, and guerrilla bands along the Mississippi River grew in the winter of 1862–63. The buildup of irregulars occurred for several reasons. The failure of the Union Army of the Southwest to take Little Rock relieved pressure on Hindman, and later Holmes, to defend the capital itself. The conventional war continued to be the focus of both sides, and new Confederate troops were raised. The Rebel loss at Prairie Grove (December 7–8, 1862), destroyed the last hope of a conventional victory for the Confederates in Arkansas, but by that time the irregulars had already established themselves in much of the backcountry of the state. For their part, the Federals focused on holding a handful of strategic towns in the state and supporting their drive on Vicksburg, ignoring the guerrillas. With the state north of the Arkansas River effectively abandoned by the Confederates, and the Union army content to garrison a few towns, the guerrilla ruled the hinterland. Still lacking logistical support, organization, or discipline, these irregulars turned to the civilian populace for support and moved to regions where they could plunder without interference. Consequently, the guerrilla companies moved from the area around Little Rock to either northwest Arkansas to prey on the large Unionist population or to the Mississippi to raid the unarmed riverboats supplying Grant's army.[33]

Rebel authorities discovered that they had lost control of their guerrillas by the winter of 1862–63, and they would never regain it. That winter, the guerrilla bands showed the first signs of turning into the plundering marauders that they would later become. To keep their units intact and motivated, some irregular commanders turned to pillaging schemes. Captain J. F. Barton, the leader of an independent guerrilla company in Crittenden County, wrote to Hindman in early 1863, attempting to explain the need to further motivate his men: "The thing we lack is incentive and motive to induce the men to risk their lives and their all to accomplish the end [defeat of the Union]." To keep his guerrillas in the field and to gain more recruits, Barton suggested that Hindman issue letters of marque and reprisal, legally authorizing the irregulars to seize and sell Union property. Barton promised he could "guarantee to [Hindman] and the Gov't. that we can organize two companies of two hundred men each who will break up the navigation of the river except for gunboats, and if they are not watchful we will get some of them." Hindman's response to the request is unknown, but it is worth noting that Barton's group was still operating as an effective guerrilla company along the Mississippi until mid-1863.[34]

After the Confederate defeat at the Battle of Prairie Grove in December 1862, Hindman was transferred to Tennessee. Prior to his departure he realized the dangers of the guerrilla force he had created. Men of military age, instead of volunteering for service in the conventional military, had opted for membership in local guerrilla bands. The reasons for this are obvious; local service meant living at home, defending one's own community, and the opportunity for plunder without retribution from military authorities. As early as July 1862, the Confederate leaders in Arkansas recognized the problems in a mass raising of guerrilla units, but the threat of imminent Union invasion stopped any attempts to rein in new independent companies. By the spring of 1863, however, the growth of these bands posed a serious threat to the conscription of new troops. In a circular to the chief of the recruiting service, Colonel A. S. Morgan, Hindman revised his earlier course and prohibited "all men between 18 and 40 years of age from joining the independent or unattached cavalry companies." Instead, Morgan was to "take all such men out of those companies and hold them for infantry service," preferring charges against county provosts marshal or guerrilla captains who attempted to stop the transfers.[35]

Sadly for the Confederacy, few independent companies were disbanded. The organized Rebel forces did not control the backcountry of Arkansas, where most of the guerrillas were located, and conventional military leaders did not want to disband the units in direct contact with the Federal armies along the Mississippi or in the northwest counties of the state. Consequently, the guerrilla companies that were threatened by Confederate conscription officers, who aimed at transferring the irregulars to infantry commands, began to resist the Rebel government's authority with force. Guerrilla bands that worked closely with the conventional army took the possibility of being dismounted or disbanded as a direct attack on the units themselves. Colonel W. P. Lane, the commander of a Texas partisan ranger outfit, printed a circular for his men to placate any fears that they would be dismounted. "Attention Partizan Rancers [sic]! All persons who have enlisted for, or squads or companies raised by authority from Col. W. P. Lane (Lane's Rangers) . . . Bring all the arms possible. We have special orders by which WE ARE NOT TO BE DISMOUNTED!"[36] The loss of privately owned horses, of freedom to come and go at their pleasure, and to fight the war as they saw fit threatened the existence of the guerrilla bands and led to the first major split between the Confederate regular and irregular forces in Arkansas.

Beginning in 1863, the Confederate army in Arkansas began fighting a three-way war between its own guerrillas, who avoided conscription and military discipline, and the Federals, who attempted to hunt the guerrillas to extinction as well as engage the regular Confederate forces. Guerrilla bands that preferred to fight their own war, outside of the influence of the Confederate army, moved to the northern half of the state. There, the Union army maintained only a handful of fortified outposts, abandoning the countryside because of a lack of men. The northern half of the state became the most guerrilla-infested region of Arkansas for the last two years of the war, as groups from Missouri, the Indian Territory, Louisiana, and Texas, as well as homegrown irregulars, preyed on the local population for survival. For the

Confederacy, and the citizens of the state, the war in Arkansas had taken a complex and cruel turn.[37]

By the fall of 1863, the Confederate guerrillas had become a major problem for the conventional Confederate army occupying southern Arkansas. The meager forces remaining after the fall of Little Rock in September were soon dispersed across the southern half of the state in a vain attempt to halt pillaging by their own guerrilla companies. In a series of general orders, the Confederate commander in south Arkansas sent warning to the guerrillas, writing in November "that gross and repeated outrages have been committed upon the persons and property of civilians in this District . . . appeals have been made to stimulate the pride of the men, and induce them to discontinue, in their comparisons, conduct disgraceful to themselves, both as men and soldiers. But the evils have not ceased, and it would appear as if the most stringent measures alone can check them."[38]

A month later, when it became apparent that the appeal to the guerrillas' conscience had failed, the Confederates responded by sending Colonel (later Brigadier General) Shelby's cavalrymen to hunt them down. Shelby, an experienced irregular cavalry leader, grew to loathe the uncontrolled guerrillas.[39] In 1864, as the cavalry commander under fellow Missourian Sterling C. Price, Shelby dealt swiftly and unmercifully with the independent guerrilla companies. Price's raid, the longest such operation of the Civil War, traversed northern Arkansas as it moved toward St. Louis. Shelby initially planned to absorb the independent companies into his own cavalry command, but discovered that the guerrillas had degenerated into brigands. As one guerrilla outfit, "Captain Parke's Independent Company," attempted to join Shelby's force, the Confederate cavalryman ordered Parke's arrest. In a statement to General Price, recommending the immediate execution of Parke and his henchmen, Shelby wrote "their [Parke's men] gross outrages committed upon Southern families, such as robbing women and children of their money and wearing apparel," was common among the guerrilla bands. Later, after arresting several of the most despicable guerrilla leaders, Shelby directed one of his battalion commanders, Lieutenant Colonel Joseph B. Love, to "shoot them whenever found . . . not one of them is to be spared."[40]

Shelby found northeast Arkansas abandoned by the Union army and filled with bands of professedly Confederate guerrillas preying on the citizenry. He wrote that they were "Confederate soldiers in nothing save the name, robbers and jayhawkers [who] have vied with the Federals in plundering, devouring and wasting the subsistence of Loyal Southerners." As for their military usefulness, he added, "the condition of the so-called Confederate forces here was horrible in the extreme. No organization, no concentration, no discipline, no law, no anything . . . riding rough over defenseless families on stolen horses, whole predatory bands of Federals—unmolested and unfought—roamed about like devouring wolves, and swept whole neighborhoods at a breath."[41]

By 1864, guerrilla companies fit Shelby's descriptions, as both Confederate and Federal riverboats became targets for the renegade guerrilla bands. Edward W. Gantt, a Confederate brigadier general who later defected to the Union cause, wrote in the fall of 1863 of one such incident. "A few days since [in October 1863], a Confederate officer was aboard a transport with his family," when guerrillas attacked the boat. The Confederate officer "stepped forward and entreated the [guerrillas] not to fire, that their friends were on board." The guerrillas, after hearing his pleas, killed him and looted the boat. Another Confederate officer, Colonel DeRosy Carroll of Franklin Country (southwest of Fort Smith), was killed for resisting a guerrilla company led by "Wild Bill" Dark, "formerly a Confederate soldier in good service." Another independent company, led by a "Captain Webb," terrorized the region around Yellville, in northern Arkansas. One resident later wrote that "after the Federal troops left Yellville, Webb's company came into town one night and burned thirty-two houses, including the Methodist church, Masonic hall, and two hotels." According to Thomas Estes, the guerrilla band was later "killed by regular Confederate troops, in their last hiding place, in Independence County, Arkansas, near Batesville."[42]

The guerrilla leaders who attempted to both obey the Confederate government and maintain their strategy of plunder soon found themselves in an unenviable position. Elmo Ingenthron's book *Borderland Rebellion* relates the story of a captured Rebel guerrilla, Solomon Roberts. The bushwhacker, who "imagined that any Federal property should of right belong to the Confederacy," was charged by the *Confederates* with breaking the rules of war. He was arrested and given one week to prepare his defense. Roberts's lawyer "advised him to leave the country; but this advice was not taken and he was tried and executed." With examples such as this, it is not surprising that the Rebel guerrillas avoided contact with their own civil and military authorities as much as possible in the last year of the war.[43]

As chapter 2 will discuss, by the winter of 1863–64 the Federals had abandoned much of the state north of the Arkansas River. The guerrillas, without either Union or Confederate interference, turned their attention to plundering as much of the region as possible. For the people of northern Arkansas, the Civil War from late 1863 to the final surrender in May 1865 was a time of terror. Any yeoman farmer, whether a Unionist or Confederate, was at risk on his isolated mountain homestead. The guerrillas, separated from any military discipline by the Union occupation of the Arkansas River towns (Fort Smith, Little Rock, and Helena), preyed on these small farmers for information, food, weapons, and mounts. Inevitably, members of these guerrilla units saw the possibility of financial gain from plundering their neighbors.

One such incident, related by an aged mountaineer in the late 1940s about his father's experience as a teenager during the war, perhaps encapsulates the trauma faced by many isolated farmers. Mr. Beach, a resident of Hindsville, Arkansas (in Madison County), recalled that "there was three of them [guerrillas, whom Beach always referred to as bushwhackers]" that entered his father's home and demanded food. The guerrilla band not only looted the home, they "took all of grandma's hogs and killed them. Didn't eat any part, mind you, but jest killed them. Same way with the mules and horses and cows."[44]

The Beach family's experience with a guerrilla band could be considered mild compared with the tales told to Silas C. Turnbo, a former Confederate and a postwar folklorist.[45] Turnbo compiled a large volume of wartime tales of the Arkansas Ozarks in the 1880s, when the experience of the Civil War still was fresh in the minds of the participants. Mrs. Elvira Eoff, a resident of Boone County, recalled the local Methodist preacher, Dan Wilson, who, with two other men, was captured by a Confederate guerrilla band. "Mr. Wilson was a prayerful man," she began, describing how "his captors tried to make him keep quiet, but he continued his devotions in spite of their threats." The resulting barbarity was still well remembered in Boone County: "One of the bushwhackers remarked that he would stop his fuss and grabbed him, and with the assistance of his partners in crime, he pulled his tongue out and cut part of it off. Soon they killed all three men."[46]

The guerrillas' rampages, along with the persecution by Confederate provosts marshal of Unionists and the Federal army plundering of pro-Confederates, forced many residents of northern Arkansas to leave. The pro-Confederate population either stayed in the region, especially those who supported the guerrillas, or headed toward Rebel lines in southern Arkansas, northern Louisiana, or Texas. Unionists headed north into Missouri, especially around the city of Springfield. Making the trek to safety meant that the refugees had to move through guerrilla-infested country. L. M. "Buck" Toney, who was a teenager during the war in Izard County, recalled that "the war progressed to such an extent that all the men had to take sides, my mother, Bethy Toney, and we children were ordered to leave Izard County, but not before all of our provisions were taken from us and all our property that we had not concealed in the forest." The Toneys, without an adult male protector, were easy prey for bushwhackers: "After getting four miles into Oregon Country [Missouri]," the helpless family was "robbed of our wagon, oxen and everything except what few clothes we had on and set adrift."[47]

However victimized the bulk of the population and the refugees were, their travails pale in comparison with the terrorizing of the avowed Unionists. For example, John Fritts, a resident of Marion County, was a well-liked and respected member of his community before the war. When war broke out, he openly supported the Union cause, but did not serve in the Federal army or hinder Confederate operations. This did not stop a band of Rebel irregulars from riding to his home on the night of July 27, 1864, and dragging him and another man into the woods and shooting them. The families of "Union men" were also victimized. David Chyle lived on the Missouri side of the poorly defined Arkansas-Missouri border, and when the opportunity came, joined the Union army as a member of the First Arkansas Cavalry. This made Chyle's family a prime target for Confederate guerrillas. He later recalled that "one day a bunch of mounted guerrillas who claimed to be Southern men rode up to our house and compelled my father who was sixty years old to go with them." The guerrillas also forced several small boys and another man to go with them. Reaching an isolated field, the guerrillas released the boys and shot the men. Later, the same Confederate guerrillas hanged two other Unionists in the neighborhood. Being an open Unionist could be a death sentence in northern Arkansas during the final two years of the war.[48]

The Unionists were targets of terrorism from even the most organized and disciplined partisan ranger companies. Lieutenant Colonel Sidney L. Jackman, a Confederate recruiting officer operating along the border of Arkansas and Missouri, recalled that he served on a drumhead court-martial against a captured Unionist. Two other Confederate officers served as judge and jury against a "union Preacher who lived near the border of Mo., and Ark," whose name he could not recall. Jackman related that the preacher was "reported a bad man. Coffee [Colonel Coffee, the ranking Confederate on the court-martial] had him court-martialed, with the hope of finding him guilty of some crime that would justify his execution." The trial began, and "no evidence of any crime whatever, was proved against him, except the fact, that he was a union man, and that he admitted himself." Although this infuriated the other two Rebel officers, who "regarded [it] as ample evidence . . . [to] justify execution," Jackman defended the minister, saying "that they could hang or shoot me, upon the same testimony." Jackman's defense of the Unionist was a surprise to the other two officers, who regularly conducted such drumhead trials against avowed Yankee sympathizers. Jackman won the old preacher's release, noting "the expression of his face, and the grip of his hand when he bade me farewell, [was] not soon forgotten."[49]

The small immigrant population in Arkansas was also singled out for brutality by the Rebel guerrilla bands. The staunchly pro-Union town of Hermannsberg, for example, experienced guerrilla raid after guerrilla raid. Karl Friedrich Hermann, who founded the German immigrant town in the 1850s, wrote that "the few fanatical neighbors [pro-Confederates] were nothing to fear; [however] the 'foreign' guerrilla bands [from outside the community] were nothing but rabble and riffraff, fighting the war on their own terms." Later, Hermann described the irregulars as "wahre Teufel," or "genuine Devils," who "plundered all Union people, [with] everyone fearing constant death [from] the robbers, who had no military organization and dressed in any uniform they pleased." The residents of Hermannsburg, after enduring constant terrorizing, finally abandoned their homes and farms in early 1863, heading to Missouri and never returning to Arkansas.[50]

By 1864, many, but not all, of the Confederate guerrillas, isolated from the conventional forces in southwest Arkansas by both the Union army and by choice, had become no more than terrorists and brigands. They habitually preyed on the civilian population and steadfastly avoided contact with the Union army. Conscription agents, and other officials of the Confederate government, were at risk of summary execution by guerrillas if caught, simply because the irregulars preferred to fight the war without official interference, including being drafted into the conventional army. Basic responsibilities of government vanished under the irregular's tyranny. For instance, the Arkansas Confederate government, despite offering ample payment, could not contract for mail service south of the Arkansas River owing to guerrilla activity, while in other areas such tasks as collecting taxes or arresting criminals became impossible. As a result, any semblance of civil order in the guerrilla-occupied regions vanished with the conventional armies, which were the only governmental elements of either side to possess the means to suppress the guerrillas.[51]

In the last year of the war, hunting their own guerrillas became a full-time occupation for the Confederate army, which hampered their actions against the Federals. Colonel John C. Wright, the commander of the Twelfth Arkansas Cavalry Regiment, noted that "in the hills and mountains south of Ft. Smith, there were bands of deserters and jayhawkers who were robbing and terrorizing the Southern people." Half of his regiment was sent to suppress the guerrilla bands in 1863 and 1864, and succeeded in breaking up the gangs as long as they were in the area. Unfortunately, "as soon as we left they would gather again. Nothing but cavalry can deal with such outlaws."[52] Where the Confederate army could not deal with the rampaging bands, local Confederate citizens organized militia companies to deal with the threat. Henry Merrell, a Northerner who had moved to Arkansas before the war, described the raising of a militia company to fight "a Capt. Greer who had been elected Capt. of a Company in Confederate service, but failing to pass the examination was reduced to the ranks; whereupon he deserted after writing passes for a number of soldiers who also deserted and met him in the mountains . . . forming the nucleus of the band." Greer's guerrillas, according to Merrell, "had to plunder in order to subsist, but it was not long before they proceeded to an attempt at murder," which led the community to organize a militia force under a Captain Morgan. Morgan's militiamen stormed the guerrillas' hideout, killing some and hanging others. In most cases, the violent solution to the guerrilla problem rarely was a permanent one: Captain Morgan was later killed by guerrillas from ambush.[53]

The cumulative effect of the uncontrollable guerrilla bands was a rapid decline in the influence and legitimacy of the Confederate government in Arkansas. Small towns, such as Yellville, in northern Arkansas, and Hot Springs, in the south-central region of the state, were given over to the guerrillas or abandoned altogether. The local governments themselves, ostensibly the command and control element in the guerrilla organization, came under attack. In Benton County, Confederate guerrillas attacked and destroyed the Confederate county clerk's home, after they found that he had moved the county records to his home for safekeeping. It was well after the end of the war before Benton County could reconstruct the legal transactions burned by the guerrillas, from marriage licenses to land titles to tax receipts. In western Arkansas, the conditions were much the same, as the hinterland was abandoned to the guerrillas. A Fort Smith newspaper reported in February 1864 that two-thirds of the farms in the region were abandoned, and of the remaining one-third, only a third of those had men working the fields.[54]

The damage caused by the guerrillas was counterproductive to both their survival and that of the Confederacy in Arkansas. Isolated from the Confederate army in south Arkansas, the guerrillas were dependent on the local populace to survive. Perversely, the Confederate guerrillas, now usually referred to as "bushwhackers" by the remaining residents of Arkansas north of the Arkansas River, stepped up their plundering and were soon seen as criminals and banditti. The result was the alienation of civilians who could have supported the guerrillas with supplies and manpower. John Bowen, writing to his brother-in-law from Waldron (in Scott County), described the unstable and dangerous conditions caused by the guerrillas: "the horse property is confuscated [by both Confederates and guerrillas] heare, and a man would not be safe to go round heare to hunt up property—bushwhackers might get a mans scalp."[55] Henry Merrill, operating a cotton mill at Royston (Pike County) that produced cloth for the Trans-Mississippi District, was forced to sell his factory to the Rebel government. His isolated location exposed his mill to "the attacks of confederated deserters . . . moreover, we were not popular with the people, and to rob us would have been regarded by many as a good joke rather than a crime. For me personally as a 'd——d Yankee' and a 'speculator,' I might look for nothing less than hanging to be my portion if they got hold of me."[56] The guerrillas, formed and organized to halt the depredations of the Federal army, instead eroded the loyalty of many Arkansans to the Confederacy and reduced the support from the locals.

The closing months of the Civil War saw the demise of the Confederate guerrilla in northern Arkansas, as Federal counterinsurgency programs succeeded in isolating and destroying the largest groups. In southern Arkansas, the guerrilla bands found their ranks swollen by deserters and other malcontents who took advantage of the relative powerlessness of the Arkansas Confederate government. Robert L. Kerby, in *Kirby Smith's Confederacy*, notes that the "legislature of Confederate Arkansas had already become a dim memory." The few remaining legislators convened at the temporary Confederate state capital at Washington, in Hempstead County, and held a final session on September 22, 1864. It "debated for a week, and [then] dispersed, never to reconvene." For all intents and purposes, the Confederate civil government of Arkansas had ceased to exist in the fall of 1864. With the collapse of the civilian authorities, only the Union and Confederate armies remained as viable institutions of law and order.[57]

The winter of 1864 was harder on the guerrillas than any previous time. The Federal counterinsurgency program managed to isolate some guerrilla bands in north-central Arkansas, denying them food and men. Additionally, the guerrillas discovered that their assault on the civilian populace had only succeeded in driving out their supporters; when they were forced away from the Federally protected enclaves, they found that the countryside was virtually abandoned. Union farm colonies, a new emphasis on pursuing and destroying the irregulars, and the capturing of some of the more notorious guerrilla leaders by the Federals resulted in the further scattering and isolation of the irregulars by the spring of 1865.[58]

The end of the war in Arkansas in May 1865 presented a dilemma to both the Union army and the remaining guerrilla bands. Some guerrillas, despite their fearsome reputation, steadfastly believed in the Confederate cause but saw the surrender of their commanders, such as Brigadier General M. Jeff Thompson, as a chance to return to civilian life without retribution. Others did not plan to stop fighting so easily. One such incident was the surrender of a group of Confederate guerrillas led by Captains Husband, Maybery, and Vaugine at Devall's Bluff in mid-May. Initially, Major General Joseph J. Reynolds, the Union commander in Arkansas, authorized the surrender only of Captain Husband and his company, which, "notwithstanding their irregularity," was not considered to be a bushwhacker band; of Vaugine and Maybery, he said, "hunt them down, of course, but don't trouble yourself about the question of outlawry." A Federal officer, Major G. W. Davis of the Thirteenth Illinois Cavalry, still attempted to convince the guerrilla chieftains to surrender, going into their camp unarmed with a civilian guide. Both Maybery and Vaugine claimed that "they

and their men had fired the last shot at [the Federals]," yet resisted surrendering owing to "threats [that] had been made against them which
made it inconsistent for them to voluntarily surrender at [Pine Bluff]."
The guerrilla commanders, knowing their reception from the local
populace they had terrorized for three years would not be a warm one,
informed the Union officer that "it was their intention to leave the
country immediately." Major Davis returned to Pine Bluff on May 11,
followed by fifteen of the guerrillas who wished to individually surrender. The guerrilla leaders had no idea what to do—they could either
surrender and hope for Union mercy, or they could attempt to flee the
area and head west. The final decision was made by Captain Maybery,
who "killed his coadjutor, Vaugine, on the 14th instant, in a personal
encounter, since which time forty-eight of his men have come into the
post and surrendered."[59]

As the guerrilla bands began their careers in bloody violence, many
ended their days by fighting among themselves, while others surrendered or simply returned home. Some of the Confederate guerrilla leaders cooperated with the Union army in hunting down the more violent
bushwhacker bands.[60] Most followed the example of men like Captain
H. Reynolds, who stated that "from the best information I can get [I]
believe we are whipped," and surrendered to the nearest Federal
authorities. Fortunately for the guerillas, the Union army in Arkansas
saw that the easiest way to prevent a continual insurgency was to grant
leniency to the surrendered bands, and by mid-June all of the organized guerrilla companies, some of which had been in the field for three
years, ceased to exist.[61]

The irregular conflict in Arkansas was a true people's war as
described by both Clausewitz and Jomini. In *On War*, Clausewitz illustrated the conditions under which a people's war would most likely
succeed—factors of terrain, national will, and the relationship of the
peripheral combat area to the industrial and political center. Arkansas,
isolated by Union military operations and on the far limits of the Confederacy, provided a fertile ground for the growth of Clausewitz's
people's war. However, it was Jomini who perhaps more clearly com-
prehended the costs of such a conflict, one in which "the excited passions of a people" become the main tool of war. In *The Art of War*,
Jomini warned that "the spectacle of a spontaneous uprising of a nation
is rarely seen; and, though there be in it something grand and noble
which commands our admiration, the consequences are so terrible

that, for the sake of humanity, we ought to hope never to see it." The Confederate guerrilla war in Arkansas, born in desperation, lacking legitimacy in the eyes of both its own people and its enemies, and without the controlling hand of a formal military structure, became the monster feared by Jomini.[62]

The guerrillas, despite their organizational and logistical failures, did represent the will of some of the state's residents. Not all the guerrilla bands were brazen looters; many, such as the groups under Captains Maybery and Husband, mentioned above, saw themselves as defenders of their homes and families from the invading Federal army. Others, such as John Cecil, former sheriff of Newton County, were wholeheartedly supported by the local populace and fought both "bushwhackers" and the Federal army.[63] Despite the intent of some patriotic Confederate guerrilla commanders, the lack of adequate control of the guerrilla war by both the Confederate government and military destroyed any widespread support for the independent companies. Out of pure survival, the "Bands of Ten" raised in 1862, armed with legal protection as provosts marshal and without supplies, used terror and extortion to stay in the field. This is not to say that all the guerrillas that were fighting in Arkansas drew their justification for existence from General Orders Number 17. Some were clearly bands of deserters, while others were no more than criminal gangs taking advantage of the chaos to terrorize their neighbors. Together, some of irregulars raised under General Orders Number 17, plus all the less disciplined guerrilla groups operating in Arkansas, began preying on the civilian populace. The wholesale looting of Unionists, immigrants, and later loyal Confederates forced the population of Arkansas to flee to areas under military protection—Union or Confederate. Ironically, as the guerrillas stepped up their orgy of pillaging, they were destroying their basis of support. With the refugees went their food supplies, information sources, mounts, weapons, and especially recruits.

In the twentieth century, Mao Tse-tung stated that "because guerrilla warfare derives from the masses and is supported by them, it can neither exist nor flourish if it separates itself from their sympathies and cooperation." In Arkansas, the guerrillas managed to alienate so much of the population that they caused a mass migration of the state's free and slave population to safer zones. This severely hampered the ability of the Rebel government and military to maintain conscription and military industries, not to mention the basic governmental duties of mail delivery and legal record keeping. The Confederate guerrillas, hailed as "an effective and captivating branch of the service" in 1862, came to terrorize the citizenry and drain the limited manpower of the Confederate army by 1865.[64]

In short, the Confederacy's guerrilla war in Arkansas, meant to serve as a temporary measure to slow the Federal advance in 1862, grew into a conflict of its own, pitting the guerrilla against the organized armies of both sides, with the prize being the civilian populace that they were ostensibly defending. Mismanagement of the guerrilla companies by the Confederate leadership, and the denial of logistical support to the units by the Rebel army, resulted in the degeneration of the bands into marauders and bushwhackers. In the defense of General Hindman and General Holmes, not all of the guerrillas in Arkansas were raised under the auspices of General Orders Number 17. As in any irregular war, malcontents, plunderers, and criminals took advantage of the situation to rob, pillage, and settle long-standing feuds with their neighbors, as noted by Silas Turnbo and others.[65] However, when the legally raised independent companies turned to plundering for survival, they destroyed any Confederate hope of using them as adjuncts to the regular forces or as a viable threat against the Federal army. The Confederacy's sole attempt at a people's war died not because of a lack of nationalism or fervor, but because of a dearth of effective leadership and organization at the operational level of war. Sadly for the Confederates, the Arkansas guerilla could have been an effective tool to support the conventional war, as evidenced by the actions on the White River on 1862.

For the Confederates, the failure to control and support the guerrillas created a vicious circle in which the only winner was the Union army. Cut off from supplies and control by military and political authorities, the guerrillas fought their own war against the Federals and pro-Union neighbors, and ultimately some guerrillas turned against the Confederates as well, especially the hated conscription officers. The widespread lawlessness caused by the irregulars and exacerbated by the Confederate authorities' indifference toward their own guerrillas, greatly aided the invading Federal army. By 1865, the Yankee invader, instead of the Rebel guerrilla, was seen as the protector of law and order by many Arkansans. Instead of a mass uprising of the populace against an invading foe, the guerrilla war became a self-inflicted wound that ultimately doomed the Rebel cause in Arkansas.

FIRE, PROVOSTS, AND TORIES

The Federal Counterinsurgency Campaign in Arkansas

Desolation is not the purpose of the North—but Conquest.
Henry M. Rector, Confederate governor to
President Jefferson Davis, April 11, 1862

In the spring of 1862, Major General Samuel Curtis, flush from his victory at Pea Ridge, prepared to become the first Federal general to conquer a seceded state. The Confederate armies raised to resist the Union invasion were scattered, underequipped, and without a strong leader. Arkansas lay at his feet.

Yet he failed to take the state capital at Little Rock in the summer of 1862, giving Arkansas and the trans-Mississippi Confederacy another lease on life. As discussed in the preceding chapter, much of Curtis's failure can be credited directly to the ways Confederates reorganized their conventional forces in 1862, as well as to the raising and employing of Rebel guerrillas. Ironically, the launching of a people's war against the Federals in 1862, and its concordant defeat of Curtis's plan of conquest, built the foundation of Federal military activities in Arkansas until 1865. These activities would ensure the rise of pro-Union Arkansans to positions of military and civil leadership, and spelled doom for the Confederate cause in Arkansas.

Beginning with Curtis, Federal army commanders tried to find ways to limit the guerrilla threat. Two programs aimed at destroying the irregulars, one to reduce the guerrillas' impact on conventional operations, and a second to pacify the state to ease its transition back into the Union. The first phase focused on protecting the Federal armies as they moved through the region. These antiguerrilla campaigns, occurring throughout the war but more common in 1862–63, brought misery to the citizenry of the state as both Union troops and Confederate guerrillas burned, plundered, and destroyed everything that hindered their operations. The second phase, counterguerrilla operations meant to catch guerrilla outfits and eliminate their hideouts, became the primary mission of many Federals, including special antiguerrilla units and the military police, or provosts marshal. In the last two years of the war, counterguerrilla operations were the paramount duties for some conventional units, especially the locally raised Unionist regiments, as the more strategically important theaters across the Mississippi drew men from the state. Of these conventional regiments, the First Arkansas Cavalry (Union), stationed at Fayetteville, conducted a model counterinsurgency campaign that managed to both eliminate irregulars and rebuild the social structure of loyal Arkansas.

The march of Curtis's victorious Army of the Southwest back into Arkansas in late April 1862 marked the beginning of the guerrilla war. The region from Salem (where his army entered the state) to Little Rock contained some of the most inhospitable environment west of the Mississippi. Swamps, mosquitoes, and poisonous snakes all served to harass Curtis's army, but two main enemies—terrain and Confederate guerrillas—undercut his mission to seize the state capital.[1] Arkansas in early May is hot and humid, and a moving army requires tens of thousands of gallons of drinkable water each day. Luckily for the Yankees, heavy spring rains ensured the rivers and creeks were full. Unluckily for them, these same bodies of water also slowed their advance to a crawl. In his haste to push into Arkansas, Curtis had neglected to move his pontoon bridges to the front of his army. Consequently, much of the first week of May 1862 was spent waiting on pontoon bridges to arrive so that the army could cross both the White and Little Red Rivers in northeast Arkansas.[2] Compounding the problem was the lack of forage for the Federal army. In a report to St. Louis, Curtis explained that he and his army had "left nothing for man or brute in the country passed over by my army, except a little saving to feed the poor."

His tenuous supply lines, stretching from central Missouri to Searcy Landing, Arkansas (about forty miles from Little Rock), were further hampered by the weather. "It rains night and day; streams are all high, mud ankle deep," Curtis wrote. To deal with the lack of forage, Curtis ordered his army to spread out as they crossed the Missouri border, further weakening his small force. It was during this time that the Federals first engaged Confederate guerrillas in Arkansas, whose main goal was the isolation of Curtis's divided army.[3]

The threat from irregulars presented sundry new problems for Curtis, who had never faced unconventional operations on the scale present in northeast Arkansas. Federal soldiers soon found themselves shot at from swamps, forests, towns, and farms. Small detachments of guerrillas constantly harassed the Federals throughout May and June 1862, eroding morale, limiting the scope of foraging expeditions, and further exacerbating their supply problems. For example, the commander of the Ninth Illinois Cavalry, Colonel Albert Brackett, reported that guerrillas murdered one of his soldiers on May 21, 1862. In a letter to his division commander, Brigadier General Frederick Steele, he wrote that "an example must be made in some way here, or our soldiers and expressmen will be assassinated on every occasion." His attitude reflected the frustration in the Federal command, as he described locals who would act like "good Union men" while concealing their true occupation as guerrillas. Having lost three men of his command (two killed and one wounded) to bushwhackers, Brackett recommended issuing a strong proclamation warning Arkansans that extreme measures would be taken against any community sponsoring such acts.[4]

The frustration of dealing with an irregular foe took its toll on the Federal troops in Arkansas. Second Lieutenant Benjamin F. McIntyre of Company A, Nineteenth Iowa Infantry, described what it was like to fight the Confederate bushwhackers. "In comeing [sic] through a gorge or defile of the Boston Mountains [in the foothills of the Ozarks, northeast of Fort Smith] we were fired upon . . . from the ridge high above us," he explained. The attack "threw our regiment into momentary confusion" but soon "a number [of] troops scaled the hills." McIntyre closed by stating that "it taught Stragglers [sic] a lesson and many who had loitered behind will remain with their regiment hereafter." The experience of the Nineteenth Iowa Infantry was not uncommon to Federal units moving in the backcountry of Arkansas in 1862–63;

such incidents did much to provoke Union troops to punish local communities for guerrilla attacks.[5]

The antiguerrilla operations of General Curtis's Army of the Southwest became the pattern for all Union forces in Arkansas until after the fall of Little Rock in September 1863. Generally speaking, antiguerrilla operations, or those aimed at protecting the conventional force from harassment or injury from enemy irregular forces, did not take into account the root causes of civilian resistance. The civilians themselves are of little importance in an antiguerrilla campaign, except in how they supply and sustain the guerrillas. Consequently, antiguerrilla operations tend to be brutal and retributive, punishing entire communities for the acts of guerrillas who may or may not be members of that community. The punitive policy in Arkansas soon developed into a pattern of retributive burnings in which homes, farms, and even small towns were burned to the ground by vindictive Federal troops. These *retributive burnings* began during the White River Expedition in the hot summer of 1862, and continued throughout the war, though becoming less common as the war continued.[6]

The Federal army initially employed conventional troops in a manner that duplicated many of the tactics used by European forces in Africa and Asia.[7] After guerrilla activity increased in an area, a punitive expedition would be launched to either find the partisans or punish the local community for harboring them. Union troops found such operations frustrating, and they rarely achieved the goal of eliminating the guerrillas. One large raid took place southeast of Little Rock on June 3, 1864; although it was conducted two years after the first Union troops began fighting the irregulars, it is indicative of antiguerrilla operations in the war. A notorious guerrilla captain, Thomas Steele, was reported to be operating out of his brother's plantation near Terry's Landing, on the Arkansas River between Little Rock and Pine Bluff. Lieutenant Colonel Robert F. Patterson led a force of 800 infantrymen of his Twenty-ninth Iowa Infantry, 80 cavalrymen, and the armed steamer *Leonora* to attack and destroy Steele's band. Patterson's plan pitted Federal strengths against supposed guerrilla weaknesses; he would use his infantry to isolate the area, preventing anyone from warning the bushwhackers. The *Leonora* and the cavalry would secure the far side of the Arkansas River to prevent the guerrillas from escaping downstream.[8]

Fifty men held the landing, while another 140 captured and held Scott's Bridge south of the plantation. Twenty-five men remained on the steamer, which moved into the middle of the Arkansas opposite the plantation. The remainder of Patterson's command moved to Pais's plantation, north of Steele's, "taking with us every person who could give information to the enemy." Patterson's main force seized Steele's plantation, capturing the owner and his family, but found no guerrillas. When he discovered that he missed capturing the entire partisan contingent by a single day, he decided to destroy the plantation to eliminate the guerrillas' base of operations. In his final analysis of the expedition, he deemed it a limited success, explaining that "the number of men under command of Roberts [Thomas Steele's second in command] and Steele will not exceed 50 and then are usually but a few of them together." He added that capturing a guerrilla unit encamped was almost impossible, since "they [the guerrillas] have no fixed equipment but go from one place to another, their object being to get Government horses, to destroy Government plantations, and to make up a company by recruiting and conscription." The failure of antiguerrilla expeditions such as Colonel Patterson's to eliminate the guerrillas infesting Union-controlled Arkansas pushed Federal officers to develop new and innovative programs, programs that often strayed far from the doctrine of the era.[9]

Like most violent solutions to complex problems, retributive burning had limitations as a persuasive tool. Widespread destruction of foodstuffs, commercial businesses, and housing ultimately led to a massive refugee problem for the Federal army. In turn, the availability of forage from the hinterland was greatly reduced simply because of a lack of farmers. The Union enlisted men and noncommissioned officers who made up the foraging expeditions often translated retributive burning for guerrilla activities into wanton destruction of all property. Sergeant James Crozier, Twenty-sixth Iowa Infantry, recalled that as his company moved down the Mississippi River in December 1862, their steamboat would stop along the Arkansas embankment to randomly burn plantations and farms without purpose or cause. "Coming down [from Memphis] we burned that trading post where the boats traded Salt for Cotton," he began, adding, "there was a large lot of Cotton that was burned also they laid the whole place in ruins." A few days later, Crozier wrote that "we run last evening untill 8 1/2 pm when tied up to Gaines Landing some of the old soldiers got ashore and burned two Cotton Gins and a couple of houses." Understandably, "the General [Frederick Steele] is awful mad about it." Such actions did little to stop guerrilla attacks, but did much to ruin any vision of Federal troops as liberators or fellow citizens of the people of the Mississippi Valley.[10]

The Federals' failure to take Little Rock, and the subsequent shift of forces to the Mississippi River, allowed the Confederates to rebuild their shattered armies and regain control of much of the state by late 1862. Excepting Helena and parts of the northwest, all of Arkansas was again Rebel controlled during the winter of 1862–63. Once more, Rebel bushwhackers were operating along the entire western side of the Mississippi River, from the Missouri border to deep in Louisiana, with Arkansas as the central base of operations for these elements. Guerrillas shot Federal troops on riverboats, ambushed unarmed transports with small artillery pieces, and managed to capture and burn several Federal supply ships. Sergeant Crozier, in October 1862, confided in a letter home that movement down the Mississippi along the Arkansas border had become so dangerous that "we shall travel with loded [sic] guns as several boats had been fired into lately & some killed." He described one riverboat as having "several shots through her smokestack and Pilot house." Even the materially rich Federal army could not afford constant sniping and ambushing of its riverine supply line.[11]

For General Grant's army marching toward Vicksburg, the situation was critical. He had to have a dependable supply route for his campaign to succeed, and the Mississippi River was the only viable course.[12] Only undisputed and uninterrupted control of the Mississippi could keep the Union army moving; guerrilla attacks on the waterway continually threatened to cut his lines. In response to this danger, Grant, through his naval commander, Flag Officer David D. Porter, requested that the navy provide "a force of marines to be carried in suitable vessels accompanying the gun-boats and to be landed at points where guerrillas were wont to assemble." The Navy Department, already stretched thin with blockade and antiraider duties, reluctantly refused to fulfill the request. The War Department, in response, authorized the raising of an extraordinary composite brigade of infantry, cavalry, and artillery specifically organized for antiguerrilla warfare, the Mississippi Marine Brigade.[13]

The Mississippi Marine Brigade was a revolutionary concept. The brigade was a self-contained antiguerrilla army, carrying everything it needed to conduct sustained operations against irregulars. It contained its own conveyances, consisting of eight troop transports equipped with special cranes and ramps for rapid unloading of artillery and mounts, a hospital transport, several steam tugs, six coal barges, and five small steamers. The assembled ground force was impressive. Nearly 1,200 soldiers belonged to the brigade, organized in a regiment of mule-mounted infantry, two cavalry squadrons, and a battery of six ten-pound howitzers. Their commander, Brigadier General Alfred W. Ellet, was the brother of Charles W. Ellet, developer and commander of the Mississippi Ram Fleet until his death in 1862.[14]

After seeing its first action along the Tennessee River, the Mississippi Marine Brigade moved to suppress guerrillas between Memphis, Tennessee, and Vicksburg, Mississippi. In keeping with what had become standard Federal military practice, the brigade resorted to retributive burning to punish suspected guerrilla sympathizers. Beginning in 1863, it destroyed towns, homes, and plantations along the Mississippi, from southern Missouri to northern Louisiana, in the hope of dissuading Confederate guerrilla attacks. Sadly for the Union, the attacks did nothing to prevent further guerrilla ambushes. Town burning was commonplace for the Marine Brigade. The staff and muster rolls of 1863 and 1864 show that the leadership of the Marine Brigade, without guidance from higher up, decided to punish the town of Austin, Mississippi, for aiding guerrillas. "A party of rebels being discovered 35 miles north of there [Helena, Arkansas] returned May 24th and disembarked," the report began, concluding with "burned the town of Austin [Mississippi] that had harboured [sic] the guerrillas and refused to give information." An Arkansas Confederate guerrilla leader, Captain J. H. McGehee, later reported that Austin had served as a staging area for several ambushes, including the destruction of several small steam tugs, steamboats, and flatboats moving between Helena and Memphis. McGehee's actual base of operations was the small town of Hopefield, Arkansas. He later admitted that he crossed the Mississippi to conduct his operations, knowing that the Federals would punish the community nearest to the ambush, leading the Federals to destroy property of innocent, and often pro-Union, civilians.[15]

By the time of Vicksburg's surrender on July 4, 1863, the entire Mississippi River line between Missouri and Louisiana had been devastated by Federal retributive burning operations. A Confederate soldier, William W. Heartsill, was aboard a steamer heading toward a Northern prisoner of war camp when he sarcastically wrote: "on the west bank of the Mississippi, extending from the mouth of the White River to this point [Helena, Arkansas], evidence innumerable WHY WE SHOULD love the 'Glorious Union,' no less than FIVE HUNDRED blackened walls and lone chimneys are standing as monuments to departed civilized warfare." Generals Grant and Sherman attempted to mitigate the wanton destruction by issuing orders to burn the property of only known Southern sympathizers. This put the onus of identifying enemy guerrillas on individual commanders, and often on individual soldiers. Consequently, units like the Mississippi Marine Brigade destroyed large areas of farmland and numerous residences out of ignorance, indifference, or both. Not all these large-scale destructive operations were managed from below; in late 1862, Sherman himself ordered a fifteen-mile stretch of the Arkansas side of the Mississippi to be completely devastated in retribution for the killing of two soldiers on the steamer SS *Catahoula*.[16]

The Mississippi Marine Brigade soon revealed several weaknesses that hampered its usefulness. Poor recruiting practices undercut the brigade's effectiveness. General Ellet scoured hospitals and stockades throughout the Midwest, advertising "Soldiering Made Easy!" and "no long, hard marches, camping without tents or food, or carrying heavy knapsacks, but good comfortable quarters, and good facilities for cooking at all times." Not surprisingly, the men he gathered were often lazy, incompetent, or shirkers—in short, men who were not wanted for various reasons by other units. In one example of the lack of discipline in the brigade, a pro-Union man, living near the Arkansas-Louisiana border, complained that members of the Marine Brigade raided his home twice, took all of his clothing, and kidnapped his brother, a local doctor. The Federals demanded that he "tell [them] where my money was," but he claimed to have none. After taking the doctor's horse, the soldiers offered to sell the animal back to him for one hundred dollars in gold. Before they left, the marines even took the knives and forks that the pair were eating with when the raid began. During the 1864 Red River campaign, Federal naval officers and pro-Union civilians accused the brigade of looting, and discipline in the unit was a continual headache for Union commanders.[17]

In addition to discipline problems, conflicts between Admiral Porter and General Ellet led to confusion on the mission and purpose of the marines. Porter did little to support Ellet's recruiting or to aid with arming and supplying the brigade. For their part, the Ellet clan refused to give the navy command of the Mississippi Ram Fleet. Porter wanted command of all ships on the Mississippi, including the Mississippi Marine Brigade's and the Ram Fleet, while Ellet believed he had to take orders only from the secretary of war since his unit was not assigned either to Grant's command or to Porter's fleet. In the operations around Vicksburg in the spring of 1863, conditions became so intolerable between the Ellets and Porter that the Marine Brigade was shifted out of the guerrilla-infested Mississippi River region entirely. While the brigade did some antiguerrilla work along the Tennessee River in support of the Federal army in central Tennessee, it never truly did the job it was designed to do—eliminate irregulars along the Mississippi River in support of Grant's drive on Vicksburg.[18]

The Mississippi Marine Brigade was only one of the conventional tools that the Federals used in their counterguerrilla war. The provost, or military policeman, required little innovation or modification to aid in fighting the Confederate irregulars, and had long been a part of the armies of many nations. In the U.S. Army, such "provost guard" duty was assigned to regular infantry or cavalry units on a rotating basis, with a senior staff officer appointed as "provost marshal." Usually, the mission of the provost guard included the policing of the soldiers, issuing passes, preventing clashes between soldiers and civilians, and closing illegal establishments that were prejudicial to the command, such as "bawdy houses" and taverns. In the trans-Mississippi during the Civil War, the guerrilla conflict led to a new role for the provosts, beginning in Missouri during the first year of the war. To assist in the counterguerrilla mission, the departmental provost marshal commanded a multifaceted organization, including a secret service branch, the military prison, and subordinate provosts marshal scattered in substations throughout Arkansas, duplicating the established provost system in Missouri. From November 1863 to the end of the war, Lieutenant Colonel John L. Chandler, former commander of the Seventh Missouri Cavalry and a combat veteran, served as Arkansas's provost marshal general.[19]

Colonel Chandler divided his scattered command into four districts, three under the assistant provosts marshal general (officers holding the rank of captain) and one under his direct control. The District of the Frontier established its headquarters at Fort Smith, and had responsibility for the westernmost counties of the state and the entire Indian Territory (modern Oklahoma). The District of Northeast Arkansas and

District of East Arkansas, operating out of Batesville and Helena, respectively, covered Union-occupied Arkansas from the north-central region to the Louisiana border. The District of Central Arkansas, commanded by Chandler, included Little Rock and the surrounding counties. The district provosts marshal maintained a substantially smaller support staff than the provost marshal general, and was responsible for administering oaths, gathering information on suspected guerrillas and other disloyal persons, and ensuring that a constant stream of vital intelligence was flowing back to Chandler's headquarters at Little Rock.[20]

Chandler saw his mission as twofold, with his primary goal the "general polic[ing] of the army and of the towns and country occupied, the arrest of stragglers and deserters and forwarding them to their Regiments, the suppressing of brawls, bawdy houses, drunkenness and disorderly conduct." These missions provided the regimental commanders and the commanding general with the discipline needed to keep their units effective, especially during the lull in combat against regular Confederate forces in the winter and spring of 1863–64. His second objective, tied directly to the guerrilla war, was the "arrest of spies, smugglers, *disloyal and dangerous persons*, carrying [out] sentences including execution," and the "enforcement of orders [and] redressing complaints of citizens against soldiers or others." Chandler's military policemen also issued passes required for merchants operating within Federal lines, seized contraband property, and gave loyalty oaths. The loyalty oaths, considered relatively ineffective in persuading ardent Rebels, had, in the words of one observer, "never made a loyal good citizen out of a rebel anymore than a penitentiary makes an honest man." On the other hand, the provosts had full authority to punish oath-breakers, and did so on numerous occasions.[21]

Two other tools were available to the Union provosts marshal—paid spies and the military prison system. The network of spies, known as the "Secret Service" branch of the provost marshal general's office, maintained surveillance on possible guerrillas.[22] Infiltrating the backcountry, these agents provided priceless information. In late 1863, Colonel Chandler sent an unidentified man into the counties of northern Arkansas, along the Arkansas-Missouri border. Names, residences, and known contacts of "bushwhackers, guerrillas, desperadoes, and bad men" were carefully cataloged and reported to the provost marshal general. Membership in the Confederate army or the irregular companies was noted. Some men, whom the secret service agents called "bad men," were often working in conjunction with guerrillas. "Andy Bickley of Prairie County" was described as "point[ing] out the effects of Union families to guerrillas." Another more sinister character, Arthur Roads, "boast[ed] of killing fed soldiers and trying their close off [trying their clothes on]," while Henry Neil was known as "a vitious [sic] rebel." Other subjects were defined by their irregular activities, such as "a man named 'Hunter' who is a rebel but not a bushwhacker." Loyal Union men, such as James Lee of Independence County, "a Union sympethizer [sic] who will give information," were valuable. Such intelligence indicated which families, and ultimately which regions of the state, were hotbeds of guerrilla activity or served as safe havens for the irregulars.[23]

The military prison at Little Rock was the last part of the provost marshal counterinsurgency triad. After the occupation of the state capital, the Federal army seized control of the state penitentiary and used it to hold convicted Federal soldiers, Rebel prisoners of war, Confederate guerrillas, disloyal citizens, and common criminals. In conjunction with the Judge Advocate General, or military judicial system, the military prison played a critical, but largely forgotten role in pacifying the state. In general, War Department regulations dictated the death sentence for captured guerrillas. This guidance was codified in General Orders Number 100, issued on April 24, 1863. According to the order, guerrillas "if captured are not entitled to the privileges of prisoners of war, but shall be treated summarily as highway robbers or pirates." Their punishment, if captured, was "death . . . by sentence of a military commission."[24] In many instances, a drumhead court-martial and summary execution was conducted in the field. In 1862 and early 1863, when security of the field forces from guerrilla harassment was paramount, Federal officers carried out executions in accordance with War Department regulations. As time passed and the pacification of Arkansas and its restoration to the Union became stated goals of the Lincoln administration, the execution of captured guerrillas declined.[25]

Beginning in the fall of 1863, Union commanders in Arkansas inventively interpreted War Department General Orders Number 30, which stated that any person convicted of "Being a Guerrilla" would be sentenced to death. Instead, Federal officers, especially now Major General Frederick Steele, the commander of Union troops in the state, commuted death sentences to "Hard Labor for the Duration of the War." Steele's actions placed the legal definition of guerrillas somewhere between that of prisoners of war and common criminals. During the war, they would serve their sentences as criminals. When the war ended, they would be released with other former prisoners of war. The program of leniency had several effects. It prevented captured guerrillas from becoming martyrs to the cause. The January 1864 execution of seventeen-year-old David O. Dodd, the "Boy Hero of the Confederacy," in Little Rock proved to the Federals that execution of captured Confederate sympathizers would do far more harm than good to both the Federal army and to the fledgling Unionist government.[26]

Through careful application of the death sentence for guerrillas, Northern commanders deterred the Confederacy from executing Federal prisoners, especially local Unionists. As described in chapter 1, both Federal and Confederate commanders came close to mass execution of captured soldiers in 1862 because of the unclear combatant status of guerrillas. Therefore, imprisoning captured guerrillas was a wise move militarily and politically. As the Federals pacified more of the state by early 1865, more Rebel guerrillas were sent to the military prison at Little Rock. The provost marshal's prison records used the euphemism "political citizens" to describe prisoners, including guerrillas, that did not easily fall under the Articles of War. Examples included not only guerrillas, but disloyal citizens, smugglers, and those who supported the guerrillas. Unlike normal prisoners of war, who would be shipped to St. Louis or New Orleans en route to the large prison camps in the North, the guerrillas stayed in Arkansas. For example, the February 1865 records of the prison noted "313 Prisoners of War, 22 political citizens, 70 Federal soldiers and 8 Federal citizens" on its muster. When the POWs were transported to New Orleans, no "political citizens" were listed on the manifest, or in the monthly report to Federal commanders in St. Louis. With the exception of a handful of guerrillas convicted in the summer of 1865, the remainder of the "political citizens" was released without fanfare after the surrender of the last Confederate units in the state. The lenient surrender terms, combined with the policy of not executing surrendered guerrillas, may have had much to do with the rapid disintegration of the irregular bands at the end of the war.[27]

The antiguerrilla operations of the Mississippi Marine Brigade and the administrative and intelligence gathering assets of the provost marshal general formed only two of the three main programs developed by the Union army in Arkansas to defeat the guerrilla menace. The raising of indigenous counterguerrilla units formed of loyal Unionists formed the third part of the Federal effort, and was mostly responsible for the Confederate irregulars' ultimate defeat. White Arkansans joined Union army units from the beginning of the war, but not until 1862 was the first all-Arkansas unit formed, the First Arkansas Cavalry Volunteers, led by an Indianan, Colonel Marcus La Rue Harrison. The First Cavalry was the most successful of the Unionist counterguerrilla units, but all of the four cavalry regiments, two light artillery batteries, and eight infantry regiments that rallied to the Union cause served in the state and fought against the irregulars.[28]

The First Arkansas Cavalry, despite poor performance against regular Confederate units at the Battle of Prairie Grove on December 7, 1862, proved to be the finest of the Union counterguerrilla units raised in the state. Based in the northwest counties of Arkansas, the unit conducted a brutal and effective counterinsurgency campaign against the Confederate guerrillas from 1863 to 1865. Their legendary hatred for the guerrillas, who had driven many of the Unionists and their families out of Arkansas in the first year of the war, fueled their desire to eliminate their foe using any means necessary. Sergeant Charles O. Musser, a soldier in the Twenty-ninth Iowa Infantry, described the skills these "Mountain Tories" brought to the Union army when he wrote that "they [the Arkansas Unionists] are already doing good service as Scouts. [T]hey are acquainted with the country and Know who are loyal and who are not." He added that the Unionists "brought in a good many Guerrillas and bushwhackers." From the unit's inception in 1862 to the end of the war, the First Arkansas Cavalry was credited with killing more than 200 guerrillas in northern Arkansas, a tally unmatched by any other Federal unit in the state.[29]

Prior to the fall of Vicksburg in July 1863, the First Cavalry and its sister units served as conventional troops, facing organized Rebel forces. However, the reduction in Federal manpower after Vicksburg led to an increased reliance on locally raised forces; the capture of Little Rock in September 1863 sped up the process. By early 1864, relatively few nonindigenous units remained in the state; many had been withdrawn in 1863 to Tennessee or for duty against rebellious Sioux in Minnesota. Union defeat in the Red River Campaign in the summer of 1864 further dissuaded the Federal high command from sending additional units to the state and resulted in the locally raised units playing a more central role in pacifying occupied regions. To further complicate the Arkansas Unionists' work, as the numbers of Federal troops declined, the activity of Confederate guerrillas increased, eroding many of the hard-earned victories of the year before.[30]

For Colonel Harrison and his horsemen of the First Arkansas, the center of their command focused on the town of Fayetteville, Arkansas, deep in the heart of loyalist country. Fayetteville was a small but strategically significant town on the Telegraph Road between Fort Smith, Arkansas, and Springfield, Missouri. In the wild and untamed Ozarks, Fayetteville represented an island of loyalist sentiment, boasting a small college, shops, and storehouses. When John S. Phelps was appointed military governor of Arkansas, he looked to Fayetteville and Colonel Harrison for support. Harrison easily rallied the locals to support the Union. "An enthusiastic Union meeting was held here to-day [January 27, 1863]," Harrison wrote to Phelps, adding that "1,000 Arkansas Union men [were] present, exclusive of Arkansas troops stationed at this post." Additionally, and more importantly to the guerrilla war, Harrison added that "fifteen home guard companies asked to be organized for militia for home defense . . . these men will require no pay, and only a little sugar, salt and coffee and will be a bulwark here in raising volunteer regiments." It was from this group of home guardsmen that Harrison recruited his counterguerrilla troops throughout the war.[31]

Throughout 1863 and well into 1864, Colonel Harrison duplicated the antiguerrilla tactics used by other Federal units. The First Arkansas constantly patrolled the Telegraph Road, the region around Fayetteville, and occasionally made longer forays deep into the Ozarks. "I moved the mounted men of my command, an aggregate of 412 men, with two 12-pounder mountain howitzers, on the afternoon of the 7th instant," began one report to Major General John Schofield, the district commander in Springfield, Missouri. During this expedition, which took place in November 1863, Harrison and his men proved the superiority of locally raised counterguerrilla troops over soldiers brought in from other regions. Harrison reported that "I felt assured that General McNeil [commander of the District of the Frontier] was not thoroughly informed as to the whereabouts of Brooks [a Confederate colonel commanding a detachment of cavalry and partisans] or his strength." Harrison, based on the reports of his men, decided to move his command in a direction opposite of that which General McNeil had commanded. Within a day, Harrison's command had engaged the Rebel force, estimated at 700 poorly armed conscripts and 500 better-trained and armed Confederate regulars. For the next several days, the First Arkansas pursued the irregular cavalry command, ultimately driving the demoralized survivors south of the Arkansas River, concluding that "no organized band of rebels is known to be now in Northwestern Arkansas."[32]

In April 1863, nearly 900 Rebel troops, both conventional cavalry and numerous guerrilla companies under the command of Brigadier General William "Old Tige" Cabbell, moved north from Ozark (on the Arkansas River) to attack Colonel Harrison's isolated command at Fayetteville. Since the Battle of Prairie Grove, where the First Arkansas Cavalry had broken and fled, the Federal command considered them useless against regular Rebel troops.[33] On Saturday, April 18, 1863, the test came. Confederate horse artillery opened fire on the regiment's encampment and the town itself, and forward elements of the Rebel force began house-to-house fighting to seize the town. Unlike in their humiliating retreat from Prairie Grove, the Arkansas Unionists held their ground. The Confederates, fearing that a Federal relief force would come to the rescue of the isolated detachment, launched a frontal cavalry charge against the well-armed and fortified Unionists. The charge was broken by a devastating cross fire from the blue troopers, and the Confederates slowly disengaged after the four-hour fight.[34] In the words of General Cabbell, "the enemy all (both infantry and cavalry) fought well, equally as well as any Federal troops I have ever seen," adding that "although it was thought by a great many that, composed as they are of disloyal citizens and deserters from our army, they would make but a feeble stand, the reverse, however, was the case, as they resisted every attack made on them, and, as fast as driven out of one house, would occupy another and deliver their fire." Harrison and his troops were rapturous with their first battlefield victory. "A just cause is ours . . . the Stars and Stripes float gallantly over us," Harrison told his men, concluding that "God is on our side. Who can be against us?"[35]

The April 18 fight revealed the relative isolation of the regiment in Fayetteville. Consequently, on April 20 Harrison moved the First Arkansas back to Springfield, Missouri, and conducted its counter-guerrilla war from there. Not until the summer 1863 campaign ended with the surrender of Little Rock did the First Arkansas return to Fayetteville. Sadly for the horse soldiers, their war, the counterinsurgency that they would fight for two long years, was just beginning.[36]

From September 1863 until the summer of 1865, the First Arkansas conducted a grueling campaign against Confederate guerrillas scattered across northern Arkansas. Harrison's cavalrymen fought the scattered bushwhackers on a daily basis, and again distinguished themselves in engagements with Confederate regulars during General Sterling Price's Missouri expedition in the fall of 1864.[37] Outside of the engagements against Price's regulars, destroying the guerrillas was the main job of the First Arkansas.

Harrison realized that he had several options to fight the guerrillas, all of which he employed at one time or another. He could continue constant patrolling in hopes of engaging the scattered bands. This approach had two drawbacks. Harrison's men lacked sufficient mounts to conduct sustained mounted operations.[38] Additionally, the poor road network of northern Arkansas, combined with the mountainous terrain of the southern Ozarks, severely hampered any pursuit.[39] Harrison's second approach to defeating the guerrilla menace was a combination of retributive burning and knowledge of the region. He had been given direct orders to safeguard gristmills and other resources necessary for the survival of the populace of northwest Arkansas. However, he was well aware that the guerrillas used the gristmills as meeting places. One was owned by Captain William "Buck" Brown, a noted partisan commander, and a thorn in Harrison's side. The troopers of the First Arkansas had a particular hatred for Brown's command, having clashed with them on numerous occasions. Colonel Harrison reported that the "disabling of mills causes more writhing among bushwhackers than any other mode of attack," and believed that by cutting off the guerrillas from food supplies and centralized meeting places he could destroy the insurgency. Consequently, the First Arkansas moved out in late August 1864, with the mission of eliminating the mills. The operation was a partial success. Three large mills were destroyed during the foray, including Buck Brown's, but Harrison himself later admitted that the bushwhackers "threatened to stay and fight me on boiled acorns."[40]

Colonel Harrison's combination of patrolling and retributive burning had failed to destroy the guerrilla menace by the fall of 1864. The Federals had clearly damaged the irregulars, but had consistently failed to bring them to battle on terms favorable to the First Arkansas Cavalry. The lack of success against the Confederates, using what looked like twentieth-century "search and destroy" tactics, became visible throughout that fall. Harrison's implied mission, to convert Rebel Arkansans into loyal citizens of the United States, was in danger of failing, and the possibility of losing northwest Arkansas to the guerrillas or the region's complete depopulation increased daily. The cycle of Federal destruction and guerrilla terrorism took its toll on the citizens of northwest Arkansas; conditions became so bad that pro-Confederates were fleeing south, while the Union sympathizers went north. In one case, John Sights, a slave owner and shopkeeper in Hinds-ville (west of Fayetteville), sent his seventeen-year-old daughter to Texas with his cash and slaves in the fall of 1864 because of the threat of seizure by foraging Federals or theft by Rebel bushwhackers. Sights's fears were not mere paranoia. Soon after his daughter departed, a local Confederate guerrilla band rode up to his house and demanded his valuables. When he refused, the irregulars held him while his legs were shoved into his fireplace. The fire burned him severely, "until the flesh on his feet was burned to a crisp and the flesh on his legs cooked half way to his knees." Incredibly, Sights survived under the care of a Fed-eral surgeon at Fayetteville, who "came and amputated both legs above the knees." Such incidents, by the fall of 1864, had become common-place in the First Arkansas's area (see map 3).[41]

The problem of refugees, guerrillas, and the Federals' isolation led Colonel Harrison to a revolutionary idea. He determined that farmers could return to their fields only if he protected them from bush-whackers, but he did not have sufficient manpower to guard every farm and hamlet. Instead, he proposed a four-point plan for establishing *fortified colonies*, or small farm villages, formed of loyal Unionists and capable of self-defense. Initially, a Home Guard company of fifty Union-ists, the core of the colony's population, was armed and organized, then moved with their families to a defensible location personally selected by Harrison. The guardsmen then built a small earthen fort or wooden blockhouse large enough to shelter the colony's population against attack. Finally, the Union colonel's officers administered oaths and other administrative requirements that bound the home guardsmen as "loyal to United States authorities; to abide by the laws and orders from the nearest military post; the laws and present constitution of [Union-ist] Arkansas; the proclamation of the President, &c., and mustered in as home guards." Each man then received a parcel of land based on vote of the community, "having nothing in common except common defense and obedience to law." All persons living within ten miles of the colony were forced to either join Harrison's program or leave.[42]

The fortified agricultural colonies soon became the centerpiece in Colonel Harrison's counterinsurgency scheme. Throughout the winter

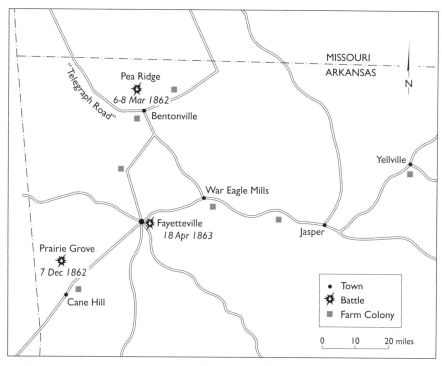

Map 3. Area of operations, First Arkansas Cavalry, 1863–65.

of 1864–65, the Unionists stockpiled munitions and supplies and gathered the displaced refugees around Fayetteville and other Federal outposts. Colonel Harrison's only shock came when Major General E. R. S. Canby, commanding the Military Division of West Mississippi, proposed the withdrawal of all Federal troops from Fort Smith, Fayetteville, and most of western and northwestern Arkansas. Harrison was livid and appealed to the main commander in the trans-Mississippi, Major General Grenville M. Dodge, to prevent the abandonment of the region to the mercies of the guerrillas. He encouraged the pro-Union civic leaders to appeal directly to President Lincoln, while he offered to stay and fight the Rebels with his single cavalry regiment: "I will hold this place with my regiment, four companies of infantry and four pieces of artillery, against 15,000 men—only give me the trial; if not, then, for the sake of these poor people, cannot some one be sent here to protect them?" Harrison's letter, along with political pressure applied by Governor Isaac Murphy, led to the Federal army's rejection of Canby's plan. For Harrison, the decision to stay and fight the guerrillas allowed him to see the results of the "post colony" program before the war ended.[43]

The farm colonies provided tangible results for the counterinsurgency program. To begin with, it freed the Federals from guarding and feeding the Unionists in the refugee camps in northwest Arkansas, releasing troops for active duty against the guerrillas. The colonies had much to offer the refugees, many of whom had lived in the area before the war. For example, the Union Valley Colony, near Prairie Grove, possessed a blacksmith shop, a wagon shop, a church, and a free public school, in addition to free farmland. The agricultural colonies also provided increased supplies for the Federal troops; Union Valley Colony alone promised Harrison a thousand tons of hay by spring 1865. Most importantly, the fortified settlements provided way stations for cavalry patrols, allowing the First Arkansas to constantly scour the territory between the colonies for guerrillas and expand the area they could deny to the irregulars.[44]

Colonel Harrison's cavalry, when combined with the farm colonies, produced rapid results. From February to March 1865, the troopers claimed over 100 bushwhackers killed and the dispersing of several of the largest guerrilla companies. The death of Harrison's nemesis in northwest Arkansas, Captain William "Buck" Brown, is indicative of the success of these operations. During a patrol between the farm colonies in Benton County, two cavalry patrols "overtook Buck Brown near his mill . . . skirmished with him; killed 3 of his men; captured 5 mules; killed Buck Brown; scattered his party and returned." In his report to General Sanborn, the Federal colonel added, "this makes eighteen bushwhackers in March," and the month was only half over.[45] Sanborn lavished praise on the First Arkansas: "I must congratulate you upon the rapid destruction of bushwhackers in your section." He also surmised that "with their leaders killed and the rapid destruction of the men generally all the guerrillas will soon leave that section." More importantly, the pacification of northwest Arkansas and southwest Missouri could continue unabated: "The people should all co-operate now, and peace and order will soon be restored in that section [northwest Arkansas and southwest Missouri]," the general concluded.[46]

The First Arkansas soon began to build up a tally of known guerrillas killed, captured, or driven away. The unit produced detailed reports of their successful activities. In another report to Sanborn, Harrison noted "seven more [guerrillas killed] in March not reported," including

"the notorious Lieutenant Burkett, who has so long infested Middle
Fork of White River with his band." A detachment led by Sergeant
Benjamin F. Johnson had engaged Burkett's guerrilla company, killing
Burkett and "twenty of his band at the same time." Such messages
became commonplace in the spring of 1865, as winter snows melted and
the Federal cavalry could return to active patrolling. When combined
with the network of fortified farm colonies now scattered across northwest Arkansas, the cavalry transformed a previously secure area for
guerrilla operations into a killing ground. Even the notorious guerrilla
band of William C. Quantrill, who had used northwest Arkansas as a
base of operations earlier in the war when Missouri became too dangerous, now avoided the region. Other Missouri guerrilla companies,
instead of staying together in Arkansas in the winter months, broke
up into smaller, less dangerous groups and returned to Missouri, where
they were easy targets for local militias and Federal troops. Harrison's
program clearly had operational-level repercussions beyond his own
few counties of northwest Arkansas.[47]

Harrison's post colonies spread rapidly. By March 15, 1865, he could
report to Governor Murphy that "I have never known anything more
enthusiastically taken hold of our people than is our colony system."
In Washington County alone, there were ten organized or partially
organized colonies; the Union Valley Colony, commanded by Captain
J. R. Rutherford, consisted of 112 well-armed and fortified home guardsmen who "think they can whip 1,000 rebels inside the fort." Another
guard unit in the same county, the West Fork Colony, was "armed and
fortified [and] have done some good service against guerrillas." Harrison claimed a total of fourteen fully armed and organized settlements,
with several more in the early stages of development. More importantly, the colonies were already beginning to isolate the guerrillas from
their main supply source—the Unionists of northwest Arkansas.[48]

The success of the post colony system soon spread throughout the
rest of Union-occupied Arkansas. Around Batesville, in northeast
Arkansas, Colonel Hans Mattson, commanding the Third Minnesota
Infantry, set up colonies in the area in May 1865, after "organiz[ing] the
people into home-guards, fight guereillas [sic], protect the people and
restore law and order." Mattson's orders were simple, to "make known
as soon as practicable to the people of that section of the State that the
chief object of occupying the country is their protection against armed
forces of whatever kind, to give encouragement to agriculture and other

peaceful pursuits, and re-establish commercial relations." At Pine Bluff, former slaves formed a colony that included one of the first schools for freedmen in the state. For the Federal army, however, the social benefits of the farm colonies were secondary to the mission of separating the guerrillas from the populace.[49]

Oddly, Harrison's plan met the greatest resistance from his immediate superior, Brigadier General Cyrus Bussey, who commanded from Fort Smith. In May 1865, as Harrison's plan entered its final stages and the guerrilla bands were finally being destroyed, Bussey claimed that "these colonies are not formed by the people, but by Colonel Harrison, who has virtually driven the people from their homes to these colonies." Bussey was absolutely correct. Harrison, by his own admission, forced every family within ten miles of a colony to join it or leave. In a letter to the assistant adjutant general in Little Rock, Bussey stated his firm belief that Harrison's program was nothing more than thinly veiled tyranny: "[A]t a public meeting in Fayetteville, Major Worthington, now dead, declared in a speech that any man who did not go into the colonies would be shot and have his house burned. . . . Colonel Harrison was present at this meeting and did nothing to correct the impression that went out—that every man must go into the colonies or be considered a bushwhacker." Bussey further claimed that "Harrison is organizing these colonies for the purpose . . . of elect[ing] him[self] to Congress next fall." Neither General Bussey nor Colonel Harrison foresaw the surrender of the guerrilla bands in the early summer of 1865; with the removal of the bushwhacker threat and the restoration of civil law following the end of the war, the farm colonies dissolved.[50]

In a statement attributed to him, Confederate General George Pickett, asked years after the Civil War why his division failed during the assault on Cemetery Ridge at Gettysburg, replied "I think the Union Army had something to do with it."[51] The failure of the Confederacy's guerrilla war in Arkansas, the closest the South came to a true Clausewitzian people's war during the Civil War, had much to with the Union army. Federal commanders in Arkansas, isolated from both guidance and influence of the War Department, developed innovative tactics and methods to deal with irregular warfare. The development of a combined-arms riverine force, although a failure, demonstrated that Union commanders in the trans-Mississippi recognized the guerrilla threat as a serious problem though commanders in the East denigrated the matter. The use of military police as spies, prison guards, and as local constabulary provided accurate and useful combat intelligence to senior commanders, as well as maintained a semblance of law and order in the occupied areas. As a consequence, the provosts marshal did much to reinforce Unionist sentiment in the state, paving the way for a smooth transition into Reconstruction. Finally, the use of indigenous loyal troops, best exemplified by the First Arkansas Cavalry, had the greatest impact on the guerrilla war. The Unionist troopers had every advantage of the guerrillas; they were familiar with the terrain and the people, and fought just as brutally as the guerrillas did. When backed by firm leadership and a well-developed counterinsurgency plan, they proved the worst nemesis of the Confederate guerrillas in Arkansas.

The Federal army in Arkansas defeated the guerrillas by the summer of 1865. The formal surrender of General Robert E. Lee's army in Virginia, and the capitulation of other major commands of the Confederate States, provided the pretext for the remaining bushwhackers to surrender without being treated as criminals. Not surprisingly, there were few guerrillas left in the backwoods of Arkansas after May 1865. After a winter and spring of being hunted by Federal cavalry and their own neighbors, the remaining irregulars were ready to surrender. The Union army, backed by loyal Arkansans, had won the guerrilla war. Far across the Mississippi, in the no-man's-land between Washington and the Shenandoah Valley, another aspect of the uncivil war was also drawing to a close. The best known of all the Confederate partisans, Lieutenant Colonel John Singleton Mosby, surrendered to Federal authorities. Mosby's partisan war, unlike the guerilla war in Arkansas, demonstrated a high level of organization and won several notable victories, but, like his fellow irregulars in the trans-Mississippi, Mosby found that the inventiveness and adaptability of the Union army limited, and finally defeated, his unconventional campaign.

John Singleton Mosby and the Confederate Partisan War in Virginia

There were probably but few men in the South who could have commanded successfully a separate detachment in the rear of an opposing army, and so near the border hostilities, as long as he [Mosby] did without losing his entire command.

Lieutenant General Ulysses S. Grant,
Personal Memoirs of U. S. Grant, 1885–1886

In the spring of 1864, Lee's Army of Northern Virginia, battered by nearly three years of war, prepared to face a new opponent, Lieutenant General Ulysses S. Grant. The Rebels, still heavily outnumbered by the Federal Army of the Potomac, attempted to conscript every available man in Confederate territory. Lee disbanded irregular units, legalized under the Partisan Ranger Act of 1862, and forcibly drafted their members into conventional units. All, that is, except one. A single battalion of Confederate partisan rangers, the Forty-third Battalion, Virginia Cavalry, remained in the field with Lee's blessing. Its commander was a physically unassuming young man, a lawyer by profession, who possessed a fiery temper and had risen from private to lieutenant colonel. He was John Singleton Mosby, and his exploits contributed more to the myth of a Confederate guerrilla war, during the war and afterward, than those of any band of Arkansas bushwhackers or brigade of Kentucky cavalry. Ultimately, Mosby would command hundreds of partisans, scattered in small detachments of fewer than thirty men, almost at the doorstep of the Federal capital, a region that became known as "Mosby's Confederacy."

Mosby became a legend in his own time—a bugbear to frighten isolated Federal detachments in northwestern Virginia and a hero to the embattled Confederacy. His fame, however, was of little consequence to the conduct of irregular warfare in the Civil War. For Mosby the "guerrilla," called so by scores of contemporaries and reinforced by over a century of historical studies, was no guerrilla at all, but the archetype of a partisan leader adroitly described by both Jomini and Clausewitz. Mosby and his companions, unlike the irregular companies prowling the northern Appalachians of western Virginia, were not proto-terrorists or forerunners of the armies of Mao Tse-tung or Ho Chi Minh. Instead, Mosby was a product of nineteenth-century military theory and antebellum Virginia culture, conducting the types of irregular warfare considered acceptable to combatant powers of the time and especially so to the people of the Confederacy. To best understand this Confederate ranger, we should see Mosby as the kind of commander who fit perfectly into the Confederacy's often romantic concept of irregular warfare, a gentleman rogue robbing from the rich Yankees to feed the poor Rebels.

The region in which Mosby's Rangers operated greatly resembled northern Arkansas. Dense forests, imposing hills and mountains, and numerous small waterways (in addition to the Potomac) provided an outstanding base of operations for irregular units. One main difference between northern Arkansas and northern Virginia was the presence of a large slave-owning population favorable toward the Southern cause. Moreover, northern Virginia had more roads and towns than Arkansas, which enabled Mosby's mounted partisans to quickly strike vulnerable Federal supply columns and escape using a network of well-constructed roads. Northern Virginia offered a smaller geographical area for irregular operations than Arkansas, but provided greater popular support and mobility for indigenous Confederate guerrillas (see map 4).[1]

Mosby's force based its style and success on several basic concepts. He understood that his command existed due to the tacit agreement of the soldiers themselves. The makeup of Mosby's Rangers—antebellum planters and professionals, Federal deserters, young men looking for

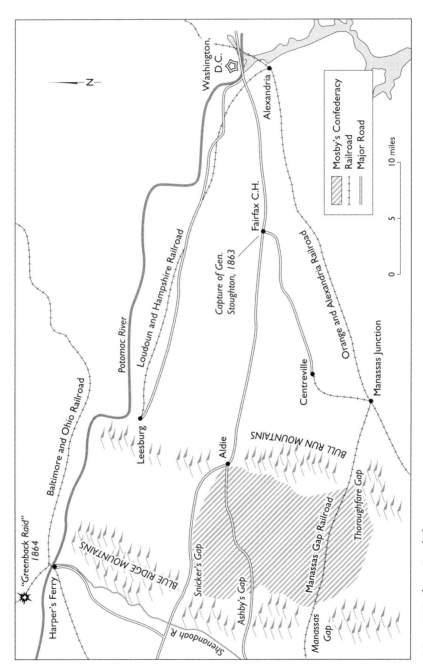

Map 4. Mosby's Confederacy.

adventure, and locals who joined out of hopes for retribution against the Yankee invader or to avoid being conscripted into the infantry—was a leadership challenge of the highest order. To motivate and command such a diverse unit behind enemy lines, Mosby was given special powers through the Partisan Ranger Act and directives from the Confederate high command. For example, he had carte blanche to seize and plunder captured Federal property; his status as a partisan ranger officer entitled him to distribute the booty to his men as rewards, much like privateers on the high seas. In this respect, Mosby's Rangers resembled the bushwhacker bands along the Mississippi River, and this facet of guerrilla motivation suggests that it was not so much nationalism and ideological fervor driving some Rebel irregulars during the last two years of the war, but the opportunities afforded to gain plunder. Also Mosby expressly forbade his men to attack or loot unarmed Unionist civilians, preferring to focus his efforts against regular Federal troops. He protected both pro-North and pro-South civilians in his area of operations, fulfilling many of the roles that the Federal army had in Arkansas. Organized Unionist military units, in contrast, were an especially fulfilling target for Mosby's battalion. By limiting the war to combatants only, Mosby avoided many of the problems that arose in Arkansas—such as the depopulation of his base of operations—and that plagued the Rebel guerrilla war in other regions. As a bonus, his fair treatment of surrendered Federals encouraged others to capitulate, and it limited, but did not eliminate, reprisals on his own captured men. Finally, Mosby rarely conducted battalion-sized operations, typically leading small ten- or twenty-man detachments aimed at specific objectives, and placed either competent officers or himself in direct command. As a result, officers of Mosby's Rangers could adequately control the small detachments and prevent the wanton looting of the civilian populace that was fatal to the Confederate guerrilla war in Arkansas.

Mosby's successes in raids and skirmishes were unquestionable, but the direct impact on the operations of the Army of the Potomac, and the forces operating independently in northern and northwestern Virginia from 1863 onward, was exaggerated then and later. It is a simple fact that with a handful of men, he successfully engaged Yankee forces much larger than his own, destroying or capturing millions of dollars in Federal property, and inflicted considerable physical and, more importantly, psychological damage on the Union cause.

However, other irregulars, including the vilified Quantrill in Missouri, hampered the Federal armies as much as Mosby, if not more. The question must be asked—why did Mosby garner such widespread praise from contemporaries and from historians as the model partisan warrior? A review of the extensive literature on the "Gray Ghost of the Confederacy" reveals several major issues. First was his official standing. Mosby was a legally commissioned officer assigned to the Army of Northern Virginia, the major field force of the Confederacy, and handpicked by General Robert E. Lee and Major General J. E. B. Stuart for his assignment. The importance of this army and Lee to the physical and moral survival of the Confederate States cannot be understated. In *The Confederate War*, Gallagher quotes a European visitor to the South in 1865 as stating that "Lee was 'the idol of his soldiers & the Hope of country.' This witness pronounced 'the almost fanatical belief in his judgement & capacity' to be 'the one idea of an entire people.'"[2] Consequently, in the postwar era, Mosby's exploits were portrayed as part of Lee's strategic and operational genius, making him, in Civil War historiography, a figure that could not be equalled by Quantrill in Missouri, bushwhackers in Arkansas, and even General John Hunt Morgan in Kentucky.

Mosby's own social background made him more acceptable to both contemporaries and later historians as a partisan leader. He represented a combination of both the yeoman and planter classes of the antebellum South, and of the redeemers of the post-Reconstruction era. He had been raised on a small farm in west-central Virginia of a solid, and slaveholding, family. He was educated at the better schools of Virginia, including the University of Virginia. Additionally, he married into an influential political family of Tennessee, the Clarke family, led by Beverly Clarke, a longtime congressman and former minister to Central America. One of Mosby's wedding guests during the December 1857 ceremony was a future president, Senator Andrew Johnson of Tennessee, who in 1866 denied Mosby's request for pardon. When Mosby passed the Virginia bar, he entered into a profession respected in Southern society. With his background and connections, it is not surprising that he became an officer in the Rebel army. Obviously, he was not a man living on the periphery of society, but a mainstream member of antebellum Southern life. As a responsible member of Southern society, Mosby fit the mold of other prominent Confederate officers in Lee's army, in sharp contrast to Quantrill,

Anderson, or other trans-Mississippi irregulars, who were not part of the eastern plantation aristocracy.[3]

Mosby's career in the Confederate army began as did that of many of his fellow officers in the Army of Northern Virginia. Volunteering as a private in the Washington Mounted Rifles in April 1861, he saw action at First Bull Run in July and in small skirmishes against the Federal army. His regimental commander, noting Private Mosby's education and talents, named him adjutant, with an equivalent rise to the commissioned ranks. It was as the adjutant of the Washington Mounted Rifles that Mosby first came in contact with Major General J. E. B. Stuart, who became his greatest supporter. Stuart recognized Mosby's aggressiveness and competence, and in early March 1862 sent Mosby and three cavalrymen on a hazardous mission. Major General Joseph E. Johnston, commander of the Confederate forces in northern Virginia, was gravely concerned over a dramatic increase in Federal military activity. Unknown to Johnston, Union commander Major General George B. McClellan was preparing to embark his army to move them to Fort Monroe for an advance on Richmond, the Peninsula campaign of 1862. Johnston's cavalry, under the command of Stuart, was tasked with gathering information on Federal plans and movements. Stuart soon found that the Federals were maintaining a thick counter-reconnaissance screen north of the Rappahannock River, hindering large cavalry operations. Consequently, Stuart decided to send Mosby and his team to find out "if McClellan's army is following us, or if this is only a feint he is making."[4] Slipping through the lines and traveling at night, Mosby's detachment eluded the larger Union cavalry forces and soon learned that the Federal force was a diversion and that the bulk of the Yankee army was heading to the Peninsula. Stuart reported this action to Johnston, and the Confederate army moved to face McClellan. Mosby had proven the value of small, well-led intelligence-gathering detachments behind enemy lines; Stuart had found a junior officer capable of independent action and audacity in the face of the enemy. It was a combination of talents that would directly lead to Mosby's career as a partisan.[5]

Having successfully proven himself, the young officer soon joined the ranks of Stuart's favorites.[6] Mosby played an important, but largely forgotten role in supporting the first of Stuart's famous raids around the Federal army. As McClellan's powerful Union force slowly crept up the Peninsula toward Richmond in the spring of 1862, the Confederate

force, now named the "Army of Northern Virginia" and commanded
by General Robert E. Lee, attempted to probe the Federals for weakness.[7]
On June 10, Stuart sent Mosby and four scouts on a reconnaissance of
the Union army. On the following day, Mosby returned with the welcome news that a weak cavalry screen covered the Federal right flank,
from the Chickahominy River to the Federal headquarters at White
House. In a letter to his wife, Mosby related that "I reported it [the Federal weakness] to General Stuart, suggested his going down; he approved
it [the ride around the Federal army], asked me to give him a written
statement of the facts." Stuart took the information Mosby had gathered to Lee, who in turn authorized the raid, which took place June
12–15. The results were impressive; Federal dispositions, strength, and
logistical capabilities were outlined for Lee, and gave him an immeas-
urable advantage in the upcoming Seven Days battles (June 25–July 1).
For Mosby, the importance of his scouting mission was twofold. He had
again proven himself to Stuart as a man who could be depended upon,
and it favorably brought him to the attention of Lee.[8]

The raid was not flawless. Captured by the Federals while carrying
messages to General Jackson, Mosby was "suspected to be a courier
with important dispatches . . . [and] was searched diligently; but none
were found." Demonstrating his flair for the dramatic that would greatly
aid him later, Mosby "frightened the enemy away from the railroad by
telling them a train of cars, loaded with infantry and artillery, would
be there in a few minutes." Taken to General Alexander McCook's
headquarters, he was identified as one of Stuart's best scouts and sent
to Washington. Ever the watchful scout, Mosby observed McClellan's
army preparing to embark at Aquia Creek, prior to joining the Army
of Virginia, under Major General John Pope, then south of Washington.
When he reached the Old Capitol Prison, he immediately identified
himself to the Confederate prisoner exchange commission and informed
them he had critical information for Lee. He was exchanged almost
immediately, and returned to Lee's headquarters. Armed with the new
information, Lee sent orders to Major General Thomas "Stonewall"
Jackson to turn to face Pope's force, a campaign that would ultimately
lead to Second Bull Run. Jackson's men struck Pope's Federals at Cedar
Mountain on August 9, 1862; Mosby would later state proudly that he
"brought on that battle."[9]

The Confederate leadership recognized in Mosby what Jomini
called a man "bold and full of stratagems."[10] Between Lee's invasion

of Maryland in September and the Confederate victory at the Battle of Fredericksburg in early December 1862, Mosby continued to serve as Stuart's preeminent scout.[11] The Rebel cavalry leader soon grew to trust the young officer, and Mosby joined the inner circle of the cavalry command of the Army of Northern Virginia. Following the withdrawal of Federal troops from Fredericksburg in late December, Mosby was given permission to take a detachment of men, first six and later fifteen handpicked troopers, to harass the retreating Yankees. A few minor successes proved to Stuart that the damage Mosby caused to the larger Federal army was well worth the risk of losing a good junior officer and a small number of elite cavalry troopers. The nascent force, which would soon become Mosby's Rangers, left Lee's army on January 24, 1863, "to threaten and harass the enemy on the border and in this way compel him to withdraw troops from his front to guard the line of the Potomac and Washington."[12]

Mosby could conduct this type of operation for one simple reason—he could take his pick of volunteers from the elite Virginia cavalry regiments under Stuart's command. In March 1863, after receiving his commission as a "Captain of Partisan Rangers" and the directive to raise a band of partisans to operate behind enemy lines, Mosby began operations. Using the fifteen men provided by Stuart, Mosby recruited another fifteen and opened the spring campaign with a thirty-man company. The partisan leader moved his force through the Union lines and began offensive operations against Federal cavalry and infantry detachments in north-central Virginia, between Washington, D.C., and Harpers Ferry, Virginia. The region, by 1865, would be known as "Mosby's Confederacy."[13]

Almost immediately, Federal authorities began misidentifying Mosby's detachment as a *guerrilla* band, referring to them as such in numerous reports. These initial reports did much to hinder the Federal operations against Mosby later in the war, simply because of a basic misunderstanding of who Mosby and his men actually were. Instead of underequipped and unorganized guerrilla bands, which Union troops had been fighting since 1861 in western Virginia, the Federals faced disciplined and motivated elite cavalrymen with a specialized mission of partisan warfare. Consequently, how the counterinsurgent forces operated should have been different; Mosby played off the Federal confusion and happily engaged small detachments of Union cavalry that would have been adequate for a counterguerrilla role. Mosby wrote, in a report to Stuart, that "the extent of the annoyance I have been to the Yankees may be judged of by the fact that, baffled in their attempts to capture me, they threaten to retaliate on citizens for my acts." Such a Federal response during the first of Mosby's raids reflects a complete misunderstanding of the nature of the partisan war; such an act, punishing civilians for military operations in their area, was a viable strategy in a guerrilla war, but not in a partisan war. From the start, the Federal authorities were blind to Mosby's actual mission—intelligence gathering and attacks on the Federal lines of communication that directly supported the Army of Northern Virginia. Hence, one of the reasons for Mosby's fame during and after the war was the failure of the Union army to grasp that it was fighting a *partisan* and not a *guerrilla*.[14]

The soldiers of Mosby's small command were initially veteran horse soldiers. As he moved deeper into Federal-occupied territory, and his detachment took casualties, the only available replacements were local volunteers. Fortunately for Mosby, Lee had also given him legal authority to raise his own troops, with the understanding that all men thus enrolled would be "mustered unconditionally into the Confederate service for and during the war."[15] The men Mosby attracted were a widely varied lot. A member of the command, J. Marshall Crawford, described the recruits as "peculiarly fitted for that kind of service, men remarkable for their courage and acuteness." Crawford adds that there were certain advantages in local recruiting for partisan operations. Two men in particular, John Bush and Sam Underwood, were memorable to Crawford; both men had lived within the Union lines for the most of the war and were intimately familiar with the Federal camps. "John, one night, while scouting between Fairfax and Alexandria, had a cowbell around his neck, and went into their camp on all-fours, and brought out five of the finest horses he could find, all belonging to officers," Crawford recalled. "Morning came; all the horses were missed, and could be found nowhere," and the Union officers, after "investigating the matter, to their mortification they found they had been duped, which so provoked them that the commanding officer ordered the bells to be taken off every cow in the neighborhood for ten miles around." Beyond being an amusing anecdote, the story demonstrates the lack of security in the Union camps as well as the familiarity of Mosby's troops with the region.[16]

The Confederate authorities further limited Mosby's recruiting base by refusing the passage of civilians into the Union lines, ostensibly to prevent desertion to the enemy. When Richmond newspapers spread the stories of Mosby's successes, especially the capture of Brigadier General Edwin H. Stoughton (recounted below), numerous civilians, paroled soldiers, and deserters attempted to join the group. Mosby generally asked few questions about a recruit's background, with the distinct exception of deserters. Having been organized under the Partisan Ranger Act of 1862, Mosby's men enjoyed certain privileges, including the ability to sell most captured Federal property. To say the least, this benefit appealed to many. In a letter, Major John Scott, one of Mosby's officers from early 1863 onward, wrote that "deserters from the regular army have begun to rally to this new and brilliant standard, under which they may partake of the comforts and pleasures of social life, and at the same time discharge the duties and receive the emoluments of the partisan soldier." Calling deserters "[an] evil, more potent than the enemy, [which] would destroy our infant command," Mosby would not tolerate their presence. Mosby was a partisan, but he was also a commissioned officer in the Confederate service who ran his organization as any conventional cavalry troop commander led his command. Scott, to his surprise, discovered that "Mosby has an uncompromising sense of military honor and duty, which has persevered him in this trial. Instead of allowing his command to become a refuge for deserters, he is, on the contrary, a most efficient ally of the conscript officer." In response, Richmond continued to support Mosby's operations as much as possible, and Confederate newspapers continued to spread his fame. When compared with bushwhacker commands in western Virginia or in the trans-Mississippi, Mosby's partisans were paragons of military virtue. Of the flood of new recruits from the unoccupied Confederacy attempting to join the rangers, one veteran ranger simply observed: "Of the regular service they [the would-be recruits] had a holy horror."[17]

According to popular Northern perceptions. Mosby's men were uncouth and barbaric guerrillas. However, a brief examination of the personnel records of his command reveals a starkly different picture. The basic requirements for service in Mosby's Forty-third Virginia Cavalry Battalion were simple: either the trooper was combat experienced, added special skills or talents to the command, or was part of what was considered the social elite of the antebellum era. The benefits to the Forty-third Battalion of soldiers in the first two categories were obvious. Examples abound of men in northern Virginia who were intimately familiar with the territory and Federal units in the area. The benefits of men on high social class to Mosby's command are somewhat less obvious. Some of Mosby's best men, both officers and enlisted, were solid members of the antebellum Virginia community. The muster rolls of Mosby's command from 1863 to 1865 contain the names of men who were graduates of West Point, the Naval Academy, Virginia Military Institute, and the University of Virginia. Following the war, many of Mosby's Raiders assumed respectable positions in Southern society. For example, several of Mosby's former privates went on to attend VMI, while others became physicians, lawyers, county sheriffs, state administrators, federal officials, and state legislators. One soldier, Private Baron Robert von Massow, was the son of the chamberlain of the King of Prussia, a veteran of seven years of service as an officer in the Prussian army, and the future chief of cavalry of the Imperial German Army. Before World War I, von Massow commanded the German IX Corps. Mosby himself would become U.S. ambassador to Hong Kong during the Hayes administration. Obviously, some of Mosby's men were ne'er-do-wells looking for an easy war away from the conventional battlefields. However, the presence of soldiers from the professional and planter classes of Virginia, mixed with a smattering of men with VMI, West Point, or Annapolis training, did much to encourage discipline and military efficiency.[18]

Despite the presence of soldiers and officers with some military experience, the relative absence of conventional military tactics and training in the Forty-third would have shocked many contemporary officers. Crawford, recalling his experiences in Mosby's Raiders, simply said: "The truth is, we were an undisciplined lot. During the twelve months of my service I learned but four commands—fall in and count off by fours, march, close up, and charge." He added a fifth command, "an order technically known as the 'skedaddle,'" which he had never heard given but maintained that "the Rangers seemed to know instinctively when that movement was appropriate, and never waited for the word." The "skedaddle" was the rangers' response to an overwhelming enemy force—they would simply disperse in all directions and rally at prearranged meeting places. When scattered rangers split up, "each man worked out his own salvation and 'struck for home and fireside' by his own particular path. We dissolved like the mist 'before their wery [sic] eyes wisibly [sic]' and left them nothing to follow." Such tactics were common for Mosby's men and greatly frustrated

Federal cavalry forces attempting to decisively engage and defeat the irregulars.[19]

Battlefield tactics closely resembled those of conventional cavalry, with a few exceptions. Mosby limited the use of sabers and captured Federal- and Confederate-issue carbines. The primary weapon was the six-shot revolver, the Colt .44 cap-and-ball (often called the "Colt Navy") being the preferred model. A Ranger would arm himself with as many revolvers as possible and, with a fast horse, charge headlong into an enemy formation. The effect was impressive. Rapid and violent attacks, usually at night or in times of limited visibility, made it seem that the rangers had many more men than they actually did. It was this tactic, more than any other, that made Mosby's men successful in combat. Ranger Crawford recalled that "if a charge was to be made we did not go into it in serried ranks and with orderly approach as if to impress the enemy with our awful dignity; but each man realized that the shorter the time from the start to the finish the less the danger was, and would clap spurs to his horse, often throw the bridle rein on its neck, and with pistol in each hand bend every energy to getting there, and making himself as numerous and influential as possible on the way."[20]

When these tactics failed, the rangers usually found themselves in serious trouble—outnumbered, outgunned, and surrounded by enemies who suddenly realized that what they thought were hundreds of wildly screaming demons were actually only twenty or so Rebel partisans. Mosby found this out himself when, in the early days of January 1864, he led a 100-man raid on Harpers Ferry. His goal was to attack and then disperse a Federal cavalry detachment near Loudoun Heights. Mosby later wrote that "by marching my command by file, along a narrow path, I succeeded in gaining a position in the rear of the enemy, between their camp and the [Harpers] Ferry." Based on the previous successes of the rangers, the capture of the Federals should have been a foregone conclusion. The partisan leader had complete knowledge of the enemy's location, numbers, and defenses, and a superior tactical position. Suddenly, everything seemed to go wrong at once. A detachment under Frank Stringfellow, one of Major General J. E. B. Stuart's scouts, came back shouting and shooting from a foiled attempt to capture the Federal commander and his staff. The Federal troopers initially responded as they had so many times before—with pleas of surrender and shouts for quarter. A Federal captain named Vernon emerged from the chaotic scene and rallied his men, and the outnumbered rangers faced what one Federal soldier later called "a perfect hell." The better-armed Union soldiers (supplied with multishot carbines) soon poured an accurate and galling fire on the rangers, killing several in the first volley. The initial loss was devastating for Mosby's men—one was a company commander, Captain Billy Smith of Company B, and another was a former British army officer, John Robinson. The rangers began to break and run on their own. Another one of Mosby's handpicked men, William Colston, was killed trying to halt the fleeing rangers. The loss had an undeniable impact on Mosby, who resisted further large-scale night attacks for the remainder of the war. Mosby's defeat at Loudoun Heights cost him irreplaceable men and demoralized the command for some months. The lesson was simple—if the rangers did not have surprise and shock on their side, they could not stand up to the Federal cavalry.[21]

Two of Mosby's most famous actions, the capture of Brigadier General Edwin H. Stoughton in 1863 and the Greenback Raid of 1864, serve as perfect examples of the abilities, limitations, and effectiveness of his partisan command. In March 1863, Stoughton, West Point trained and, at the time, the youngest general officer in the Union army, commanded a brigade of Vermont troops posted around Fairfax Court House. Mosby's troopers, consisting of the original fifteen volunteers from Stuart's cavalry and fourteen new recruits, had been operating in the area throughout the early spring, and Federal patrols were thick. Fortunately for Mosby, one of his new recruits was a Federal deserter, James Ames. Ames was an unexpected boon to Mosby. Unlike many Union deserters, Ames was a noncommissioned officer and a veteran of hard service from October 1861 to February 1863 in the Fifth New York Cavalry. Ames, some of Mosby's men felt, was not to be trusted under any circumstances. Mosby later recalled that he "never cared to inquire what his [Ames] grievance was," but one of his officers, Captain Walter Frankland, did. According to Frankland, Ames had deserted "on account of the Emancipation Proclamation, which, he said, showed that 'the war had become a war for the Negro instead of a war for the Union.'" Mosby could not care less—what mattered was that Ames knew the passwords of the Fifth New York and the gaps in the Federal picket line. Using this information, the partisan leader formulated a plan.[22]

Mosby knew exactly how to penetrate the Federal lines with a small group of men, and return safely. As his target, he selected General

Stoughton and his command. Colonel Sir Percy Wyndham, a British soldier of fortune who had recently called Mosby a horse thief in Washington newspapers, commanded the Federal cavalry in the area and was the specific target of Mosby's raid. The partisan planned to capture Wyndham and turn him over to the authorities at Richmond—a humiliation beyond compare. On the night of March 8, 1863, Mosby and his twenty-nine troopers left Dover, in Loudoun County, for the Federal lines. Only Mosby initially knew the objective; he told Ames, whom by now was called "Big Yankee" by the rangers, after the raiding party left Dover. Ames led the detachment to a break in the picket cordon between Centreville and Chantilly, and in the midst of thousands of Federal troops, the rangers headed toward Fairfax Court House. Mosby would later write that, as his force moved deeper into hostile territory, "the enemy felt secure and was as ignorant as my men." The darkness aided the rangers greatly, and allowed them to approach to hand-to-hand combat range with the few pickets on the outskirts of Fairfax. Once inside the town, Mosby dispatched troopers to capture Wyndham and any other Federal officers there. Wyndham, to the rangers' dismay, was in Washington that night; however, Ames managed to capture his former commanding officer, Captain Elmer Barker. Ames "seemed to take great pride in introducing him to me [Mosby] as his former captain."[23]

Mosby now realized the raid had caught the Federals completely by surprise. Taking six men with him, Mosby rode to the commanding general's headquarters, knocked on the door, and calmly stated "Fifth New York Cavalry with a dispatch for General Stoughton." The Union officer just inside, a Lieutenant Prentiss, opened the door and was made prisoner by Mosby. Mosby then quietly moved to Stoughton's room, where the general lay sleeping. Mosby related the scene:

> There was no time for ceremony, so I drew up the bed-clothes, pulled up the general's [night]shirt, and gave him a spank on his bare back and told him to get up. As his staff officer was standing by me, Stoughton did not realize the situation and thought somebody was taking a rude familiarity with him. He asked in an indignant tone what all this meant. I told him he was a prisoner, and that he must get up quickly and dress.
>
> I then asked him if he had ever heard of "Mosby," and he said he had.

"I am Mosby," I said. "Stuart's cavalry has possession of the Court House; be quick and dress."[24]

The rangers captured Stoughton and several of his staff officers in the midst of "several thousand troops, with several hundred in the town." Strangely, no one sounded the alarm or attempted to escape. Mosby later recalled that "there were three times as many prisoners as my men." The rangers, after spending nearly an hour in town, departed before sunrise. Because of the darkness, several of the prisoners, including Lieutenant Prentiss, managed to escape, but by that point Mosby's Rangers were nearly back to Confederate lines. Moving through Centreville, his detachment "passed so close to the [Federal] fortifications there that the sentinels on the redoubts hailed us, while we could distinctly see the bristling cannon through the embrasures." Returning to his commander, Major General Fitzhugh Lee, he turned over his prisoner, who had been Lee's roommate at West Point. Mosby expected praise for his exploits; however, he concluded that "the reception I received convinced me that I was not a welcome person at those [Fitzhugh Lee's] headquarters."[25]

Mosby's successful capture of Stoughton brought instant attention to the rangers from both North and South, and began the legend of the "Gray Ghost" that grew larger as the war progressed, and for decades afterward. In Richmond, Mosby was hailed as another Stuart, and both Stuart and Lee recommended him to Jefferson Davis for commissioning as a "Captain of Partisan Rangers." In Washington, Lincoln, when informed of Stoughton's capture, as well as the loss of Union cavalry mounts seized by Mosby, quipped, "Well, I am sorry for that—for I can make brigadier-generals, but I can't make horses." Ultimately, the success of the Fairfax raid led to Mosby's commissioning as a major and the permission to raise the rangers to full battalion strength. As a case study of his partisan operations, the raid is unequalled. It succeeded by combining a small number of experienced cavalrymen, locals familiar with the area, assistance from a Federal deserter, and considerable luck. Mosby had the ability to move quickly and tightly control his men. Little contact was made with the civilian population in the area, since Mosby had a specific objective in the operation and not a wide-ranging mission to win popular support or keep the flame of rebellion alive behind Federal lines. Lastly, the rangers controlled their aggressiveness throughout the raid; not a single Federal or Confederate soldier was killed during the mission. Consequently, the Federals did not have a chain of alerted outposts to notify them of Mosby's approach or departure. Overall, the mission was a professional operation from start to finish, a factor recognized and rewarded by the Confederate leadership.[26]

Following the success at Fairfax Court House, Mosby's men continued to raid and harass Federal outposts, and pass information on to Stuart. During the Chancellorsville campaign in May 1863, Mosby concentrated his force on the supply lines of Major General Joseph Hooker's Army of the Potomac, with the mission of hindering Hooker's offensive strength. After the Federal disaster during the Battle of Chancellorsville on May 2–3, 1863, Mosby and his men were assigned to observe and report on the disposition and composition of Hooker's army. According to several observers, reports to Lee from Mosby on Federal troop strengths and objectives encouraged Lee to launch his raid into Pennsylvania. During the Gettysburg campaign in June and July 1863, Stuart ordered Mosby to stay in northern Virginia and continue his partisan activities, with the mission of confusing and hindering the Army of the Potomac. Although his partisans fell short of complete success, his efforts were not in vain, as the Confederates gained several critical days' march on the Federals without Hooker's knowledge. With the defeat of the Army of Northern Virginia at Gettysburg on July 3, and the army's subsequent retreat back into Virginia, Mosby's Rangers were again isolated behind enemy lines. From Gettysburg until the end of the war, contact with Stuart and Lee was intermittent at best for the rangers. Mosby was on his own.[27]

Much of the impact of Mosby's operations was its effect on the Federal troops detailed to picket duty or guarding the railroads in northern Virginia. For them, Mosby was larger than life, a monster that would spring out of the darkness to attack isolated outposts and sentries and steal horses, supplies, and weapons, before fading back into the countryside. Private Nathan Middlebrook, an artilleryman who had been wounded and sent to the Federal hospital at Fairfax, wrote home of the constant stress and alarms caused by Mosby's mere presence in the region. Receiving word of a possible raid, Middlebrook and 200 of his fellow patients who were capable of fighting were pulled out of their beds and ordered to dig earthworks and draw muskets. Although rumors placed the raiders within twenty miles of the courthouse, the alert was a false alarm.[28]

Closely tied to the impact of Mosby's actions behind the lines was his influence on how Federal forces reacted to irregular attacks. Private Clement Hoffman and his regiment, the Sixth Pennsylvania Volunteer Cavalry, served as Headquarters Guard for the Army of the Potomac in late June 1863. In a letter home, he wrote that "a band of guerrillas [Mosby's] made their way through our lines yesterday [June 22, 1863] and attacked one of our wagon trains." In response, Hoffman's squadron was detached from guard duty and ordered to chase the guerrillas down. When the troopers arrived, they found that Mosby had "burned and destroyed the whole train" and that "when we got to the trane [sic] the rebbels [sic] had gone." The ability of Mosby's men, along with the scattered guerrilla bands, to operate inside the lines of the largest army of the Union led another Federal soldier to remark that, while in winter quarters, "[we] are trying to pass the time in as merry a way as possible . . . as we can surrounded, as we are by enemies who are constantly watching for some opportunity to annoy us."[29]

In the last two years of the war, Mosby's operations spread from West Virginia to the fortifications of Washington. The rangers struck Federal supply trains, raided isolated outposts, and harassed cavalry sent after them. The famous Greenback Raid of 1864 exemplifies the weaknesses and strengths of the partisan ranger concept as demonstrated by Mosby's Forty-third Virginia better than any event in the final two years of the war. In this operation, the rangers again exhibited the daring and effectiveness that they had shown in other raids, but many contemporaries noted with dismay the lengths and measures Mosby had to go to keep his men in the field against a continually strengthening foe.

The summer of 1864 began with Mosby's men attempting to slow the Army of the Potomac, now under Grant, as it advanced steadily toward Richmond. Grant himself almost became a victim of Mosby's scattered operations when the newly appointed general in chief moved to join the Army of the Potomac in the field. Grant related in his *Memoirs* that, as his unguarded train moved through Warrenton Junction, a cloud of dust was seen disappearing in the distance. The single dispatcher at the train station, when queried by Grant as to the nature of the dust, stated that Mosby had just ridden through in pursuit of a detachment of Federal cavalry. Had the train arrived a few minutes earlier, or Mosby a few minutes later, history could have taken a different turn. Grant, in a model of understatement, simply recalled that "had he seen our train coming, no doubt he would have let his prisoners escape to capture the train," and taken the unprotected Grant prisoner. Luckily for the Union, the partisan leader missed him, and Grant was able to join his army as it prepared to move into the Wilderness.[30]

As the massive Federal army pushed toward Richmond, Mosby's partisans were tasked by the Confederate command with striking at Grant's supply lines. As in most campaigns of the American Civil War, railroads served as the primary mode of supply transportation for armies in the field. Therefore, Mosby concentrated his force on attacking the primary rail line through his region—the Baltimore and Ohio, commonly called the B&O. Throughout the summer and into the fall of 1864, as Lee's army was being forced into the entrenchments of Petersburg, Mosby ran his private war against the B&O. In October 1864, a raid on a B&O train, which netted the partisans over $168,000 Federal dollars, made Mosby even more infamous in the North, and provided the Confederacy with one of its few bright points in that year. October 1864 was a bloody time for the Federal railroad system and cavalry operating in northern Virginia. Mosby's partisans struck bridges and blockhouses and destroyed rails between Harpers Ferry and Fairfax with near impunity. In response, the Federal authorities began a counterinsurgency campaign against "guerrillas" in the region that Mosby, as a partisan, ignored. Regardless, the damage the rangers caused was substantial enough to force the Federals to use armed escorts on trains. The presence of armed Federal troops encouraged Mosby and his rangers to begin attacking the trains themselves, despite the presence of civilians, including women and children, on many of them. When one of Mosby's men, Jim Wiltshire, discovered a gap in the Federal blockhouse and patrol defenses on the B&O between Harpers Ferry and Martinsburg, the partisan commander planned to ambush any trains coming down the line. To set his ambushes, he acquired a timetable of trains passing through the area, and picked the largest one, a westbound passenger train.[31]

On the evening of October 13, 1864, eighty of Mosby's Rangers, led by their commander, moved to attack the passenger express out of Baltimore. After allowing an eastbound train to pass, Mosby ordered his men to remove a rail. At 2:00 A.M., the westbound train approached, unaware of the ambush. Ranger (Major) John Scott recalled what happened next in a letter home. "At two o'clock P.M. [sic] he [Mosby] was roused by the whistle, followed by the explosion of the boiler." Mosby then ordered an immediate attack on the now-derailed train, where "a wild scene of confusion was presented." Women "screamed with terror" until, according to Scott, they were assured of their safety by Mosby's officers. For an entire passenger car filled with newly arrived German immigrants, in contrast, the reception given by Mosby's Rangers was somewhat different. The Germans, not understanding what had happened, "made no motion to leave their seats when ordered to do so." In response, one of Mosby's men quipped, "they don't understand English . . . perhaps they understand fire," and promptly set the car ablaze amid the screams and curses of the German families.[32]

Thus far, the Greenback Raid was following the pattern of any attack on a train in the American Civil War by a conventional cavalry force. The military passengers were taken prisoner, civilians taken off the train and safeguarded, and military stores seized or destroyed. Then the situation suddenly changed. Mosby's men begin to rob the passengers of their belongings, focusing on watches, money, and jewelry. Food, clothing, or other supplies normally needed by an isolated detachment behind enemy lines were ignored for loot. Mosby allowed the robbery to continue, and even ordered the searching of mail cars and other freight for more valuables. His men discovered a locked paybox, containing over $168,000 in Federal greenbacks, and secured the money. After ensuring that the passengers had been robbed, and that the handful of Federal soldiers on the train were sent to Richmond under guard, the partisans dispersed to a prearranged meeting point. The rangers later met and divided the plunder, with each partisan, excepting Mosby, who refused to take any, getting nearly $2,000 in cash. The raid quickly made headlines throughout the North and South, and Mosby was condemned as a robber or hailed as a hero.[33]

The robbery of unarmed civilians by organized military forces was one of the South's major complaints against the Federal armies during the Civil War. Mosby himself had pursued and eliminated numerous isolated detachments of Federal foragers, which he had described as "plunderers, for they were robbers rather than soldiers, had not only taken with them the horses of citizens, which in this war are regarded as contraband, but had stripped such dwelling-houses as lay in their course of all valuables which they could carry off, including silver spoons, jewelry, and the clothing of ladies."[34] Defending his own band's looting, Mosby explained that he tended to turn a blind eye to such activities by his men. After the war, he wrote that "whether my men got anything in the shape of pocketbooks, watches, or other valuable articles, I never inquired, and I was too busy attending to the destroying of the train to see whether they did," adding that "we left all the civilians, including the ladies, to keep warm by the burning cars, and the soldiers were taken with us as prisoners."[35] The second justification he and his men gave was that under the laws of the Partisan Ranger Act, any nonmilitary items captured were considered the fair plunder. The use of the Partisan Ranger Act as a justification for looting had much to do with Mosby's ability to raise and field an effective force. From the inception of the rangers, he understood that more than patriotism for the new Confederacy would be needed to motivate his volunteers. Hence, when General Lee and President Davis determined to promote Mosby to "Captain of Partisan Rangers" in 1863 and to raise troops behind the line "on a footing with all troops of the line, and to be mustered unconditionally in the Confederate service for and during the war," Mosby refused.[36]

The partisan leader's logic in refusing to enlist the Forty-third Virginia Cavalry as regular Confederate troops was simple. The law governing regular troops forbade personal plunder; all captured items, including valuable contraband, became the property of the government. A loophole in the Partisan Ranger Act allowed seized booty to be treated differently. According to the act, captured items (except horses and weapons) were treated as personal property, somewhat as when a privateer seized an enemy ship on the high seas. One of Mosby's officers, Major Scott, explained Mosby's attitude toward plunder in relation to his ability to motivate and recruit new rangers. "With the power to distribute spoil among his [Mosby's] men taken from him, which was the meaning of the letter of instructions [from Lee], he felt conscious that his opening career in the partisan service must necessarily be brought to naught, for he had said before that his command resembled the Democratic party at least in one respect, that it was held together by the cohesive power of public plunder." Despite Lee's misgivings, the secretary of war awarded Mosby's battalion partisan ranger status in 1863. Lee would later say that Mosby was the only successful partisan ranger officer, recommending that the Forty-third Battalion be kept as a partisan unit, while advising the disbandment of the other partisan ranger units operating in the Army of Northern Virginia's area.[37]

The end of the war led to the end of "Mosby's Confederacy." Throughout the winter of 1864–65, the partisans continued to struggle against the growing Federal cavalry. The Union army, stung by Mosby's operations in late 1864, stepped up their counterinsurgency campaign, duplicating many of the patterns seen in Arkansas in 1862–63, such as execution of captured partisans, wholesale destruction of supposed guerrilla-infested towns, and forced evacuation of civilians from partisan-friendly areas. As Grant's Federals slowly bled the Confederate army to death, more and more conventional military responsibilities fell upon Mosby. On March 27, 1865, as the commander of a scattered partisan battalion perhaps numbering only 200 men during its largest operations, he found himself defending nearly all of Confederate-held northern and northwestern Virginia. Lee ordered Mosby to "collect your command and watch the country from front of Gordonsville to Blue Ridge and also [the Shenandoah] Valley," adding, "your command is all now in that section." Lee's orders reflect two growing realities in the last month of the Civil War in Virginia: the Confederate army was clearly on its last legs, and Mosby and his men had risen to a level of trust and confidence from Lee and the Confederate government unequaled by any other partisan, guerrilla, or irregular command in the war.[38]

After Lee's surrender, Mosby, realizing that many of his men would be shot as bushwhackers, ordered his command to disperse back to their homes while he alone surrendered to Federal authorities. In effect, Mosby's Rangers were never disbanded, leading many observers and historians to conclude that they were truly guerrillas, fading back into the populace from which they had sprung. Mosby had a different opinion, especially in light of the execution of several of his partisans by Brigadier General George Custer's cavalrymen in the last year of the war.[39] Additionally, he wanted to "save the country from being a desert. If any one doubts this. Let him read [Major General Winfield Scott] Hancock's report. If it was legitimate for Hancock to lay waste the country after I had suspended hostilities, surely it was equally so for Grant to do it when I was doing all the damage in my power to his army." Grant ordered Hancock to accept Mosby's surrender; Hancock sent a subordinate to bring in Mosby and his men. Mosby was the only partisan awaiting capture at the agreed upon location, noting later that to send a general officer to capture a lieutenant colonel "shows that we did him [Grant] a great deal of harm."[40]

In the final analysis, the Forty-third Virginia Cavalry had some notable successes, the best known of which were the capture of General Stoughton and the Greenback Raid. In Southern newspapers, Mosby and his battalion were regaled as heroes, and in Northern papers reviled as brigands. Mosby's fame—and infamy—was tied directly to his success, and he succeeded where the majority of other partisan ranger units in the war failed. The Forty-third Virginia succeeded for several obvious, but often ignored, reasons. Mosby handpicked his men, from private to major, based on their talents and background. By doing so, he could ensure that the members were men of the "correct" social class or possessed critically needed skills for the battalion. In some ways, his unit closely resembles the First U.S. Volunteer Cavalry of the Spanish-American War, the Rough Riders, with its wide variety of members. Prussian nobles, Yankee deserters, former West Point cadets, and pro-Southern locals formed his band, complementing the abilities of one another.

The Confederate army, from Lee to Stuart, supported Mosby and his battalion. For the conventional forces, the partisans performed a unique mission that gave immediate support to the army in the field. Mosby's Rangers gathered information, attacked supply trains, and scouted ahead of Lee's army on its northward campaigns. For the conventional army, the risk of losing one exceptional officer and a handful of cavalrymen paid great dividends throughout the war. Federal units, while not directly taken from the front lines to pursue Mosby, were often delayed on their movement to the front for short-term counter-partisan work. Union troops who would usually feel safe in rear area logistical and support units, found themselves having to man block-houses, railcars, and earthworks against the chance of a raid by Mosby. Letters home from these troops, and other evidence, show that many of them lived in a semiconstant state of alert. In exchange for performing these benefits for the Confederacy, Lee ensured that Mosby's battalion stayed in existence, supplying it with arms and equipment on occasion and, more importantly, preserving the status of the Forty-third Virginia as the only effective partisan ranger command in the Army of Northern Virginia's area. As other units were disbanded in the last year of the war, Lee pressured Jefferson Davis to preserve Mosby's Rangers; the partisans had become an integral part of the Army of Northern Virginia, allowing it to affect the battlefield far from the front lines. The impact of the rangers was not only on the battlefield. Mosby's exploits, more the stuff of legend than the realities of the trenches of Petersburg, provided the Southern people with a morale boost when it was most needed. The Gray Ghost's capture of Federal generals, money, and troops, without being caught, fired the imagination of the demoralized Confederate home front at a time when it seemed the Federal war machine was grinding the Southern cause into dust.

Finally, Mosby's Rangers succeeded because of the efforts of Mosby himself. He was an extraordinary figure. Well educated, but without military experience, he possessed an inherent leadership ability and charisma admired by all, including Grant, who would hand carry Mosby's pardon to President Johnson in 1867.[41] Mosby understood what motivated his men. Some fought because, like him, they were Virginians and their state had been invaded, but he also knew that many fought with him because it was near their homes and easier than service in Lee's army. The Partisan Ranger Act gave him the legal authority to plunder Federal soldiers and civilians without penalty. As with the bushwhacker bands along the Mississippi in 1863, Mosby recognized and needed the ability to reward his men for their service, and ensure that they would come back to him when called.

Despite Mosby's successes, the fact remains that the Federal army ultimately defeated him as well as the rest of the Army of Northern Virginia. The Federals, long mistaking Mosby's partisan war for a guerrilla war like the one raging in the trans-Mississippi, lost numerous small fights to the Forty-third Virginia between 1863 and 1865, and did much to aid the partisans indirectly. The failure of the Union high command to deal with a partisan threat, in contrast to a guerrilla war, ultimately would lead to widespread reprisals against prisoners of war, civilians, and entire regions. As Yankee frustration grew, the antiguerrilla campaign against Mosby would take a darker turn, resulting in some of the most brutal acts of the entire Civil War. Oddly, for the residents of northwestern Virginia in the spring of 1865, Mosby's "guerrillas," reviled in Northern newspapers as brigands and cutthroats, would represent the only legally appointed governmental body in the region. It was the Federals who were seen as plunderers, burners, and murderers.

MISREADING THE ENEMY

The Union Army's Failed Response to Partisan Warfare in Virginia

Although I have never adopted it, I have never resented as an insult the term "guerrilla" when applied to me.

John S. Mosby, *Memoirs*, 1899

Mosby's surrender to Federal military authorities in June 1865 concluded an antiguerrilla campaign aimed at killing or capturing the partisan leader and his battalion. From mid-1863 until the end of the war, the Union army allocated substantial assets to eliminate Mosby's partisan rangers. Moreover, inventive and original programs were launched to destroy the Forty-third Virginia as well as other irregulars in northern Virginia, and new and vigorous Yankee commanders—including such men as Philip Sheridan, George Custer, George Crook, and Wesley Merritt—took to the field to fight against the partisans. None gained the upper hand. Mosby and his men survived until the end of the war, a constant threat to Federal military forces behind the front lines and a continual source of positive propaganda for the Confederacy.

Mosby succeeded in maintaining his operations despite the Federal army's attempts to destroy him for two reasons. One is Mosby's own leadership talents and organizational skills, discussed in chapter 3. The second reason for Mosby's success is less obvious, but played a much greater role in guaranteeing the survival of the Forty-third Virginia Cavalry Battalion until the end of the war. The Union army and its leaders, from company commanders to general officers, applied the wrong tactics and concepts against Mosby. Instead of battling Mosby the *partisan*, the Federals chose to fight Mosby the *guerrilla*. Consequently, Union plans to eliminate Mosby's Rangers duplicated Federal antiguerrilla operations in other theaters of the war. Some of the commanders sent to stop Mosby, such as Generals George Crook and David Hunter, had experienced irregular warfare on the antebellum frontier, while others had their first actions in the Civil War against pro-Southern guerrillas and bushwhackers in the mountains of western Virginia. These experiences led Union commanders to incorrectly identify Mosby as a guerrilla and not a *partisan*—an understandable conclusion, since in the Civil War the forces of Mosby in Virginia and John Hunt Morgan in Kentucky (during his 1861 and early 1862 operations) were the only true partisans, in the nineteenth-century sense of the term.[1]

Federal antipartisan operations in Virginia became hopelessly mixed with antiguerrilla tactics from the beginning of the war. Yankee responses to both developed simultaneously, and can be summarized into three basic modes of operation. The most common response to irregular warfare in Virginia was an active antiguerrilla campaign aimed at catching and destroying irregulars. A variety of methods fell under this approach, including large cavalry sweeps and the use of specially trained counterguerrilla units. Passive defensive actions were aimed at keeping the guerrillas and partisans away from strategically important targets, such as the extensive railroad system running from Washington, D.C., to Wheeling, West Virginia, and from friendly combat units. Of these measures, a useful one was the building of a chain of fortified blockhouses at vulnerable points on the railroads; the most original was the introduction of heavily armed and armored locomotives for patrolling the rails.[2] Lastly, retributive procedures, especially those in the Shenandoah Valley, aimed at punishing the civilian populace for supporting irregular forces. All three methods—active, passive, and retributive—often took place at the same time throughout the conflict; however, there are distinct periods in which all three developed and reached their final, but ultimately unsuccessful, stage of development.

From the time that the first Federal troops entered western Virginia until 1865, many Federal officials (both civilian and military) believed that active methods, as demonstrated in an aggressive antiguerrilla campaign aimed at eliminating the most active irregular units, were the solution to the partisan problem. After the tactics of continual small-unit patrolling failed, Union officers favoring active methods turned toward the development of specialized antiguerrilla units to hunt down the partisans and fight them on their own terms. Much as in the failed experiments with the Mississippi Marine Brigade in 1863–64, specialized conventional units were a disappointment overall, but offered one of the few possible solutions to the partisan dilemma. In the final year of the war, the Union abandoned many of its more innovative antiguerrilla procedures, instead reverting to proven active methods, such as increased cavalry patrols between Washington and the Bull Run Mountains, until Lee's surrender at Appomattox.[3]

To fully understand the evolution of active Federal counterguerrilla efforts against Mosby and other guerrillas and partisans operating in western and northwestern Virginia from 1863 to 1865, it is necessary to examine how the Union army dealt with irregulars in Virginia from the start of the war. After the attack on Fort Sumter in April 1861, and President Lincoln's subsequent call for 75,000 volunteers, four more slaveholding states seceded. Virginia left the Union reluctantly, reflecting the Old Dominion's close ties to the Federal system and its influential pro-Union population in the northwestern highlands. As mentioned in the introduction, western Virginia's mountain region served to isolate its inhabitants from the political and economic system of the rest of Virginia; instead, the people of what would become the state of West Virginia in 1863 more closely resembled the Ohioans living across the Ohio River than the state's slave-owning aristocrats. As with locales in Arkansas and Tennessee, the political and geographical isolation of western Virginia aided the growth of irregular warfare. And irregular warfare began in all three states early in the war.[4]

The northwestern counties of Virginia, running from the Bull Run Mountains to the Ohio River, were the battlefields for the uncivil war in the Old Dominion, and Federal military forces quickly took advantage of the divided loyalties of the region. In June 1861, delegates of the western twenty-six counties of Virginia met at Wheeling to form the loyal state of "Kanawha," the future West Virginia. To support the new pro-Union government and to secure the strategically important B&O

Railroad, Major General George B. McClellan launched a series of campaigns to seize the region. From the July 1861 battles of Laurel Hill,
Rich Mountain, and Corrick's Ford until the end of the war, Federal
forces occupied the gaps and thoroughfares into the Allegheny Mountains. With the exception of pro-Southern guerrillas and partisans and
the occasional raid by small conventional cavalry detachments, the
highlands of western Virginia were permanently Union.[5]

In 1861, the Confederate irregular war in western Virginia aimed
at controlling the pro-Union population. Small detachments of pro-
Confederate bushwhackers took to the hills to escape their Unionist
neighbors, who raised Home Guard units and sent volunteer regiments
to the Federal armies. Isolated from the state government at Richmond,
and prior to the establishment of the Unionist government in late
1861, the citizens of the region suffered from a breakdown of civilian
authority. Unlike in Arkansas and Tennessee, western Virginia did not
enjoy any period of Confederate governmental control, and initially
the Federal authorities—expecting a short war—did not concern themselves with day-to-day workings of civilian government. Hence, the
breakdown in law and order seen in Tennessee and Arkansas after
Union invasions was evident in western Virginia from the start. For
example, in Wood County, located along the Ohio River in extreme
northwestern Virginia, unorganized bushwhackers ran many of the
local authorities out of the county's small towns if they were not pro-
Confederate. By the summer of 1861, as one historian notes, "lawlessness was so rampant that the [newly] organizing [Confederate] guerrillas made their headquarters in the county courthouses." Some of the
secessionists, isolated from communication with Confederate military authorities at Richmond, took matters into their own hands and
launched a terror campaign against their Unionist neighbors. One victim of such activities, Israel Forman, a merchant in Grafton, wrote that
"the rebels here took possession of the property of local citizens before
open hostilities commenced and then threatened them with the guard-
house and hanging if they said anything against it."[6]

In addition to the local guerrillas, migrating irregulars—both partisans and guerrillas—entered the region from other parts of Virginia.
Mosby's Forty-third Virginia Cavalry was the best known of the irregular units, but others, including Colonel Harry Gilmore's Maryland
partisan ranger battalion, operated in western Virginia from mid-1863
onward. Although these men fought in the region from time to time,

much of the violence of the western Virginia irregular war was perpetrated by unorganized bushwhacker bands or small guerrilla detachments that had little contact with Richmond. As in Arkansas and Tennessee, these unorganized bands soon began to prey on everyone, victimizing both pro-Confederate and pro-Union citizens. The Federal army's experiences against these unorganized guerrilla bands in 1861 shaped how it fought the much more disciplined and militarily effective partisan ranger forces of Mosby and Gilmore, and did much to encourage the development of later antiguerrilla methods.[7]

The early successes against unorganized bushwhackers and hastily organized guerrilla companies occurred for several reasons. In contrast to the partisans, the Northern units were well disciplined and well armed, reinforced by a sprinkling of U.S. Regulars and led by both regular and volunteer officers.[8] Newly raised Ohio and Illinois regiments were backed by the seasoned troopers of the Second U.S. Cavalry and the "Cottonbalers" of the Seventh U.S. Infantry, and by two Unionist Virginia regiments. In May 1861, General George B. McClellan took this force into the region, sweeping aside the bushwhacker companies attempting to stop its advance. For Colonel (later Major General) George Crook, the terrain alone prevented his Thirty-sixth Ohio Infantry from annihilating the irregulars, whom he considered nothing more than "counterfeiters and cut-throats before the war." McClellan's successes at Philippi, Grafton, and Charleston provided the impetus for the counties west of the Alleghenies to declare their secession from Virginia in October.[9]

The withdrawal of the last organized Confederate force in November gave the Federal army full control of the region for the rest of the war. Its only remaining opponents were the bushwhackers scattered throughout the mountains. According to Colonel Crook, this region "was well adapted for [guerrilla] operations, for, with the exception of a small clearing here and there for the cabins of the poor people who inhabited it, it was heavily timbered, with thick underbrush, rocky and broken, with dense laurel thickets here and there." Having spent the majority of his antebellum career fighting Native Americans on the frontier, Crook said that the "thoroughfares and country roads that traversed this country were like traveling through a box canon [canyon] with the forest and underbrush for walls." As the tide of war moved to other theaters, Crook's Ohioans found themselves in an antiguerrilla campaign. The guerrillas' "suppression became a military necessity, as they caused us to dispatch much of our active force for escorts, and even then no one was safe. It was an impossibility for them to be caught after shooting into a body of men, no difference as to its size," he later wrote. Crook decided that an active antiguerrilla campaign was the solution. "Being fresh from the Indian country where I had more or less experience with that kind of warfare," he determined that the best way to deal with the guerrillas was to handpick competent company officers and "[scatter] them through the country to learn it and all the people in it, and particularly the bushwhackers, their haunts, etc."[10] Crook's men soon captured or killed numerous members of the small detachments and thought they were making progress toward eliminating the threat, when additional guerrillas from surrounding counties entered the region and began the process anew. Much like commanders in the trans-Mississippi and General Sheridan in 1864, Crook turned toward retributive burning as an antiguerrilla tactic. He recalled that "Webster, one of the counties adjoining Nicholas, in which Summersville was located, was so bad that we had to burn out the entire county to prevent the people from harboring them [guerrillas]."[11]

In addition to carrying out punitive expeditions, such as by Crook's Thirty-sixth Ohio, Northern commanders and local Unionist leaders decided upon a two-pronged approach that involved a meshing of active and passive measures. For instance, the locals would raise antiguerrilla units within the Home Guard organizations, and the Federals would concentrate on securing the main routes of communication through the region, especially the B&O. As Union commander in the area, Major General John C. Fremont ordered patrols to chase down and destroy the guerrillas. In practice, these guerrilla bands consisted of fewer than thirty ill-armed, poorly disciplined, and unorganized Southern sympathizers, who ran at the approach of a Federal detachment half their size. Consequently, victories against these guerrillas encouraged Fremont to disperse his forces, pursue the bushwhackers, and destroy them. The result was a Federal army stationed in company-size detachments in hamlets and key passes. Fremont did not like this dispersement of his forces: "the troops of my command, however, though equal to the maintenance, for the time being of lines established, were, owing to their necessarily scattered condition, unavailable in any large proportion to form active or movable columns or for operations of a general character against the enemy."[12] The lessons learned by the Federal army in western Virginia—that the key to beating

guerrillas was dispersing the army into small antiguerrilla patrols—
planted the seed that would blossom into an unsuccessful antipartisan
campaign against Mosby.

For the individual Union soldier fighting the guerrillas in western
Virginia during the first two years of the war, the behavior of these unorganized bushwhackers did much to encourage later brutal Federal
actions. Sergeant John B. Forsythe, a trooper in Company B, Loudoun
County (Virginia) Rangers, wrote that the bushwhackers in the region
did much to infuriate his fellow pro-Union Virginians: "They infested
the mountains of Virginia, and were the most cowardly and desperate
of all guerrillas." For the Unionists, the war against the Rebel bushwhackers was to the death. Federal soldiers captured by one band, commanded by Captain John Moberly, "were taken into the hills and placed
upon their backs, and great boulders put upon their limbs, and left to
die of slow starvation." Forsythe recalled that a "number of skeletons
were found at the close of the war thus pinned to the ground, presenting a most horrible and ghastly appearance, shocking to the sensibili-
ties of a civilized person, and challenging the barbarities of savages."[13]

Union officers below general ranks also saw the problems with
scattering Yankee troops in small detachments. Lieutenant Charles
Rhodes, a Regular army officer and West Point graduate assigned to
the Sixth U.S. Cavalry, bemoaned the problems of cavalry operating in
western Virginia. As with many young officers wanting the glory of
the battlefield, Rhodes noted despairingly that "the Federal cavalry in
West Virginia had performed no conspicuous deeds." Instead, he found
"the country was ill-suited for maneuvering large bodies of cavalry;
but for scouting and reconnoitering small bodies could be made very
useful, as shown by the value to [General George B.] McClellan of the
hybrid commands known as McMullen's Rangers, the Ringgold Cavalry, and Burdsall's Cavalry. In fact, partisan warfare was a distinct
feature of the operations in West Virginia throughout the war." The
frustration in chasing an elusive foe soon told on the individual soldiers, who became more likely to use punitive measures on the local
civilian population—an unfortunate, but often militarily successful,
outcome of counterguerrilla warfare.[14]

Many of these antiguerrilla patrols could be quite lengthy, and cover
considerable territory in a short time. Sergeant John Black, Twelfth
Pennsylvania Volunteer Cavalry, wrote of these operations to his family
in late 1863. Black described one patrol as making a 100-mile circuit of

northwestern Virginia, from "Kearneysville, from there to Charlestown, from there to Berryville, [and] from there to the Shenandoah River, where we crossed at Snicker's Ford and put up for the night in the Gap, having traveled 35 miles through the hot rays of the sun." The next day, the patrol moved another thirty-five miles, arriving at their camp at Harpers Ferry at 2:00 P.M. For their efforts, his detachment "met a few rebels, only stragglers. We captured five." Black added, "I am well pleased I was along for I saw the hardest 'Secesh' part of the country in our travel that I ever saw before." Noteworthy is the fact that Black's patrol was conducting a mission aimed at capturing or killing guerrillas—not a counterinsurgency mission aimed at controlling the local populace. Black's patrol was much the same as many others conducted by Federal cavalry in 1863, and was significant to Black only because they actually managed to catch a few "stragglers."[15]

As the Federal army fought an antiguerrilla war to suppress marauding bands in West Virginia, in 1863 a new threat arose in the region between Harpers Ferry and Washington, D.C. As described in chapter 3, Mosby began operations in the area in the summer, focusing his attacks on Union supply trains, foraging detachments, and on the Yankee rail system. The Union high command, having earlier seen promising results against guerrillas a few miles away in the Alleghenies, assumed Mosby and his men were nothing more than another locally raised guerrilla band aiming at conducting petty terrorism on the populace or sniping at passing Federal locomotives. They could not have been more wrong.

Passive measures against unorganized guerrillas operating in northern and western Virginia, like the active measures discussed above, were employed from the beginning of the war. From the posting of flankers and pickets for conventional forces to the use of specially designed armored trains, passive defense played an important part of the Federal counterguerrilla campaign in Virginia. Active and passive antiguerrilla measures differ in several respects, but can complement one another in a cohesive strategy. Passive defensive measures tend to be much costlier in men and material, as they aim at defending a large area against enemy attack. Additionally, passive measures give the guerrilla or partisan complete tactical initiative, allowing him to pick his own time and place for attack. Against untrained bushwhackers early in the war, the latter was never an important issue; against Mosby and the other partisans after 1863, it became a fatal flaw.

Two major strategic issues consumed Federal leaders throughout the war, and led them to develop a complex and advanced passive anti-guerrilla system. In the region occupied by Federal troops from north-western Virginia to the Chesapeake Bay, the defense of Washington was paramount. Called by one historian "the sword, shield and symbol" of the Republic, the national capital was the single most important location for the Federals; the fall of the city could mean the end of the Union. Consequently, a minimum of 30,000 men and upwards of 700 guns occupied its defenses from 1861 to 1865, which surpassed in depth and strength the legendary works at Sevastopol during the Crimean War. Tied directly to the defense of the city was a second strategic asset that preoccupied Federal commanders throughout the war, the Baltimore and Ohio Railroad.[16]

The B&O served as a vital lifeline to Washington, linking the capital to the western states. Although other lines existed farther north, the lengthy roundabout route that men, munitions, and material would have to travel made the B&O a critical part of the Federal transportation network. For irregulars, the railroad provided a perfect target for raids and ambushes. It ran through the mountainous terrain of north-western Virginia, giving partisans and guerrillas the opportunity to strike quickly and retreat into their mountain hideouts. Moreover, the rails themselves could be easily cut where they crossed over defiles, creeks, and gullies on flammable wooden bridges. Lastly, the length of the route, especially the vulnerable run from Wheeling, West Virginia, to Frederick, Maryland, placed heavy demands on Federal forces. When Mosby began his operations in mid-1863, the civilian officials of the B&O and the military officers protecting it soon discovered that many of their previous solutions, adequate to stop the lone bushwhacker or gang of unorganized guerrillas, failed against the Forty-third Virginia Cavalry.[17]

From the beginning of the war, Federal commanders realized the importance and the vulnerability of the B&O. Consequently, from 1861 to mid-1862, Union troops patrolled the entire length of the route between Wheeling and Frederick, spread out in small detachments for nearly every half mile of its length. The scattered Northern troops were successful in preventing the type of minor terrorism that had occurred outside of Baltimore in April 1861 when Southern sympathizers burned several railroad trestles leading into Washington, but were found to be nearly useless against conventional Confederate forces. Following the

Figure 2. Federal Organization and Personnel Assigned to
　　　　　Western Virginia, 1861–65

Date	Name of Command	Troops Present for Duty	Commander	Main Irregular Threat
Oct. 1861	Dept. of Western Virginia	38,671	Gen. William Rosecrans	Unorganized guerrillas
Dec. 1862	District of Western Virginia	28,433	Gen. Jacob Cox	Unorganized guerrillas
June 1863	Dept. of West Virginia	15,918	Gen. B. F. Kelley	Unorganized guerrillas
June 1864	Dept. of West Virginia	36,509	Gen. David Hunter	Partisan rangers
Aug. 1864	Dept of West Virginia	26,010	Gen. George Crook	Partisan rangers
Dec. 1864	Dept. of West Virginia	18,719	Gen. George Crook	Partisan rangers
Mar. 1865	Dept. of West Virginia	15,517	Gen. George Crook	Partisan rangers

SOURCE: *Official Records*, in the following order by year: *OR*, series 1, vol. 5, 636; ibid., vol. 21, 963–64; ibid., vol. 25, pt. 2, 185; ibid., vol. 37, pt. 1, 573; ibid., vol. 43, pt. 1, 974–75; ibid., vol. 43, pt. 1, 848; ibid., series 3, vol. 5, 137.

NOTE: All data are from monthly personnel returns for each major command. Although personnel numbers fluctuated month to month, the given sample is representative of the total available personnel (minus troops on detached duty or otherwise assigned, but not present).

poor showing of the patrolling system during Lee's 1862 Maryland campaign, Federal commanders decided that it was a waste of valuable manpower. A succession of Federal officers attempted to mitigate the problem, from General Fremont in 1861 to General McClellan in 1862, but their focus on defeating the Confederate field armies preoccupied them. Therefore, a subordinate command structure was employed to oversee the defense of the B&O and of western Virginia (see figure 2).[18]

Of the commanders assigned to defend the B&O, none were as inventive and controversial as Brigadier General Benjamin F. Kelley. Kelley was not a professional soldier, but a native of Wheeling and an antebellum employee of the B&O. After assuming command of the Department of West Virginia in early 1863, Kelley focused on dealing with both a conventional and unconventional threat against the railroad. To him, the quandary was how to form a force strong enough to resist conventional cavalry raids but dispersed enough to cover the entire line against irregular attacks. The solution came in two parts—an extensive blockhouse system and armored trains.[19]

The blockhouses were miniature fortresses, containing sufficient ammunition, food, and water to resist a siege for several days. Two basic models of blockhouses were constructed. One was large, capable of holding small artillery pieces and about fifty men. The second was a simpler style, often referred to as an outpost, and was most often used to cover the approaches to railroad bridges, with one on each end of the bridge. Built of logs of between twelve and fourteen inches in diameter, and twenty-four feet long on each side, the blockhouse was a formidable obstacle for an irregular detachment. Even a conventional cavalry unit, unless it had field artillery, would find a blockhouse difficult, if not impossible, to storm. Inside the blockhouse, which was built on high ground with cleared fields of fire surrounding it, upward of thirty men lived and fought. One Union officer described them as "timbered on top to keep shells out and . . . notched through the sides for the purpose of shooting through above the earthwork" that surrounded the blockhouse. Strengthening the defenses were abatis. The blockhouses, similar to ones used by the British years later in the Boer War, met the Federals' need for protection with a minimum expenditure of manpower.[20]

General Kelley's second solution was even more modern. Encouraged by the success of naval ironclads, he directed his officers to build a rail-mounted version of the *Monitor*, calling them "ironclads." These armored railcars gave the blockhouses the added firepower needed to respond to large conventional or unconventional attacks, while using only a fraction of the field artillery strength that would have been necessary to provide guns to each outpost. An average ironclad train carried a "battery, three guns in each, covered with railroad iron at each end, and four cars iron-lined and musket-proof between the two." Against an enemy armed with artillery, the trains were easy targets, but when facing lightly armed irregulars, the behemoths were unstoppable. The ironclads were so successful in scaring away irregulars that they were often used to protect construction crews repairing the rail line after attacks. Although Kelley was later relieved of command because of differences with his commanders in Washington, the passive measures he employed stayed in effect until the end of the war.[21]

The extensive passive defense measures along the B&O, coupled with active antiguerrilla operations in the mountains of northwestern Virginia, kept irregulars restricted to minor operations that, in the words of one Union officer, the Army of the Potomac noticed no more than "the ox did the fly on his horn."[22] When Mosby began his partisan operations in the summer of 1863, the Federal authorities found that the partisan species of fly was somewhat more of a nuisance than the bushwhacker species. Initially, Federal commanders, believing Mosby's twenty-man partisan detachment to be no more than another guerrilla band, began an active approach to capture him. Following his raid on Fairfax Court House, where he captured General Stoughton, Mosby became the number one target for cavalry patrols operating between Washington and the Shenandoah Valley (see chap. 3). If a Federal commander in the region heard rumors of the Forty-third Virginia Cavalry, or any other irregular detachment, Yankee troopers rode off in hot pursuit—regardless of the validity of the rumor. Later, when Union officers realized that such an approach would never work against irregulars who knew the terrain and were often better mounted than the Northern cavalry, a more proactive approach was used—constant patrolling of suspected guerrilla-infested areas. This tactic, while occasionally successful, led to boredom and frustration for the soldiers involved. One trooper, Captain William Hyndman of Company A, Fourth Pennsylvania Cavalry, called these patrols "guerrilla scouting tours," and noted in his postwar memoir that his company was continually conducting them in hopes of catching Mosby. He stated that "frequently we reached as far as Warrenton, and met parties of guerrillas, occasionally, with whom we had some sharp skirmishes. During the winter [of 1864–65] we captured several of these." Twice during that last winter of the war, Hyndman's company caught up with Mosby's men, only to find that Mosby's camp was "vacated both times—the wily rebel having almost miraculously got wind of our intention." The Federal captain's description of Mosby reflected his aggravation with the partisan chieftain's operations. "He was a singularly active, vigilant and subtle foe. It was impossible to even surprise him, to say nothing of effecting his capture."[23]

General George Crook returned to the Shenandoah Valley and western Virginia in 1864, as part of Sheridan's command. He found it a completely different environment in 1864 than in 1861, when the main threat had been scattered bushwhacker bands. In 1864, he came against organized partisan ranger outfits, especially those of Mosby, Gilmore, and McNeill, as well as isolated guerrillas in the Alleghenies and the Blue Ridge Mountains. Crook began work immediately, falling back on the lessons he had learned while fighting Native Americans—that a successful insurgency could be fought only with competent and motivated soldiers organized into special units. The first he developed was the cavalry detachment under Captain Richard Blazer, "who evinced an adaptability for that kind of work, and became so efficient that he was not long in ridding the district infested with these people [the unorganized bushwhackers]."[24]

Active antiguerrilla operations formed the dominant method of Union attempts to destroy Mosby and the other partisan rangers. Of all the active operations developed to hinder Confederate partisan warfare, the use of specialized antiguerrilla units against Mosby and other irregulars was the most successful and promising, though they ultimately failed because of mismanagement, Confederate counter-counterguerrilla operations, and the impatience of the Union high command. Federal leaders, including Sheridan and Crook, sponsored the employment of such detachments beginning in 1863, and the units provided numerous benefits to the Union high command. Often called "scouts," these volunteer detachments were led by handpicked officers known for their loyalty, competence, and aggressiveness. In this respect, they closely resembled the Confederate officers of Mosby's command, who were selected by the partisan leader for the same reasons (see chap. 3). These scout detachments, in addition to their primary antiguerrilla mission, also provided critically needed combat information to Sheridan and his subordinate generals in the 1864 Shenandoah Valley campaign. Despite some successes, the specialized units failed to hunt down and destroy the Confederate irregulars, and in at least one famous case were themselves the prey of Mosby's Rangers.

The initial idea for special detachments came from General Crook, who placed Captain Blazer, a West Virginian who enlisted in the Ninety-first Ohio Infantry at the start of the war, in command of a small unit of highly mobile and efficient troopers, armed with the newest Spencer repeating rifles and the best mounts that Crook could provide.[25] Their mission seemed simple—find and destroy Mosby's Rangers and any other irregular detachment in the area of operations, running from the Alleghenies to the Bull Run Mountains. Since much of this area was behind enemy lines, Blazer's men often wore civilian clothes or even Confederate uniforms to gather information. Mosby later acknowledged that "Blazer's Independent Scouts" posed the single greatest threat to his command during the war. Another member of Mosby's Rangers agreed with his commander, describing the lengths to which the Confederates went to trap and eliminate Blazer's scouts at every opportunity.[26]

Throughout the early fall of 1864, Captain Blazer's command pursued Mosby and his men across the region. As they became familiar with the area and the people within it, they learned the advantages of a lenient policy toward the citizenry and captured irregulars. Captain J. Marshall Crawford, one of Mosby's company commanders, later stated that "I must say they [Blazer's men] had more of the instincts of men, and the feelings of humanity about them on that day [September 2, 1864] than any we ever met before. Our wounded they carried to houses in the neighborhood, and requested every attention to be shown to them until removed."[27] Another of Mosby's men, John Alexander, wrote that "his [Blazer's] kindness to citizens was proverbial, and everywhere within range of his activities the citizens were ready to bear honorable testimony to his character," adding, "he was certainly a thorn in Mosby's side."[28]

The Federal scouts aggressively targeted Mosby's Rangers, chasing down rumors of the partisans' location at every opportunity. Occasionally, acting on such rumors paid off. In late September 1864, Blazer, who reported directly to Sheridan, informed his commander that his troop had ambushed "Mosby's guerrillas, 200 strong, at this place [Myer's Ford, West Virginia], and after a sharp fight of thirty minutes we succeeded in routing him, driving them three miles, over fences and through corn-fields." The partisans were stubborn and "fought with a will, but the seven shooters [Spencer carbines] proved too much for them," and the Union officer claimed one officer and six men killed, and six Rangers captured. This was a seemingly small exchange for the Federals, but based on Mosby's dependence on a cadre of motivated and experienced irregulars, any losses were considered critical.[29]

Blazer's success in gaining popular support and in capturing isolated partisans was truly a thorn in Mosby's side, and he decided to pluck the thorn. In the words of partisan Major John Scott, "Mosby and Blazer could not long inhabit opposite sides of the Blue Ridge Mountains, and Mosby was resolved to bring the rivalry to a speedy and decisive issue."[30] Mosby decided to split his force, sending a detachment under Major Adolphus A. Richards to "hunt Blazer up."[31] On November 18, 1864, Richards's and Blazer's columns made contact, with the Rebel partisans gaining the initial surprise. Richards realized that he could not give Blazer's Federals time to react, since the latter possessed exceptional firepower from seven-shot Spencer carbines. Outnumbered nearly two to one, Blazer's small command broke under the assault. All semblance of military discipline was lost as men attempted to escape as best they could. The Rangers lost one man killed and five wounded, while Blazer's casualties were drastic—sixteen killed, six wounded, and eleven captured, including the guerrilla hunter himself. According to Sheridan, Blazer had only 62 men and had lost nearly one third of his force during the initial volley, while the partisans numbered nearly 115.[32]

Blazer's defeat did not halt the use of specially organized Federal units for antiguerrilla operations. Following the initial successes of Blazer's troop, Sheridan raised an even larger detachment, led by Major H. K. Young, First Rhode Island Infantry. Young was given a full battalion (nearly 400 men) and the mission of hunting down Mosby and other irregulars, and gathering intelligence for Sheridan. In the first respect, Young's battalion failed, as a unit of such large size could never hope to catch Mosby's scattered detachments. In the field of combat intelligence, in contrast, Young's battalion fared extremely well, and Sheridan credited them with greatly aiding the victory at Winchester on September 15, 1864.[33] Young's battalion could mark one major success against the partisans, the capture of Colonel Harry Gilmore, the Marylander whose exploits were surpassed only by Mosby. It must be noted that in this incident, Major Young discovered Gilmore's presence because of an informant and sent only a handful of men to capture the Rebel. Sheridan marked this as Young's greatest victory against irregulars in Virginia, and encouraged further actions against the Confederate partisans.[34] For the Confederates, the actions of specialized antiguerrilla units, such as Captain Blazer's company and Young's battalion, hampered but did not halt their use of partisan warfare.

A final active method was employed to end the partisan war, the use of Federal spies and local sympathizers. The volunteers who came forward for such duty were well aware of the consequences if they were captured, but their commanders, who would happily defend hanging or shooting guerrillas in Federal uniform as spies, completely justified the use of Union troops dressed as Confederates to gain information. Frank Reader, a captain in the Fifth West Virginia Cavalry, said that the volunteers "were required most of the time to be dressed in confederate uniforms, thus exposed to all the risks and dangers of spies, and were expected to be ready to go at any hour, day or night, when the commander of the forces ordered." Masquerading as Rebels greatly aided the scouts, since "being dressed as confederates, they would pass as good southern men, and many a letter was given them by mothers and daughters to carry to Lee's command, from which they frequently obtained very valuable information; yet in the very midst of the enemy's country they would often meet strong, faithful union men and women, to whom the general sent them for information." Additionally, pro-Union civilians "kept the scouts posted in regard to all movements of the enemy, and were valuable aids to the union cause and true friends to the scouts." As assets in the irregular war in Virginia, these West Virginia spies and their pro-Union civilian contacts were invaluable, but Federal use of them eroded many of the legalistic arguments for wholesale execution of captured irregulars in civilian clothing or Union uniforms, as supported by Major General Henry Halleck in 1862.[35]

Passive defensive methods were nearly useless in limiting Mosby's operations. As noted earlier, Mosby often knew when and where trains were running, and could pick the easiest targets. Understandably, he avoided attacking blockhouses, and General Kelley's ironclad railcars apparently worked to keep Mosby away from the land dreadnoughts. The most commonly used passive defense against Mosby was the stationing of outposts and detachments throughout the region; unfortunately for the Federals, these were easily captured by Mosby's men on numerous occasions. Compounding the confusion over the tactics needed to end Mosby's operations, many units conducted a mixture of both active and passive measures, often frustrating the soldiers involved. Lieutenant C. J. Rawling, an officer in the First Virginia Infantry (Union), described the lengths to which the Federal troops went to protect their supply trains from the Rebel irregulars in the fall of 1863, just to keep themselves and their mounts fed. When not guarding their own supply wagons, his entire regiment, along with other Union troops, conducted great "sweeps" across the Yankee-occupied region in hopes of catching guerrillas. Most were abject failures. "On the 15th of August [1863] the regiment, with the Fourteenth West Virginia, a troop of cavalry, and a battery of light artillery, moved to Petersburg, Hardy County, and there were engaged in scouting through the mountains, the country being infested with bushwhackers, who were citizens at times and soldiers when there was promise of gain," he recalled. Not only unorganized guerrillas, but Confederate partisans were a threat, since "any stores or supplies being moved by wagons were almost sure to be captured by these partisans, unless strongly guarded, and weak [Federal] detachments were often [captured] by them." Attempts to pursue and eliminate the partisans were futile, exacerbated by the brutal terrain of the Blue Ridge and Allegheny Mountains and by the rapidity and surprise of partisan attacks. According to Lieutenant Rawling, the partisans "[knew] the country well, and the roads intersecting one another in the mountain regions in a remarkable way, offering the best facilities for the prosecution of this species of warfare, of which they were not slow to avail themselves." Pursuits became exercises in endurance for both the Federals and the Rebel partisans, and often "resulted in finding that enemy on the alert, and usually absent, at least not in the place desired and expected by his pursuers, hence the latter, as it often happened, had their labor for their trouble and nothing more; in short, there was neither profit nor honor in this service." Lieutenant Rawling's experiences, sadly for the Union army, were the norm and not the exception as they attempted to conduct large antipartisan operations in western Virginia.[36]

A second passive antipartisan measure was the establishment of static guard posts. An extensive chain of these outposts played a role in suppressing the small guerrilla detachments. But positions were ripe for harassment or capture by Mosby. William Beach, an officer in the First New York Cavalry, described how attacks on these isolated posts by Mosby and other partisan rangers increased the frustration of the Union troops: "Hardly was there a night when there was not some post attacked. The report would quickly reach headquarters when the command, 'Saddle Up' would ring out and half the reserve would be out on a wild ride over the mountain roads. Such skulking attacks were so common that constant vigilance was necessary."[37] Charles Lynch, an enlisted man in the Eighteenth Connecticut Volunteer Infantry, wrote

in December 1863 that he and his regiment "are all the time watching the mountain passes and the fords" against guerrillas "who know
every foot of this country and section of Virginia." For most soldiers,
spending the war watching for guerrillas was boring, but the presence
of irregulars haunted them constantly. Lynch wrote that the "guerrillas and scouts keep us on the alert all the time as they are liable to
show up at any time." Speaking of Mosby's Rangers, Lynch stated that
"they raid trains on the B&O R. R." and "seem to know when they can
make a good haul." The long and frustrating antiguerrilla duty led to
some acts of brutality against the few irregulars that were caught.
While marching toward Cedar Creek in May 1864, Lynch wrote: "our
scouts brought in a bushwhacker, a tough looking specimen of humanity," and noted that "not much mercy is shown to them." In general,
according to Lynch, "Old Mosby keeps us busy" by attacking the B&O
(which Lynch's unit was tasked to guard) and by "manag[ing] to steal
horses, and get the best."[38]

A third passive measure against irregulars, used throughout the Civil
War in every area that had a high level of irregular activity, was the
requirement to escort wagon trains needed for logistical support. In the
Shenandoah and in northern Virginia, armed convoys became the norm
rather than the exception. The activities of Mosby's men and other partisans, along with those of the unorganized guerrillas in the region,
forced Union commanders to assign troops to escort duties. Sergeant
Lynch of the Eighteenth Connecticut described the problem of supplying Sheridan's army in 1864 in a region populated by irregulars, writing
"we are seventy miles from our base of supplies, which must be brought
to us in wagons under a strong guard." Lynch believed only cavalry could
do the job adequately, and even they "have much trouble from the guerrillas under Mosby and others," who "keep concealed in the woods along
the pike" and can see up and down the Valley from their mountainous
hideouts. Sergeant Lynch stated simply: "don't like that kind of duty,"
especially after several wagons were "cut out of a train" under the
Connecticut regiment's protection.[39] For Captain Elisha Hunt Rhodes,
Mosby's Rangers were a constant threat in July 1864. As soon as his regiment, the Second Rhode Island Infantry, passed Leesburg, Virginia,
"Mosby's Rebel Cavalry attacked our trains and captured a number of
sick and wounded men," including five Rhode Islanders.[40]

By giving the partisans the ability to pick their own targets at their
leisure, passive defensive measures were flawed from their inception.

Although the deterrent quality of some passive actions, such as the larger fortified blockhouses and armored trains, limited the targets of the partisans, the reality was that passive measures would only succeed in reducing, not eliminating, the partisan threat.

Union antiguerrilla operations from 1861 to 1863 focused on catching and eliminating guerrilla bands scattered throughout the region, and met some success in suppressing the operations of the small, unorganized, and undisciplined bushwhacker bands. As Mosby began his operations in mid-1863, the method of Confederate irregular warfare changed to a partisan strategy, but Federal response did not. Against Mosby, Union commanders still tried to operate using constant cavalry patrols and specialized antiguerrilla detachments. Mosby was able to use the Federal dependence on antiguerrilla tactics in his favor, gobbling up the small Yankee detachments. Part of the problem with Federal understanding in the changed irregular war was that prior to Mosby's operations in 1863, the Union high command had treated guerrillas as a nuisance and seemingly as a separate entity from the Confederate field armies. The Federals' experience in western Virginia, Missouri, and Arkansas reinforced this belief. Mosby was different, taking orders directly from Lee and Stuart, and understanding the intent of his operations to the extent that he could act independently for extended periods. He was not a talented bushwhacker, but a skilled partisan officer—a fact that Union military leaders never recognized during the war.

Mosby's headline-grabbing actions both frightened and embarrassed the Federal high command and called for a new approach. Having used large-scale retributive burning in Missouri, Arkansas, and along the Mississippi River to halt guerrilla attacks, and having found success in the punishment of pro-Confederate communities in western Virginia early in the war, Federal commanders decided to try the same approach against Mosby. Over the objections of men actively fighting guerrillas in the region, one of the most destructive military campaigns in American history—the 1864 Shenandoah Valley campaign—was launched.[41]

Sheridan's 1864 campaign has long been used by historians as evidence of the totality of warfare in the Civil War.[42] Others, concentrating on the role Sheridan played in denying the rich agricultural resources of the Valley to Lee's army in 1864–65, have seen the 1864 Valley campaign as a critical part of Grant's war of attrition against the Confederacy. Yet there is a third reason that Sheridan launched his incendiary campaign in 1864, one that is often forgotten or ignored.[43] Sheridan, in his own words, began the burning of the Valley as a response to attacks by Confederate partisans, especially Mosby's Rangers, on his scouts, pickets, and supply trains.[44]

Before Sheridan began his campaign, the attitude of the Federal military authorities, especially those in the Army of the Potomac, toward the guerrilla problem was indifference. As put succinctly by Captain Walter S. Newhall, Second Pennsylvania Cavalry, in late 1863: "the phlegmatic Army of the Potomac isn't going to bother its head about a few guerrillas, so they are allowed to pursue their pleasing devices." His frustration was evident when he described how guerrillas burned bridges, killed couriers, and raided supply trains with relative impunity. The tone of this letter, and several of his diary entries, indicates that Captain Newhall preferred a more retributive and permanent solution to the guerrilla problem than the capture-and-return methods of the Army of the Potomac provost marshal general. When Sheridan began burning the Valley in the late summer and early fall of 1864, Captain Newhall, and many of his peers, believed it was the best method to deal with the partisan threat.[45]

Retributive burning reached its apogee during the Valley campaign. As the Federal troops marched through the region, destruction of farms and homes and the threat to burn entire towns became a reality. Captain Rhodes of the Second Rhode Island Infantry, wrote in his diary of one such incident at Newtown on September 27. There, a "Negro told me that Mosby and some of his men were in town and would attack us as we passed through." Responding to this information, Rhodes found a local citizen to go into Newtown with a message: "[I] sent him to Colonel Mosby with my compliments and told him to get out of the town or I would burn it." The irate citizen-messenger demanded to know if Rhodes had orders to burn the town; Rhodes responded by saying "we would have the fire and get the orders afterwards." Mosby took Rhodes's demand seriously, leaving the town but staying within visual range of the Yankee column. The town was spared, and the wagon train escorted by Rhodes continued through the town to link up with Sheridan's army.[46]

As an example of the arbitrariness of the burning, Newtown, which had survived Captain Rhodes's incendiary threats, was burned approximately two months later on Sheridan's order. Sitting on the route between Winchester, Sheridan's base of supply, and the location of the forward armies, Newtown was a perfect base of operations for irregulars. Alexander Neil, a brigade surgeon in Sheridan's army, wrote that "we were attacked by Guerrillas, and six of our men killed, 13 wounded & 15 captured, a Colonel and a Surgeon on the Staff of Genl. Sheridan, were mortally wounded, the doctor since died." In response, Sheridan "burned Newtown and all the houses within 5 miles of the place." The burning of Newtown, as could be expected, only served to encourage the irregulars, who "attack [Federal] trains everyday & are a perfect nuisance."[47] Sheridan dispatched General Wesley Merritt's cavalry division to the area to "operate against Mosby, taking care to clear the area of forage and subsistence, so as to prevent the guerrillas from being harbored there in the future." Merritt cleaned the area of all foodstuffs that could be carried and then burned what he could not move. For the people living in the Valley, especially those living along the main thoroughfares through the region, the level of destruction soon reached catastrophic proportions.[48]

The burning of the Shenandoah Valley came as a surprise to the civilians caught in the maelstrom of fire and destruction. They had survived offensives and counteroffensives for nearly three years on a semiannual basis. Confederate and Federal armies would march and fight throughout the region, yet little wholesale destruction occurred. In the fall of 1864, everything changed. Federal attempts to destroy both Lee's food supply and Mosby's hideouts encouraged the Yankee commanders to take decisive action. Robert Hugh Martin, who was a young boy during the war, later wrote of his experiences; the burning of the Valley left the largest mark in his memory of the entire war. "All during the war, as I had picked up from overheard conversations," Martin recalled, "there had been Federal officers who had threatened to burn the town under one pretext or another, but these threats had not been particularly alarming." Martin blamed the early threats on Yankee "swashbucklers," who delighted in terrorizing the helpless population. In early October 1864, this changed. Federal troops set barns and a gristmill afire, panicking the locals. As a child, Martin "was terribly frightened [and] lifted up my voice and wept loudly, the first and only time during the war from fright at the war's events." His reason for crying was simple—the adults began discussing the real prospect of starvation in the coming winter. He added: "Santa Claus forgot to come to the Shenandoah Valley in the closing years of the war. . . . I had heard about him but understood he did not come because of the war."[49]

General Merritt summarized the campaign as one aimed at damaging Lee's supplies and intended as an antiguerrilla measure. Writing after the war, Merritt believed Sheridan burned the Valley to prevent his being tied down in a manpower-intensive counterinsurgency campaign. He recalled that "Sheridan was opposed to the proposition submitted by the others [General Grant, President Lincoln, and Secretary of War Stanton], which was to operate against Central Virginia from his base in the Valley, . . . the general reasons for his opposition [being] the distance from the base of supplies, the lines of communication, *which in a country infested by guerrillas it would take an army to protect*, and the nearness, as the campaign progressed, if successful, to the enemy's base, from which large reinforcements could easily and secretly be hurried and the Union army be overwhelmed." Merritt fully supported his commander's concept. He ordered his men to conduct methodical destruction of anything that could aid the enemy, an act he acknowledged as "a severe measure, and appears severer now in the lapse of time; but it was necessary as a measure of war." The cavalry commander's justification for the order, tellingly, was not to end the war more quickly by starving the Army of Northern Virginia, but because "the country was fruitful and was the paradise of bushwhackers and guerrillas," who "had committed numerous murders and wanton acts of cruelty on all parties weaker than themselves." The murder of Federal soldiers, in Merritt's opinion and that of the Union high command, completely justified retributive burning operations as a counterguerrilla tactic. Much as with the guerrilla war in Arkansas, the Federal attempt to defeat Mosby ultimately became an incendiary campaign aimed at eliminating logistical support for the irregulars.[50]

The burning of the Shenandoah Valley changed the nature of the war between the Blue Ridge and Allegheny Mountains. The retributive character of Sheridan's operations soon led Union soldiers, Confederate guerrillas, and partisans into a vindictive, brutal, and personal conflict, perhaps equaled only in the most divided regions of southern Missouri. In June 1864, A Company, Fourth Pennsylvania Cavalry, was operating in Sheridan's force along the Pamukey River in the Shenandoah Valley. As the company patrolled the area, protecting Federal supply trains and attempting to chase down guerrillas, logistical support became less available through the normal supply channels. Consequently, the company, along with most of Sheridan's army, began to live off the well-provisioned countryside—in other words, to randomly forage at every farm and village in the region. Captain William Hyndman, the company commander, remembered that Sheridan's army "literally 'cleaned out' the section of everything edible for man or beast, operating over strips of country four miles wide, all along the line of march, both right and left," justifying the "rather rough deeds perpetrated by us in Virginia, at this time, out of sheer necessity." The farmers of the Valley were left without food to feed their families, much less Lee's army, after Sheridan's troopers "came down upon them like swarms of locusts, eating up the very seed for their next harvests."[51]

Hyndman's experience could have been useful to Sheridan and Crook, who were surprised by the increase of guerrilla activity as the army moved through the Shenandoah Valley. They had surmised that such actions would decrease the number of guerrillas, believing that both the bushwhackers and partisans would move because of a lack of supplies or that the citizenry would cease supporting them out of fear of Federal retributive measures. Hyndman's observation of the destructiveness of the Federal army was only surpassed by his keen insight, as when he noted that "on account of this [the plundering of the Valley], maddened by the intrusion, what few men were left in the country, hovered around in the shape of guerrillas, picking up any stray foragers they found, and making summary examples of them." For Hyndman and other company officers in Sheridan's force, the war turned more brutal than ever before, as a destructive cycle of "Federal plunder—guerrilla ambush—Federal burn" began. Hyndman wrote angrily: "it was no uncommon sight to see our dead comrades suspended conspicuously from the limbs of trees along our line of march, and labeled 'Such will be the fate of every forager caught!'. . . [T]hese scare-crows, horrible and revolting as they were, only whetted the operations of our men, giving to their movements sometimes a slight coloring of vengeance. Several of the bodies I saw suspended in this manner, I recognized as those of well-remembered soldiers of our command." Another officer, in a letter home, wrote that "it would be a great blessing to rid the Country of this terrible land pirate [Mosby]," adding "we string his men up whenever caught, but they still hover around murdering & robbing."[52]

By August, Sheridan's men had been plundering and burning much of the Shenandoah Valley. In practical military terms, the campaign was a complete success at both the operational and strategic levels of war. It led to the defeat, and near annihilation, of several large Confederate forces and secured the main invasion route into Maryland and Pennsylvania from future Rebel invasions. For Sheridan's men, in contrast, the actions in the Valley revealed the darkest side of irregular warfare and actually led to an increase in the number of unorganized irregulars. Hyndman, who several months before had pitied the citizens of the Valley, now described them as "military outlaws, the cowards and felons of the war," lacking, in his words, "a spark of true manhood, to say nothing of courage or valor, in their composition—the very scum of the foul wave of treason, as it rolled and blackened along the Union lines; the foetid decomposed humanity which even the rebel cast off from his living armies; a paltry, weasel-spirited horde, who were drafting about bodies [from] which they had robbed the Potter's fields of the South, ever since their first escape from the gallows. " He, the other troopers of his regiment, and most likely many of Sheridan's men, believed the only way to stop the guerrilla atrocities against the Federal soldiers was to execute all captured irregulars. To Hyndman's dismay, this did not always occur. "Strange to say, when we captured any of these [irregulars], by the humane provisions of our government, they were treated as prisoners of war." But he added: "I never caught one nor saw one, without bitterly gulping down impulses, which unrestrained, would have wrenched out their tongues till they blackened in death, or hung them without ceremony."[53]

The Federal troops, as the campaign progressed, became more willing to take part in punitive measures against the civilian populace. Lieutenant H. H. Chipman, Company F, Sixth Michigan Cavalry, reported to his commander, Captain C. H. Safford, of his actions against one group of accused guerrillas. His account exemplifies the tragic circle of violence that the guerrilla war in the Shenandoah Valley produced. After losing a soldier to a sharpshooter, Chipman explained that "a sergeant from the First New York Dragoons, in command of the picket reserve, informed me that he had sent twelve men and a noncommissioned officer out to where Briggs was shot, with orders to get his body, arrest what men he found near there, and burn the houses, &c." Lieutenant Chipman and his detachment arrested two men, whose homes were in the area. Based on the witness of a Federal soldier, who believed he saw the smoke from one of the houses, Chipman proceeded to the home, where he found the man's "wife and two small children. The men and their families were very abusive in their language, saying they wished all of us were shot, 'Served him right,' meaning Briggs, and other very insulting remarks." Chipman commended his men during this action, stating, "while I was making these inquiries it was only by the greatest effort that I could keep the men from killing them on the spot." The Federals, assuming that the inhabitants were guerrillas, burned the houses to the ground. Chipman later stated that he "heard cartridges explode in one of the houses burnt, thus proving that they had arms and ammunition concealed, which the men in their search did not find, and in contradiction of the prisoners, who had stated they had none about their premises." The Union lieutenant then sent his men on a search for ropes to hang the men; not finding any, he decided on a firing squad. The Federals executed both men, releasing a young boy to return to the fiery remains of his home and his now widowed mother.[54]

As the number and ferocity of attacks on isolated Federal detachments increased, Sheridan and his subordinates became more punitive in their actions. General Crook ordered the men under his command to "send expeditions to the sections of country where these bushwhackers are harbored, and destroy all subsistence for man or beast," in order to "make a belt of devastation between your lines and the enemy's all around your front."[55] Legal actions were also taken by the Federal authorities to attempt to limit the civilian support given to irregulars in the Shenandoah Valley. For example, General Orders Number 23, issued on November 17, 1864, was intended to protect the railroad from Harpers Ferry to Winchester by holding local citizens responsible. Sheridan, with the blessing of higher command, ordered that if the railroad was attacked, he would "arrest all male secessionists in the towns of Shepherdstown, Charlestown, Smithfield, and Berryville, and in the adjacent country, sending them to Fort McHenry, Md., there to be confined during the war; and also to burn all grain, destroy all subsistence, and drive off all stock belonging to such individuals, turning over the stock so seized to the Treasury agent for the benefit of the Government of the United States."[56]

General Halleck, from his headquarters in Washington, ordered even harsher measures, calling for the destruction of all property within five miles of the rail lines if attacks occurred. Halleck especially targeted "males suspected of belonging to, or assisting, the robber bands of Mosby" for imprisonment, while their property would be destroyed or confiscated and their families sent as refugees "north or south, as they may select." Halleck closed his directive by warning the populace of northern Virginia that "the inhabitants of the country will be notified that for any further hostilities committed on this road or its employees an additional strip of ten miles on each side will be laid waste, and that section of country entirely depopulated."[57]

In a larger sense, Sheridan's destructive campaign, while damaging the logistical foundation of Lee's army, failed to eliminate the irregular threat in the region. When Mosby arrived to take command of all remaining regular and irregular forces in the Shenandoah Valley in the spring of 1865, he found the populace welcoming to him and his men, and the citizens willing to feed him and his troops. While neither new Confederate volunteers nor food reached Lee's starving army, Mosby could and did draw troops and supplies from the surrounding countryside. New recruits came forward, despite the deepening demoralization throughout the rest of the South, and by the end of the war Mosby's battalion, unlike so many other isolated Confederate commands, kept the Valley orderly, peaceful, and steadfastly pro-Southern.[58]

In April 1865, after Mosby had agreed to a cease-fire to negotiate the surrender of the Forty-third Virginia, Colonel James Harvey Kidd, commander of the Michigan Cavalry Brigade, wrote that "the region to which we were going [the Shenandoah Valley] was one of the favorite haunts of Mosby and his men and it produced a queer sensation to thus ride peacefully through a country where for four long years, the life or liberty of the union soldier caught outside the lines had been not worth a rush, unless backed by force enough to hold its own against an enemy." In effect, Mosby the *partisan*, because of Federal retribution on the citizens of the Shenandoah, became the semblance of legal authority in the region, fulfilling the role that the Union army in Arkansas played in providing law and order. A companion of Colonel Kidd, shocked that ambushes and sniping were not occurring, was told that "Mosby's word was law in that section. His fiat had gone forth that there was to be a truce, and no union men were to be molested until it should be declared off." If any single statement so refutes the Union army's antiguerrilla campaign (to eliminate Mosby) or counterinsurgency campaign (to defeat the unorganized guerrillas and build up pro-Union support), the simple recognition that "Mosby's law" and not that of the Federal government could bring peace to the war-torn Valley demonstrates the failure of the Northern counterguerrilla strategy.[59]

When Mosby surrendered and dispersed his battalion, the final organized irregular unit of the Confederacy ceased to exist. Elsewhere, Confederate guerrillas, bushwhackers, and partisans had been defeated by the Federal army. The irregulars outside of "Mosby's Confederacy" found themselves isolated from the population, treated like criminals, or scattered into ineffective bands of five or ten men in the hinterland of the Upper South. But not so in Virginia. For Federal soldiers, the region adjacent to the national capital, possessing some of the strongest fortifications in the world and a minimum of 30,000 men on garrison duty, plus the Army of the Potomac allocated to its defense, was never a secure area. Outside of the fully fortified and heavily manned Union picket lines, the Confederate partisan ruled. Mosby survived not because of Federal incompetence at the tactical level, but because of failures at the highest level of Union command. Misreading the doctrine of the time, as espoused by Jomini and reinforced by experiences in West Virginia in the first two years of the war, Northern generals believed that Mosby and other partisans were no more than scattered bushwhackers, much like the bands operating in the Ozarks and the southern Appalachians. Consequently, they ordered their men to conduct operations using tactics fitting for an antiguerrilla campaign—active measures, such as constant patrolling with cavalry, backed by occasional sweeps by larger combined-arms forces, and the extensive use of specialized antiguerrilla troops, and passive measures, such as the use of static defenses along the B&O Railroad. When these tactics failed, Federal commanders adopted a retributive approach to punish the civilians who supported the irregular war, the most famous example being an adjunct to the 1864 Shenandoah Valley campaign. In a guerrilla war, as exemplified by the conflict in Arkansas, such measures would have met with some success. In a partisan war, burning towns and plundering the countryside aided the irregulars, who gained ample support from the civilian populace, and, since they were seen as legitimate members of the Confederate military, were seen as representatives of a legal government with all the authority therein.

The Union army never succeeded in eliminating Mosby's partisan rangers. The reasons for this failure are numerous, from Mosby's own insistence on small-unit operations and his personal leadership abilities, to Federal confusion over the doctrinal differences between bushwhackers, guerrillas, and partisans. Regardless, Mosby survived the war with his command intact, no mean feat considering the resources dedicated to his defeat. Against the bushwhackers of the Alleghenies, the Union was fairly successful in limiting the damage caused to railroads and other infrastructure through a combination of active and passive measures, backed by a loyalist population and Unionist military activities. The overwhelming preponderance of Federal troops and logistical support in the region prevented Mosby, with his small band of men, from causing enough damage to have a strategic effect on the war.

The third region of the Upper South to suffer under an "uncivil war" for four years was the center of the Confederacy, encompassing the states of Kentucky and Tennessee. In the irregular war in this region, the Confederates fought a conflict Jominian in character, with the unconventional aspects focusing more on the use of raids by conventional cavalry instead of either a guerrilla or partisan war. Although bushwhackers and guerrillas operated throughout the Upper South during the war, the main focus for the Confederates was in raiding operations. Fortunately for the Rebels, they had two of their most skilled partisan cavalry leaders of the war—John Hunt Morgan and Nathan Bedford Forrest—to fight this irregular war. Unfortunately for the South, the Federal measures that failed against Mosby in Virginia worked exceptionally well in destroying the third method of Confederate irregular warfare, the mounted raid.

5

THE HEYDAY OF
RAIDING WARFARE

Morgan and Forrest in
Tennessee and Kentucky, 1862

The author of the far-reaching "raid," so different from the mere
cavalry dash, he accomplished with his handful of men results which
would otherwise have required armies and the costly preparations
of regular and extensive campaigns.

Brigadier General Basil W. Duke, *Morgan's Cavalry*, 1906

The Confederacy's irregular war against the Union possessed three
distinct aspects. Guerrilla warfare, or people's war, was the least
popular with the Rebel high command but was being conducted by individuals and small companies wherever Federal troops occupied the
South. Partisan warfare, legitimized by the Partisan Ranger Act, was
more acceptable, especially when led and organized by the social elite
of the antebellum South, such as John S. Mosby in Virginia. The third
part of the triad of irregular war was the most palatable to Confederate
civil and military leaders. The mounted raid, conducted by regular cavalry forces specifically organized and detailed for that purpose, smoothly
fit the concepts of irregular warfare in the nineteenth century, and produced a hybrid of conventional and unconventional warriors—the raider.

Raiding, unlike guerrilla or partisan warfare, presented few legalistic issues to muddy the waters. The raiders were members of uniformed

Map 5. The western theater—Tennessee and Kentucky.

and legally constituted regiments; these were not part-time guerrillas, but full-time soldiers. Under contemporary understandings of combatant status, there were no questions on the conduct of their actions. Raids were seen as part of the conduct of any well-oiled campaign, especially a defensive one. Reflecting much of the general attitudes on the subject that grew out of the Napoleonic Wars, both Clausewitz and Jomini wrote extensively on mounted raids. In *On War*, Clausewitz advocated attacking the enemy's line of communications as one of the key facets of both defensive and offensive operations. He considered the raid, when conducted as "an actual diversion aimed at reducing the strength of the opposing side" as a defensive measure; when used for "the purpose of retribution or sacking for the sake of booty," a raid became an offensive tool. Jomini, in *Grand Military Operations*, also acknowledged the destructive capabilities of mounted raiders, but believed they were better suited toward defensive operations. In this respect, the Confederate leadership in 1862 followed a more Jominian approach toward raiding, which fit well with their strategic situation in the late summer of that year.[1]

It turned out that 1862 was a banner year for irregular warfare. In Arkansas, Confederate guerrilla companies ravaged the advancing Federals. Virginia saw the first inklings of a great partisan leader in the scouts and raids of John Singleton Mosby. In the center of the Confederate perimeter, specifically Tennessee and Kentucky, bushwhackers of both sides preyed on one another and on isolated conventional forces. Into the maelstrom of irregular war being waged in the West was introduced the concept of the mounted raid, led by two of the greatest cavalry leaders of the Civil War, Brigadier Generals John Hunt Morgan and Nathan Bedford Forrest. These men, along with their elite horse soldiers, conducted the most strategically successful raids of the war. They not only hindered Federal operations but invigorated Southern morale, developing and executing concepts of successful deep raiding that became the standard by which all other Confederate cavalry operations were measured.

The mounted raid had long been a mission of conventional cavalry. From the earliest days of mounted soldiers to the nineteenth century, cavalry had conducted punitive expeditions, attacked enemy supply trains, and seized key objectives using their speed and shock effect to surprise unwary enemies. By 1862, most Confederate cavalry units were capable of conducting raiding operations as part of their normal duties. The organization of Forrest's and Morgan's raiders was similar to that of other mounted regiments in the war. These two officers also closely resembled the socially acceptable leadership that Mosby demonstrated in Virginia. They were not bushwhacker commanders, but competent, conventionally focused soldiers who were part of the social and economic leadership of the prewar South. Their soldiers, unlike the ragged guerrillas in Arkansas, were conventional horsemen, but in contrast to Mosby's Rangers, they were not necessarily handpicked. Instead, these regiments of Rebel cavalry, raised from men available for enlistment in late 1861, matured into specialized raiding troops under the leadership of Morgan and Forrest. During 1862, and culminating with the December, or "Christmas" raids, few cavalrymen on either side could claim successes equal to those of the two "partisan" cavalry brigades of the Army of Tennessee.

John Hunt Morgan, much like Mosby, came from the upper strata of antebellum Southern society. His ancestry traced back as far as the mid-1600s in America, and his forbears served in the Revolution and under General Andrew Jackson during the War of 1812. Calvin Morgan, the future raider's father, married the daughter of the wealthy and influential John Wesley Hunt of Lexington, Kentucky, in 1823. Hunt, in the opinion of one historian, was "the wealthiest man west of the Allegheny Mountains," and on numerous occasions rescued his daughter's family from bankruptcy.[2] Young John was a perfect model of the Southern gentleman. His family practiced plantation agriculture as their main form of income, owned many slaves, and he spent much of his youth riding, hunting and, on at least one occasion, dueling in defense of his honor. It is not surprising that when he rose to fame in the Civil War, he was held as a paragon of Southern virtue.[3]

Morgan began his military career as a volunteer in the Mexican War, serving with the Kentucky cavalry regiment at the Battle of Buena Vista, returning home in June 1847. After the war, and an unsuccessful attempt to have his volunteer commission transferred to the regular army, Morgan settled into business in Lexington and soon established himself as one of the leaders of the community. In addition to running a thriving business, Morgan was active in the local militia and formed an infantry company, the Lexington Rifles, in 1857.[4] As the specter of war arose in 1860, it was natural for many in the South to turn to men like Morgan for military leadership based on both their standing in the community and martial experience. When the war began, Kentucky's claim of neutrality prevented Morgan and his pro-Confederate compatriots from seeing action in the opening battles. In September 1861 he and other like-minded members of the Lexington militia slipped out of town and headed south to join the Confederate army in southern Kentucky. These men formed the core of Morgan's cavalry in 1862, and many would rise to command companies and battalions under his leadership.[5]

Following his commissioning as a captain in late October 1861, Morgan began operating in an unconventional manner. He occasionally dressed his company in Federal uniforms to slip behind the lines, usually to gain information or conduct foraging operations. During the winter of 1861–62, and into the early spring, he and his men operated extensively in southern Kentucky and northern Tennessee, raiding Federal outposts and burning bridges. As one historian adroitly states, "in five and a half months of guerrilla warfare, Morgan had done nothing of military significance, but for a captain in command of a single company, it was an outstanding record."[6]

Morgan's cavalry company included a variety of men, some of whom belonged to the influential classes of antebellum Kentucky society, while others were "farmers and poor men."[7] One of his lieutenants was a kinsman, his brother-in-law Basil W. Duke, who rose to the rank of brigadier general by 1865 and became Morgan's biographer in the postwar era. After the reorganization of the Lexington Rifles into the Second Kentucky Cavalry Regiment in the winter of 1861, recruits from diverse backgrounds joined the unit. George St. Leger Grenfell, a former British cavalry officer, was one of the most useful to Morgan's command. Grenfell was a highly experienced professional soldier who had served in the Crimean War, on the Northwest Frontier in India, and in South America. Consequently, Morgan placed Grenfell in charge of the training of the Second Kentucky. Grenfell based his training regimen on British methods, emphasizing horsemanship and the use of firearms from horseback. Such skills were needed, despite the fact that all of the Kentuckians were experienced horsemen, to weld the unit together as an effective fighting force. The dislike of rigid military discipline so often associated with the Confederate soldier was even more evident in Morgan's command and grew with every raid and expedition. Morgan needed men like Grenfell and Duke to keep a rein on the fiercely independent raiders, much as Mosby made use of West Pointers, VMI graduates, and foreign officers to keep his rangers in line.[8]

The makeup of Morgan's command closely resembled that of Mosby's Rangers. One observer, Bennett Young, who served with Morgan in 1862 and 1863, recalled that "the division then comprised a remarkable body of young men" who "represented a full share of the chivalry and flower of the states of Kentucky and Tennessee." Doctors, lawyers, farmers, woodsmen, clerks, and even clergymen filled the ranks, and a "large proportion of these were liberally educated." Young's evaluation was that the experience with horses and firearms acquired by many men in antebellum Southern society made them perfect cavalrymen, because "they were proud, and that made them brave."[9] Another historian described Morgan's men as being "like most Kentuckians" who were "fond of a horse and outdoor sports, and sat a saddle like a centaur."[10] Ignoring the flowery prose, it is obvious that Morgan led a body of men who were socially far from the quality of western bushwhackers and who were familiar with mounted operations. Together, these factors gave the Second Kentucky Cavalry a good start toward becoming effective irregulars.

Nathan Bedford Forrest, often portrayed as a semiliterate racist with a thirst for blood, came from a different background than John

Hunt Morgan. As Morgan had in Lexington, Forrest had made a name for himself in Memphis, Tennessee. A self-made man, Forrest, despite his lack of education, rose close to the elite of Memphis society.[11] He enjoyed a sizeable income from his cotton plantation and his slaves, and began dabbling in local politics before the war. Elected as an alderman for Memphis in the late 1850s, Forrest sold much of his real estate and slave-trading businesses and focused on his numerous plantations, earning nearly $30,000 in 1861.[12]

When the war began, Forrest enlisted as a private in the Seventh Tennessee Cavalry; his position in Memphis society led several influential citizens to appeal to Governor Isham Harris to allow Forrest to raise his own cavalry battalion. Harris agreed, and Forrest was given permission to raise "a battalion of mounted rangers." Equipping the men was a problem, as Tennessee had exhausted its supplies of arms. Consequently, Forrest went to "neutral" Kentucky and convinced local Confederate sympathizers to aid in the purchase of weapons and equipment. While there, Forrest persuaded a local cavalry company to join his nascent battalion; when he returned to Memphis, he discovered his adjutant had also been recruiting. Unlike the homogeneous forces of Mosby or Morgan, Forrest's battalion contained only one company of men from Forrest's hometown of Memphis. In addition to the Kentucky cavalry company, a second Tennessee company joined, along with several companies from Alabama and a company from Texas. Forrest's first command was, in effect, a hodgepodge outfit that included men from four different states. Well into 1862, Forrest was still recruiting men, some of whom had been in independent partisan ranger companies in western Tennessee. For example, Private James Hamner wrote that the unit he belonged to, "Capt Little's Co of Partisan Rangers," joined itself to Forrest in October 1862 without any direction or orders from the Confederate army. The rangers felt that Forrest fought the war in a manner they liked, so they joined him. Such a wide variety of troops presented numerous disciplinary and organizational challenges to Forrest, and proved an excellent training ground for higher leadership.[13]

Despite his best efforts, Forrest's battalion still only had enough modern weapons for half the men; the rest were using shotguns brought from home. Forrest pushed ahead with training despite the equipment shortages, and his unit was ready for duty by late October 1861. It was immediately dispatched to the area around Dover, Tennessee, near the site where Fort Donelson would be built. Forrest had already begun to impress his superiors. Colonel Samuel Tate, a Confederate officer and president of the Memphis and Charleston Railroad, wrote to General Albert S. Johnston that "Colonel Forrest's regiment [of] cavalry, as fine a body of men as ever went to the field, has gone to Dover or Fort Donelson," adding, "give Forrest a chance and he will distinguish himself." Johnston placed Forrest's battalion under General Lloyd Tilghman, and the troopers spent the winter of 1861–62 patrolling and scouting the area around the Cumberland and Green Rivers. The benefit of this duty greatly enhanced the ability of Forrest and his soldiers to conduct raids in the area in the following years.[14]

Throughout the winter and spring of 1862, Morgan's and Forrest's growing commands continued to perform conventional cavalry missions in support of General Albert S. Johnston's Army of Tennessee.[15] Following the fall of Forts Henry and Donelson in March, the raiders conducted rearguard actions on the approaches to Nashville. As Johnston's army fell back through the city, Morgan and Forrest continued to delay the Federal Army of the Ohio, under Major General Don Carlos Buell, burning the Confederate quartermaster stores in the city before rejoining Johnston's army.

After the Battle of Shiloh and the death of Johnston, Morgan began planning the first of his large-scale raids into north-central Tennessee and south-central Kentucky. Johnston's replacement, General P. G. T. Beauregard, supported Morgan's concept of the operation, which aimed at destroying railroads and supplies behind the advancing Federal armies, now unified under Major General Henry W. Halleck. Morgan's raiding plans were nearly derailed when General Braxton Bragg, previously the commander of the II Corps, assumed leadership of the army from Beauregard in mid-April. However, Bragg's plans could not have pleased Morgan more. Instead of a raid by a single understrength cavalry brigade, the bulk of the army, nearly 27,000 men, would be shifted from Corinth to Chattanooga, and launch an invasion of eastern Tennessee and Kentucky by the end of August 1862.[16]

Morgan was dispatched with his Second Kentucky Cavalry, a regiment of Georgia partisan rangers, plus Colonel A. A. Hunt and a squadron of Texas rangers, to attack isolated Federal outposts, destroy bridges over the Cumberland River, and, in general, to create chaos behind the Union lines.[17] Forrest was assigned to a similar expedition to the west, focusing on harassing the Federals around Nashville. In effect, Bragg launched a two-pronged raiding campaign ahead of the main body of his army to disrupt the flow of reinforcements and to act as a counter-reconnaissance element (both Morgan and Forrest considered the destruction of enemy cavalry as one of their main goals) to blind and confuse the forces commanded by Major General Buell. To further aid the success of the operation, Bragg ordered Generals Earl Van Dorn and Sterling C. Price, who had moved their trans-Mississippi troops to Corinth in late April, to begin an offensive toward western Tennessee (see map 5).[18]

In conventional terms, the campaign would begin with a stunning Confederate victory on August 30 at Richmond, Kentucky, which "practically caused the evacuation of all of Kentucky east of Louisville and south of Cincinnati."[19] Unhappily for the Rebels, the campaign would end with a decisive defeat at Perryville on October 8–9 that led to the retreat of the army back into eastern Tennessee. During the campaign, while Bragg attempted to reestablish a Confederate Kentucky by force of arms, the cavalry forces of Morgan and Forrest began their second raiding campaign against the Federals.[20]

That campaign was conducted from July 4 to July 28, 1862, beginning and ending at Sparta, Tennessee, and is often referred to as the "First Kentucky Raid." During this operation, Morgan developed tactics that became hallmarks for his brigade. His men abandoned the saber, "which they found as useless as a fence post," and trained dragoon style to fight dismounted with rifles, instead of fighting on horseback with carbines. Horses delivered Morgan's brigade to the battlefield, where it engaged the enemy on foot.[21] The raid itself had several objectives, including the primary mission of disrupting the flow of men and materials to Buell's pursuing army, to inspire pro-Confederate sentiment in central Kentucky, and to allow the troops to remount and resupply in the untouched Kentucky countryside. In the first case, the raid had some success. Buell had stripped central Kentucky of troops, and isolated detachments and Home Guards of questionable value were the only forces left behind to fight Morgan. Consequently, the raiders were able to defeat several bodies of Federal troops at Tompkinsville, Lebanon, and Cynthiana, Kentucky, driving within eighty miles of the Ohio-Kentucky border before turning back for Tennessee.

In his secondary mission of stirring up popular support for the Rebel cause, Morgan was less successful. Although he enjoyed the adulation of the crowds, happily drove off Federal provosts marshal from Kentucky towns, and won the accolades of his fellow Rebel soldiers, few of the expected recruits came forward, as few would come forward to join Bragg's army as it moved into Kentucky toward Perryville that fall.[22] As during every raid Morgan conducted in the Bluegrass State, "Kentucky was to [the Confederate raider] a land flowing with milk and honey, where he feasted royally." The raids became a perfect time for the troopers to replace worn-out mounts, contact friends and relatives behind the lines, and take new equipment from Federal depots.[23]

It was during this period that Morgan's men began to be called *guerrillas* by the Federal authorities. He vehemently denied that "foul aspersion," contending that his raiders "came not to molest peaceful individuals or to destroy private property, but guarantee absolute protection of all those not in arms against us." Most pro-Confederates believed Morgan's statements; those of an Unionist bent, and the Federal army, reacted differently as Morgan became more successful in his raiding career. In military terms, Morgan's first Kentucky raid managed to slow Buell's advance, capture over 1,000 Federals, and destroy nearly a million dollars in Federal property, but it had the unintended consequence of alerting Federal authorities to the weakness of Kentucky's defenses and to the danger of Morgan as a raiding chieftain. Responding to the 1862 raids, new cavalry regiments were raised in Indiana, Ohio, and Illinois and sent to Kentucky. These troopers would form the core of the pursuit forces that would annihilate Morgan's command in the summer of 1863. Unbeknownst to Morgan or the Confederate high command, the clock was ticking on the effectiveness of the mounted raid as a useful strategy.[24]

In Tennessee, Forrest's men were also wreaking havoc with the Union troops. On July 9, his column of nearly 1,400 men left Chattanooga, aiming to damage the 300-mile-long supply line of Buell's army. Buell had shifted his main supply base from Corinth, Mississippi, to Louisville and Nashville to support his upcoming campaign toward Chattanooga. When Forrest launched his raid, Buell's engineers had just finished repairing the Nashville and Chattanooga Railroad, and fresh supplies began flowing to the Union army. For the raider, the most logical place to strike the rail line was Murfreesboro, where the Federals had stockpiled railroad repair materials, food, and ammunition. Another factor made Murfreesboro appealing to Forrest: destruction of the flammable railroad bridges spanning Stones River would halt Federal supplies until repaired. The raid on Murfreesboro, because of its strategic importance and wildly successful outcome, became, in Forrest's own words, "the brightest feather in my cap."[25]

The newly promoted brigadier general, accompanied by his Tennessee cavalry regiment, the Eighth Texas Cavalry, the Second Georgia Cavalry, and two companies of Kentucky cavalry, arrived at Murfreesboro in the wee hours of July 11, 1862.[26] After capturing the outlying pickets, Forrest's troopers divided into three attack columns. Two columns would strike the Federal camps outside the town, while the third went for the town itself. The Eighth Texas, commanded by Colonel Wharton, hit first and charged through the camp of the Ninth Michigan Infantry and Seventh Pennsylvania Cavalry. The colonel of the Ninth Michigan was severely wounded, as was Colonel Wharton, and the fight bogged down into a sniping match between the now-fortified Federals and the Texans. The second attack, on the camp of the Third Minnesota Infantry, was turning out much the same, with the Northerners having an advantage due to the presence of a supporting artillery battery. Forrest personally led the assault on Murfreesboro itself, and "after two or three hours' hard struggle the court-house was fired and surrendered to Colonel Morrison." With the courthouse came the added benefit of capturing Brigadier General Thomas L. Crittenden and his staff. Forrest then turned his men against the Minnesotans, forcing their surrender. Having recombined two-thirds of his brigade, Forrest moved to support the Texans' assault. After surrounding the Federals, the Rebel commander sent a message under a flag of truce; the message later became evidence of Forrest's irregular style of war. The raider simply wrote: "I must demand an unconditional surrender of your force as prisoners of war or I will have every man put to the sword. You are aware of the overpowering force I have at my command, and this demand is made to prevent the effusion of blood." The Yankees surrendered and Forrest moved his command back to its base of operations at McMinnville. During the July 9–14 raid, Forrest had managed to destroy nearly a half-million dollars in property, including railcars and stockpiled supplies, and captured a badly needed four-gun battery of new ten-pound rifled Parrot guns and nearly 1,200 officers and men. Oddly, the orders to burn the railroad bridge were not carried out because of a miscommunication, and one of the main objectives of the raid was not accomplished. Forrest had become, in the words of a Federal officer, "the counterpart to [Stonewall] Jackson . . . with this striking distinction between them, that, while the latter was always invoking the aid of the Lord, the former never ceased to be in close alliance with the Devil."[27]

The launching of Bragg's Kentucky campaign, and the aftermath of the Battle of Perryville, presented a golden opportunity for cavalry raids. The poor condition of the transportation network in central and eastern Tennessee and Kentucky meant that an invader would have long, and vulnerable, supply lines. It was against the logistical tail of Buell's army that the raiders, operating in units ranging in size from 10-man squads to 600-man battalions, harassed, slowed, and ultimately halted the Army of the Ohio's campaign toward Chattanooga in the summer of 1862, and opened the way for Bragg's invasion of Kentucky. The impact of the raiders' actions, both militarily and for Confederate morale, should not be understated. Following Buell's relief, his detractors blamed his failure to advance faster in eastern Tennessee and destroy Bragg's army on the work of Morgan and Forrest. "If the army had supplies enough to justify the long delay for the purpose of reconstructing lines, which were cut almost as rapidly as they were connected," began one member of the "Buell Commission" investigating the campaign, "I hold that he had sufficient [force] to seize and hold East Tennessee, and the better way to get Morgan and Forrest from his rear was to keep them busy at his front." Buell defended himself from the accusations, stating that "not more than about 4,000 troops, mostly infantry, were left behind" to defend against raiders, while the rest moved south with the army. These regiments "were scattered over the principal part of the State, more as a police force and to guard railroads than to prevent invasion." Buell declared that he had asked for additional cavalry regiments to guard his rear, having seen the consequences of Confederate cavalry raids during the Corinth campaign. In early July, he received five newly raised regiments, none of them fully equipped or trained. Consequently, they "were in no condition to render much service at the time of Morgan's first raid" in July 1862.[28]

In response to the raiders, Federal authorities began several programs to reduce the effectiveness of Morgan and Forrest. First, following the pattern repeated throughout every occupied area harassed by irregulars during the Civil War, Federal authorities pushed for the recruitment of local troops. These forces gave two great advantages for countering irregular warfare—they freed up first-line troops for conventional combat missions, and they were familiar with the area in which they operated. The high command of the Federal army turned to men who had proven themselves adept at training and employing Unionist anti-irregular forces. One such officer was General George Crook, who had been successful in fighting bushwhackers in the mountains of western Virginia. Crook was sent to Tennessee to aid the Unionists in resisting both guerrillas and raiders. He found, to his chagrin, that the situation in Tennessee was somewhat different from in Virginia. The quality of the local troops was poor in the extreme; equipment, military training, and discipline were in short supply. Writing after the war, Crook recalled that when his command arrived in Carthage, Tennessee, the Unionists disembarked off the riverboat and immediately began looting the town. Later, he was given the First Tennessee Infantry (Union), which had "been sent away from the Army of the Cumberland to get rid of this element of discord." When Crook tried to discipline the miscreants, "they accused me of disloyalty." Luckily for Crook, Rosecrans supported his attempts to whip the unit into fighting shape. During his assignment in Tennessee, Crook complained that "I had my hands full, what with looking out for the enemy and restraining the lawlessness of our own people."[29] Unfortunately for the Federal cause, this behavior exemplified many of the Tennessee Unionist units, while those in Kentucky were often undermanned or underequipped. Against these pro-Union troops, the Confederates threw their elite cavalry and irregular forces.[30]

Buell also introduced a blockhouse system, duplicating the efforts taken to defend the Baltimore and Ohio Railroad in northern Virginia, concentrating on protecting railway bridges, tunnels, and other locations necessary for the operation of the Louisville and Nashville Railroad. In concept and construction, Buell's blockhouses copied those in Virginia—an earthen berm surrounding a wooden stockade or bunker, occupied by approximately fifty men. The difference between Buell's system and that discussed in chapter 4 was its intent. The Federals in Tennessee and Kentucky expected the blockhouses to not only limit guerrilla attacks, but to delay or halt major incursions by raiding cavalry. Against guerrillas, the blockhouses were remarkably successful. At no time during the war did unorganized irregulars overrun or destroy a single blockhouse. The blockhouses also worked well against Confederate raiders without artillery support. Private Adolphus Montague, a trooper in Company B, Seventh Tennessee Cavalry (Confederate), wrote that the blockhouses were "the most dangerous places as those within could turn their guns on us from all directions, while they were protected by huge timbers in the [block]house and the dirt thrown up against it." Unless the Rebels had overwhelming numbers, and prepared for heavy losses, the stockades were impervious to assault without artillery support.[31]

Lastly, the Federals reorganized and reinforced their mounted forces. Buell rightly believed his cavalry to be underequipped and ill trained, but failed to note that one of the reasons for the poor condition of his horse soldiers was tactical misuse. The Federals were deploying their troopers in a manner consistent with an antiguerrilla campaign; prior to Morgan's August raid, it was common for Tennesseans to see small antiguerrilla cavalry patrols and detachments throughout the state. During the August raid, Northern commanders found themselves unable to reform the scattered cavalry before Morgan had struck his objective and slipped back into friendly lines. One former Union officer later wrote that from April to October 1862, nearly 12,000 Federal horsemen were in the district commanded by Buell, but "they were widely scattered, broken up into small detachments, doing guard, picket, courier, and ornamental duties; just enough in one place to be easily driven or captured, and no force large enough anywhere to make successful resistance." Yet Buell still demanded additional cavalry from Washington after the July raids, and blamed the success of Forrest and Morgan on his lack of troopers.[32]

The July 1862 raids by Morgan and Forrest had consequences beyond the loss of property. For the Confederates, the raids represented an opportunity to slow down the enemy armies as they built up their strength for a decisive battle, and gave the Southern cause a new pantheon of heroes. For the Union, Morgan's and Forrest's successes forced them to recognize the importance of anti-raiding defenses throughout Tennessee and Kentucky. Added to Buell's problems, the staggering of the raids—Morgan's on July 4 and Forrest's on July 9—resulted in the Federal army rapidly shifting troops from one area to another, unable to coordinate a pursuit of either Rebel column. The officers of the Army of the Ohio learned many lessons from their humiliation by Morgan and Forrest in the summer of 1862, and the conduct of counterirregular warfare in the region shifted from an antiguerrilla strategy to an antipartisan/antiraider strategy. The raids of July 1862 also demonstrated the value of such operations to the Rebel leadership, as Buell's offensive toward Chattanooga ground to a halt and gave the Confederates an opportunity to launch an aggressive campaign into eastern Kentucky.[33]

For the Federals, August 1862 was no better than the previous month. Bragg launched his raiding team of Morgan and Forrest on another coordinated strike to cut Buell's logistical tether, again focusing on the vulnerable railroad bridges and tunnels. In what one historian considers "the most strategically significant action of [Morgan's] career," the raider struck the twin tunnels of the Louisville and Nashville Railroad seven miles north of Gallatin, Tennessee. The tunnels, one 600 feet long and the other 1,000 feet, were a perfect target. That rail line led directly to Buell's army and served as its main supply artery. Their destruction would prevent the use of the line for months, if not years, crippling the Federal advance on eastern Tennessee for the foreseeable future.[34]

Bragg's plan was for the two cavalry forces to work in conjunction with each other, as they had on the operational level in July. Morgan had the mission of destroying the tunnels, while Forrest would occupy the enemy forces around Nashville and central Tennessee, taking the city if the Federals weakened the garrison to chase Morgan. After sending out scouts in civilian clothes to make contact with Confederate loyalists in the area, Morgan's command set out on the raid. On August 10, Morgan struck Gallatin, capturing the town and many of the 375 Kentucky Unionist troops guarding the area. Taking a train, the raiders filled its flatcars with wood and set it ablaze, sending it into the thousand-foot "Big South Tunnel." The fiery train set the supports aflame, collapsing the tunnel and closing it to the Federals for over three months. One Federal officer concluded that this was the single most destructive act committed on a railroad during the war.[35]

While Morgan attacked Gallatin, Forrest kept the Federals busy. The successful raids by the Confederates in July had made their destruction a high priority for the Army of the Ohio. Consequently, Buell ordered the bulk of his cavalry, 1,200 troopers, to join a mixed infantry-cavalry force under Brigadier General William Nelson, and another 700 horse soldiers, commanded by Brigadier General R. W. Johnson, to eliminate the Confederate raiders. The result was utter disaster. Buell had hoped to "concentrate all the cavalry I can to operate in force," while he rushed the construction of small stockades, capable of holding up to 100 men, to defend the vulnerable bridges. He recognized the weakness to this plan: These small outposts were unable to defend themselves against large groups of raiding cavalry. In the vain hope of using his understrength and inexperienced cavalry as a counter-raiding force, he sent Nelson and Johnson to pursue Forrest and Morgan, respectively.[36]

Nelson's division of cavalry and infantry met Forrest for the first time in late July, as the Confederates struck targets around Nashville.[37] It was here that Nelson discovered the poor condition of the Federal cavalry. In his opinion, he could "settle this part of the country and stop Morgan and Forrest and be in position to receive any forces from Chattanooga, if I can get my orders obeyed." The troops assigned to him were either so poorly trained as to be useless as cavalry, or lacked sufficient mounts to pursue Forrest's troopers, or were so scattered on antiguerrilla duty that they could not be reconstituted into an organized command in time to be effective.[38] After a fruitless pursuit of the Confederates, Nelson admitted defeat. He wrote to Buell that "to chase Morgan and Forrest, they mounted on race horses, with infantry this hot weather is a hopeless task."[39] Forrest was able to raid the Federal lines at will, ranging throughout central Tennessee with little hindrance from the Union forces, all the while keeping the enemy from defending against Morgan's cavalry. The Federal army, although it outnumbered its opponent, found itself stymied by two cavalry commanders leading small brigades on their flanks and rear; ultimately, the Army of the Ohio would grind to a halt because of their aggressive raiding.[40]

The pursuit force under Johnson finally caught up with Morgan near Gallatin. Having destroyed the tunnel and severely damaged the Federal facilities in the town, Morgan ordered his raiders back to Confederate lines. On August 19, a force of 300 Federal troops reoccupied Gallatin and began conducting house-to-house searches, arresting every able-bodied male over twelve years old, informing them that they would be taken to Nashville and "hanged as spies for aiding Morgan." Morgan turned his brigade around and halfway between Nashville and Gallatin attacked the Federal column. He dispersed the Union troops, chasing the bulk of the force to Edgefield Junction. There the Federals took refuge in one of the newly built blockhouses. Despite his lack of artillery, Morgan assaulted the position. After taking heavy casualties, the raiders left the remains of the Federal force in the stockade, returning to Gallatin with the prisoners. Morgan would remember the cost of attacking these seemingly impregnable blockhouses without artillery support, and later ensured that artillery accompanied his raiders for such a contingency.[41]

The return to free the Gallatin prisoners cost Morgan time, allowing Johnson's cavalry to catch up to the raiders. On August 21, as Morgan's command encamped in Gallatin, word came that Johnson's cavalry was closing in. Morgan alerted his brigade, and the raiders moved north out of the town. Realizing that he could not outrun the Federal cavalry, the raiding chieftain decided to stand and fight. It was here that Morgan's raiders turned to their other role of mounted infantry. Had his men been armed with pistols and carbines, it is likely that his command would have been mauled, if not destroyed, by Johnson's horsemen. That was not the case. Morgan dismounted his men and had them take up fighting positions along a split-rail fence paralleling the Gallatin-Hartsville turnpike. The Federal cavalry, finally seeing their prey, broke into a charge, sabers drawn. The Rebels, armed with rifled muskets, shattered the Union assaults. Johnson's men rallied and attacked again, and were again repulsed. Realizing that he was not facing an overpowering force, Morgan ordered a general advance, sweeping the field of Federals. Johnson himself was captured, and more than half his force killed, wounded, or taken prisoner.[42]

The destruction of Johnson's cavalry, and the exhaustion of Nelson's entire division in the pursuit of the Confederate raiders in July and August 1862, had consequences far greater than the Federal tactical defeats. Buell realized that he required even more cavalry regiments to prevent his entire rear area from going up in flames, while Bragg found that raiding cavalry could buy him the time he needed to prepare for the inevitable Federal onslaught. As part of his overall plan, Bragg decided to launch his invasion of Kentucky. Although it ended in failure, it did lead to the relief of Buell and the dislocation of Federal offensive plans in the fall of 1862. Much of the credit for these results lies with Morgan and Forrest, who had established themselves in the first rank of Confederate cavalrymen. Their stellar successes created a serious misunderstanding by the Confederate high command. Looking only at the outcome of the Gallatin and Murfreesboro raids, it is easy to extrapolate that the weak link had been found in the Federal armor, yet this concept is true only if the Union army failed to adapt to the raiding strategy. To the Confederates' future dismay, the Yankees already had begun to adapt their forces from an antiguerrilla to an antiraiding role. Blockhouses were constructed in large numbers, guarding vulnerable tunnels, bridges, and crossroads, duplicating the system in northern Virginia (see chap. 5). Buell, and his replacement,

Major General William S. Rosecrans, pushed for new cavalry regiments with the express mission of countering raids. While these units lacked seasoning, much like Federal cavalry everywhere during the first two years of the war, they would provide the mobility and reconnaissance desperately needed to stop the raiders. A final outcome of the raids for Federal plans was the development of militia units for local defense throughout the region. In the Unionist counties of Kentucky, and in the states north of the Ohio River, the Home Guards, as the militia was generally referred to, were of questionable military effectiveness, but they were of sufficient numbers to hinder any raid in their area.[43]

In the postmortem of Buell's career, a special commission was convened in Nashville to evaluate the Federal commander's failures. In one discussion, the subject of Morgan's raid on the Gallatin tunnels came up. In the many biographies and studies of Morgan and his command, few scholars have noted this debate, since it dealt less with the actions of the raiding chieftain than with how his opponent tried to deal with him. During the hearings, Buell mentioned the impact of Morgan's raid on his logistics in August 1862, referring to the Gallatin raid as the single most damaging Confederate operation conducted against him. In response, a member of the committee, agreeing with newspaper accounts labeling Morgan and Forrest as guerrillas, asked why Buell had not conducted a retaliatory raid on the civilians in the area, whom the commission considered as directly supporting "these parties of guerrillas." Buell, to the surprise of the commission, responded: "I object to this term 'guerrillas' as applied to these troops. They are as much troops as any in the rebel service. I think there is a difference between the cavalry of Morgan, Forrest, and Starnes and what we understand by 'guerrillas.' I know of no reason for giving them a character which does not belong to them, for they are not 'guerrillas' in the proper sense of that term."[44]

Buell understood that in the summer of 1862 he was not opposed by guerrillas, meaning small bands of unorganized bushwhackers, which he considered little more than a nuisance, but by conventional cavalry with the specialized mission of raiding. The Federal general added that neither were Morgan or Forrest to be considered partisan rangers, stating that "these troops are not of that character." Despite Buell's adroit observations, and the presence of such in the *Official Records*, contemporaries and later scholars categorized both Forrest and Morgan as guerrillas or partisan rangers.[45]

Responding to the success of the raiders in slowing down Buell's army, Bragg decided to launch his own counteroffensive in hopes of raising the flag of rebellion in slave-holding Kentucky, and driving the enemy out of war-torn eastern Tennessee. A two-pronged invasion of the Bluegrass State was launched on August 28, one column spearheaded by Bragg's 27,000-man Army of Tennessee moving toward Bowling Green, while a 6,000-man division, led by Major General E. Kirby Smith and styled the "Army of Kentucky," moved from Knoxville, Tennessee, toward Lexington, Kentucky.[46] From the start, the campaign experienced difficulties. Bragg and Kirby Smith cared little for one another and consequently failed to coordinate their offensives.[47] Kirby Smith focused on clearing out eastern Tennessee and pursuing the forces of Federal Major General William Nelson after the latter's defeat at Richmond, Kentucky, on August 30.[48] Bragg had hoped that Kirby Smith's penetration of Federal-held Kentucky would draw Buell's army out from central Tennessee and create an opportunity to retake Nashville. Despite his drubbing at the hands of Forrest and Morgan, Buell was no fool, and he shadowed Bragg's army as it advanced into central Kentucky, preventing the Confederates from attacking westward. Delayed by the resistance of the Union garrison at Munfordville, Kentucky, Bragg's scouts finally reached their objective, Louisville, in the last days of September, only to find that the Army of the Ohio had gotten there first. Bragg pulled back his outnumbered army near Perryville and regrouped. The October 8 battle at Perryville, while a tactical draw, was a strategic defeat for the Confederacy. Bragg realized that he could not defeat Buell's armies, which totaled nearly 80,000 around Louisville and another 45,000 in Cincinnati. On October 13, Bragg joined forces with Kirby Smith and retreated into eastern Tennessee. The Federals followed.[49]

The retreat left Bragg's army in shambles. Nearly 15,000 men were in hospitals by late November, suffering from exhaustion and malnutrition. Additionally, Bragg himself was under pressure from all quarters to go on the offensive again and regain what was lost by the Kentucky invasion. Governor Isham Harris convinced Jefferson Davis, who in turned convinced Bragg, to attempt to draw the Federal army out of Nashville and defeat it in an offensive-defensive campaign. The Confederates hoped to regain the Tennessee capital and divert U. S. Grant's army, then advancing on Vicksburg, to meet the new threat. Preparing for the new offensive, Bragg began to reorganize his army, including his cavalry. Prior to November 1862, Confederate cavalry in the Army of Tennessee was dispersed, with one battalion or regiment assigned to each infantry brigade or division, depending on availability. As a result, few effective cavalry forces existed, with the exception of Morgan's and Forrest's regiments. Bragg rebuilt the cavalry, taking the scattered regiments and forming them into three brigades, commanded by Morgan, Forrest, and Brigadier General Joseph Wheeler. Although Wheeler was the lowest ranking and least successful of the three, he was promoted to "chief of cavalry" for the army and placed in overall leadership of the mounted forces.[50]

Wheeler, with Bragg's approval, further changed how the cavalry was organized. Instead of three cavalry brigades, in direct support of each of Bragg's three corps, he created five brigades. Three of them, totaling 5,000 men, were designated as "regular" cavalry and were attached to the infantry corps. Forrest's and Morgan's brigades were designated "partisan," with the specific mission of raiding.[51] Unlike Confederate armies on other fronts, the Army of Tennessee had half of its cavalry, nearly 5,000 troopers, specifically organized and designated for conducting raids on a permanent basis. These men were not partisan ranger companies or semiorganized guerrilla commands, but conventionally organized and disciplined cavalry given the distinct and, at this point, critical mission of harassing the enemy's supply lines—raiding warfare of the kind imagined and described by both Clausewitz and Jomini. The first test of Wheeler's new regular/partisan organization came in December 1862, as Bragg faced a new opponent in Major General Rosecrans, who now had the task of capturing Chattanooga.[52]

Bragg built up an army of approximately 40,000 effectives by early December in the area around Murfreesboro, hoping that the Federals would pour out of Nashville and attack him. Although weakened by transfers to Mississippi, and frustrated by a shuffling of units in the region, Bragg prepared his plan.[53] He decided to use Morgan's and Forrest's partisan brigades to first prod the Federals into action, and then send the troopers to destroy the enemy's supplies while he engaged the Federals with the bulk of the army. Having seen the successes of raiders the previous summer, Bragg believed such actions made perfect sense. His intent was not to fight a strong and well-informed enemy, but a weakened, blinded foe whose strength could not be brought to bear. To do this, he had to have the utmost performance of his raiding chieftains. In the "Christmas Raids" of 1862, both Morgan and Forrest proved to Bragg that his confidence in their abilities was well placed.[54]

The campaign to defeat Rosecrans's Federals was as much an irregular as conventional campaign. If the irregulars failed to cut Rosecrans's supply lines and deny the enemy accurate and timely information, Bragg's smaller army could not hold back the Federal juggernaut. His plan for the raiders closely resembled that of the summer before. He would stagger the raids, Forrest leaving on December 11 and Morgan moving out eleven days later. Forrest would strike the Mobile and Ohio Railroad in western Tennessee, with the twofold mission of cutting Grant's supply lines in northern Mississippi and forcing Rosecrans to send troops to pursue the raiders. Morgan would move northeast of Nashville into central Kentucky, with the objective of burning two 500-foot-long railroad trestles at Muldraugh's Hill, five miles north of Elizabethtown, Kentucky. Actually, the deployment of Forrest to western Tennessee and Morgan to Kentucky had certain disadvantages. Since the summer raids, Union commanders had focused on building blockhouses to defend vulnerable locations, raising troops and Home Guards for local defense, establishing a formal railroad defense system, and deploying new cavalry forces. Additionally, the absence of half his cavalry on raids reduced Bragg's ability to gather information or to screen the army. As a result, when Nashville newspapers began publishing accounts of Forrest's and Morgan's exploits, Rosecrans began moving his army south, believing the shortage of cavalry would prevent proper screening by the Confederates. This unexpected consequence of the raiding campaign was one of the main reasons that Bragg was caught by surprise by Rosecrans's advance toward Stones River on December 26.[55]

The Federal army was greatly concerned with Confederate irregulars, especially Morgan and Forrest in the early winter of 1862.[56] Continual improvements to General Buell's blockhouse system were made and additional troops detailed to guard vulnerable spots along the Louisville and Nashville Railroad. In mid-November, for example, Major General Horatio G. Wright, the commanding officer of the Department of the Ohio, informed a concerned Rosecrans that a full infantry brigade at Munfordville, along with three regiments assigned to patrol the roads and man blockhouses, were protecting the railroad. By the time that Morgan began his raid, nearly 7,000 Federals were guarding the Tennessee section of the Louisville and Nashville, while 3,500 were performing the same duty on the Kentucky sections of the line.[57]

Despite the apparent strength of the Union forces, there was still one glaring weakness. Yankee cavalry was still undermanned and underequipped in contrast to approximately 10,000 Confederate horsemen. Added to the equation was the presence of unorganized bushwhackers operating throughout the region, further depleting the available cavalry strength. Rosecrans and Wright faced continual demands from Unionist civic and military leaders to provide mounted troops to eliminate these irregulars. As a result, the sparse Federal cavalry was further spread out in futile antiguerrilla operations, preventing the organization of a pursuit force envisioned by Buell the summer before. The shortage of cavalry became so acute that Rosecrans was forced to plan his offensive toward Chattanooga with that fact clearly in mind. Rosecrans later wrote that "the enormous superiority in numbers of the rebel cavalry kept our little cavalry force almost within the infantry lines, and gave the enemy control of the entire country around us," and he blamed "clans of mounted men, formed into a guerrilla-like cavalry" for his inability to discern Bragg's movements or intentions prior to Stones River. The situation reached the point where Rosecrans wrote directly to Secretary of War Edwin Stanton, pleading for "revolving arms or breech loading carbines" to save his "half armed and two-thirds demoralized" cavalry. It would be mid-1863 when the Federals completed their cavalry reorganization and redeployment, just in time to surprise Morgan during his "Great Raid" north of the Ohio River (see chap. 6).[58]

Morgan departed Alexandria, Tennessee, with his command on December 22, heading north toward his key objectives, the railroad trestles at Muldraugh's Hill, Kentucky. His division numbered only 3,100 men, all mounted, and seven field guns. Morgan divided the division into two brigades, one commanded by his brother-in-law, Colonel Basil H. Duke, and the other by Colonel W. C. P. Breckinridge. He split the artillery between the two brigades, having learned in the summer raids that the Federal blockhouses were all but impervious to small-arms fire.[59] By this point in Morgan's career as a raider, he had developed his own concept of how such operations would be conducted. According to Colonel Duke, Morgan would depend on speed to gain the enemy's rear area, since it was assumed that any delay at the front lines would bring the response of large, combat-ready forces. Once past the forward troops, Morgan would send raiding detachments out on his flanks as he advanced toward his objective, burning bridges and destroying rail lines. Their goal was to hinder pursuit; if small detachments of Federals could be surrounded and forced to surrender, all the better, but large forces would be avoided at all costs. Artillery dealt with blockhouses; if the stockade resisted bombardment, it would be bypassed without risking the cavalry in an assault. Once the objective of the raid had been destroyed, a successful withdrawal to friendly lines depended on the ability of the raiders to avoid fighting enemy units of any size, since a delay of only a few hours would give time for pursuers to catch up. These concepts guided the conduct of the Christmas Raid.[60]

For the first four days of the raid, the Confederates fought a series of skirmishes against Union outposts, never becoming decisively engaged, and crossed the Cumberland and Green Rivers with a minimum of combat. On the 26th, Morgan reached Nolin, Kentucky, where his men forced the surrender of a seventy-six-man detachment of the Ninety-first Illinois Volunteer Infantry, burning the bridge and blockhouse, and paroling the prisoners. The next day, the Confederates encountered the remaining 700 men of the Ninety-first Illinois and forced their surrender after a half-hour fight.[61]

The Confederates, barely affected by these skirmishes, reached their objective on December 28. The twin trestles at Muldraugh's Hill were protected by the 700 men of the Seventy-first Indiana Volunteer Infantry, but they had no artillery. Morgan quickly developed a plan to hit both trestles at the same time, sending Breckinridge's brigade against the 200 Federals guarding the southern trestle and Duke's larger brigade against the remaining 500 Union troops protecting the northern trestle. Adequate Federal troop strength did not compensate for the disadvantages: The blockhouses and earthworks had not been completed, and not one field gun was allocated to the defense of this strategic site. After a three-hour bombardment, Morgan demanded the surrender of the garrison. The entire regiment, including twenty-seven officers, capitulated, and the two bridges were burned to the waterline. Additionally, large stores of medical, commissary, and quartermaster supplies that were stored in warehouses near the bridges were burned (see map 6).[62]

The Federals were not without hope at this point. Unbeknownst to Morgan, a large force, 2,300 infantry and a battery of artillery commanded

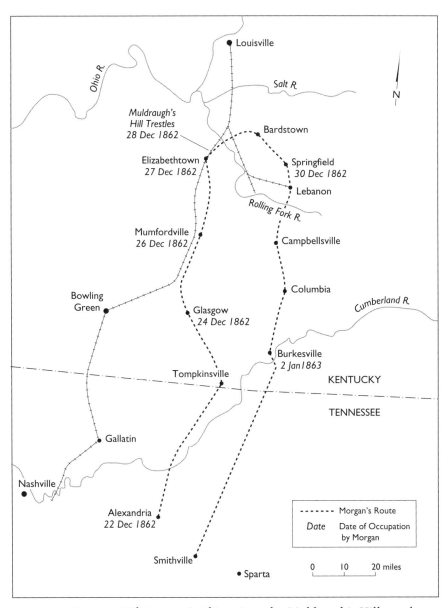

Map 6. Morgan's "Christmas Raid" against the Muldraugh's Hill trestles, December 1862.

by Colonel John M. Harlan, was pursuing the Confederates from the south, following the Louisville and Nashville rail lines. Simultaneously, the Twelfth Division of Major General George H. Thomas's corps, commanded by Brigadier General Joseph J. Reynolds, was dispatched from Rosecrans's army outside of Nashville and sent knifing across north-central Tennessee and central Kentucky in an attempt to get in front of the raiders and prevent their return to Southern lines.[63] A third force of 3,300 men under Colonel William A. Hoskins closed in from eastern Tennessee. Rosecrans's plan was to box Morgan in by having Harlan's pursuit force drive the Rebels into Reynolds's 5,000-man division and using Hoskins's men to stop any escape to the east. On December 29, Colonel Harlan finally caught the raiders, blocking a ford at Rolling Fork, Kentucky, and the ability of the Federal army to destroy Morgan's raiders was brought to a test.[64]

The fight at Rolling Fork was, if anything, anticlimactic. Harlan's artillery pounded Confederates attempting to cross the ford. Colonel Duke, commanding the rear guard, was severely injured by shell fragments, and for a time it seemed that the raiders had been caught, but the exhausted Twelfth Division infantry could not continue the pursuit and the raiders slipped farther south. The weather hindered the Yankees, as a slushy snow began to fall on December 29, slowing both the fleeing raiders and their pursers. The limited Union cavalry, which had been used extensively on the back roads and byways of rural Kentucky to search for Morgan, was already spent. The Confederates, in contrast, had captured an unguarded supply depot at Campbellsville and had eaten their fill before burning it. General Reynolds's column reached the town twelve hours after the raiders had departed. Morgan and his men returned to Confederate lines on January 2, too late to take part in the New Year's fight at Stones River.[65]

The second half of Bragg's raiding offensive was that under Forrest. General Forrest's command, unlike Morgan's, did not have a specific objective but was instead meant to get behind Grant's lines and destroy bridges, rails, and supply depots wherever they could be found. To conduct such an operation successfully took a combination of planning, audacity, and leadership, all traits associated with Nathan Bedford Forrest. On December 11, Forrest and 2,100 cavalrymen, along with a battery of four field pieces, rode toward Clifton, Tennessee, from their camps at Columbia.[66] On December 15, the cavalry brigade forded the Tennessee River. The river crossing is an interesting example of Forrest's careful planning of a raid. He sent scouts to the area prior to beginning the campaign, and they had procured enough flatboats to move the brigade. Forrest ordered them to sink the boats until the troopers arrived, when they would raise the boats, move across the river, and then sink them again in order to recover them on the return trip. Luckily for Forrest, the boats were not found by Federal patrols during the period and were available in January when the raid concluded (see map 7).[67]

On December 18, Forrest's column ran into the first major Federal forces on the raid at Lexington, 800 horse soldiers and two cannon of the Eleventh Illinois Cavalry, led by Colonel R. G. Ingersoll. Forrest ordered his men to attack, shattering the Federal troopers, who withdrew to the well-fortified town of Jackson, leaving Colonel Ingersoll, 147 of his men, and the artillery in Forrest's hands. The additional guns were a boon to the raider, who was now able to provide artillery support for each of his three columns. Survivors of the skirmish at Lexington fled into the works at Jackson, spreading rumors that Forrest was reported to "be from 10,000 to 20,000 [in strength] and still crossing the river." Consequently, the Federal commander at Jackson, Brigadier General Jeremiah Sullivan, ordered his 10,000-man garrison to prepare for attack, pulling in his outlying pickets and patrols. In effect, Sullivan surrendered all of western Tennessee to Forrest, based on the inaccurate reports of Ingersoll's broken regiment.[68]

By now, Forrest, who had a fairly good idea of Sullivan's strength, decided to isolate the garrison at Jackson, thus giving his columns a few more days to finish their incendiary work. On the 18th and 19th, Forrest sent two forces, one, led by Colonel George Dibrell, and another, under Colonel A. A. Russell, to strike north and south of Jackson, respectively, while he feinted at the city itself. The Federals reacted just as Forrest hoped, abandoning the isolated garrisons struck by the two colonels while digging in against what was perceived to be a huge attacking army. At Carroll Station, Dibrell's men burned the depot, captured over 100 Federals, and replaced all their old flintlocks with captured percussion cap rifles. South of Jackson, Russell burned the trestle leading toward Bolivar, preventing the rail movement of reinforcements to Sullivan. Successful in his December 18th attacks, Forrest decided the jig was up and began withdrawing from the area before his true strength was realized. Later that day Forrest repulsed a weak Federal counterattack; he took it as a sign that General Sullivan was beginning to move out of the earthworks. On December 20, Forrest

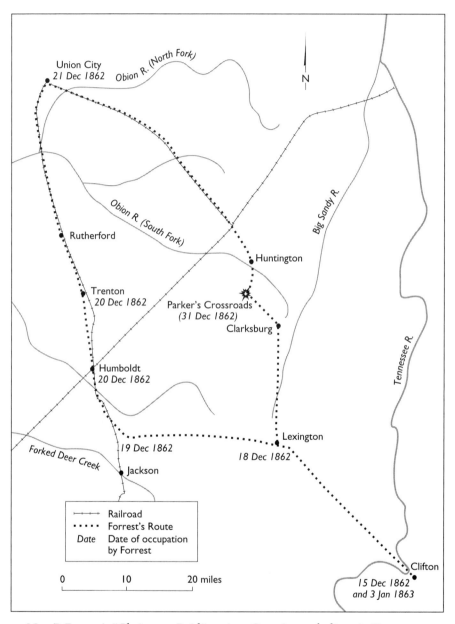

Map 7. Forrest's "Christmas Raid" against Grant's supply lines in Tennessee, December 1862.

left a screen of troopers to cover the movement of his brigade and turned toward the railroad bridge over Forked Deer Creek, and the towns of Humboldt and Trenton.[69]

Colonel Dibrell's column suffered the first failure of the raid as it attempted to seize the Forked Deer Creek bridge, guarded by a strong force of Federal infantry. At Humboldt, Colonel J. W. Starnes and his Tennesseans easily overpowered the weak garrison, burning everything they could not carry off. Forrest ran into some trouble at Trenton, where Colonel Jacob Fry's Sixty-first Illinois Infantry had taken hogsheads of tobacco and cotton bales and assembled a hasty fort. Creating a second strongpoint, Fry ordered his men to cut loopholes in the walls of the stone-masonry rail depot. Forrest's initial attack was repulsed by the heavy Federal rifle fire. In response, the raider ordered his artillery forward. After taking a few cannon shots, the 700 began to surrender. The Confederates immediately paroled the prisoners so they would not have to be guarded or taken with the column. The experience at Trenton presented a good lesson to both the Rebel raiders and Federal defenders; an attacker with artillery could always beat a defender without it, even if defenders were in a blockhouse or earthworks.[70]

The action on December 20 spread panic throughout the Union lines, doing much to build up Forrest's later reputation as a fearsome opponent. Garrisons pulled in their pickets lest the raiders capture them, and hurried to dig earthworks at every small crossroads, town, or hamlet. Some Federal officers went even further. On the Mississippi River, Brigadier General Thomas A. Davies, commanding the fortifications at New Madrid, Missouri, and Island No. 10, ordered the huge shore batteries spiked and the powder thrown into the Mississippi to prevent its capture by the raiders. Davies also called for gunboats from Cairo, Illinois, to prevent Forrest from crossing the Mississippi with his "force of more than 7,000 [cavalry] and ten pieces of artillery . . . backed by a heavy infantry force." Davies even imagined Forrest attacking his defenses in conjunction with Confederate troopers in the trans-Mississippi, or assaulting Columbus, Kentucky, to close the Ohio River. Such panic pervaded the region, as Forrest's columns seemed to expand and contract in size with every report. In this respect, Forrest's raid demonstrates the power of raiding cavalry behind the enemy's lines, especially when the combination of green defenders and poor communications tended to exacerbate the threat. By his audacity, Forrest managed to prevent nearly 20,000 Federal troops from taking immediate action against him and gave himself additional time to damage the rail network of western Tennessee.[71]

For the next ten days, Forrest continued to gobble up small Federal detachments and burned the rails. As the raiders moved north, they discovered two disturbing facts—that General Sullivan was pursuing them out of Jackson, and that the bridges across the Obion River had been burned. Luckily for the Confederates, Sullivan's force was moving slowly because of the destroyed bridges left behind by the raiders, and one intact but dilapidated bridge was discovered over the Obion. After rebuilding the bridge, Forrest's men crossed the river and rode hard for two days, finally resting near Parker's Crossroads. There, the 1,500-man Fiftieth Indiana Brigade, commanded by Colonel C. L. Dunham, caught the raiders and brought them to battle. Forrest dispatched four companies to cover his avenue of escape, the road to Clarksburg, Tennessee, and prepared the rest of his 2,500 men to meet the oncoming Union troops. Placing the bulk of his artillery in the center of his line, Forrest allowed the Yankees to launch a series of poorly coordinated and unsupported attacks on the artillery, while he ordered two strong cavalry forces to envelop the enemy from both flanks. The plan worked exceedingly well, with Rebel cavalry capturing the Federal supply train and equipage and scattering the Union troops. It seemed that Forrest had chalked up one more victory, but suddenly another Federal regiment attacked the Confederate rear. The Rebel cavalry dispatched to protect the escape route had taken the wrong road, allowing the Federals to slip in behind Forrest. Instead of gathering up prisoners, Forrest ordered them released while he withdrew the remainder of the brigade. For five hours both sides had fought one another, finally forcing Forrest's retreat. The raiders recrossed the Tennessee River on January 3, 1863, returning to the safety of friendly lines.[72]

The bloody battlefield of Stones River, with its seemingly meaningless outcome, was a dark spot for both the Northern and Southern home fronts on New Year's Day, 1863. The news of Morgan's and Forrest's successes, and their limited casualties, became headline news across the Confederacy.[73] Morgan had done it again—he had ridden behind the enemy's lines and burned and destroyed at will, capturing isolated outposts and detachments with apparent ease. Forrest had humiliated Union officers from Cairo to Memphis and panicked every Yankee outpost in the region. The Rebel high command grew even fonder of raiding as a strategy to wear down the Federals, and with officers like Morgan and Forrest leading the charge, it was expected that future raids would be even more successful.

The Confederates, however, had made several miscalculations and errors in judging the outcome of Morgan's Christmas Raid, as have several historians and biographers of the raider. The first negative result for the Confederates was the virtual blinding of Bragg's army on the eve of Stones River, akin to the separation of Stuart's cavalry from Lee's army prior to the Battle of Gettysburg. Bragg sent half of his cavalry to raid the enemy's supply lines, with the intent of slowing or stopping their forward momentum. What Bragg did not know was that Rosecrans was a leader of the McClellan ilk—careful planning and preparation were his strong points. Hence, when Rosecrans took charge of the Army of the Ohio, he immediately began to build up supplies in huge depots. Unlike many generals in the Civil War, Rosecrans did not stockpile ammunition, food, and other necessities out of antebellum concepts of warfare—he was hoarding stores in expectation that Morgan or Forrest, or both, would raid and try to destroy the vulnerable Louisville and Nashville Railroad. When Morgan destroyed the Muldraugh's Hill trestles, closing the railroad for five weeks, he gained Southern acclaim and boosted Confederate morale but accomplished very little. Rosecrans had ample stockpiles to supply his army for several months, and the Cumberland River had risen, allowing resupply by river. In effect, other than the movement of Reynolds's 5,000-man division in a futile pursuit of the riders, Morgan's 3,100 cavalrymen did not have a major impact on the strategic level.[74]

Forrest succeeded for many of the same reasons as Morgan. The Federals in western Tennessee, much as in central Kentucky, were still dispersed in small detachments guarding blockhouses, depots, and villages. The Union troops there were almost totally without artillery, vulnerable to any Rebel force having even a single field gun. Also, the sheer destructive power of a raiding column hampered pursuit. General Sullivan's mostly infantry force, upward of 3,000 men and eight guns, had difficulty catching Forrest's mounted troops. In the inexorable logic of irregular warfare, the larger the force, the more difficult it is to move the force quickly. By depending so much on infantry to pursue Forrest, Sullivan reduced his chances of catching the raider, provided the Confederates did not halt or become delayed. The fight at Parker's Crossroads occurred only because Forrest decided to rest his weary men and horses for two days prior to the last sprint for home. The influence of

Forrest's personality and leadership cannot be understated. He was often in the front lines, personally leading attacks and counterattacks, and was the first over the rickety bridge across the Obion River. Forrest's innate military skills, which became more pronounced throughout the war, intuitively led him to order double-envelopments of enemy forces, to continually raid and harass detachments lying along his line of movement, and to plant rumors and other false information with Union parolees, who consistently exaggerated the size of the Confederate force.[75]

As important as the military influence of the raiders on the survival of Confederate Tennessee in 1862 was their effect on the Rebel home front. The Confederacy had, at times, barely survived the year. Federal troops had threatened Richmond, repulsed Lee's September invasion of Maryland, and, in the West, had driven Rebel forces out of Kentucky, Missouri, northern Arkansas, and most of Tennessee. Every battle seemed to be a mass bloodletting with little to show for it—Shiloh, Stones River, and Antietam being significant examples. Into this sequence of disappointments Confederate raiders injected success, the equivalent of chivalric knights, riding rings around the powerful Federal armies. Mrs. Irby Morgan, writing thirty years after the war, still recalled the powerful feelings generated by the raiders. On meeting General Forrest, she remembered that "the ladies came in troops to hear what their brave chieftain had to say. You can't imagine in this day [1892] how excited and enthusiastic the women became. The news of victory [at Murfreesboro and Morgan's first Kentucky raid] was like an electric spark that set us all on fire." For the Confederate soldiers in the Army of Tennessee, the raids "infused a new life and energy at once in their movements, inspired a self-confidence which had been materially shattered by previous miscarriages and disaster, and gave an assurance of the judgment and capacity" of Forrest and Morgan. When Forrest abandoned raiding as a tactic, and Morgan was captured at the end of his disastrous July 1863 raid, the concordant negative impact on morale was just as great. Presenting the raiders as national heroes by placing them alongside conventional generals such as Lee, Jackson, and Stuart as unbeatable commanders was a two-edged sword. Victories built up Confederate hopes, while defeats contributed to national demoralization.[76]

The issue of the public perception of the raiders leads to a second consideration, assessing the raids themselves. Artillery, specifically the lack of guns to support the Federal blockhouses, and the untrained condition of many Union regiments, were major factors in the successful Confederate raids in 1862. Both Morgan and Forrest acknowledged the critical importance of artillery on these expeditions. The Federal blockhouse system enabled small detachments of Union troops to hold off irregulars or raiders, provided the Rebels did not have cannon; any field gun doomed the detachment defending a blockhouse. In the December raids, the Confederates easily forced the surrender of hundreds of Federal troops by simply opening fire with their horse artillery, the best example being that of Colonel Fry's capitulation at Trenton on December 20. Before Forrest's battery had gotten into position, Fry's makeshift fort had easily held off direct assaults. When the Rebel guns arrived, the Federals surrendered after the third shot.[77] In addition to their shortage of artillery, the Federal troops on outpost duty tended to be second-line troops, either newly raised regiments or those who had proven themselves poorly in battle. In both Grant's and Rosecrans's armies, the better units were kept in the front lines, while less competent commanders and units were placed in forts and depots in the rear area. It was these second-rate Federal units who fought some of the most aggressive and experienced Confederate cavalry regiments of the Civil War.[78]

Another outcome of the 1862 raiding campaigns was the illusion that the summer and December raids had crippled the Federal advance toward both Vicksburg and Chattanooga, buying time for the beleaguered Confederacy. In 1863, the Rebels, faced with a series of Union campaigns, attempted the same strategy again, but with a much different outcome. The Confederate belief that the raids stopped the Federals is partially true. Buell's campaign was severely hindered by Forrest's capture of Murfreesboro, and by Morgan's destruction of the Louisville and Nashville Railroad tunnel at Gallatin. In both cases, the raiders hit a specific target for a specific goal—closing choke points for the Federal supply system. In neither one of the August raids were there any attempts to burn every railroad bridge in sight, nor did the raiders attempt to push too far from the safety of Confederate lines. The raids followed a sharply focused plan aiming at a single objective, and were conducted with speed and stealth. The December raids had less well defined goals, producing general harassment of the enemy rear areas, but were successful nonetheless, for a variety of reasons already discussed. However, none of the successful raids truly crippled the Federal army. Rosecrans, having seen the perceived impact of raiders on Buell's campaign, stockpiled huge amounts of supplies. He decided that the army should be able to survive without resupply for several weeks. When the December raids hit the railroads supporting his advance, Rosecrans was not overly concerned, since he had spent from November 26 to December 26 building up enough materials "to insure us [the Army of the Ohio] against want from the largest possible detention likely to occur by the breaking of the Louisville and Nashville Railroad."[79]

The Federals learned several lessons from the 1862 raiding. First, the blockhouse system was only as effective as the men placed in the fortifications. The use of green troops in the defense of strategically important locations was a disaster; the men in the blockhouses began drilling, and inspections were conducted by high-ranking staff officers on a regular basis. Buell had called for more cavalry, and though he was replaced by Rosecrans, the governors of the midwestern states responded. New regiments were raised in the winter and spring of 1862–63, and were reasonably well equipped and ready for action by early summer. Additionally, both Grant and Rosecrans authorized ending the practice of assigning cavalry regiments as support to infantry brigades; instead, the troopers would belong to cavalry brigades and divisions, led by competent cavalry officers and supported by artillery. Constructing new blockhouses, training of the infantry in those stockades, and developing effective cavalry stopped the Confederacy's raiding war in the summer of 1863. Unhappily for the Southern forces, the Federal plan began to bear fruit just as the Rebels started to place even greater emphasis and hopes on the raiding strategy and looked to expand the size of their raiding brigades and the depth of their forays. Disaster was looming on the horizon for the Confederacy in 1863.

Major General Thomas C. Hindman, commander, Trans-Mississippi District, 1862. As commander of Confederate forces in Arkansas, Hindman authorized the organization of guerrilla forces under his "Bands of Ten" order of 1862. Courtesy Alabama State Archives.

Colonel, later Brigadier General, M. La Rue Harrison, commander, First
Arkansas Cavalry (Union), 1862–65. Harrison's Unionists fought a two-year
war against Confederate guerrillas operating in northwest Arkansas. Courtesy
Washington County (Arkansas) Historical Society/Shiloh Museum of Ozark
History.

Lieutenant Colonel John Singleton Mosby (left), Forty-third Battalion, Virginia Cavalry, and unknown gentleman, 1864. Library of Congress.

Locomotive operating on the B&O Railroad, near Union Mills, Virginia, 1864. Such rough terrain greatly aided the partisan campaign of Mosby's Rangers. Library of Congress.

Heavily fortified blockhouse near Arlington Heights, Virginia, 1864. This type of fortification was commonly used as part of the Federal antipartisan efforts against Mosby in the last two years of the war. Library of Congress.

Fortified bridge across the Cumberland River near Nashville, Tennessee, 1864. In response to Morgan's and Forrest's 1862 raids, the Federal army fortified strategic locations such as bridges and rail hubs. Without artillery, such locations were nearly impossible to capture. Library of Congress.

Large blockhouse along the Tennessee River, late 1863. To house larger detachments, the Federals built temporary fortifications capable of sustaining a short seige. In conjunction with cavalry, these small forts played a critical role in the failure of Morgan's 1863 "Great Raid." Library of Congress.

Brigadier General John Hunt Morgan, 1862. Morgan's successes of 1862 could not be repeated in the summer of 1863. Ultimately, Morgan was a victim of the Union army's reforms—blockhouses, cavalry, and organization. Courtesy Alabama State Archives.

Brigadier (later Lieutenant) General Nathan Bedford Forrest. Considered one of the greatest untrained military leaders of American history, Forrest first earned his fame as a raider in the winter of 1862. Courtesy Alabama State Archives.

6

GREAT RAIDS, GREAT REFORMS AND GREAT DISASTERS

The 1863 Spring and Summer Raiding Campaign

> In cavalry experiences [using raids] it is sometimes easier to get in than to get out.
>
> Private Bennett H. Young, Company B,
> Eighth Kentucky Cavalry Regiment,
> Morgan's Division, *Wizards of the Saddle*

As the smoke settled over the battlefield at Stones River, both Union and Confederate armies moved into winter quarters, warily watching each other, a mere eighteen miles apart. The Northern troops sat south of Murfreesboro, while the Southerners shielded Chattanooga. The lull in fighting gave time for both sides to replace the 23,000 casualties.

Moreover, the antagonists had time to evaluate the performance of the raiders, especially Morgan and Forrest, in the previous year. The Rebels had much to celebrate about their raiding chieftains—thousands of captured Yankees, millions of dollars in enemy property destroyed, and a new set of heroes to boost the sagging morale of the Confederate home front. Union commanders saw one unmitigated disaster after another; from the early summer until the late winter, Morgan and Forrest had run rings around their cavalry, burned needed supplies, crippled strategic railroads, and demoralized their armies. The year 1863, they determined, would be different. Extensive reforms of every aspect of antiraiding operations were implemented and enforced by rigid standards. The Confederates, in contrast, were content to continue raiding as they had in 1862, and waited for the late spring, when the roads were dry and forage plentiful, to launch a widespread raiding campaign to bring the Union armies to a halt. The most famous of these, General John Hunt Morgan's "Great Raid" through Kentucky, Indiana, and Ohio, would test the new Federal defenses in July 1863. The results ultimately destroyed Morgan and his command and validated that the Federal army in Tennessee and Kentucky was capable of stopping a planned and organized irregular campaign, just as the Federals had won against unorganized guerrillas in Arkansas and partisans in Virginia.

A significant change in the strategic situation in 1863 was the increase of Union forces in the region. During the December raids by Morgan and Forrest, two major Federal campaigns, one led by Rosecrans toward Murfreesboro and the other by Grant toward Vicksburg, absorbed nearly all available Union troops in Tennessee and Kentucky (see chap. 5). By early summer 1863, the influx of new regiments enabled the Federals to raise a third major army under Major General Ambrose Burnside, the Department (later designated as the Army) of the Ohio, to focus on the liberation of eastern Tennessee. Along with Rosecrans's Army of the Cumberland, the Federal armies in Tennessee and Kentucky were built up during the spring of 1863 for a dual summer offensive toward Knoxville and Chattanooga. In addition to the task of striking toward Knoxville, Burnside was also given control over all Federal troops north of the Cumberland River. This was done for several reasons, including command and personality differences between Rosecrans and General in Chief Henry W. Halleck, as well as differences between Rosecrans and Burnside, and to support President Lincoln's long-held desire to liberate eastern Tennessee. The result was a new focus: combat the raiders, reduce their effectiveness, or even eliminate them (see map 8).[1]

The revamped Federal antiraiding campaign of 1863 showed improvement in several ways. These included reforming the Federal cavalry, rebuilding blockhouses along the railroads, integrating the Union navy into the antiraiding forces, improving the efficiency of the army, and initiating direct counter-raiding expeditions aimed at exhausting the Confederate cavalry. The development of the Federal cavalry received

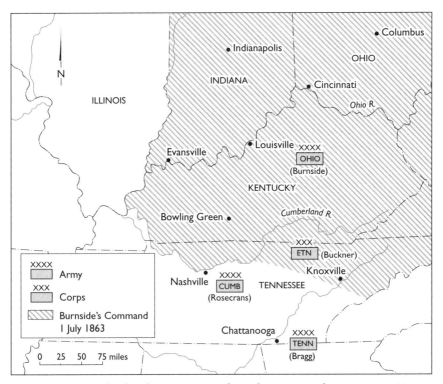

Map 8. Major Federal military commands in the western theater, 1862–63.

the foremost priority; for the Union troopers to win, they needed equipment, horses, numerical superiority, and experience. Generals Buell and Rosecrans pushed for more and better horse soldiers throughout 1862; in early 1863, the new cavalry regiments were raised and assigned to both the Army of the Ohio and the Army of the Cumberland. Most of these were positioned and ordered to act against raiding, but others were formed into raiding commands themselves, leading to an alternate approach toward the Confederate raiders—that of Union counter-raids aimed at both hitting vulnerable Confederate supply lines and tying up Rebel cavalry. Counter-raiding had multiple benefits, including giving experience to the untested troopers and encouraging a more aggressive role for the Union cavalry. General Rosecrans bluntly asserted: "I wish to have cavalry enough to destroy the enemy cavalry."[2]

The first issue to face Rosecrans was the arming and mounting of his troopers. With his army slowly recovering from the New Year's bloodletting at Stones River, he began to pressure the War Department for new horse regiments, and for equipment to improve those he already had. Many of the new units reporting for duty that spring, such as the Second and Tenth Ohio Cavalry, lacked both firearms and horses.[3] To overcome these shortages, Rosecrans wrote to General in Chief Halleck on an almost daily basis, beginning in late January. The content of this exchange was anything but civil. Noting that he had "three regiments of Tennessee cavalry," and the Second Indiana Cavalry, all of whom "are now without arms," he demanded an increase of cavalry weapons, specifically repeating carbines, for his army. In short, Rosecrans told Halleck, "if we cannot arm our cavalry, we had better disband it." As expected, Halleck reacted negatively to the reproach, chastising Rosecrans for his remarks, calling them "without reason," and ending by telling him that his cavalry was as well armed as that of General Samuel Curtis in Arkansas or General Grant in Mississippi. What Halleck did not fully understand is that Rosecrans, after the raids of Morgan and Forrest the previous year, wanted to eliminate the raiders once and for all, and to do so required the best cavalry force he could possibly muster. Apparently thinking his abrupt reply was sufficient for Rosecrans, Halleck was shocked on February 3 when he saw a telegram Rosecrans had sent directly to Secretary of War Edwin M. Stanton, asking for cavalry weapons. Rosecrans begged for enough equipment to "mount infantry brigades for marches and enterprises" and to equip his 1,000 cavalrymen who did not have horses, and the 2,000 who were without weapons. "This matter is so clearly in my mind of paramount public interest that I blush to think it necessary to seem to apologize for it," he wrote. The general in chief was furious, as is evident in the telegraphic exchange between Tennessee and Washington in early February 1863, insisting that the best arms had already been sent to Rosecrans, while Rosecrans kept wiring back that he could not stop raiders with what he had. Halleck refused to send more weapons, but Rosecrans's appeal to Stanton circumvented him. On March 1, a shipment of 2,480 Burnside carbines and 500 Colt revolving carbines arrived in Louisville. Rosecrans finally had the firearms for his cavalry.[4]

Without sufficient cavalry horses, the improved armament meant little. Having solved the weapons problem, Rosecrans pushed to gain enough horses to sustain a lengthy antiraiding campaign. The War Department, as always, resisted his efforts to upgrade his horse soldiers. A number of issues emerged during his quest to gain sufficient mounts. Since Kentucky was officially a Union state, he could not go about seizing horses without purchase; Tennessee, thanks to the work of Wheeler, Forrest, and Morgan, had no horses left.[5] Consequently, Rosecrans sent quartermasters to Louisville and Lexington to purchase mounts, which the locals happily increased in price to meet the demand.[6] The first batch of mounts left much to be desired. For example, between January and May 1863, the Army of the Cumberland received 9,119 horses from the Department of the Ohio (which covered northern Kentucky), and returned 8,212 horses as "unserviceable." Nearly 11,500 cavalry horses still remained in the army, of which "at least one-fourth" were considered "worn out and unfit for service."[7] As with the carbines, General Halleck and Quartermaster General Montgomery C. Meigs found themselves bombarded by constant requests for horses from Rosecrans. One can almost hear the frustration and growing annoyance in Halleck's telegrams, when he told Rosecrans that "I regret very much to notice the complaining tone of your telegrams in regard to your supply of horses. You seem to think the Government does not do its duty toward your army. . . . [We] here have done all in [our] power to supply your wants, and I venture to say that for no other army has greater care and solicitation been felt or given."[8] Halleck and Meigs provided the money to purchase horses and pulled cavalry regiments from other commands to support Rosecrans. From a logistical standpoint, the Federal cavalry in the West was well mounted and equipped to fight by early May. Rosecrans, through his dogged telegraphing, had gotten his wish—an antiraiding force capable of meeting and defeating the forces of Morgan and Forrest.[9]

To complement the improved cavalry, the weak fortification system was rebuilt, from batteries and redoubts at major cities to the blockhouses guarding the railroads. The Federals were well aware that the blockhouses, unless fully manned, well fortified, and provided with artillery, were vulnerable to the raiders. In February, Rosecrans wrote Halleck on the subject, stating that, in their present condition, "the occupation of the points [blockhouses] . . . will not [be permanent], nor in such manner as to leave the posts as baits for rebel enterprise." Luckily for the Federals, the atrocious late winter weather had set in, and brought most operations to a halt, which gave them time to evaluate and improve the blockhouse system. First, the commanders of regiments and detachments scattered along the railroads and key towns had to be either combined into stronger units or reinforced. In a purely antiguerrilla role, small detachments were an efficient and effective way to spread an army's presence across a large area. Against organized cavalry conducting a raid, such outposts were easily gobbled up by any large force. According to the Federal commander in Kentucky, when asked by Rosecrans to garrison the entire line of the Cumberland River, "the forces which could be assigned to the various points would not be strong enough to hold them against any serious attack, and even to place small garrisons at those points would involve the serious weakening of the garrisons at points on the railroad which it is important we should hold."[10] In effect, the Federal forces in the region were slowly concentrating into larger forces, based around fortified towns and blockhouses, and with the main mission of protecting the railroad. This tacit rejection of an antiguerrilla role and its replacement with an antiraiding defense paid great dividends when the summer raiding season began.

The repair of the fortification system, especially the blockhouses and stockades protecting vulnerable bridges and depots, received a high priority. Competent engineer and artillery officers were tasked to survey and evaluate the condition of the blockhouses and stockades, both along the Louisville and Nashville Railroad and at key towns and locations. As the weather improved, and the ground became more pliable, the work began. New depots to support the planned summer campaigns were laid out and fortified against raiders, and the existing fortifications were given additional artillery and reinforced. At places such as Louisville, Frankfort, and Lexington, Kentucky, detailed plans and "directions for such extensions and improvements as circumstances required" were left by engineers for the garrisons to implement. Special care was taken with the railroad bridges at Muldraugh's Hill (target of Morgan's December attacks), Munfordville, Bowling Green, and elsewhere along the Louisville and Nashville. After the engineers had left, however, it was up to the individual garrisons to maintain the blockhouses. Although it was not put in orders until September, Rosecrans's guidance to the commanders of these garrisons is clear in its intent. The commanders had to conduct weekly inspections of each blockhouse and stockade under their command, and report their findings to headquarters. The reports themselves were fairly detailed, and included "the present state of the defenses in regard to their security from artillery; the state of the ground around them; any possible cover for an enemy in their vicinity; and the state of the supplies of wood, water and rations." The officers were instructed to cut down trees and undergrowth for 100 yards from each blockhouse, which was to also have an earthwork intended to "mask it wholly or in part from artillery fire." To guarantee that the work was being done, Rosecrans's chief engineer was instructed to inspect the fortifications on a regular basis and report on his findings. The Federal army was placing emphasis on the blockhouse system, and improving units and deployments, to prevent a repetition of the results of the fall and winter 1862 raids. Rebel artillery alone would no longer force a surrender. The strengthened blockhouses, and their well-protected garrisons, would now have to be assaulted by dismounted raiders—something no Rebel cavalry commander wanted.[11]

In addition to devoting their overwhelming material wealth into fortifications, the Federal army ensured that their growing fleet of gunboats was tied into the antiraiding plan. Tennessee and Kentucky possessed several wide and navigable waterways that provided both a supply line and a means to deliver naval firepower to the Federals. The Ohio, Tennessee, and Cumberland Rivers, along with hundreds of creeks and streams, crisscrossed the region. Many locations most vulnerable to raiding, such as supply depots, were near the rivers. Consequently, Union naval vessels, many with large-caliber guns, could easily repulse irregular contingents as well as block fords and other crossing sites. Rosecrans and other Federal generals in the region, as well as some naval officers, were quick to realize this. General in Chief Halleck attempted to coordinate with the Navy Department for continual patrols along the Tennessee and Cumberland, but the shortage of shallow-draft ships, capable of crossing the upper reaches of both rivers in the summer, hampered his efforts. Rosecrans even offered infantrymen to man the gunboats, understanding that without control of the rivers, not only could the raiders cross the rivers at will, but his main logistical lifeline—the rivers themselves—could be easily cut by a few artillery pieces placed along the banks. Finally, by pressuring Halleck, who in turn pressured the Navy, a small flotilla of gunboats began patrolling the rivers in late January.[12]

Luck assisted Rosecrans and his plan to defeat the raiders that he knew would be coming in force in the summer. The naval officer appointed to command the patrols along the Tennessee, Cumberland, and Ohio Rivers was Lieutenant Commander Leroy Fitch, who had been running a one-man counterguerrilla war in the region since August 1862. Fitch had initially been ordered to suppress bushwhackers and guerrillas operating along the Ohio and Tennessee. He had been fairly successful. Fitch was not only a competent combat commander, but he had a knack for improvisation. Starting out with a single lightly armored steamer, the *General Pillow*, he had pushed his commander, Captain A. M. Pennock, to arm every craft that could carry a cannon. By January 1863, Fitch's flotilla numbered six gunboats, and one of them carried powerful eight-inch naval guns that outclassed any Confederate field artillery in the region. Throughout the winter months, the flotilla escorted supply convoys to Rosecrans's army and dominated the rivers, sending guerrilla parties scurrying for cover as they approached. The effectiveness of the gunboats should not be underestimated. During Wheeler's and Forrest's attack on Fort Donelson in February, Commander Fitch's vessels demolished the attacking Confederates, pouring shot and shell into the massed Confederate ranks as they prepared for a final assault on the works. Later in 1863, during Morgan's Indiana-Ohio raid, Fitch and his gunboats would play a pivotal role in bringing about a Federal victory.[13]

Closer integration of naval and land forces required more than the allocation of warships to patrol the rivers. How the Army of the Cumberland and the Department of the Ohio operated both between the services and internally had to be dealt with. Army cooperation with the Navy, as always, was problematic, so much so that President Lincoln became involved in the dispute.[14] Internal organizational changes and administrative reforms, in contrast, were easily made. In conjunction with the engineer operations mentioned above, officers were appointed to oversee the defense of the railroads specifically. Lieutenant Arthur L. Conger, 115th Ohio Volunteer Infantry, was one such officer. Although he did not become "assistant inspector of railroad defenses" until June 1864, his experience was common for the position. Lieutenant Conger covered a relatively small area, from Nashville to Murfreesboro, and was constantly on the move overseeing the defenses of his seven blockhouses. He and his fellow inspectors moved on the daily trains and checked everything relating to the status of the defenses, including rations on hand and the condition of personal firearms. Such constant inspecting and reporting to higher headquarters ensured that senior Federal commanders, for the first time, had a grasp of the conditions and readiness of the railroad defenses.[15]

A second administrative change perhaps had the greatest influence on the individual officer and soldier. Rosecrans and Burnside well remembered the surrender of thousands of well-armed troops and millions of dollars in government property to Morgan and Forrest during the previous year, and decided to make surrender a less viable option to Federal officers. On January 27, 1863, Rosecrans issued General Orders Number 5, directing that "such disgraceful conduct on the part of both officers and men, intrusted with duties so important, renders them both morally and legally responsible for the loss of life and public property which so frequently ensues." Officers who surrendered when their men still had means to resist, or whose negligence caused the surrender of the command, "shall forfeit all pay and allowances that shall be due him, and be dishonorably dismissed [from] the service." If an officer sent out a poorly guarded supply train, and the train was captured, the officer was "held pecuniarily responsible for any injury such trains may sustain, and moreover, be punished as for misbehavior in the face of the enemy."[16] The Federal commanders took the issue seriously. In one case, Colonel A. S. Hall, the commander of the Second Brigade, Fifth Division, XIV Corps, faced a court-martial due to the loss of a supply train. General Joseph J. Reynolds, his commander, warned him that he would be held responsible for the loss, totaling nearly $100,000 in property, as well as "an diminution of confidence or military spirit that may result from this most uncalled-for disaster." A later investigation exonerated Colonel Hall, but not Captain B. W. Canfield, the commander of the wagon train. Rosecrans ordered the captain dishonorably discharged, adding that he "regrets his inability to inflict the extreme penalty of the law upon one so deserving an ignominious death." Publishing such findings throughout the entire Departments of the Cumberland and Ohio may have had the desired effect, as the *Official Records* do not reflect any further court-martials that spring.[17]

Not only were soldiers punished for not stopping raiders and other irregulars, those who did their duty were rewarded. General Rosecrans established a "Roll of Honor," and published the deeds of men who fought off irregular attacks and demonstrated courage and valor under fire. By using a combination of "Special Field Orders" outlining the soldier's deeds and issuance of a small red lapel ribbon signifying his membership in the Roll of Honor, Rosecrans directly rewarded those who fought.[18] The majority of examples in the spring of 1863 focused on irregular warfare. For example, Sergeant Thomas Branch, Company I, Tenth Michigan Infantry, was the first member of the roll, appointed on February 5, 1863, for his actions in defending a construction crew on the Nashville and Chattanooga Railroad. After irregulars fired on the train, Branch responded quickly, ordering his twenty-five-man detachment to return fire. Ultimately, he had his men fix bayonets and charge the enemy, estimated at twice his numbers. The Federal sergeant put out the fires started on the construction train, got it back on the rails, and returned it and its cars intact to Murfreesboro.[19] Such acts of courage, when published for the entire command to see, appeared to have a beneficial effect on morale.

While the Federals attempted to rebuild the organization and morale of their antiraiding forces, the Confederates concentrated on striking the Federals wherever they could. General Wheeler's cavalry, especially the brigades (later divisions) of Forrest and Morgan, hit isolated Federal outposts around Murfreesboro almost every day in January and February, and Bragg's army slowly reconstituted itself after the Battle of Stones River. However, internal dissent within the Army of Tennessee's high command, especially the constant bickering between Bragg and his senior commanders, led to chaos within the Confederate leadership. Major Confederate campaigns were suspended until late spring, when it was expected that the roads would have improved enough to support operations. During this period, the only offensive operations that the Rebels could conduct were raids, led by officers who were outside of Bragg's staff.[20]

The largest raid of the winter of 1862–63 was against Fort Donelson; General Wheeler, along with brigades commanded by Forrest and Colonel John A. Wharton, struck the fort on February 3. Wheeler's objective was to block the river as a supply line for the Federal army, for after the destructive Christmas Raids of 1862, the Union logistics had become increasingly dependent on the Cumberland and Tennessee Rivers. Wheeler believed that the garrison at the fort and the nearby town of Dover, Tennessee, were weak and ripe for the taking. Initially, he sent off Forrest and Wharton with the idea of blocking the river for only a short time; later he concluded that seizing Fort Donelson would be the best solution to the problem. Forrest later complained that his men had not been issued enough ammunition for such an operation and that he had been ordered only to ambush a few riverboats and retire. He tried to talk Wheeler out of the attack, considering it not worth the cost in men and horses. Wheeler ignored this recommendation and ordered the assault. A thousand of Forrest's dismounted cavalry, weakly supported by artillery and poorly coordinated with Wharton's brigade, stormed the 800 Federals in the fort several times and were repulsed. At a cost of nearly 150 killed and 600 wounded, Wheeler's raid managed to capture a single cannon and eighty prisoners, kill twelve Federals, and destroy a riverboat loaded with hay. The demoralized troopers withdrew to Confederate lines. As Wheeler wrote his report on the action to Bragg, he spoke to both Forrest and Wharton on the performance of their soldiers. Wharton took responsibility for the poor performance of his men, which exposed Forrest's assault to the full brunt of Federal firepower. Forrest exploded in fury at both Wharton and Wheeler. "General Wheeler," Forrest began, "I advised against this attack, and said all a subordinate officer should have said against it, and nothing you can say or do will bring back my brave men lying dead and wounded around that fort tonight. . . . [T]here is one thing I want you to put in that report to General Bragg—tell him that I will be in my coffin before I fight again under your command." Although they would work together in the upcoming campaigns at Tullahoma and Chattanooga, Forrest thereafter considered himself outside of Wheeler's influence. The relationship between Wheeler, Forrest, and Morgan, which had won so much for the Confederate cause the previous fall, had begun to deteriorate.[21]

The deteriorating relationship between Wheeler and Forrest, and the latter's heavy losses at Fort Donelson, led to the transferring of Forrest and his command to assist General Earl Van Dorn's operations on the left wing of Bragg's army. On March 4, the combined troopers of Van Dorn and Forrest won a substantial victory at Thompson's Station, Tennessee, twenty miles south of Nashville.[22] On March 15, Forrest was given a full cavalry division, consisting of his brigade and that of Brigadier General Frank Thompson. Nine days later, Forrest launched them on a quick raid against Brentwood, Tennessee, where a stockade protected a bridge outside of Nashville. Forrest managed to capture the garrison of nearly 750 men, with little loss.[23] The Confederates had signaled the beginning of the raiding season to the Federals, who responded by launching raids of their own, aiming to exhaust Forrest's command.

Forrest's division was again tested in late April, during the famous raid through northern Alabama by Federal troopers led by Colonel Abel Streight. The raid was launched for several reasons. The Unionist population of hilly northern Alabama was one concern to the Lincoln administration, and the Western and Atlantic Railroad, running between Chattanooga and Atlanta and Bragg's main supply artery, was the other. Streight's mission was to cut through northern Alabama, encouraging the locals, and head for Georgia. Once there, he was to demolish as much of the railroad as possible before returning to Federal lines. The 1,700-man, mule-mounted brigade, supported by General Grenville Dodge's 8,000-man infantry division, departed on April 21 from East-port, Mississippi, and was immediately detected by the Confederates. Dodge's force stayed at Tuscumbia, Alabama, while Streight pushed for-ward. The Confederates reacted rapidly, shifting Forrest's entire divi-sion to support the cavalry attempting to hold back Dodge's division and Streight's brigade. On April 29, Forrest began pursuing Streight, fighting a series of skirmishes as he pushed the Federals farther and far-ther away from their lines. For four days, the Confederates pursued the Federal raiders, not giving them a moment's rest. The Yankee troopers, by the end of the raid, were so exhausted that some were falling asleep while under fire. The discovery that the bridge was burned over the Chattanooga River, the last chance to escape, led to the brigade's sur-render. Nearly 1,600 exhausted Union soldiers went to prisoner of war camps, while Forrest was rewarded with the thanks of the Confederate Congress.[24] Seemingly, this Federal raid had been an abject failure.

Streight's defeat, although a tactical and operational loss, may be viewed differently on the strategic level. By drawing Confederate cav-alry away from the front lines, Streight aided the upcoming plans of the Army of the Cumberland to advance on Chattanooga. In respect to the Federal antiraiding strategy, Streight managed to tie up nearly 5,000 Confederate cavalry for almost two weeks, exhausting horses and men that the Rebels could ill afford to lose. Unlike infantry, cavalry could not operate over a long period of time; horses could literally be ridden to death if not given proper food and rest. The Federal raid managed to tire out the mounts of Forrest's division, making the possibility of a Confederate repeat of the western Tennessee raid in December much less likely. The horses, in the words of one observer, "were generally of the best 'blooded stock' of Middle Tennessee and Kentucky; but the hardships of the expedition had been so extreme and prolonged, that it had perceptibly affected them." Weakened by constant riding, 250 of 550 horses in one battalion, and 95 of 120 artillery horses, died of disease and exhaustion by the time Forrest reached Rome, Georgia, on May 6.[25]

A second unexpected incident also changed the nature of the Con-federate raiding campaign. Forrest's capture of Streight, combined with the actions during the raids south of Nashville, led to his recognition as a Confederate national hero. The death of General Van Dorn in May had left open the command of the cavalry of the left wing of Bragg's army; Bragg offered it to Forrest, who accepted. Forrest had, in effect, been promoted out of the echelon of small-scale raiding. His new responsibilities effectively removed him from the cut-and-slash actions that made him famous. Although many of his later expeditions during the war would be labeled as "raids," the combined exhaustion of his division and his promotion ended Forrest's raiding career before the summer raiding season of 1863.

For the Confederates, their best hope of a successful raiding campaign in the summer of 1863—the combined cavalry of Forrest and Morgan—had been cut in half. Any major raids now fell on Morgan alone, enabling the Union army to concentrate their antiraiding forces against one, not two, raiders. Perhaps the surrender of Colonel Streight's command did more good for the Federal cause in Tennessee, and ultimately the war, than anyone expected—it removed Forrest from the summer 1863 raiding war as effectively as if someone had killed him.[26]

While Forrest spent the early spring in raids on Fort Donelson and chasing Colonel Streight's brigade, Morgan spent the winter conducting a combination of conventional cavalry missions and small-scale raiding. The screening of Bragg's army took a toll on the men and mounts of Morgan's command. One soldier of the Ninth Kentucky Cavalry later recalled that "this long and arduous service almost completely unfitted the Regiment for active service when the campaign began in June 1863."[27] In addition to carrying out constant patrols, Morgan's men operated in an unproductive region of the state, an area known as the "Barrens of Tennessee." Food was scarce, and replacement horses almost impossible to find. The Ninth Kentucky, for example, was left behind during the Great Raid simply because there were not enough horses to mount the majority of its troopers.[28] On the other hand, the scouting and screening missions kept the raiders busy until early summer, and provided additional experience to the men. According to one observer, "although the armies were idle for months after [the Battle of Stones River], the cavalry was never so."[29]

As Morgan's troopers skirmished and patrolled that spring, the high command of both sides planned the upcoming campaign. Federal leaders eyed two big objectives, Chattanooga and Knoxville, while the Confederates fretted over their ability to hold the gateway into the Deep South. On the strategic level, the early summer of 1863 represented one of the last hopes for a negotiated peace with the Union that would lead to Confederate independence. In the East, General Robert E. Lee's Army of Northern Virginia, coming off a victory at Chancellorsville in May, prepared to move northward and invade Pennsylvania, a campaign that would culminate at Gettysburg. In the trans-Mississippi, scattered Confederate forces gathered in south-central Arkansas to attack the city of Helena on the Mississippi River, in the vain hope of drawing Grant's formidable army away from Vicksburg. And in the West, Bragg's army of 45,000 sat eighteen miles away from the growing power of Rosecrans's Army of the Cumberland, now numbering over 56,000 infantry and 9,000 cavalry.[30]

In early June, the Confederates first detected movement in the Federal army around Murfreesboro, as Rosecrans, under pressure from Washington to support Grant, prepared to launch an offensive. Following a winter and spring of raids and counter-raids, the beginning of a conventional campaign was a welcome turn of events to Rosecrans. On June 23, the Federals advanced from Murfreesboro, headed southeast toward Bragg's army. For the next six days, Rosecrans's Federals skirmished and maneuvered against the Confederates, driving them back on their base at Tullahoma. Unluckily for the Rebels, Morgan and his command had already departed for a daring raid into Indiana and Ohio, reducing the number of cavalry for screening and information gathering by nearly one third. Wheeler and Forrest, with the bulk of the cavalry, fought a skillful delaying action while Bragg pulled the army toward Chattanooga. On July 1, the Federals entered Tullahoma, continually harassed by the Confederate horsemen. By July 6, Bragg's army reached Chattanooga, having succeeded in preventing its encirclement by Rosecrans's forces, but also placing an even greater distance between friendly lines and Morgan's raiders.[31]

Following the tepid results of the spring raiding campaign, Morgan worked on executing a much bolder operation, one that would stop the expected Federal invasions of eastern Tennessee and northern Georgia, bring the war onto northern soil, and place him in the forefront of Confederate celebrities. He and 2,500 men would slice across Kentucky, feinting along the route to confuse Federal pursuers, cross the Ohio River into Indiana, and cut a swath through that state and its neighbor, Ohio. Having completed the mission, the raiders would either push across the middle Appalachians into Virginia, or into West Virginia to link up with General Lee's victorious army in Pennsylvania.[32]

Displaying immaturity as an officer, and a lack of military courtesy, Morgan told neither Wheeler nor Bragg of his plan. Instead, he presented the operation as a short movement into Kentucky with the singular objective of striking Louisville and its 300-man garrison. Wheeler approved the idea, as did Bragg, who added that the force should primarily be Kentucky troops, since they could gather new recruits during the raid. Bragg also agreed to the raid in the hope that it would draw off enough Federal cavalry to allow his army to disengage from Tullahoma and fall back on Chattanooga without interference. Needing all the cavalry he could get, Bragg wisely denied Morgan's request for his entire 5,000-man division for the raid, initially only allowing for 1,500 men and a few artillery pieces for the operation. By June 18, Morgan had convinced both Wheeler and Bragg to increase the expedition's strength to 2,000 troopers. The Confederate raider kept silent on his true intent to all but a few confidants, such as his brother, Captain Thomas Morgan, and his brother-in-law, Colonel Basil Duke.[33]

Wheeler wanted Morgan's cavalry back into position as soon as possible. The success of the Christmas Raids had come at a cost, that of tactical blindness prior to the Battle of Stones River. Senior officers of the Army of Tennessee remembered well that the movement of Forrest's and Morgan's cavalry was the spark that ignited the Federal army into action, and were specific in their orders to Morgan. In Special Orders No. 44, Morgan was instructed to "proceed to Kentucky with a force of 2,000 officers and men," to "break up and destroy the Louisville and Nashville Railroad . . . [and], if practicable, destroy depots of supplies in the State of Kentucky." Wheeler specifically ordered Morgan to return to Confederate lines as soon as his objectives were met. Morgan agreed with Wheeler's guidance, thanking him for intervening with Bragg for the additional 500 men; no one suspected Morgan's true intent.[34]

Morgan controlled sufficient men and equipment for raid, along with competent and experienced cavalry officers to use them. His First Brigade was led by Colonel Duke, and the Second Brigade by Colonel Adam R. "Stovepipe" Johnson. Duke's brigade was formed around many of the men who had been with Morgan since 1861, and included the Second Kentucky, Fifth Kentucky, Sixth Kentucky, Ninth Kentucky, and Ninth Tennessee Cavalry regiments. The Second Brigade was similarly organized, and consisted of the Seventh Kentucky, Eighth Kentucky, Tenth Kentucky, Eleventh Kentucky, and Fourteenth Kentucky

Cavalry. Attached to the division were two artillery batteries, one of two three-inch rifled Parrott guns and another of two twelve-pound howitzers. All totaled, the expedition consisted of 2,460 men, the single largest raiding force that Morgan had ever commanded.[35]

Morgan moved his small division into a staging position near Alexandria, Tennessee, and prepared to cross the Cumberland River on June 11. As soon as he relocated his command, Federal forces began to harass him. A small, 550-man cavalry brigade, under Colonel F. W. Graham, detected the movement of some of Johnson's Second Brigade south of the Cumberland River at Mud Camp Ford. Graham, believing only 300 Confederates were in the area, launched his men into an attack. Luckily for Graham, the bulk of Johnson's 1,200-man brigade had withdrawn, along with the rest of Morgan's division, in an attempt to engage a Federal raiding column returning from Knoxville. The Federal colonel was not dismayed, and turned his men westward along the south bank of the Cumberland, burning and destroying any resource of use to the Confederates, and defeating Major O. P. Hamilton's battalion of Johnson's brigade near Kettle Creek, Kentucky. The Federals captured two artillery pieces, supplies, and "scattered the entire command." When Morgan found out what happened, he warned Wheeler that "there is now no force on the Cumberland River, and the entire rear of this flank is exposed to raids, which no doubt the enemy will attempt, and, if successful, with most disastrous results." What is important from this seemingly meaningless engagement is that the once derided Federal cavalry was now showing initiative and looking for Morgan's men in hopes of destroying them; these horsemen were capable of conducting destructive raids on the same scale as the Confederates. Additionally, Graham's foray showed that the Federals north of the Cumberland River were expecting a raid by Morgan at any time, and had stationed a thick screen of cavalry to detect and defeat such an operation. It did not appear to have occurred to Morgan that the Union cavalry had matured into a formidable fighting force and that his raid had little chance of succeeding against a competent and alert foe (see map 9).[36]

If Morgan needed more evidence of the dramatic change in the Federal cavalry, it should have been the 1,500-man expedition launched by Burnside against Knoxville. Morgan had planned to depart for his raid in mid-June, but was ordered by Wheeler at the last minute to shift his forces to Monticello, Kentucky, to stop the Federal raiders. It was

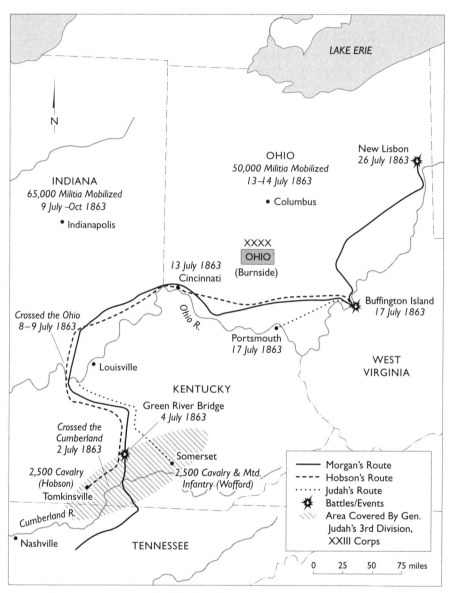

Map 9. Morgan's "Great Raid" of 1863.

during this change of bases that the Union cavalry crossed the Cumberland and defeated Major Hamilton's battalion. Morgan rushed his troopers through the heavy spring rains that turned the roads into a quagmire. From June 11 until June 24, Morgan exhausted men, horses, and supplies in a fruitless search for Colonel William P. Sanders's

Yankee raiders. Sanders, after burning three bridges, capturing several hundred Confederates, and destroying large amounts of supplies, hurriedly retreated into Federal territory before Morgan's division arrived. The portents for Morgan's raid were not good; he had lost the element of surprise along the Cumberland River crossing sites, fatigued his men and horses hunting Union raiders, and his own scouting expedition alerted all of Indiana and Ohio to his coming. The Federal raid toward Knoxville, in effect, achieved many of the same goals as Colonel Streight's raid in northern Alabama; it exhausted the very Rebel cavalry who were expected to lead the raiding war.[37]

Morgan spent the latter half of June preparing for his big raid, allowing men and mounts to recover and replacing supplies, and planned to set out on July 2. Beginning in early June, scouting parties slipped past the Federal pickets into Kentucky, often dressed in civilian clothes, to verify the depth of the rivers and fording points. A detachment under Captain Henry Hines, Company E, Ninth Kentucky Cavalry, was sent under secret orders from Morgan to cross the Ohio River into Indiana and gather information. A detachment from Colonel Duke's brigade proceeded under similar orders to examine crossing points on the Ohio River north of Louisville. Thus, before the raiders had left Tennessee, Morgan indicated his true objectives—the disapproved raid into Indiana and Ohio—by sending detachments to find the best entrance and egress across the Ohio River. His stubborn adherence to his original plan, and his desire for greater fame, would cost the Confederacy much in the upcoming month.[38]

Captain Hines's scouts set out on June 8 to begin the survey of Morgan's route. Dressed in Federal uniforms, his eighty-man company covered several parallel paths toward the Ohio River, avoiding the pro-Union areas, calling it "Home Guard country," and recommending that it "was good policy to avoid a collision with [Home Guards] if possible." Regardless of his stealth, Hines and his company were reported to Federal authorities, who dispatched cavalry to pursue them. For six days, the Union cavalry followed the scouts, giving them little time for rest. Hines later recalled that "the men were much worn down with fatigue—their legs and feet were so much swollen that many were unable to wear their boots—the continual pressure of their legs upon the saddle had caused their skin to slough, and the flesh laid bare from the calf of the legs to the hips." Hines, and ultimately Morgan, should have taken this as a warning regarding the sharp change in Federal counter-raiding strategy from the previous winter. Any Confederate raiders detected crossing into Kentucky would face Home Guards as well as regular Federal troops on static guard duty and Yankee cavalry.[39]

Having rested only twelve hours in six days, the scouts were literally collapsing with exhaustion. After crossing the Ohio River on June 14, one exhausted man failed to wake up when his detachment moved out in the darkness. Federals captured him and he revealed Hines's route. Hines recalled that "the news spread like wild fire over the country, the sounds of the conch shells [which the Home Guards used for communication] were heard on all sides." The countryside was alerted and the Indiana militia was taking to the roadways and forests throughout the area. Soon, "every hilltop was illuminated by the signal lights of the enemy, and every thicket concealed the now alarmed and watchful home guards." The scouts attempted to speed up their tiring mounts and complete Morgan's reconnaissance. Hines's troopers tried to cross the Ohio River on June 19, but failed, finding nearly 800 Federal troops and two gunboats blocking their escape. Knowing that Morgan's success depended on his information, Hines swam the river with fifteen of his men, while the remainder, too exhausted to carry on, surrendered to the surrounding Union troops. Helped by local Confederate sympathizers, the scouts finally linked up with Morgan's command as it moved northward in July. In microcosm, the scout anticipated the eventual fate of Morgan's entire command—isolated by Federal gunboats and infantry, harassed by home guardsmen, and chased by a surprisingly competent and aggressive Union cavalry.[40]

Because of the failure of Hines to slip in and out unnoticed, the entire region was now on alert. Luckily for Morgan, the scouts had succeeded in scattering some of the Federal cavalry assigned to the area between the Cumberland and Ohio Rivers. In the wee hours of July 2, 1863, Morgan's division began to cross the Cumberland River towards Indiana.

The crossing of the river was an event itself. Finding only small canoes available for the crossing, many of the Rebel troops disrobed, placing their uniforms and weapons in the small boats, while they swam the river with their mounts. Startled Federal pickets fled after being attacked by naked, pistol-armed cavalrymen emerging from the river. Duke's brigade continued to cross at Burkesville throughout the night, and by midmorning on July 2 the entire command was across. Johnson's troopers, crossing a few miles down at Turkey Neck Bend, were shot at continually by Union skirmishers, who withdrew once a strong force had crossed the river. A mere twelve miles away, the Federals at Marrowbone, Kentucky, under Brigadier Generals Benjamin Judah and Edward Hobson committed what one historian calls "a critical error in judgment." Believing the river to be too swollen to cross, they had not placed strong enough forces at the fords, and allowed the entire raiding force to get across the river with little resistance.[41]

Major General Judah, an experienced officer whose career went back to the antebellum army and the Mexican War, and his Third Division of the XXIII Corps, covered the north bank of the Cumberland River precisely where Morgan planned to cross. The Federal general's patrols had seen the buildup of Morgan's raiders south of the river, reporting "from 5,000 to 7,000" Confederates across from the fords at Burkesville on July 1. He had a strong force at his disposal: two full brigades of cavalry and infantry, plus a third brigade, under Brigadier General James Shackelford, attached to the Third Division command after Morgan's abortive attempt to cross the Cumberland in June. Through his skilled scouts and patrols, Judah surmised that Morgan would cross at two sites along the river and alerted his superior, Major General George Hartsuff, to expect the enemy at any time. Naval support was also requested to shell the assembling Confederates. In northern Kentucky, Burnside ordered the movement of an additional two regiments from Hartsuff's corps to Judah, but the former demurred, arguing that he needed more time to move the men. When Morgan crossed the river on July 2, Judah was still waiting for his reinforcements and the gunboats.[42] To conduct his pursuit, Judah divided his division into three parts. One, under General Hobson, was at the crossings near Burkesville and at the town of Marrowbone, twelve miles northwest. A second force was at Somerset, under General Shackelford, and consisted of nearly 2,500 mounted infantry and cavalry. Judah's third element consisted of 1,200 mounted troops he led personally, stripped from his First Brigade. Altogether, Judah commanded nearly 8,000 officers and men, all of whom were used to pursue the raiders.[43]

Major General Judah made several severe tactical errors. First, he did not expect the Confederates to cross the Cumberland initially, since the heavy rains of the previous weeks had caused the river to rise. His second major mistake was shifting his forces from contesting the crossing sites to Tomkinsville and Marrowbone, where he planned to gather his forces and wait until he determined exactly how many men

Morgan had. Consequently, Morgan, after fighting a skirmish with Judah's cavalry at Burkesville, which cost him his chief scout, Captain Quirk, discovered that no Federal forces were between him and the Green River, his next obstacle.[44]

Morgan pushed his men hard, knowing that speed was vital. The raider had hoped to avoid contact with Federal troops until he was well north of the Ohio River. Instead, his expedition had been discovered from the outset, and Union troops could be expected to resist all along the route of march. The Confederates reached the Green River crossing site, near Columbia, Kentucky, early on July 3, and discovered the bridge was held by Federal infantry. Not only were the Federals entrenched in hastily built breastworks, the bridge itself had a stockade to protect it. Morgan responded as always, bringing up his field guns to force a Union surrender. What happened next was unexpected, to say the least. His cannoneers fired a few shots into the Yankee breastworks, and then sent a flag of truce demanding the Federals' surrender. Colonel Orlando H. Moore, and 200 men of his Twenty-fifth Michigan Infantry, were in no mood to give up without a fight and responded that "the Fourth of July was no day for me to entertain such a proposition." Clearly, the men behind these breastworks were different from those Morgan had faced only six months before, soldiers who would surrender a fortified blockhouse after a few cannon shots; one Confederate soldier remembered that "the tone of his [Moore's] reply boded trouble."[45]

Morgan ordered his men to open fire, determined to take the breastworks and stockade by storm. His men rushed forward under the blazing fire of Moore's Michiganders, who steadfastly refused to abandon the fortifications. At times, the sides were separated only by the logs of which the breastworks were built, and fighting was "nearly hand-to-hand." For three and a half hours Morgan launched attack after attack against the Union troops. Finally, Morgan had had enough. Thirty-six of his men lay dead, including a regimental commander, Colonel Walter Chenault of the Eleventh Kentucky Cavalry, and nearly fifty were wounded. Moore lost six killed and twenty-three wounded. The raiders, realizing that the Federals were too strong and well entrenched to be dislodged, sidestepped Moore's Michigan regiment and crossed six miles downstream at a newly discovered ford.[46]

The fight at Green River Bridge, when considered by itself, is of little import. Throughout the war, strongly held fortifications almost always delayed any attacker, and if the attacker was not willing to take heavy losses in storming them, were nearly impregnable. What makes the Federal defense at Green River different is that Colonel Moore's *200* soldiers faced the three full regiments of Morgan's division, and, despite the lack of artillery, repulsed seven charges against the breast-works. Again, the increased competency of the Federal army in the western theater was becoming more evident. Six months before, entire Yankee brigades surrendered to Forrest and Morgan's raiders; now mere infantry detachments, no larger than a full-strength company and lacking field guns, were defeating multiple elite cavalry regiments with artillery support.

Once across Green River, the raiders expected the resistance to decrease, since, based on their experiences the previous winter, the bulk of the units in Kentucky were either locally raised Union regiments or second-rate Federal commands. However, that was not the case. The experience of the Christmas Raids, and the continual raiding and counter-raiding of the spring, had hardened many of the green Yankee regiments into effective fighting machines. One such unit was the Twentieth Kentucky Infantry, commanded by Lieutenant Colonel Charles S. Hanson, and it sat astride Morgan's path to the Ohio River at the town of Lebanon, Kentucky. Hanson had received news of the clash at Green River Bridge, and ordered his 380 men to fortify the town against assault. The actions taken by Colonel Hanson perfectly demonstrate the changed leadership of the Federal forces in the region. Since he had no cavalry, Hanson seized citizens' horses and mounted some of his junior officers to act as scouts. Since he had no artillery, and expected Morgan to have plenty, he prepared two stone buildings in the town center for defense, cutting firing holes in the masonry. To buy time for reinforcements to arrive, he sent the bulk of his meager force, 280 men, to act as a skirmish line against the enemy, whose battle line was "about 2 miles in length" and armed with artillery. For two hours the skirmishers fought from farmhouses, barns, and stables, slowly being forced back into the town. Morgan offered Hanson surrender terms, which the Federal colonel refused. Seeing that he could only hold the stone railroad depot, Colonel Hanson ordered his men to conduct a fighting withdrawal to the building, and burned the stock-piled quartermaster supplies in the town. Morgan sent in a second flag of truce, demanding the Federal surrender or "the town would be burned and no quarter shown." Colonel Hanson again refused and continued to fight. Finally, after seven hours of continual fighting, Morgan ordered the Second Kentucky Cavalry to rush the depot. During the final assault, his brother, Captain Thomas Morgan, was killed.[47]

The death of young Tom shocked many of the Second Kentucky, who considered him the favorite of the regiment. Soon, some of the Confederates began to abuse the prisoners and threaten to kill the lot, including Colonel Hanson, until cooler heads prevailed. To punish the Federals, Morgan ordered the prisoners double-timed for nine miles to Springfield, where they were paroled. Along the route, several prisoners died, including two who collapsed from exhaustion and were purposefully run over by artillery carriages, and one who was clubbed to death when he collapsed. Never before had Morgan's men, who still considered themselves the models of Southern chivalry, committed such atrocious deeds. As soon as Colonel Hanson was paroled, he headed for the nearest telegraph station and reported Morgan's strength to Burnside, along with the fate of his men. Morgan never explained why he treated his prisoners with such cruelty, but several factors clearly played a major role. The death of his brother was the spark that set off the flame, but the true reason may have been the growing frustration of Morgan's entire command. In 1862, his raiders easily captured Federal troops and supplies, often without firing a shot. Now, the raiders faced not just a single stubborn enemy regiment, but an entire enemy army that was defending every ford, crossroads, and bridge with dogged determination. Regiments that had fought since 1861 relatively unscathed were now being cut to pieces by accurate rifle fire, and being ordered to storm fortified entrenchments and blockhouses. A final factor added to Morgan's concerns. General Judah's nearly 5,000 Yankee cavalry and mounted infantry, with plenty of artillery, closed the distance with every delay.[48]

Following the capture of Lebanon, Morgan pushed on toward Brandenburg, Kentucky, which Captain Hines's scouts determined as the best crossing point of the Ohio River. Morgan's force, by the time it reached Brandenburg on July 8, had lost nearly 400 men, and now numbered approximately 2,100. While most troopers were riding out of Lebanon, an advance detachment of 100 men, commanded by Captains Taylor and Merriwether, rode directly for Brandenburg, arriving there on July 7. The steamboat *John T. McCombs* docked at the wharf at 2:00 P.M., and was immediately captured by the raiders. A short time later, the steamer *Alice Dean* hove into view, and using emergency signals, the raiders convinced it to pull alongside. It too was seized, and Morgan had his cross-river transport. On the morning of July 8, the remaining 2,000 men and four cannon arrived, and the ferrying of the troops began. After midnight on July 8–9, the last of the Confederate troops were across the river, with the only excitement during the day being an attack by Indiana home guardsmen and the gunboat *Springfield* that was easily driven off by the raiders.[49]

Historians and biographers, and Morgan's men, have considered the actions of the Federal army on July 8 to be a weak response—confused, blinded, and disrupted by the hard-charging Confederate cavalry. Few have considered the fact that a handful of Indiana home guardsmen, most without military training, nearly stopped Morgan's Great Raid. When Morgan's men seized the two steamboats, locals found out almost immediately and notified the Home Guard. Around midnight on July 7–8, just as Morgan's main force arrived at the crossing site, Lieutenant Colonel William J. Irvin, a militia officer from Mauckport, Indiana, had managed to alert both Federal and state authorities to Morgan's position. Then Colonel Irvin did the unexpected. He seized a small steamer, the *Lady Pike*, and had it transport a six-pounder and 100 militiamen to a point several miles from the crossing site. To transport the gun, which did not have a carriage or caisson, the militiamen acquired a farm wagon, and lashed the piece to it. Before dawn, they were in place across the river, ready to contest Morgan's 2,500 men with thirty untrained artillerists and a single cannon tied to the bed of a rickety farm wagon. Normally, such an occurrence would be cause for laughter, but the Confederates did not laugh. As the fog rose, a six-pound shot smashed into the *McCombs* and scattered the waiting Rebels. The more numerous and better trained artillery of the raiders responded, driving the militia away from their gun. Morgan ordered two regiments into the steamers, to force a landing on the far shore for the rest to follow. When the Confederate guns lifted their fire for the crossing, the Indiana militia returned to the cannon and fired a few more shots before the Rebels landed. Morgan's men easily drove off the militia once they had crossed, and believing the danger to have ended, began ferrying men and horses across the river. Suddenly, a small, dark vessel came into view and began firing. The Union gunboat *Springfield*, carrying four small howitzers, bombarded the troops on both shores, and for a full hour prevented further crossings of the river. Only when the *Springfield* ran out of ammunition did it finally retire, and the crossing continued. Later, the gunboat *Elk* repeated the performance, doing little damage to the troops on the shore, but further delaying the raid.[50]

What Morgan and his officers did not realize, despite the information given to him by Captain Hines, was that the militia, though untrained, was not timid, and numbered in the tens of thousands. Prior to this summer, the Home Guards were objects of ridicule for front-line soldiers of both sides, many of whom considered the militia nothing more than bodies of organized draft dodgers. Regardless, a handful of militia and two underarmed gunboats succeeded in delaying Morgan's raid for several more critical hours, and allowed the cavalry pursuit forces of General Hobson to close within a few hours of the raiders. Morgan's rear guard began skirmishing with the lead elements of Hobson's cavalry around midnight, but fog rolled in and covered the Rebel retreat. With the last men across the river, the *Alice Dean* was set aflame, and the *McCombs*, owned by a family friend of Morgan's, was sent upriver to Louisville. The Union cavalry had lost the race to cut Morgan off south of the Ohio River, but now the raider was in the unenviable position of having his route of retreat cut off by Federal gunboats descending from all directions. For the Yankees, the time spent in developing the Home Guards had paid off, but was offset by the poor performance of General Judah's cavalry, who could not close the forty-eight-hour head start given to Morgan when he crossed the Cumberland.[51]

At Corydon, Indiana, on July 9, Morgan's men gained a nickname that tainted the Great Raid for decades afterwards. The handful of militiamen who had resisted the crossing retreated toward Corydon, skirmishing as they went. Morgan's men took no losses and found homes and farms abandoned by their occupants upon hearing of the approaching raiders. The hungry Confederates began looting the homes for food and valuables. The locals reacted to the raiders as could be expected— outlying foraging parties were shot at from houses and barns, while others ran to inform the militia of the raiders' location. Morgan had entered a hornet's nest south of Corydon, with militiamen abandoning the local area to defend the town, while sharpshooters harassed his column. Duplicating Federal retributive burning policy, Morgan ordered houses and farms where suspected ambushers lived burned to the ground. This action further hardened the locals toward the raiders. One of the Confederates, John Ashby, later made a statement that could have easily come from a Federal trooper in the Shenandoah Valley or northern Arkansas, when he said, "we expected actions like that [sniping] from soldiers regularly in the opposing army but not from civilians."[52] At Corydon itself, about 450 home guardsmen were formed on a small hill south of town to resist the Confederates. The poorly armed and drilled militia had little chance of winning. After losing eight killed, and watching the bulk of his men driven from the field, the local commander surrendered his remaining 345 men. In the short skirmish, Morgan lost eleven killed and several wounded. In punishment for resisting his invasion, Morgan released his men to loot the town. Confederate troopers stole cash, jewelry, new horses, and a variety of attractive items—including bolts of calico cloth tied to their saddles—later leading to the derisive name of the expedition, the "Calico Raid."[53]

For the next few days, Morgan's raiders smashed militia unit after militia unit, paroling hundreds of Indianans between Corydon and the Ohio border, but losing irreplaceable hours with each encounter. Having finally crossed the Ohio River, Generals Hobson and Shackelford, with their combined strength of nearly 5,000 cavalry and mounted infantry, continued the pursuit, but were now a full day behind Morgan. From July 9 to July 19, the Federals pushed Morgan's men harder and harder, while Yankee gunboats attempted to cover every crossing north of Louisville, Kentucky. In front of Morgan, the governors of Indiana and Ohio mobilized a total of 115,000 home guardsmen to defend key cities and to delay and harass the invaders. Burnside dispatched additional regular troops on transports to back up the guardsmen and to push General Judah's force forward. Judah, with a full brigade of infantry and cavalry, moved by transport to Portsmouth, Ohio, arriving there on July 17. After sending a messenger to Hobson to continue to push Morgan hard, he moved his troops toward Buffington Island, on the Ohio River, where he guessed Morgan would try to cross. So determined was the Federal pursuit that Morgan had to stop for two full hours on July 15 just to reorganize his division, which had become scattered during the never-ending engagements with the Yankee militia and in fighting rearguard skirmishes with the approaching pursuers.[54]

Morgan was indeed heading toward Buffington Island, where Colonel Duke's scouts had discovered a fording point several weeks before. Duke's scouts had informed Morgan that the water was too shallow for Yankee gunboats, not knowing that Lieutenant Commander Fitch's vessels were specially built shallow-draft vessels capable of crossing the lowest depths in the Ohio River, in contrast to the larger ironclads the raiders had seen along the Tennessee and Cumberland. As he drove forward, Judah demanded that all five available gunboats get to Buffington's Island as soon as possible. In the early hours of July 19, he arrived at the crossing point just as three regiments of Colonel Duke's cavalry were beginning to cross the river. In the river, Fitch's flotilla emerged from the darkness and began pouring shells into the Confederates. Judah's cavalry was initially taken by surprise by the Confederates, who drove the first Federal troopers back. But by 8:00 A.M., Duke's command was in desperate straits. General Hobson's 2,500 troopers had arrived, and the Rebels were being torn by shot and shell from three sides—Judah in the west, Hobson in the north, and Fitch's gunboats on the river. By 9:30 the battle was over. Duke and 573 of his men were prisoners, but they had allowed Morgan and nearly 1,100 cavalrymen to escape the trap.[55]

For the next seven days, Morgan continually lost men to militia ambush, the pursuing regular cavalry, and to exhaustion. Years after the war, Colonel D. Howard Smith, commander of the Fifth Kentucky Cavalry (Confederate), remembered that the "fatigue was fearful," and that many of the troopers slept in their saddles as comrades led their horses. Suddenly, every ford and crossing that had been reconnoitered by Morgan's scouts seemed to crawl with Union troops. On July 20, near Eight Mile Island (in the Ohio River, opposite of Cheshire, Ohio), a group of 300 of Morgan's men, who had been separated from the command after the fight at Buffington Island, attempted to cross the river, but instead slammed directly into General Shackelford's force. After a short truce, the 300 raiders surrendered to the Federal cavalry. Leaving a small guard detachment to cover the prisoners, the remainder raced northward.[56] Militia detachments gobbled up small groups of the raiders who had been drawn away from the main force; 54 surrendered on July 21, 100 more on July 23, an additional 200 on July 25. Morgan, with his remaining 400 men, tried to cross the Ohio one last time, and make a break to freedom in the mountains of West Virginia. His objective in the last days of the raid was the bridge at New Lisbon, Ohio. What Morgan did not know was that, in addition to the estimated 10,000 Federal cavalry converging from all directions, three companies of fresh militia protected the bridge and had mined it for destruction. As Morgan approached the town, he sent a flag of truce to try to convince the local militia commander to allow his men passage on the bridge, promising not to burn New Lisbon in return. During the negotiations, the raiding chieftain had a change of heart. Many of his men were wounded and all were barely capable of riding a horse. So instead he offered the surrender of the remainder of his command to the militia. Knowing that the regular troops were only an hour or two behind, Morgan tried to convince the militia captain that he and his men should be paroled and set free in lieu of going to prison camp. The militiaman agreed, and at 12:30 P.M. on July 26, 1863, twenty-four days and nearly a thousand miles later, the tattered remnants of Morgan's command surrendered. An hour and a half later, the first pursuing column arrived on the scene and its commander, Major George W. Rue, Ninth Kentucky Cavalry (Union), voided the surrender terms and took Morgan and his 336 men as prisoners of war. The Great Raid was over.[57]

Since the end of the Great Raid, scholars and participants have tried to find a silver lining to Morgan's defeat. Some, such as Colonel Duke, contend that the raid managed to tie down Federal troops that would have denied the Confederacy the victory at Chickamauga in September. Others assert that Morgan managed to delay Burnside's invasion of eastern Tennessee and that his actions saved the Confederacy from a disaster and, combined with the millions of dollars in damages that the raiders caused, justified the operation.[58] There is no direct evidence for either hypothesis. First, the troops who chased Morgan did not come from the Army of the Cumberland, but from the Department of the Ohio. The men of the XXIII Corps, especially General Judah's Third Division, accomplished the mission they were specifically ordered to perform—to detect and destroy Confederate raiders crossing into Kentucky. Rosecrans marched his army from Tullahoma to Chattanooga with little resistance, and without dispatching a single soldier from his command to chase Morgan.

As for the second theory, that Morgan delayed Burnside's Army of the Ohio, there is some evidence to demonstrate that the Federals were delayed, but not to the extent proposed. Burnside's army, with the exceptions of Hartsuff's XXIII Corps and much of the cavalry, had not taken an active part in the pursuit but had held its position in eastern Kentucky and southern Ohio, preparing for the upcoming campaign toward Knoxville. When the Federals began the eastern Tennessee campaign on August 20, the maximum delay that Morgan's raid could be credited with was only twenty days. Had the Great Raid not taken place, and Morgan's force still existed, Burnside would have been forced to leave substantial numbers of men behind to cover the vulnerable railroads and depots of central Tennessee and Kentucky. With Morgan out of action, Burnside was able to bring the entire XXIII Corps, nearly 15,000 men, along as the primary fighting force of the invasion. Few troops were left behind to guard against raids simply because with Morgan gone and Forrest locked into screening Bragg's flanks, there were no Confederate raiders left. Rather than hampering Burnside's offensive by his raid, Morgan's defeat and capture guaranteed the overwhelming of the undermanned defenses of Knoxville by freeing up an entire Federal corps.[59]

The third, and perhaps most damaging, outcome of the Great Raid was that it closed the end of Morgan's career as a raider. His capture spelt the end of the elite regiments he had brought with him from Kentucky in 1861. Their experience and skills were forever lost to the Confederacy. Morgan himself, who had been applauded as a "Southern Paladin" in newspapers, suddenly was perceived as a maverick by Confederate leaders. After his spectacular escape from the Ohio State Penitentiary in November 1863, Morgan was denied a field command for months.[60] When he did return to active duty, he was given what one historian calls "the worse soldiers in the Confederacy." His final raid into Kentucky in 1864 was a feeble reflection of his previous glory. Morgan succeeded in capturing a few home guardsmen and destroying some easily replaceable Federal property. His new troopers, in contrast to the disciplined ranks of his 1862–63 raiders, were accused by citizens in Kentucky of a range of crimes, from attempted rape to pillaging. The attitude of many Southerners toward Morgan changed after the Indiana-Ohio raid. Mrs. James B. Clay, writing to her husband, summarized the entire raid for many Confederate civilians: the Great Raid "seems to be, so far, but a feeble effort attended by some sad events."[61] Confederate officers, such as staff officer Captain Edward O. Guerrant, who had previously praised Morgan, now attacked him. In one diary entry, written in June 1864, Guerrant noted that "people [are] generally down on Morgan. [It was] published in the Bristol paper that he was 'safely back with five fine horses.' They cost 500 men."[62] His attitude was much like that of the Confederate leaders at the time, that Morgan "was a very clever man, but don't admire him as a General."[63] Morgan tried to win back his status as a great raider, an attempt that ultimately cost him his life. In contrast, his companion in the 1862 operations,

Forrest, graduated to the higher levels of military leadership and removed himself from small-scale raiding forever.[64]

The beginning of 1863 boded well for the Confederate raiders, based on the events of 1862. Forrest's and Morgan's cavalry had run rampant over the dazed Federal defenders, leaving burning bridges, demoralized soldiers, and looted depots in their wake. As 1863 began, both armies evaluated their performance in this oldest form of organized irregular warfare. For the Confederacy, raiding had proven to be a useful strategy that took full advantage of the legendary Southern capability of independent, aggressive action and horsemanship. Additionally, the raider chieftains themselves provided a needed morale boost to the home front, especially in light of the carnage at Shiloh, Antietam, and Stones River. Thus, the new year promised to hold even greater possibilities for their raiders, and grand schemes were concocted for Morgan and Forrest to execute.

The Federal army, in stark contrast, evaluated its defenses against raiding and found them sorely wanting. Blockhouses were half finished and poorly armed, units assigned to secure the railroads were second rate at best and demoralized by their defeats at the hands of the raiders, and the Federal cavalry was lacking everything from qualified troopers to horses. The Confederates, confident in their ability to repeat their 1862 performance, were content to replace their lost mounts and men and continue the raiding war in the spring. The Federals, realizing that the deeper they moved into the interior of the South the more vulnerable they became to raiding, initiated sweeping changes in their antiraiding strategy. Federal officers, especially General Rosecrans, used the Northern dominance in manpower and industry to develop the Union cavalry into an effective fighting force, rebuild the dilapidated blockhouses and railroad defenses, and implement administrative changes within the army itself to prepare for the expected summer raiding campaign. These reforms transformed the Federal armies in Tennessee and Kentucky into forces perfectly suited for antiraiding operations.

The Confederates, hampered to some extent by overconfidence from their wildly successful raids of the previous year and by internal dissension within the high command of the Army of Tennessee, launched their late spring and early summer raids against the Union army. The early raids only served to warn the Federals that the raiding season had begun. Federal raids against the Confederates at Chattanooga, such as Streight's disastrous raid into northern Alabama, were failures, but served to exhaust the available Confederate cavalry.

When Morgan launched his Great Raid, he rode into a maelstrom and did so without the support of other raiding expeditions. Part of the Confederate success in 1862 was based on hitting the Federals at different points, and keeping the defenders scrambling about looking for them. In the Great Raid, Morgan was on his own; Bragg's withdrawal from Tullahoma to Chattanooga relieved even more pressure on the Federal army and freed additional units to pursue Morgan. Initially, the Federals made several tactical mistakes and allowed Morgan's division to cross the Cumberland River without seriously impeding its advance. Some historians have seen this as a tactical failure on the part of the Union army, and evidence of the superiority of the Rebel horsemen. In reality, Morgan's crossing of the Cumberland encouraged him to go deeper into Federal territory and farther away from friendly lines. As he pushed farther north, Union units closed in behind him, isolating him from retreat along the same route. Ahead of him, militia forces, although limited in effectiveness, appeared in huge numbers, and were soon joined by regular Union cavalry and infantry from across the northwest. Ultimately Morgan's entire division was rendered hors de combat. Many were captured with no chance of parole or exchange, denying the Confederacy what was arguably the single most effective cavalry division of the Civil War.

Confederate overconfidence, combined with the inventiveness and flexibility of Federal commanders in confronting the raiding threat, negated raiding as a strategy in 1863. After that summer, the Confederacy tried other raids, but when facing a veteran Union cavalry, fortified rail lines, the overwhelming material might of the North, and the slow attrition of their own mounted units, they had little chance of changing the course of the war. The summer of 1863 was the last real opportunity for organized raiding by conventional cavalry forces, the most acceptable form of irregular warfare to the Confederate army, to have a decisive role. The surrender of Morgan on a riverbank in Ohio was, in an important way, evidence to the Confederacy that the Federal antiraiding campaign had decisively beaten them, confirming that the successes of 1862 would never happen again.

CONCLUSION

The End of the Uncivil War

Any man who is in favor of a further prosecution of this war is a fit
subject for a lunatic asylum, and ought to be sent there immediately.
Nathan Bedford Forrest, 1865, in
*May I Quote You General Forrest? Observations and
Utterances from the South's Great Generals*, 1997

On a misty April morning, a group of weather-beaten and exhausted
men gathered in one of the few remaining tents belonging to a
once-proud army. General Robert E. Lee and his officers assembled for
one last meeting, to discuss the advisability of surrendering their starving
men to the Federal Army of the Potomac and the Union commander,
General Ulysses S. Grant. The last hope of the Rebel army, the supplies
at Appomattox Station, had just been captured by Yankee cavalry, and
blue-coated infantry had closed off every route of escape.

As Lee spoke to his officers, the possibility of further resistance
was suggested by his chief of artillery, thirty-year-old Brigadier General Edward P. Alexander. Alexander proposed that the entire 25,000-
man army be broken up into small groups with orders to report to their
state governors for duty, to carry on a guerrilla war now that the conventional war had ended. Lee allowed Alexander to finish speaking,

and then simply stated: "We must consider its effect on the country as a whole . . . already it is demoralized by the four years of war. If I took your advice, the men would be without rations and under no control of officers. They would be compelled to rob and steal in order to live. They would become mere bands of marauders, and the enemy's cavalry would pursue them and overrun many sections they may never have occasion to visit. We would bring on a state of affairs it would take the country years to recover from. . . . [Y]ou young fellows might go bushwhacking, but the only dignified course for me would be, to go to General Grant and surrender myself and take the consequences of my acts." Alexander later wrote: "I had not a single word to say in reply. He had answered my suggestion from a plane so far above it that I was ashamed of having made it."[1]

In a letter to Confederate president Jefferson Davis, Lee repeated his contention that a guerrilla war was not only militarily unsound but also inhumane. "A partisan war may be continued, and hostilities protracted, causing individual suffering and the devastation of the country," Lee wrote, "but I see no prospect by that means of achieving a separate independence." With few exceptions, mostly in the isolated Ozarks and Appalachian Mountains, Confederate soldiers surrendered their weapons, swore their allegiance to the Union, and tried to rebuild their lives.[2]

Some Confederate leaders, most notably President Davis, attempted to push the concept of a widespread guerrilla war, despite the advice of Lee and others. Even Davis's own cabinet, especially Secretary of State Judah Benjamin, recommended surrender over guerrilla warfare. Benjamin wrote Davis on April 22, 1865, telling him that since the conventional forces were unable to continue fighting, "the struggle can no longer be maintained in any other manner than by a guerrilla or partisan warfare. Such a warfare is not, in my opinion, desirable, nor does it promise any useful result." Almost verbatim to Lee's admonition to his officers calling for surrender over guerrilla war, Benjamin added: "It [guerrilla warfare] would entail far more suffering on our own people than it would cause damage to the enemy; and the people have been such heavy sufferers by the calamities of the war for the last four years that it is at least questionable whether they would be willing to engage in such a contest unless forced to endure its horrors in preference to dishonor and degradation."[3]

But why? Why did the Confederates lay down their arms after one of the most bitter and destructive wars in the nineteenth century? Lee's personality and example, and Confederate adoration for "Marse Robert," clearly had some influence, but why did Lee's surrender end an irregular war in the backwoods of Arkansas, the hidden valleys of the Blue Ridge Mountains, or the barrens of Tennessee? Exactly why didn't the South continue the war, using the concepts of irregular warfare accepted and understood in the nineteenth century?

This difficult question, which has been debated by scholars since 1865, is answered in every chapter of this work. The Confederacy tried irregular warfare during the war, and in each attempt was thwarted by the Union army. While the Federal successes were never a hundred percent cure for irregular warfare, the experience against Mosby being the most obvious example, the Union army proved that it could mitigate the damage, or even roll back the effects, of any irregular war. Consequently, the three methods of irregular war known and accepted in the nineteenth century—guerrilla, or "people's war," partisan warfare, and raiding warfare—had been tested by the Rebels and found wanting. Numerous reasons exist for the failure of each type of unconventional warfare. At the heart of the matter was a lack of a cohesive Confederate strategy for irregular operations. With the exception of congressional support for partisan warfare through the Partisan Ranger Act of 1862, Confederate leaders at Richmond did all in their power to prevent or hinder the growth of irregular warfare, clearly preferring conventional war. Tight controls were placed on the mobilization of additional guerrilla and partisan ranger companies; most of these men ended up as regular infantry. In 1864, at the insistence of General Lee and other commanders, the Partisan Ranger Act was revoked, and only a few state-sponsored partisan units, Lieutenant Colonel John S. Mosby's Forty-third Virginia Cavalry, and the irregulars west of the Mississippi were kept intact.[4]

In Arkansas, Confederate authorities attempted to raise the masses to stop the Federals' invasion in 1862 and released the terror of state-sponsored guerrilla warfare on the region. Using General Orders Number 17, Confederate General Thomas C. Hindman gave legal protection to ten-man bands of guerrillas that sprang up across the state. Initially they were successful in harassing the Federals while Rebels built a new conventional army. The Confederate defeat at Prairie

Grove in December 1862, and the abandonment of the guerrilla companies, doomed the irregular campaign in the state.

In contrast, the Union army progressively improved and developed their counterirregular program and ultimately defeated the Rebel guerrilla war. The Federals initially used an antiguerrilla response in 1862, content to beat back the cloud of irregulars surrounding their armies. Later, when reconstructing the state became an issue, the Federal command showed its inventiveness and flexibility by converting to counterinsurgency. Loyal Arkansans were organized into counterguerrilla units and given the responsibility to secure the hinterland from the guerrillas. A variety of programs were introduced to restrict and reduce popular support for irregulars, including fortified farm colonies, punitive raids and expeditions, and the use of spies and the Federal military law enforcement system. The Rebel guerrillas found themselves, by April 1865, hunted by both Union and Confederate forces, hated by their neighbors and the government that sponsored them. The Confederate experiment in "people's war" was a disaster, as the guerrillas were denied needed oversight by conventional military forces, logistical support, and finally moral support of the populace. The Arkansas guerrilla bands became bushwhackers, preying on the weak and helpless to survive.[5]

Partisan warfare, a concept that had a long history in America, took root in northern Virginia. Unlike the guerrillas in Arkansas, the most successful of the Confederate partisans, Colonel Mosby and his Forty-third Virginia Cavalry, won the admiration and support of the Confederate high command. On the surface, widespread use of partisan warfare appeared to have a greater chance of success than guerrilla warfare. But the success of Mosby's Rangers turned out to be an aberration. Mosby's personality, innate leadership abilities, and support from Confederate military leaders, especially Lee, allowed him to keep his battalion operating behind enemy lines. Helping Mosby's cause further, his officers and many of his men were of the upper classes of antebellum society; they were men who did not want to change the social status quo, who knew their place within their culture, and tried to uphold their personal concepts of chivalry and honor throughout the war. The Forty-third Virginia was an exception to partisan warfare during the Civil War, and Lee and other Southern leaders understood that. Despite all the advantages of class and training within Mosby's battalion, the danger of losing control of the partisans was always present.

Consequently, the rangers' most successful operations were those involving only a handful of men led by Mosby and his most competent officers. The weaknesses of the partisan system were evidenced by Mosby's inability to gather large numbers of irregulars on a constant basis, and by his use of captured materials as bribes to his men to keep them loyal and motivated.

Mosby's partisan operations were the most successful of the Confederacy, yet the Federal army succeeded in limiting the damage he could cause. In response to Mosby's operations, the Union army built a system of blockhouses to defend vulnerable railroads and other strategic targets, and stationed a large number of men in the area between the Blue Ridge Mountains and the defenses of Washington, D.C., to hinder partisan operations. When those programs did not stop Mosby, a punitive expedition was launched down the Shenandoah Valley to sweep it clean of both food for Lee's army and irregulars for Mosby's war. General Philip Sheridan's 1864 Valley campaign was both a conventional operation and an antipartisan sweep, and was moderately successful in both cases. Although Mosby continued his operations until the end of the war, the damage he caused was negligible when compared with the overwhelming resources available to the Union. Robbing a few trains, destroying some railroad track, and capturing a Federal general were embarrassing to the Union, but never threatened its ability to field and support the largest of its armies. Mosby's raiders had also been beaten by the Union army, through both their antipartisan operations and programs and by the might of the Northern industrial machine. Operating against the developed transportation network of northern Virginia and with his small group of men, Mosby could neither destroy enough Federal property to affect the war nor damage the numerous road and rail supply lines to the Army of the Potomac.

The third and final aspect of the Confederacy's irregular war was the raiding war. Although this work concentrates on Kentucky and Tennessee in the western theater, organized raiding occurred as well in the East and the trans-Mississippi region. What made Tennessee and Kentucky different from Virginia or Arkansas was that the Confederates formed cavalry brigades, and later cavalry divisions, and gave them the specific mission of raiding. Two of the greatest cavalry leaders of the war, John Hunt Morgan and Nathan Bedford Forrest, applied their considerable skills and abilities to achieve this mission. Through their actions, the possibility existed for the Confederates to use large-scale raiding by *conventional cavalry* forces to disrupt Union plans and as a viable defense against the Federal armies. In 1862, both Morgan and Forrest enjoyed numerous successes, destroying millions of dollars in Federal property and bringing General Don Carlos Buell's 1862 campaign to a halt in middle Tennessee. In December 1862, both Rebel horsemen again demonstrated their skills by hitting the vulnerable railroads supporting Grant and Rosecrans.

As in Arkansas and Virginia, the Confederates had initial success, only to be countered by the Federal army. The winter and early spring of 1862–63 was a time of reform for the Union forces in the western theater, as an antiraiding strategy was developed and implemented. They improved their cavalry, built fortifications, constructed gunboats, and raised Home Guards and militia throughout the Old Northwest. A series of Federal counter-raids, including the failed operation of Colonel Abel Streight and several successful cavalry expeditions into eastern Tennessee in the spring of 1863, exhausted and weakened the Confederate troopers before the summer raiding season had even begun. When Morgan launched his Great Raid into Indiana and Ohio in July 1863, it was doomed from the start. For nearly a month, the raiders were pursued by the Union army and shelled by navy gunboats, and in the process lost nearly 2,500 irreplaceable cavalrymen and severely damaged Southern morale without appreciable gain. Although raids continued in all theaters until the end of the war, their use was much more limited than during 1862–63. The end of the raiding war in Tennessee and Kentucky in 1863 marked the end of raiding as a major part of the Confederacy's strategy to win its independence.

Despite the Rebel failure to win the irregular war, scholars since 1865 have discussed why the South did not turn to guerrilla warfare after Appomattox. In the 1970s, with the recent defeat in Vietnam still stinging the American consciousness, some Civil War historians began to ask why the South did not adopt a Maoist "war of national liberation" and achieve independence by eroding the North's will to fight.[6] Several major factors argue against the possibility of such a war. The first group of factors can be generally classified as moral issues, ideas that are intangible but vital to a widespread guerrilla war in the twentieth century. These include the lack of a cohesive ideology in the South to unify all Southerners to support the Confederacy, antebellum political and economic divisiveness that hindered national unity, and the varying reasons individual Rebels fought, such as to resist invasion, win independence, and support the slave system. Added to the equation was the lack of a political system diametrically opposed to that of the enemy and the lack of Confederate nationalism. Unlike wars in the twentieth century, the Civil War did not present two divergent political systems in conflict; in fact, it represents one of the few examples of two democracies at war. Southern nationalism, according to some historians, was so weak that it barely existed in sufficient amounts to support a conventional war, much less a brutal guerrilla conflict. In the realm of ideas, the Confederacy lacked those critical components—ideology and nationalism—necessary for a successful guerrilla war.[7]

The second reason the Confederacy could not fight a guerrilla war after 1865 is the subject of this work—military constraints. In the twentieth century, theorists and guerrilla leaders, such as Mao Tse-tung, Vladimir Lenin, and Che Guevara, developed a doctrine for guerrilla warfare based on Marxist ideology that included both an ideological and a military component. Such a concept did not exist in the nineteenth century. Clausewitz and Jomini, if accepted as reflecting the ideas and feeling of their time, presented a simplistic framework for irregular warfare focused on military concepts alone. As one would expect from members of the European elite, both authors contended that irregular warfare existed with the threat of anarchy looming in the background. Only stern discipline administered by conventionally trained officers could control irregulars, and ensure that they adhered to a campaign strategy aimed at fighting a single, decisive battle. This concept was proven in the American Civil War by the operations of Mosby in northern Virginia. Of the three modes of irregular warfare of the era, only the Clausewitzian "people's war" comes close to a twentieth-century concept of guerrilla warfare, which was considered by both the Union and Confederate armies as no more than brigandage. Their attitude was backed by military convention of the period and by international law and custom; the fate of captured guerrillas in Arkansas varied little from the fate of Turkish partisans captured by Russians in 1806, and that of Spanish guerrillas and Russian raiders executed by the French in 1809 and 1812, respectively.

Finally, the basic military concept of logistics is often overlooked by historians focusing on intangibles such as national morale and ideology. The simple reality of fighting a guerrilla war is that the guerrilla fighters must be supplied and sustained from somewhere. Since European assistance was clearly out of the question by 1865, given the overwhelming naval and military power of the United States in the Western Hemisphere and its apparent eagerness to use that force on any regional threat, the Confederates could only look to the Southern populace for logistical support.[8] General Joe Johnson, commanding the Army of Tennessee in April 1865, quickly rejected that possibility in his decision to surrender to General William T. Sherman, noting that "the impossibility of recruiting our little army, opposed by more than ten times its number, *or of supplying it except by robbing our own citizens*, destroyed all hope of successful war."[9]

Other factors played importantly in the mix and provide perhaps the central reasons that Lee and his men did not take to the hills and fight in April 1865. As demonstrated in Arkansas, Virginia, Tennessee, and Kentucky, the Federal army was substantially more inventive and original than has been acknowledged before, and developed a wide variety of counterinsurgency techniques, including the use of loyalist units, farm colonies, blockhouses, and specialized anti-irregular units. Finally, the Confederates themselves were adverse to a "people's war," unless it was one based on their own concepts of states' rights and rule by the antebellum planter class. Theirs was a conservative revolution, aimed at maintaining the status quo and guaranteeing additional rights and privileges to the upper classes. A Confederate "people's war," if fought as such conflicts were in the twentieth century, would have forced the South to appeal to the poorest rural farmers and laborers, who would form the guerrilla armies needed to fight such a war. The Vietnamese and Chinese revolutions, for example, used land reform and the redistribution of wealth to motivate the working classes to fight, both of which were unthinkable to the Southern aristocracy in 1861. A second option, used extensively by Mosby and many of the less organized guerrilla bands, used the cohesive power of plunder for motivation. A twentieth-century-style guerrilla war would have depended on the lower classes to provide the needed manpower, which would have disrupted the precariously balanced Southern society as permanently as the emancipation of slaves. The second option, allowing the guerrillas to plunder at will, would have resulted in much of the South, previously untouched by war, resembling Arkansas in 1865, with burned houses, refugees, and a strong Federal counterinsurgency army built around Unionists and freed slaves.[10]

When Lee and his generals stood around a smoldering campfire and made their decision not to continue the war, they had more to consider than the perceived inhumanity of guerrilla warfare and their part in continuing the war through irregular means. Although they might not have dwelt on it in detail, the simple fact existed that the Confederacy had been fighting an irregular war, as defined in nineteenth-century military theory and practice, since early in the conflict. In some areas, unorganized bushwhackers had taken to the hills as soon as the war began. In passing the Partisan Ranger Act in April 1862, the Confederate Congress had signaled that irregular warfare was part of its overall strategy to win the war and gain independence, but the Rebels had been conducting such a war well before it was codified in law. The entire spectrum of unconventional warfare, from guerrillas to partisans to raiders, was used since 1861, and each failed. The collapse of the Rebel irregular war was due to Confederate mismanagement and other administrative failures, lack of support for the program from conventionally trained officers, and tactical mistakes by irregular leaders that gave the Federal army the opportunity to beat the Rebels on the open field. Ultimately, the collapse of the Confederacy in April 1865, and the rejection of a postwar guerrilla conflict by most Confederate leaders, ended the guerrilla war.

Underlying the Confederate mistakes are the Union successes. The Northern armies have long been seen as a lumbering monolith, slowly beating their enemy through overwhelming manpower and industry.[11] The irregular war was different; much as the Confederate leaders found the entire effort distasteful, so did many Federal commanders. Consequently, Union officers fighting irregulars often did so with second-rate and underequipped troops and locally raised forces. The only exceptions to this were when the irregulars became a serious threat to conventional operations, as in Tennessee and Kentucky in early 1863. The Federal army won through a combination of inventive counterinsurgency programs, creative use of their material superiority to save manpower in rear-area defensive missions, and by raising and training their own specialized antiguerrilla, antipartisan, and antiraiding forces.

In 1865, when the generals of the Army of Northern Virginia stood around Lee and argued for an irregular war in lieu of surrendering, of course they did so with a vision of unconventional warfare based on the era in which they lived. The young officers whom Lee allowed to speak had little understanding or experience outside of the conventional forces, while Lee, who had been privy to the high command of the Confederacy since its inception, had a larger view of the war. When Lee spoke against dispersing his army as guerrillas, he understood something that his generals did not: Irregular warfare had been tried and had been beaten as surely as his army had been.

APPENDIX A

The Partisan Ranger Act

GENERAL ORDERS No. 30.

WAR DEPARTMENT,

ADJT. AND INSP. GENERAL'S OFFICE,

Richmond, April 28, 1862.

I. The following acts, having passed both Houses of Congress, were duly approved by the President, and are now published for the information of the Army:

AN ACT to organize bands of partisan rangers.

SECTION 1. The Congress of the Confederate States of America do enact, That the President be, and he is hereby, authorized to commission such officers as he may deem proper with authority to form bands of partisan rangers, in companies, battalions or regiments, either as infantry or cavalry, the companies, battalions or regiments to be composed each of such numbers as the President may approve.

SEC. 2. Be it further enacted, That such partisan rangers, after being regularly received into service, shall be entitled to the same pay, rations and quarters during their term of service, and be subject to the same regulations as other soldiers.

SEC. 3. Be it further enacted, That for any arms and munitions of war captured from the enemy by any body of partisan rangers and delivered to any quartermaster at such place or places as may be designated by a commanding general, the rangers shall be paid their full value in such manner as the Secretary of War may prescribe.

Approved April 21, 1862.

V.—ADDITIONAL CORPS—GUERRILLA SERVICE.

12. Under the prohibition of this act against the organization of new corps, no further authority for that purpose can be given, except that specially provided for in the act of Congress entitled "An act to organize bands of partisan rangers." For this latter purpose applications must be made through the commanding generals of the military departments in which the said corps are to be employed.

By command of the Secretary of War:

S. COOPER,
Adjutant and Inspector General.

The Partisan Ranger Act was only a small part of the entire War Department general order issued in April 1862. It included directives on the raising of new conventional units, the use of substitutes, and the election of officers as well. The selection here includes only those sections applicable to irregular warfare. See *OR*, series 4, vol. 3, 1094–1100.

APPENDIX B

GENERAL ORDERS NUMBER 17
HEADQUARTERS, TRANS-MISSISSIPPI DISTRICT

HDQRS. TRANS-MISSISSIPPI DISTRICT,
Little Rock, Ark., June 17, 1862.

I. For the more effectual annoyance of the enemy upon our rivers and in our mountains and woods all citizens of this district who are not subject to conscription are called upon to organize themselves into independent companies of mounted men or infantry, as they prefer, arming and equipping themselves, and to serve in that part of the district to which they belong.

II. When as many as 10 men come together for this purpose they may organize by electing a captain, 1 sergeant, 1 corporal, and will at once commence operations against the enemy without waiting for special instructions. Their duty will be to cut off Federal pickets, scouts, foraging parties, and trains, and to kill pilots and others on gunboats and transports, attacking them day and night, and using the greatest vigor in their movements. As soon as the company attains the strength required by law it will proceed to elect the other officers to which it is entitled. All such organizations will be reported to these headquarters

as soon as practicable. They will receive pay and allowances for subsistence and forage for the time actually in the field, as established by
the affidavits of their captains.

III. These companies will be governed in all respects by the same
regulations as other troops. Captains will be held responsible for the
good conduct and efficiency of their men, and will report to these headquarters from time to time.

By command of Major-General Hindman:

R. G. Newton,
Assistant Adjutant General.

"General Orders Number 17," 17 June 1862, *OR*, series 1, vol. 13, 835.
Officially, because General Hindman was commander of the entire Trans-Mississippi District, his directive applied not only to Arkansas but also to much
of Texas, Missouri, and Louisiana.

NOTES

INTRODUCTION

1. The issue of tactics versus strategy is critical in understanding irregular warfare. Often, a force fighting from ambush is credited as a "guerrilla" unit, while in reality it could have been a conventional organization using terrain and concealment to their advantage. Such misnomers are common even early in the twenty-first century, as media outlets often call any attack from ambush a "guerrilla attack."

2. Lieber, *Guerrilla Parties*, 12. Emphasis added.

3. The concept of light infantry was first introduced in America during the French and Indian (Seven Years') War by British officers serving in North America. General William Howe, who commanded British forces during the first years of the American Revolution, had much to do with its development. Howe's idea was for a light-moving, elite striking force able to fight the French and their Indian allies on equal terms. The light infantry was so successful that the development of light companies within the British infantry regiments became common practice. In many ways, the light troops of the French and Indian War are forerunners of Civil War partisan rangers, such as Lieutenant Colonel John S. Mosby's Forty-third Virginia Cavalry, "Mosby's Rangers" (see chaps. 3 and 4). See Leckie, *George Washington's War*, 145–46; and Matheny, "Impact of the Frontier." The initial concept of light infantry was developed by the famous military theoretician and commander Marshal de Saxe in his *Reveries* (1732). Several excellent works trace the beginnings of the light infantry approach. See Fuller, *British Light Infantry*; and Quimby, *Background of Napoleonic War*.

4. Roughly translated, *jägers*, or hunters, are light infantry and cavalry especially trained to operate in small detachments. They are the forerunners of modern light infantry forces, such as parachute, commando, and Ranger units. See the introductory essay in Ewald, *Treatise on Partisan Warfare*, 29–31.

5. Ibid., 21–22, 24, 27. The analysis by Selig and Skaggs, translators of *Treatise on Partisan Warfare*, of Von Ewald's contribution is excellent; however, they tend to see the American Revolution as the first so-called revolutionary war of the pattern that became notable in the twentieth century. The concept of the American Revolution as a "people's war" has been debated for decades, and is still open to discussion. For contrasting views of this topic, see Higginbotham, *War of American Independence*, and Weigley, *American Way of War*.

6. Lieber, *Guerrilla Parties*, 17.

7. John R. Eakin, "Guerrillas!" Washington (Arkansas) *Telegraph*, 21 May 1862; a similar editorial calling for guerrillas was written in the Richmond (Virginia) *Enquirer* in late May 1861, as noted by Stan Cohen in *The Civil War in West Virginia*.

8. Letter from Captain W. J. McArthur, Assistant Adjutant General to Brigadier General J. O. Shelby, to Lieutenant Colonel Joseph Love, 7 June 1864, U.S. War Department, *The War of the Rebellion: A Compilation of the Official Records of the Union and Confederate Armies*, series 1, vol. 34, pt. 4, 653 (hereafter *OR*).

9. Stated by Charles Lieb in his biography, *Nine Months in the Quartermaster's Department: Or the Chances of Making a Million* (Cincinnati: Moore, Wilstach, Keys, and Co., 1962), cited in Matheny, *Wood County*, 50–51

10. Heartsill, *Fourteen Hundred and 91 Days*, 221.

11. Carl von Clausewitz, trans. J. J. Graham, *On War* (London: N. Trubner and Company, 1873),4:174. Although Graham's translation was one of the first in English, many historians consider the 1976 Michael Howard and Peter Paret translation to be superior. In this case, the Graham and Howard/Paret translations are basically the same. See Clausewitz, trans. Michael Howard and Peter Paret, *On War*, 480. The 1976 translation will be used throughout this work.

12. For many years, scholars doubted the influence of Clausewitz on Western military thought prior to the late 1870s. Christopher Bassford, in his *Clausewitz in English*, rejects this assumption. Bassford contends that knowledge of Clausewitz's work had spread to the United States by the 1850s, and that the first publication of Clausewitz in America (in 1873) was a response to demand. The possibility exists that Civil War generals and political leaders had some knowledge of *On War*, but the influence the work did or did not have during the era is unclear. See Bassford, 50–55.

13. In his book on U.S. Army counterinsurgency in Vietnam, Larry Cable defines two types of irregular warfare in the twentieth century, partisan and insurgent. Cable ignores nineteenth-century unconventional warfare, but uses the terminology of Clausewitz and others to try to define the war in Vietnam. Consequently, Cable's definition of *partisan* is based on World War II unconventional warfare in the Soviet Union and the Balkans, while his insurgent

model draws on Communist guerrilla movements led by Mao Tse-tung and Ho Chi Minh. See. Cable, *Conflict of Myths*, 4–5.

14. Clausewitz, *On War*, 481.

15. The terrain of the Upper South played a major role not only in respect to the conduct of irregular warfare but in the development of pro-Union forces in the region. Arkansas, Virginia, and Tennessee all had strong Unionist populations, concentrated in the mountainous regions of each state. The reasons behind these Unionist sympathizers include the lack of slave-based agriculture, immigration patterns, and mistrust of strong central authorities, especially after the Confederate Conscription Acts of 1862. For a discussion of Unionists in Arkansas, see Dougan, *Confederate Arkansas*; Woods, *Rebellion and Realignment*; Thompson, *Arkansas and Reconstruction*. Tennessee is discussed in Ash, *Middle Tennessee Society Transformed*, and Virginia's Unionists are examined in Shanks, *Secession Movement in Virginia*.

16. The influence of Jomini's teachings on the West Point-trained senior officers of both the Union and Confederate armies is debatable. West Point, in the antebellum era, did not have a specific course on military history or military theory. Instead, Professor Dennis Hart Mahan integrated teachings on the art of war in his engineering courses, and sponsored a "Napoleon Club" that included both George McClellan and Henry Halleck as its members. From this evidence, some historians have surmised that the teachings of Jomini, through Mahan, were passed to the cadets who later led the armies of the Civil War. For additional information on the debate, see Dupuy, *Men of West Point*, 12–24; Dupuy and Dupuy, *Military Heritage of America*, 191–94; Perret, *Country Made by War*, 252–53; Morrison, "Best School in the World," 96–98; Millis, *Arms and Men*, 107–108; Cunliffe, *Soldiers and Civilians*, 389–92; T. Harry Williams, "Military Leadership"; Connelly and Jones, *Politics of Command*; McWhiney and Jameson, *Attack and Die*; and Vandiver, *Their Tattered Flags*, 88–89.

17. Jomini, *Art of War*, 246.

18. Ibid., 201–202.

19. Jomini, *Treatise*, 336.

20. Jomini, *Art of War*, 204–205. The Partisan Ranger Act is discussed in chapter 3 and 5 and is included verbatim as appendix A. French experiences in North Africa may have also had some impact. In *Military Thought in the French Army, 1815–51*, Paddy Griffith contends that the bloody guerrilla war in Algeria and the domestic revolts in France in the 1820s and 1830s helped to shape French military thought, as reflected in the works of Jomini and other theorists. See Griffith, 32–50, 56–57. See chapters 5 and 6 for a discussion of the reorganization of Confederate cavalry in 1863 in Tennessee.

21. Weigley, *American Way of War*, 18–39; see also Leach, *Arms for Empire*. Matthews, ed., *Public Laws of the Confederate States*, 48. Letter from General R. E. Lee to General Samuel Cooper, 1 April 1864, in Lee, *Wartime Papers*, 688. U.S. Congress, Senate, *Journal of the Congress of the Confederate States*, 58th Cong., 2nd sess., S. Doc. 234, vol. 6, 801–802, 828.

22. All definitions are either directly taken from the U.S. Army's *Field Manual FM 31-16: Counter-Guerrilla Operations*, 4–6, and *Field Manual FM*

90-8: Counter-Guerrilla Operations, or are extrapolations by the author from modern texts on counterinsurgency warfare.

23. Asprey, *War in the Shadows,* 110–11, 161–62; General Orders Number 2, 13 March 1862, *OR,* series 1, vol. 8, 611–12.

24. Major General W. T. Sherman to Major General T. C. Hindman, 17 October 1862, *OR,* series 1, vol. 13, 742–43.

25. Edwards, *Noted Guerrillas;* Williamson, *Mosby's Rangers.*

26. Beller, *Mosby and His Rangers,* 11–12, 85–88; Siepel, *Rebel;* Ramage, *Gray Ghost.* Books on John Hunt Morgan include James Ramage's *Rebel Raider;* Dee Alexander Brown's *The Bold Cavaliers;* and Bennett H. Young's classic *Confederate Wizards of the Saddle.*

27. Castel, *William Clarke Quantrill;* Goodrich, *Bloody Dawn.* Quantrill is often portrayed in movies and novels as a lower-class bandit, a butternut-wearing highwayman. This image has been disproved by several historians. See Bowen, "Quantrill, James, Younger, et al.," and "Guerrilla War in Western Missouri."

28. Brownlee, *Grey Ghosts of the Confederacy;* Fellman, *Inside War;* Goodrich, *Black Flag.*

29. Barksdale, "Semi-Regular and Irregular Warfare."

30. Castel, "Guerrilla War."

31. Grimsley, *Hard Hand of War,* 94, 119, 151–62.

32. Carl Beamer, "Gray Ghostbusters"; Gates, "Indians and Insurrectos"; Birtle, *U.S. Army Counterinsurgency.*

33. Asprey, *War in the Shadows,* 104–108; Callwell, *Small Wars;* Cross, *Conflict in the Shadows;* Gann, *Guerrillas in History.*

34. Kerby, "Why the Confederacy Lost."

35. Beringer et al., *Why the South Lost,* 342, 343, 346–47.

36. Gallagher, *Confederate War,* 120–23, 126, 127.

37. Mitchell, "Perseverance of the Soldiers," 124–25.

38. Sutherland, ed., *Guerrillas, Unionists, and Violence.* Specific essays on Arkansas (Robert R. Mackey, "Bushwhackers, Provosts, and Tories: The Guerrilla War in Arkansas"), Virginia (Daniel E. Sutherland, "The Absence of Violence: Confederates and Unionists in Culpeper County, Virginia), and Tennessee (B. Franklin Cooling, "A People's War: Partisan Conflict in Tennessee and Kentucky") are especially pertinent to this work.

39. Sutherland provides an excellent overview of the status of irregular warfare and Civil War historiography in the March 2000 issue of *Civil War History.* See Sutherland, "Sideshow No Longer." For information on the guerrilla war in Arkansas, see Sutherland, "Guerrillas."

40. North Carolina also possesses several of the above-mentioned features, but was not considered for this work because of the lack of Federal military involvement in the state. Although Union troops occupied several seaports along the coast, these enclaves were only intended to isolate the main contraband routes and increase the effectiveness of the naval blockade. A Unionist irregular war did occur in the mountains of western North Carolina and was brutally repressed by the Confederacy, using many of the same methods that it condemned the Union army for employing. For an excellent

retelling of war in the North Carolina mountains, see John Inscoe and Gordon McKinney, *The Heart of Confederate Appalachia*. For a more personal view of the bloody guerrilla war in North Carolina, see Philip S. Paludan, *Victims*. Missouri did not quit without a fight, and would continue to be a battleground for both conventional and unconventional warfare until 1865. See Michael Fellman, *Inside War*, for details on Missouri's internal war, and Robert Leckie's *None Died in Vain*, 145, 151–53, 175–85, for an overview of the military operations to secure the Border States. McPherson, *Battle Cry of Freedom*, 278–79, 282, 297–299.

41. Shea, "1862," 44, 46–47. An excellent overview of the complex issues in Arkansas is Carl H. Moneyhon, *Arkansas and the New South*.

42. Some Confederates realized the importance of the western theater as the decisive theater in the Civil War. See Hattaway and Jones, *How the North Won*, 277–83.

43. Gallagher, *Confederate War*, 95.

44. Lee to Cooper, 1 April 1864, in Lee, *Wartime Papers*, 689.

CHAPTER 1

Correspondence between Governor Rector and Governor Pickens can be found in the Arkansas History Collection, Box 1, File 8, Special Collections Division, University of Arkansas, Fayetteville (hereafter UAF).

1. Clausewitz, *On War*, 479. Emphasis added.

2. Arkansas has many of same geographical, social, and political factors that faced other Upper South states, such as Kentucky, Virginia, and Tennessee. The introduction discusses why Arkansas, Tennessee, and Virginia were selected as case studies of irregular warfare during the Civil War.

3. Shea and Hess, *Pea Ridge*, 256, 262, 265.

4. Arkansas produced 17.7 million bushels of corn, 955,000 bushels of wheat, and possessed over 570,000 cattle and 106,000 horses in 1860, a substantial part of the agricultural wealth of the trans-Mississippi Confederacy. See U.S. Department of Agriculture, *Report of the Commissioner of Agriculture for the Year 1866*, 568–70.

5. Hartje, *Van Dorn*, 166–68; Moore, ed., *Rebellion Record*, 5:11–13; Davis, *Papers of Jefferson Davis*, 8:194.

6. Dougan, *Confederate Arkansas*, 87–89.

7. "Document 6: Governor Rector's Address, 5 May 1862," in Moore, ed., *Rebellion Record*, 5:11–13.

8. Jefferson Davis to Earl Van Dorn, 20 May 1862, in Davis, *Papers of Jefferson Davis*, 8:193–94.

9. General Orders Number 59, Headquarters, Western Department, 26 May 1862, *OR*, series 1, vol. 8, 28.

10. Gallaway, *Ragged Rebel*, 35.

11. Letter from R. W. Johnson and others to President Davis, 15 April 1862, *OR*, series 1, vol. 8, 814–15.

12. Shea and Hess, *Pea Ridge*, 289, 296–97; Neal and Kremm, *Lion of the South*, 117–19.

13. Washington (Arkansas) *Telegraph*, 18 June 1862; Major General Thomas C. Hindman, "Report of Maj. Gen. Thomas C. Hindman, C.S. Army, of operations May 31–November 3, 1862," *OR*, series 1, vol. 13, 36 (hereafter "Hindman's Report").

14. C. C. Danley, editorial, "Let Us Fight as Civilized Men," *Arkansas Gazette*, 11 May 1861; Major General Thomas C. Hindman, "General Orders Number 17," 17 June 1862, *OR*, series 1, vol. 13, 835. Emphasis added.

15. Pro-Union guerrillas in Arkansas did exist, but were never given sanction by the Federal authorities. Instead, pro-Union sympathizers joined volunteer Union regiments raised in the state. See Barnes, "Williams Clan."

16. Letter from Van Dorn to Brigadier General J. S. Roane, 19 May 1862, *OR*, series 1, vol. 13, 831–32.

17. Newspapers played an important role in Civil War Arkansas. Due to the largely rural population of the state, newspapers became the only dependable way to spread information, including general orders issued by the military command. A sampling of the Washington *Telegraph* and the Little Rock *Arkansas Gazette* from 1862 and 1863 reveals that a substantial portion of each, upward of a full one fourth of some issues, was devoted to Confederate orders and directives.

18. Both Jomini and Clausewitz emphasized the necessity for firm controls over irregular forces. See the introduction for details. "General Orders Number 18," 17 June 1862, Headquarters, Trans-Mississippi Division, War Department Collection of Confederate Records, Box 78, Record Group 109, National Archives and Records Administration (hereafter RG 109, NARA); *Arkansas Gazette*, 14 June 1862. Neither of the main newspapers in Confederate Arkansas, the Washington *Telegraph* and the Little Rock *Arkansas Gazette*, published the full General Orders Number 18, but both published the complete General Orders Number 17.

19. "Hindman's Report," *OR*, series 1, vol. 13, 43.

20. "C.D." letter in Indianapolis *Daily Journal*, 20 February 1862, cited by Shea, "Semi-Savage State," citation from original; "Hindman's Report," *OR*, series 1, vol. 13, 35–36; "Operations on White River, Ark.: Reports of Col. Graham N. Fitch, Forty-sixth Indiana Infantry, Commanding Expedition," *OR*, series 1, vol. 13, 104–105.

21. "Operations on White River, Ark.," *OR*, series 1, vol. 13, 106.

22. "To the Inhabitants of Monroe County, Arkansas from G. N. Fitch, Colonel, 46th Regiment, Indiana Volunteers," ibid., 106–107.

23. See chapter 2.

24. Letter from Major General T. C. Hindman to Colonel G. N. Fitch, 25 June 1862, *OR*, series 1, vol. 13, 108.

25. Letter from Colonel G. N. Fitch to Major General T. C. Hindman, 28 June 1862, ibid., 108–109.

26. "Fight at Waddell Farm, Ark., Colonel Brackett's Report," and "Jacksonport *Cavalier* Account," in Moore, ed., *Rebellion Record*, 5:190–92.

27. Letter from Brigadier General Albert Pike to President Jefferson Davis, 19 November 1862, *OR*, series 1, vol. 13, 921–22; Neal and Kremm, *Lion of the South*, 132–35.

28. The Confederate government reorganized the region, changing the title from "Trans-Mississippi District" to "Trans-Mississippi Department" in August 1862. General Holmes was given the overall command of the department, while Hindman became the commander of the "District of Arkansas," and later a divisional commander at Prairie Grove and under the Army of Tennessee. The other two districts of the region, the District of Louisiana and the District of Texas and Arizona, were commanded by Major General Richard Taylor and Major General H. O. Hebert, respectively. See *OR*, series 1, vol. 13, 877.

29. Neal and Kremm, *Lion of the South*, 133–34.

30. Letter from Major General W. T. Sherman to Major General T. C. Hindman, 28 September 1862, *OR*, series 1, vol. 13, 682–83. The subject of Sherman's relationship to the concept of total, or "hard," war is the focus of Mark Grimsley's *The Hard Hand of War*. The portrayal of Sherman as the first modern general began after World War I. Historians such as B. H. Liddell Hart, in his *Sherman: Soldier, Realist, American*, and T. Harry Williams, in *Lincoln and His Generals*, continued the evaluation of Sherman as a "modern" general.

31. Letter from Major General Theophilus Holmes to Major General Samuel Curtis, 11 October 1862, *OR*, series 1, vol. 13, 726–28.

32. Letter from Major General W. T. Sherman to Major General T. C. Hindman, 17 October 1862, ibid., 742–43. Alternative punishments for guerrilla activities were introduced by the Union army in Arkansas, varying from imprisonment to death. See chapter 3 for details. According to the records of the First Arkansas Cavalry Regiment (Union), several of their captured members were "shot at Fort Smith, Ark., while a prisoner of war, by order of Major Gen. Hindman." See "Report of the Adjutant General of the State of Arkansas for the Period of the Late Rebellion, and to November 1, 1866" (39th Cong., 2nd session, 1867, S. Doc. 53), 14.

33. For information on the Battle of Prairie Grove, see Shea, *War in the West*, 94–103; Coombe, *Thunder along the Mississippi*, 128–29; Hattaway and Jones, *How the North Won*, 212–13.

34. Captain J. F. Barton to Major General Thomas C. Hindman, Thomas C. Hindman Papers, Box 121, 1863 File, RG 109, NARA; grammar and spelling as in the original. "Report of Captain J. H. McGhee, Arkansas Cavalry," 2 March 1863, *OR*, series 1, vol. 22, 232. Colonel John S. Mosby's partisan rangers in Virginia operated under a similar system. See chapters 3 and 4 for details.

35. "General Order Number 20," *Arkansas Gazette*, 12 July 1862; circular dated 28 February 1863 from Headquarters, Hindman's Division, Little Rock, to Colonel A. S. Morgan, Chief of Recruiting Service, Major General T. C. Hindman Papers, Box 1, 1863 File, RG 109, NARA.

36. "Attention Partizan Rancers!" circular issued at Washington, Arkansas, 15 August 1862, Special Collections Library, Duke University, Durham, North Carolina. Capitalization and spelling from original.

37. The Confederate Congress became disturbed over the growing number of independent companies throughout the South and attempted to limit them. In General Orders Number 53, issued June 17, 1864, the Confederate

Congress published an act "To Promote the Efficiency of the cavalry of the Provisional Army, and to Punish Lawlessness and Irregularities Thereof." The act called for dismounting any mounted soldier or irregular whom "misbehaves before the enemy, or is guilty of illegally wasting, spoilating or appropriating for his own use, any private property or doing violence to any citizen." As a result, Confederate guerrillas avoided the conventional forces after early 1864, preferring to fight their own war. See "General Order Number 53," Confederate States General Orders, Civil War Collection, Box II-1-1, University of Arkansas at Little Rock Special Collection (hereafter UALR-SC).

38. General Orders Number 49, 3 November 1863, Departmental Records, Trans-Mississippi Department, District of Arkansas, RG 109, NARA; General Orders Number 60, ibid.

39. Shelby himself was not averse to foraging from loyal Confederates in Arkansas to feed his men, but would generally punish those who pillaged items not necessary for military survival. See Oates, *Confederate Cavalry*, 54–55.

40. Brigadier General J. O. Shelby to Lieutenant Colonel Joseph Love, 7 June 1864, *OR*, series 1, vol. 34, 653.

41. Special Orders Number 4, 24 September 1864, Military Departments: Special Orders and Letters Sent, Brigadier General J. O. Shelby's Command, Department of the Trans-Mississippi, 1864, RG 109, NARA; Special Orders Number 37, ibid.; Brigadier General J. O. Shelby to Lieutenant Colonel J. F. Belton, 31 May 1864, ibid.

42. "Address of Brigadier General E. W. Gantt, C. S. A., Given on October 7, 1863, at Little Rock, Arkansas," Pamphlet 113, Pamphlet Collection, Civil War Collection, UALR; Moneyhon, "Disloyalty and Class Consciousness," 241; Estes, *Early Days and War Times*, 10–11.

43. Ingenthron, *Borderland Rebellion*, 205. Emphasis added.

44. Sutton, *Early Days in the Ozarks*, 44.

45. Silas C. Turnbo served in the Twenty-seventh Arkansas Infantry (Confederate) from 1862 to 1865. His literary career began in the 1870s, with local newspapers. Soon he was a regular contributor to many of the state's newspapers as well as the Goodspeed county histories. His first published work was *Historical and Biographical Sketches of the Early Settlement of the Valley of White River* in 1877, and he continued to write throughout his life; his personal papers number nearly 2,500 pages of transcribed text organized into twenty-eight volumes, and are housed at the Springfield-Greene County Public Library in Springfield, Missouri. He was a close friend of William E. Connelly, an early historian of guerrilla warfare in Missouri. Following Turnbo's death in 1925, Connelly purchased his notes and unfinished manuscripts from Turnbo's widow. When Connelly died in 1930, the Turnbo collection was sold to various institutions and individuals, and is presently scattered in numerous colleges, universities, and libraries throughout Arkansas and Missouri. See Ingenthron, "Silas Claborn Turnbo."

46. Allen, ed., *War and Guerrilla Stories*, 133. Allen's 1987 printing was transcribed from one of the few surviving original 1890 editions in the archives of the University of Central Arkansas, Conway, Arkansas.

47. Ibid., 31. The Toney family, consisting of five children from ages one to fourteen, were saved from starvation and exposure in their February 1863 journey by the chance meeting of an old neighbor. The neighbor "piloted us within sight of where a company of Federal soldiers were in camp." The Federal officers gave the family rations and clothing. Such actions as this won the loyalty of many of the refugees, enabling the Union army to conduct a wide variety of pacification operations in the final year of the war in northern Arkansas. See chapter 2 for details.

48. Ibid., 38–39, 111–12.

49. Sidney L. Jackman memoir, 45–46, Arkansas History Collection, Manuscript Collection Number 613, UAF.

50. Nanny Hermann Diary, 21 November, 12 December 1862, Hermann Family Collection, Bochum Immigrant Letter Collection, Ruhr University, Bochum, Germany. Translated from original text. Hermannsburg ceased to exist during the war, but the homes and farms were reoccupied by others after the conflict. The town is now known as Dutch Mills, in Washington County, presumably due to the slang of the early nineteenth century that referred to all Germans as "Dutch," the American bastardization of "Deutsch."

51. Mail Contracts in Arkansas, 1864–65, District of Arkansas, Trans-Mississippi Department, RG 109, NARA.

52. John C. Wright, "Memoir of Colonel John C. Wright, C.S.A.," 116, Manuscript Collection, UAF. Wright spoke highly of the Confederate guerrillas in northwest Arkansas, justifying their attacks on the Unionist population as equivalent to the Federal recruitment of Arkansans into Arkansas Unionist units. See chapter 2 for more details.

53. Merrell, *Autobiography*, 319–20. Merrell noted that he did not take part in the vigilante justice of the time, for several reasons. "First, we were employed day & night carrying on the Factory, and our duty was there. Second, I would never take part in the hanging of any man, however much he might deserve it, without a fair trail & that by law," not considering his status as a Northerner in Confederate-occupied southern Arkansas. Ibid., 319.

54. Catalfano-Serio, *Effect of the Civil War*, 20; Fort Smith *New Era*, 20 February 1864.

55. John Bowen to Samuel Haney, 2 February 1864, Haney Family Papers, Manuscript Collection Number 860, UAF; grammar and spelling as in the original.

56. Merrell, *Autobiography*, 321–22.

57. Kerby, *Kirby Smith's Confederacy*, 392, 425. When the Confederate army in Arkansas surrendered in late May 1865, Confederate governor Harris Flanagin attempted to convince the Federal authorities to allow him to call the state legislature in order to revoke the secession acts of 1861. Realizing the powerlessness of the Confederate government in Arkansas, the Unionist governor, Isaac Murphy, and the Federal commander in Arkansas, Major General Joseph J. Reynolds, rejected his proposal. Instead of being treated as a legally elected state governor, he was told to go home. See ibid., 425–26 for details.

58. See chapter 2 for details on the Federal counterinsurgency program in 1864.

59. Letter from Lieutenant Colonel John Levering to Brigadier General Powell Clayton, 12 May 1865, *OR*, series 2, vol. 48, 418; Letter from Brigadier General Powell Clayton to Lieutenant Colonel John Levering, 14 May 1865, ibid., 440; Letter from Major G. W. Davis to Captain S. M. Cambern, 15 May 1865, ibid., 451–52; Letter from Major General Joseph J. Reynolds to Captain Joseph McC. Bell, 16 May 1865, ibid., 466.

60. One guerrilla leader, Captain M. V. Raibon, operating in the region around Devall's Bluff, wrote the local Union commander that "it has been my constant business and duty to suppress jayhawking and attend to all lawless strollers through the country in the garb of soldiers, which business I have endeavored to execute, and which duty I have endeavored to discharge to the best of my ability." Ibid., 450–51.

61. Ibid., 450; see chapter 2 on the reasons for Federal leniency at the end of the war.

62. Clausewitz, *On War*, 480; Jomini, *Art of War*, 26.

63. Lackey, *History of Newton County*, 137–41. As many families who lived in Arkansas during the Civil War, the Cecil clan was split between pro-Confederate and Unionist causes. John Cecil's brother, Samuel, was first sergeant of D Company, Second Arkansas Cavalry (Union), and fought several skirmishes against his brother's guerrilla band.

64. Washington (Arkansas) *Telegraph*, 7 May 1862; additionally, in late November 1863, several editorials calling on Confederate authorities to halt the depredations of Confederate guerrillas were published in the Washington *Telegraph*, the sole remaining pro-Confederate newspaper in the state. See ibid., 25 November 1863, for one such example.

65. Jayme Milsap Stone, contends that the Confederate guerrilla forces in Arkansas, especially after 1863, were largely made up of deserters from the Confederate army. While this may be true, no recorded data exists as to the makeup of all Confederate guerrillas in Arkansas; more than likely, large numbers of the guerrillas had some sort of experience in the Rebel army. See Stone, "Brother against Brother," 196–97.

CHAPTER 2

1. Northeast Arkansas during the late spring of 1862 was summarized in the words of one Federal soldier, who wrote that it was "one of the most rantankerous [sic], half-manufactured sections of the country you ever saw." Another described it as "the roughest, meanest country God ever made," while a third stated that "I doubt if few of the habitable portions of the globe presents a more dreary and uninviting wilderness." See "Correspondent" letter in Chicago *Tribune*, 2 May 1862; "C.D." letter in Indianapolis *Daily Journal*, 20 February 1862; and Henry Cummings to his wife, 21 April 1862, H. J. B. Cummings Papers, State Historical Society of Iowa, Des Moines, cited by Shea in "Semi-Savage State," 313.

2. Major General Samuel L. Curtis to Brigadier General W. Scott Ketchum, 12 May 1862, *OR*, series 1, vol. 13, 379; Curtis to Carr, ibid., 405; Shea and Hess, *Pea Ridge*, 292–99.

3. Curtis to Captain J. C. Kelton, 19 April 1862, *OR*, series 1, vol. 13, 364–65.

4. Colonel Albert G. Brackett to Brigadier General Frederick Steele, 24 May 1862, ibid., 397. Steele was later promoted to major general and served as the commander of the Army of Arkansas until late 1864.

5. McIntyre, *Federals on the Frontier*, 82–83; grammar and spelling as in the original.

6. "Retributive burning" is the author's term for punishing local communities for guerrilla activities. It does not appear to be a phrase used in the Civil War. Colonel Fitch's June–July 1862 White River expedition is discussed in chapter 1.

7. The use of punitive expeditions to punish irregular attacks had become common by the mid-nineteenth century. Examples of such operations during the French conquest of Morocco and Algeria, operations in Indochina, and British operations on the Indian frontier all indicate proclivity of commanders to use conventional forces to punish entire regions for guerrilla attacks. See Asprey, *War in the Shadows*, 72–74, 96–103.

8. "Report of Lieutenant Colonel Robert F. Patterson, 29th Iowa Infantry, June 3, 1864," Department of Arkansas and Seventh Corps and Fourth Military District, 1862–70, Box 6: Letters, Reports and Other Records of the Subcommands of the Seventh Army Corps, 1863–67, Record Group 393 (Army Continental Commands), National Archives and Records Administration, Washington, D.C. (hereafter RG 393, NARA). Terry's Landing no longer exists. It was near what is now Terry Lock and Dam, fifteen miles south of modern Little Rock. None of the locations mentioned in Lieutenant Colonel Patterson's report survived the war.

9. Ibid.; Mackey, "Self-Inflicted Wound," 81–83.

10. Sergeant James G. Crozier, Twenty-sixth Iowa, to "Dear Lucy," 23 December 1862, "Diary Letters of the Civil War by Captain James G. Crozier, 1862–1865," Special Collections, U.S. Military Academy, West Point, New York (hereafter USMA-SC; grammar and spelling as in the original). Crozier detested the leniency of General Steele toward the civilian population of Arkansas, all of whom he considered traitors.

11. Crozier to "Dear Lucy," 23 October 1862, "Diary Letters," USMA-SC, grammar and spelling as in the original.

12. Although rail lines existed connecting Grant's army in Mississippi to the North, they were being constantly raided and destroyed by Confederate cavalry under General Nathan B. Forrest and others. See chapter 6 for details.

13. Porter, *Naval History of the Civil War*, 333; Bailey, "Mississippi Marine Brigade," 34.

14. Numerous members of the Ellet clan served either in the Ram Fleet or the Marine Brigade until both were disbanded in 1864. See Bailey, "Mississippi Marine Brigade," 34–36, and Chapman, "Ellet Family," 61, 63–64; for an overview of the Marine Brigade's major operations, see Hearn, *Ellet's Brigade*, 143–64.

15. "Mississippi Marine Brigade, General and Staff Muster Roll, May and June 1863," Records of the Record and Pension Office of the War Department,

1784–1919, General Records, Service Histories of the Volunteer Force of the United States Army, 1861–65, the Mississippi Marine Brigade, Microfilm M594, Record Group 94, National Archives and Records Administration, Washington, D.C.; "Report of Brigadier General Ellet, commanding Marine Brigade," 5 June 1863, U.S. Navy Department, *War of the Rebellion: A Compilation of the Official Records of the Union and Confederate Navies*, series 1, vol. 25, 128–29 (hereafter *ORN*); "Report of Captain J. H. McGehee, Arkansas Cavalry," 2 March 1863, *OR*, series 1, vol. 22, pt. 1, 232. Later, when the Federals realized McGehee's base of operations was at Hopefield, Arkansas, Major General Stephen A. Hurlbut, commanding XVI Corps at Memphis, ordered it burned also. He ordered the Sixty-third Illinois Infantry to proceed with the gunboat *Cricket* to the town and allow the residents "one hour to remove their effects, after which every building will be burned." The town ceased to exist. See "Special Orders Number 10, Headquarters Sixteenth Army Corps," 18 February 1863, ibid.

16. Heartsill, *Fourteen Hundred and 91 Days*, 101, capitalization as in the original; "Special Orders Number 283," 18 October 1862, *OR*, series 1, vol. 17, pt. 2, 280–81; Major General William T. Sherman to Major John A. Rawlings, 21 October 1862, ibid., 285; see also Grimsley, *Hard Hand of War*, 113–19.

17. Chapman, "Ellet Family," 63–64; letter from C. J. Field to Rear Admiral David D. Porter, 26 December 1863, *ORN*, series 1, vol. 25, pt. 1, 697–98.

18. Hearn, *Ellet's Brigade*, 82, 87, 132–33, 137, 148–51. Ellet's brigade was sent to Tennessee to aid in Colonel Abel Streight's raid in northern Alabama, but arrived too late to take part. According to Hearn, this was a common problem with the marine brigade—it always seemed to arrive too late to do any actual fighting. See ibid., 153–56; Brigadier General Charles P. Stone to Major General James B. McPherson, 29 March 1864, *OR*, series 1, vol. 34, pt. 2, 768; James A. Greer to Rear Admiral David D. Porter, 21 December 1863, *ORN*, series 1, vol. 25, 697; Porter to Sherman, 29 October 1863, ibid., 524; see also Bailey, "Mississippi Marine Brigade," 39–41.

19. Fellman, *Inside War*, 33–34, 78, 93–94. General Steele appointed Colonel Chandler to the position of provost marshal general of Arkansas on November 25, 1863, following his successful command of the Seventh Missouri Cavalry at the battle of Bayou La Fourche, Louisiana, in September 1863. See "General Order Number 44," 25 November 1863, Headquarters, Army of Arkansas, Civil War Collection, File A5, Series 2, Box 1, File 6, UALR-SC; "Report of Lieutenant Colonel John L. Chandler, 7th Missouri Cavalry," *OR*, series 1, vol. 22, pt. 1, 500; letter from Lieutenant Colonel John L. Chandler to Lieutenant Colonel William Wood, 23 August 1864, Letters of the Provost Marshal General, Headquarters, VII Army Corps and the Department of Arkansas, vol. 108, RG 393, NARA.

20. The Frontier District covered Johnson, Franklin, Yell, Sebastian, Crawford, Washington, Benton, Madison, Carroll, and Newton Counties in addition to the Indian Territory; Northeast Arkansas District covered Independence, Van Buren, Searcy, Marion, Izard, Fulton, Lawrence, Jackson, Poinsett, Craighead, Greene, and Randolph Counties; Eastern Arkansas District covered Phillips, Crittenden, St. Francis, Mississippi, Desha, and Chicot Counties; and

Central Arkansas District covered Pulaski, Prairie, White, Conway, Pope, Saline, Perry, Jefferson, Hot Spring, and Drew Counties. See "Orders and Accounts," 26 April 1864, Provost Marshal General of Arkansas, Headquarters, Department of Arkansas, vol. 111, RG 393, NARA.

21. Ibid.; General Orders Number 6, 14 January 1865, Department of Arkansas General Orders, vol. 20 (1865–67), RG 393, NARA, emphasis added; Denby, *War in Arkansas*, 12. An example of the pass system is best shown in General Orders Number 26, dated May 28, 1863, and issued from the post of DeVall's Bluff. It states: "From and after this date the lines of this post will be open for the ingress and egress of loyal Citizens upon passes to be issued by the Provost Marshal and countersigned by the Commanding Officer of the District, Forces or Post. Any persons convicted of abusing the privileges conferred by this order by attempting to correspond with, or communicate information to the enemy, or to pass contraband goods through the lines, will be summarily punished in the severest manner known to military law." Department of Arkansas, 1863–65, vol. 296, Miscellaneous Records, RG 393, NARA. Sampling of the Department of Arkansas Adjutant General records reveals charges against civilians for "violation of loyalty oath," and stiff sentences, usually hard labor for two years, for those so convicted. See ibid.

22. In a letter from assistant Provost Marshal General Captain Samuel McLaugton to Lieutenant Colonel W. H. Wood, the provost marshal general of West Mississippi, the responsibilities of the Arkansas provosts were outlined. Unlike Louisiana, Captain McLaugton maintained, the provosts marshal in Arkansas did not serve as judges (see letter dated June 14, 1864, from Colonel James Bowen, provost marshal general of the Department of the Gulf), but concentrated more on gathering intelligence for use by the field forces and maintaining order within the Army of Arkansas. Provost Marshal General Affidavits, 1864, and vol. 5553A, Letters and Telegrams Received, Military Division of West Mississippi, vol. 5551, RG 393, NARA.

23. "Lists of Bushwhackers and Guerrillas," 1863–64, Department of Arkansas records, vol. 361, RG 393, NARA; grammar and spelling as in the original. The same file also identifies guerrillas that were from Missouri but used Arkansas as a safe haven, and also noted men who were suspected of supplying ammunition to the guerrilla bands.

24. General Orders Number 100, 24 April 1863, *OR*, series 2, vol. 5, 676–77; General Orders Number 30, 22 April 1863, *OR*, series 1, vol. 22, pt. 2, 238.

25. Bolden, "So Long as Strangers Are the Rulers," 27–31.

26. Dodd was convicted of spying on January 5, 1864, after he was captured attempting to leave Little Rock with a coded message outlining the Federal defenses of the city. Despite his pleas of innocence, he was hanged on January 8, 1864. See Sutherland, "1864," 105–107; Mackey, "Bushwhackers, Provosts and Tories," 175–77. General Frederick Steele, a West Point classmate of U. S. Grant, and brother of John B. Steele, a Democratic congressman from New York, came under severe criticism from Radical Republicans, and later Arkansas Unionists, for his lenient policy toward former Confederates. See Bolden, "So Long as Strangers Are the Rulers," 7–11, 34–36.

27. "Classification of Prisoners," Orders and Accounts, Provost Marshal General of Arkansas, Department of Arkansas and VII Army Corps and Fourth Military District, 1862–70, vol.111, RG 393, NARA; General Register of Prisoners, New Orleans, 1863–65, Records of the Provost Marshal General, RG 109, NARA; General Register of Prisoners, New Orleans, vol. 3, 1865, ibid. The provost marshal in Little Rock noted five classifications for prisoners: prisoners of war, citizens arrested for violation of the laws of war, Federal military prisoners, citizens arrested for criminal offenses, and Confederate deserters. Following the end of the war, several trials were held at Little Rock for guerrillas captured from the winter of 1864 to summer 1865. Those who had violated their oath of allegiance in addition to being a guerrilla were the worse treated. For example, Edmore Stratton, a resident of Brownsville (in Prairie County), was sentenced to fifteen years hard labor at the federal penitentiary at Columbus, Ohio, for violating his oath, being a guerrilla, and larceny, on May 26, 1865. See "Registers of Federal Soldiers, Rebel Deserters and Civilians Confined and Released," February 1864– December 1866, Little Rock Penitentiary, Department of Arkansas and VII Army Corps and Fourth Military District, 1862–70, vol. 383 and 385, RG 393, NARA.

28. Arkansas's white volunteer regiments, and their dates of organization (or date of organization to date of disbandment) are as follows: First Cavalry (June 1862), Second Cavalry (July 1862), Third Cavalry (February 1864), Fourth Cavalry (December 1863), First Light Artillery Battery (January 1863), First Infantry (March 1863), First Infantry Battalion (July–December 1862), Second Infantry (October 1863), Fourth Infantry (January–October 1864), Fourth Mounted Infantry (October 1863–June 1864); Arkansas also raised several black regiments from freed slaves. All black units were eventually reclassified as U.S. Colored Troops (USCT) and passed out of state control. These units were the First Infantry Regiment, African Descent (changed to Forty-sixth USCT), Second Infantry (54th USCT), Third Infantry (56th USCT), First Light Artillery Battery, African Descent (Battery H, Second U.S. Colored Light Artillery), and two USCT recruited regiments, the 112th and 113th Infantry. Nearly 10,000 white and 15,000 black Arkansans fought for the Union, against an estimated 60,000 who served with the Confederacy. All information is from Dyer, *Compendium of the War of the Rebellion*, 113, 997–1000; U.S. House, Committee on War Claims (14 June 1898), "Fourth Mounted Infantry Claims," 55th Cong., 2nd sess., 1898, vol. 6, H. Doc. 9219, Report 1550, serial 3722; Current, Lincoln's Loyalists, 73–79, 216.

29. Musser, *Soldier Boy*, 85; Report of Colonel M. La Rue Harrison, 8 April 1864, *OR*, series 1, vol. 34, pt. 1, 876; Britton, *Civil War on the Border*, 2:521; "Arkansas Volunteer Units (Union), General and Staff Muster Rolls, June 1862 to December 1865," Records of the Record and Pension Office of the War Department, 1784–1919, General Records, Service Histories of the Volunteer Force of the United States Army, 1861–65, Arkansas Volunteer Units (Union), Microfilm M594-1, RG 94, NARA.

30. Sutherland, "1864," 123; Hattaway and Jones, *How the North Won*, 519–23.

31. Colonel M. La Rue Harrison to Military Governor John S. Phelps, 27 January 1863, *OR*, series 1, vol. 22, pt. 2, 78. An excellent description of prewar Fayetteville from a Unionist perspective is in William Baxter's *Pea Ridge and Prairie Grove*, 2–35, citation from original.

32. "Report of Expedition from Fayetteville to Frog Bayou, Ark. and skirmishes near Huntsville and near Kingston, Colonel M. La Rue Harrison, First Arkansas Cavalry (Union)," *OR*, series 1, vol. 22, pt. 2, 749–53.

33. The First Arkansas Cavalry was the lead element of General Francis Herron's division on December 7, 1862, as it moved from Fayetteville toward Cane Hill. At dawn, it clashed with Confederate horsemen, led by Brigadier General John S. Marmaduke, and was routed and sent fleeing back into the Federal infantry. Herron later reported that the First Arkansas "came back on me 6 miles south of Fayetteville, at 7 a.m., closely pursued by at least 3,000 cavalry. It was with the very greatest difficulty that we got them checked, and prevented a general stampede of the battery horses; but after some hard talking, and my finally shooting one cowardly whelp off his horse, they halted." Such behavior tainted the reputation of the then inexperienced cavalrymen. Colonel Harrison's tenacious defense of Fayetteville in 1864 erased many of the doubts of his commanders in respect of the combat ability of the First Arkansas Cavalry. See "Report of Brigadier General Francis J. Herron," *OR*, series 1, vol. 22, pt. 1, 102–103; "Report of Colonel J. O. Shelby," ibid., 148–51; Shea, *War in the West*, 88–91.

34. The Arkansas Confederate troops referred to Unionist volunteers as "Mountain Tories."

35. DeBlack, "1863," 68–69. Report by Brigadier General W. L. Cabbell, C. S. Army," *OR*, series 1, vol. 22, pt. 2, 310–13; General Orders Number 16, 19 April 1863, ibid., 309–10.

36. DeBlack, "1863," 56–96.

37. Paradoxically, Price's defeat created further problems for Harrison, as large numbers of isolated Rebel detachments scattered across northern Arkansas, including deserters and stragglers, joined local guerrilla companies. See Albert Castel's *General Sterling Price and the Civil War in the West* for further details. Colonel Harrison and the First Arkansas Cavalry, as soon as they learned of Price's invasion, refused to withdraw from Fayetteville. Instead, they repaired the fortifications prepared in September 1863, sent out aggressive reconnaissance patrols, ambushed Confederate scouts and guerrillas attempting to join Price, recruited additional militiamen, and prepared for the assault. As a result, Harrison again held off a determined Confederate attack on Fayetteville from October 26 to November 4, 1864. A force estimated at 1,200 Confederate cavalry and guerrillas under Major General James F. Fagan attempted to besiege and capture Fayetteville, in order to secure lines of communication for Price's main force. Harrison's horse soldiers and Home Guards defeated Fagan's troopers, and after being relieved by the Federal Army of the Border on November 4, took part in the pursuit of the defeated Rebel command. See Colonel Robert R. Livingston to Lieutenant Colonel John W. Stephens, 11 May 1864, *OR*, series 1, vol. 34, pt. 3, 548; Livingston to Major William D.

Green, 12 May 1864, ibid., 562–63; Harrison to Brigadier General John B. Sanborn, 9 April 1864, ibid., 109.

38. The lack of proper mounts became an issue of contention between the War Department and Major General Frederick Steele. Apparently Steele liked to race the best horses in his command for the entertainment of himself and his officers. This led the chief of cavalry for the Cavalry Division to state that "he could scarcely get a squadron of one regiment to trot in line, so completely had the stock been spoiled for cavalry service." The lack of suitable horses directly affected the counterguerrilla war, as the cavalry units, such as the First Arkansas, could not sustain long patrols or rapid pursuits. U.S. Senate, "Administration of the Department of Arkansas", 38th Cong., 2nd sess., 1864, serial 1214, S. Rept. 142, 78; Clausewitz, *On War*, 480.

39. As described in the introduction, one of Clausewitz's requirements for a successful people's war, that "the country [in which the guerrillas operate] must be rough and inaccessible," adroitly describes the region in which the First Arkansas Cavalry operated.

40. Harrison to Sanborn, 31 August 1864, *OR*, series 1, vol. 41, pt. 1, 267–68; "Reports of Expedition in Washington and Benton Counties, Arkansas, with Skirmishes," ibid., 266–70; Hughes, "Wartime Gristmill Destruction," 175–76, citation from original.

41. Allen, ed., *War and Guerrilla Stories*, 131–32.

42. U.S. Senate, "Report of the Adjutant General of Arkansas for the Period of the Late Rebellion, and to November 1, 1866," 39th Cong., 2nd sess., 1867, serial 1278, S. Doc. 53, 267.

43. Harrison to Major General Grenville M. Dodge, 22 December 1864, *OR*, series 1, vol. 41, pt. 4, 917.

44. Harrison to Governor Isaac Murphy, 15 March 1865, *OR*, series 1, vol. 48, pt. 1, 1177–78; Harrison to Colonel William A. Phillips, 15 March 1865, ibid., 1179; Harrison to Brigadier General John B. Sanborn, 29 March 1865, ibid., 1293–94.

45. Harrison to Sanborn, 16 March 1865, ibid., 1174. Harrison had been promoted to full colonel in the winter of 1864–65, after his performance during the siege and battle of Fayetteville in November.

46. Sanborn to Harrison, 16 March 1865, ibid., 1176.

47. Harrison to Sanborn, 13 March 1865, ibid., 1161; Schultz, *Quantrill's War*, 292–94. John N. Edwards, in *Noted Guerrillas*, quotes Quantrill as saying, "This side of the Mississippi river the war ended with the abandonment of Missouri by General Price. All the West is overrun with Federal soldiers. No food, no forage, no horses, no houses, no hiding-places." In the past, Quantrill could always retire to northern Arkansas and hide in the Ozarks; Colonel Harrison's cavalry, combined with the farm colonies, prevented that. Edwards, *Noted Guerrillas*, 382–84.

48. Harrison to Governor Isaac Murphy, 15 March 1865, *OR*, series 1, vol. 48, pt. 1, 1177–78; Harrison to Colonel W. A. Phillips, 15 March 1865, ibid., 1179. Colonel Harrison not only had to worry about bushwhacker bands preying on the fledgling colonies, but bands of destitute Native Americans from the Indian Territory. In the letter to Colonel Phillips, he complained that "the

Indians cross the line and drive off cattle and other stock . I would respectfully request that you give such orders as will prevent these raids, as all the stock this side of the line will be absolutely required to sustain the Union people who belong to the colonies." See Harrison to Phillips, 15 March 1865, *OR*, series 1, vol. 48, pt. 1, 1179.

49. Hans Mattson, *Early Days of Reconstruction*, 7, Pamphlet Collection, Pamphlet 5188, UALR-SC; letter from Hans Mattson to wife, 14 May 1865, "Correspondence & Miscellaneous Papers, 1855–1866," Box 1, Hans Mattson and Family Papers, Minnesota Historical Society; Hans Mattson to wife, 19 May 1865, ibid.; Neal and Kremm, "An Experiment in Collective Security," 175–76, 178–81.

50. Brigadier General Cyrus Bussey to Colonel John Levering, 9 May 1865, *OR*, series 1, vol. 48, pt. 2, 368–69.

51. The quotation is probably apocryphal. According to one source, the statement was cited in a 1908 *McClure's Magazine* article by General Pickett's wife, LaSalle Corbell Pickett, entitled "My Soldier." See Boritt, *Gettysburg Nobody Knows*, 122.

CHAPTER 3

1. Shanks, *Secession Movement*, 1–3.

2. Gallagher, *Confederate War*, 140, citing Conolly, *Irishman in Dixie*, 52.

3. Jones, *Ranger Mosby*, 19–21, 28–29. Jones continues the tradition of considering Mosby both a guerrilla leader well ahead of his time and a gentleman; additionally, he describes Mosby as a reluctant Rebel, joining the cause only after Virginia's secession. Also, like many of the Virginia upper class, Mosby did not start out as an officer. Initially he was a private in an elite cavalry regiment, until commissioned in 1862. James Ramage, in *Gray Ghost*, takes a somewhat different approach toward the partisan leader than Jones, attempting to examine his psychological background and his postwar career as well as his military exploits. Ramage praises Mosby highly, both as a partisan leader and as a man, stating that, "Understanding this mystery [the duality of Mosby as a charming *bon gallant* and as a cold and calculating battlefield leader] provides the key to appreciating the strengths and weaknesses of this great man." Ramage's work puts Mosby in the best light and, despite his excellent and detailed research, lacks the objectivity of other studies. Additionally, Ramage makes the same error as other scholars of irregular warfare in the Civil War, and identifies Mosby as a "guerrilla" and freely uses that term and "partisan" interchangeably without attempting to tie in the concepts of irregular warfare in the nineteenth century. However, Ramage does describe the development of the Partisan Ranger Act, and how Mosby's Rangers creatively applied the regulations therein. See Ramage, *Gray Ghost*, 10. Another interesting view of Mosby is that of A. Kendall Royston in his unpublished thesis, "The Legal Mind Fights the Illegal War." Royston contends that Mosby's legal training gave him special insights into the legality of partisan warfare that enabled him to walk the thin line between brigand and irregular soldier.

4. Siepel, *Rebel*, 31–46, 50–51; Mosby, *Memoirs of Colonel John S. Mosby*, 106. At the time, Mosby technically was a private again. Fitzhugh Lee, with whom Mosby would share a lifelong antipathy, had taken over command of the Washington Mounted Rifles, and relieved Mosby as adjutant in order to appoint another officer to the position. As a result, Mosby returned to the ranks, but was still visiting Stuart as part of the inner clique of the Army of Northern Virginia. It was during one of these visits that Mosby was selected by Stuart for the reconnaissance of McClellan's army. See Emory Thomas, *Bold Dragoon*, 111; Ramage, *Gray Ghost*, 56–57.

5. Siepel, *Rebel*, 51; Jones, *Ranger Mosby*, 58–59. Not all historians agree with this assessment. For example, in an unpublished thesis, Richard L. Tripp maintains that Stuart alone was responsible for the planning and gathering of combat intelligence for the Confederate forces at the time, and that the actual executor of the mission, Mosby, had little to do with its success. See Tripp, "Cavalry Reconnaissance," 48–49. Emory Thomas credits Stuart with selecting Mosby for the mission, but gives Mosby credit for its success. See Thomas, *Bold Dragoon*, 111.

6. Mosby had actually been relieved as adjutant of the Washington Mounted Rifles when a new regimental commander was appointed. Consequently, Mosby reverted to enlisted rank, adjutant being a nominative rather than commissioned title. Mosby then joined Stuart's staff as a courier, having proven himself, in the cavalry commander's view, during the actions leading up to the Peninsula campaign. See Siepel, *Rebel*, 52.

7. Lee assumed command of the Army of Northern Virginia following the Battle of Seven Pines, on April 31, 1862. Major General Joseph E. Johnston, the previous commander, had been gravely wounded during the fight. Johnston would later command other Confederate field armies, but would never return to Virginia. See Warner, *Generals in Gray*, 161–62.

8. Mosby, *Letters of John S. Mosby*, 24–25; Jones, *Ranger Mosby*, 59–62.

9. Quotations are from Crawford, *Mosby and His Men*, 54–55, 59–60. Crawford was one of Mosby's handpicked officers, the commander of Company B, Forty-third Battalion, Virginia Cavalry, and the story was related to him by Mosby and others; see also Siepel, *Rebel*, 61.

10. Jomini, *Art of War*, 204.

11. Emory Thomas, *Bold Dragoon*, 235, 240.

12. Mosby, *Memoirs*, 148–49, quotation from 149–50.

13. Crawford, *Mosby and His Men*, 63; "Commission as Captain, Partizan Rangers," 19 March 1863, John S. Mosby Papers, U.S. Army Military History Institute, Carlisle Barracks, Pennsylvania (hereafter USAMHI).

14. "Report of Capt. John S. Mosby, Virginia Cavalry," 4 February 1863, *OR*, series 1, vol. 25, pt. 1, 5. Federal commanders, from Colonel Sir Percy Wyndham, commander of the First New Jersey Cavalry, to Major General Joseph Hooker, commander of the Army of the Potomac, continually referred to "Mosby and his guerrilla band" in reports in the *Official Records* for early 1863.

15. Major W. H. Taylor to Captain John S. Mosby, 23 March 1863, *OR*, series 1, vol. 25, pt. 2, 857.

16. Crawford, *Mosby's Men*, 76–77. Crawford also contended that non-aligned "bushwhackers" before the end of the war killed Bush and Underwood. This is an odd fate for men considered guerrillas by the Federal authorities.

17. Scott, *Partisan Life*, 34. The reprint of this work is an exact facsimile of the 1867 edition, which is a series of letters written by Scott to friends and relatives; Crawford, *Mosby and His Men*, 95.

18. Keen and Mewborn, *43rd Battalion Virginia Cavalry*, 291, 334, 342, 351, 360, 378. This work is part of the regimental history series commissioned by the State of Virginia, and the compilation of the service records of Mosby's Rangers are directly from the Compiled Service Records, Confederate States Army, Forty-third Battalion, Virginia Cavalry, National Archives. Notable in Keen and Mewborn's listing are the names of numerous men dismissed by Mosby for "military inefficiency," and released back to either conscription officers or to their prior commands in Lee's army. Details on Baron Von Massow come from Mosby's *Memoirs*, 270–71, and Keen and Mewborn, *43rd Battalion*, 378.

19. Crawford, *Mosby and His Men*, 19–20.

20. Keen and Mewborn, *43rd Battalion*, 14–16; Mosby, *Memoirs*, 150–52; Crawford, *Mosby and His Men*, 18.

21. Mosby, *Memoirs*, 268–70; Siepel, *Rebel*, 103–106; Wert, *Mosby's Rangers*, 133–37. Also wounded in the attack were Mosby's brother, William, and another of his best rangers, Fount Beattie. All totaled, Mosby captured five Federals and approximately sixty horses in the raid but lost four killed, nine wounded (four mortally), and one captured.

22. Carrington, *Ranger Mosby*, 84; Mosby, *Memoirs*, 168; Williamson, *Mosby's Ranger*, 28–29. Ames would rise to the rank of second lieutenant in Mosby's command. He was killed in action on October 9, 1864, near Piedmont, Virginia, after being cornered by a detachment of Federal cavalry and refusing to surrender. The Forty-third Virginia Cavalry survivors would later put a monument to Ames in Richmond's Hollywood Cemetery. Keen and Mewborn, *43rd Battalion*, 291.

23. Carrington, *Ranger Mosby*, 90–91; Mosby, *Memoirs*, 172–74; "Report of Capt. John S. Mosby, Virginia Cavalry," 9 March 1863, *OR*, series 1, vol. 25, pt. 1, 1121–23.

24. Mosby, *Memoirs*, 175.

25. Ibid., 179, 182–83; "Mosby's Report," 9 March 1863, *OR*, series 1, vol. 25, pt. 1, 1122.

26. Mosby, *Memoirs*, 182–83; Wert, *Mosby's Rangers*, 48; Siepel, *Rebel*, 75; Ramage, *Gray Ghost*, 72. Wert takes a different approach in his analysis of the raid, using a psychohistorical methodology. He maintains that Mosby's raid on Fairfax fit with his prior history; Mosby spent a short time in jail as a young man (before law school) for trying to kill a man who had supposedly wronged him. Wert asserts that the attempt to capture Colonel Wyndham was a personal vendetta against an enemy. Interesting though it is, Wert's analysis lacks little beyond circumstantial extrapolation of the facts of Mosby's antebellum life. In his memoirs, Mosby exonerated Wyndham of any fault in the raid, stating that "Wyndham ought not to be blamed, because he did not anticipate an event that

had no precedence." For a man who supposedly is driven by vindictiveness, such generosity to an enemy is odd indeed. Mosby, *Memoirs*, 187. According to Ramage, Mosby's postwar views on Wyndham may have been affected by the latter's death in India after the war ended.

27. Williamson, *Mosby's Rangers*, 71–75; Scott, *Partisan Life*, 104–107; Mosby, *Memoirs*, 207–14; Scott, *Partisan Life*, 108–10. Part of Mosby's mission, with additional troopers from the Fourth Virginia (Black Horse) Cavalry, was the screening of Federal units covering the gaps in the Blue Ridge Mountains. For details of this successful cavalry operation, see "June 3–August 1, 1863: The Gettysburg Campaign, No. 400, Record of a Court of Inquiry convened to investigate the evacuation of Winchester and Martinsburg," *OR*, series 1, vol. 27, pt. 2, 88–201.

28. Private Nathan B. Middlebrook to "Dear Sister," 27 May 1863, Nathan B. Middlebrook Papers, USAMHI.

29. Private Clement Hoffman to "Dear Mother," 23 June 1863, Clement Hoffman Papers, USAMHI; Sergeant George Daughtery to "Dear Friends," 3 January 1863 and 22 January 1863, George W. Daughtery Papers, USAMHI. Daughtery was likely referring to the irregular company commanded by Captain Hanse McNeill, as they were operating in the region around Romney, Virginia, where the Twenty-second Pennsylvania Cavalry was stationed in the winter of 1863. His attitude was not abnormal for Federal troops after Mosby began his operations that winter, and may have led to Union commanders blaming any guerrilla attack on Mosby's command in 1863–64.

30. Grant, *Memoirs*, 393.

31. Wert, *Mosby's Rangers*, 220–35; Mosby, *Memoirs*, 312–13. See chapter 4 for details of the Federal counterinsurgency program in northern Virginia. Mosby picked a westbound passenger train for the attack for purely propaganda reasons. In his Memoirs, he stated that "the western-bound passenger train was selected from the schedule as I knew it would create a greater sensation to burn it than any other" (313).

32. Scott, *Partisan Life*, 334–36; Mosby, *Memoirs*, 314–16.

33. Mosby, *Memoirs*, 312–19; Scott, *Partisan Life*, 334–39; Wert, *Mosby's Rangers*, 232–36; Brigadier General John D. Stevenson to Secretary of War Edwin M. Stanton, 14 October 1864, *OR*, series 1, vol. 43, pt. 1, 368; Stevenson to Stanton, 15 October 1864, ibid., 380–81.

34. Scott, *Partisan Life*, 30.

35. Mosby, *Memoirs*, 317–18.

36. Scott, *Partisan Life*, 75.

37. Ibid., 75–77; General Robert E. Lee to General Samuel Cooper, 1 April 1864, Lee, *Wartime Papers*, 688–89.

38. Wert, *Mosby's Rangers*, 273–77; Colonel W. H. Taylor to Mosby, 27 March 1865, *OR*, series 1, vol. 46, pt. 3, 1359. In the winter months of early 1865, Mosby was ordered to Richmond, where he received the thanks of the State of Virginia. The entire affair was clearly a propaganda move by the demoralized Confederates, who hailed him as one of the greatest Confederate heroes. See Wert, *Mosby's Rangers*, 273–74.

39. The Mosby-Custer feud is a long-standing debate among both the participants involved and historians. Regardless, Mosby assumed that the impact of the executions would result in his having difficulty in surrendering to Federal units in the area. See Mosby, *Memoirs*, 371. For details on the debate, see Fagan, "Custer at Front Royal: 'A Horror of the War'?" and Urwin, *Custer Victorious*, 174–75.

40. Mosby, *Memoirs*, 371.

41. Grant ordered Sheridan in 1864 to "hang any of Mosby's men if captured," including their commander. See Grant to Sheridan, 16 August 1864, *OR*, series 1, vol. 43, pt. 1, 811. Grant's attitude toward Mosby, and Mosby's toward Grant, changed significantly after Lee's surrender in April 1865. After the Army of Northern Virginia laid down its arms, Mosby ordered the disbanding of the Forty-third Virginia Cavalry Battalion, returned to his boyhood home, and awaited the Federal authorities. General Winfield Scott Hancock, commander of Union-occupied northern Virginia, offered a $5,000 reward for Mosby's capture, and rumors spread that the partisan had been involved in the Lincoln assassination and had fled to Mexico. In late May 1865, Mosby sent a letter to Lee requesting he intercede with Grant for a pardon. Grant refused. Later, the Federal generalissimo relented and sent General John Gregg to offer Mosby parole. General Henry Halleck, on finding out that Grant was planning on paroling Mosby, sent a second message to Gregg ordering Mosby's arrest. On meeting Gregg, and being told that no pardon would be issued, Mosby left the meeting place, surrendering only after Grant personally intervened. Despite threats from local Unionists, Mosby returned to his law practice. Due to Grant's leniency toward the partisan, Mosby became a staunch Republican, campaigning for Grant during the 1872 election. His loyalty to Grant and the Republican Party, despite attacks by Democrats in the South, was rewarded with an appointment as consul to Hong Kong in 1879. In this respect, Mosby's postwar history closely parallels that of James Longstreet, as both were victims of Democratic attacks led by Jubal Early. The old ranger lived until Memorial Day 1916, when he died at the age of eighty-two. He is buried in his hometown of Warrenton, Virginia. For Mosby's postwar life, see Ramage, *Gray Ghost*, 265–68, 284–85, 340.

CHAPTER 4

1. See the introduction for definitions of key terms.

2. Wooden stockades and blockhouses had been used extensively before the Civil War on the American frontier, during the American Revolution, and during the French and Indian War. What makes the blockhouse system defending the railroad system around Washington different from previous incarnations is that it was built specifically to prevent irregulars from attacking the railroads. In the past, larger fortifications were employed to protect immigration routes, such as the Oregon Trail, or strategically important locations, such as the invasion route along Lake Champlain. The small 50–100-man blockhouses scattered throughout an area would have been useless against large

conventional forces, as the Federals found out during Lee's 1862 (Antietam) and 1863 (Gettysburg) invasions of the North. Similar blockhouses were used in Tennessee and Kentucky following the 1862 Confederate winter raids. For the past history of blockhouses, fortifications, and their impact on warfare in America, see Francis Paul Prucha's *The Sword of the Republic: The United States Army on the Frontier, 1783–1846* (New York: Macmillan, 1969); F. Paul Prucha, *Broadaxe and Bayonet: The Role of the United States Army in the Development of the Northwest, 1815–1860* (Madison: State Historical Society of Wisconsin, 1963), and Herbert M. Sylvester, *Indian Wars of New England*, 3 vols. (Boston: W. B. Clarke Co., 1910). The blockhouse concept was also used after the Civil War in numerous irregular warfare campaigns, from the French in Indochina to the British in South Africa.

3. Information on nineteenth-century irregular warfare doctrine is discussed in the introduction and in Jomini, *Art of War*, 202–204.

4. Shanks, *Secession Movement*, 1–3.

5. Wert, "West Virginia," 816–17.

6. Matheny, *Wood County*, 45–46; Israel Forman to "Dear Brother," 25 November 1861, Forman Family Papers, Manuscript and Special Collections, Civil War Miscellaneous Collection, USAMHI.

7. Matheny, *Wood County*, 121, 211–14, 226–27. Confederate authorities attempted to legally commission the officers of the guerrilla bands in 1861, by sending a parcel of blank Confederate army commissions with a courier into the mountains. The commissions were signed and returned to Richmond; the Federal authorities were not fooled by this legal trickery, and refused to accept them. See ibid., 227. For Federal response to Virginia governor John Letcher's attempts to commission irregulars, see "Report of Major General John C. Fremont," *OR*, series 1, vol. 15, 5–6.

8. From army commander Major General George McClellan to division commander Brigadier General William Rosecrans to company grade officers, West Point graduates and U.S. Army regulars were used extensively to lead and train the volunteers from Ohio, Illinois, Indiana, and Virginia that fought in the 1861 western Virginia campaign. Several officers received their first combat commands during this campaign, including Brigadier General Joseph J. Reynolds, who later commanded the Army of Arkansas in 1864–65, and future generals Colonel George Crook and Captain Nelson Miles. In the Shenandoah Valley in 1861, numerous regular units fought, including the Seventh Infantry and Second Cavalry regiments, and several batteries of regular artillery. In the western counties of Virginia, the bulk of the troops were from Ohio. See "Report of Operations in the Shenandoah Valley," *OR*, series 1, vol. 2, 156, and troop lists mentioned in *OR*, series 1, vol. 5, 146, 636.

9. McPherson, *Battle Cry of Freedom*, 299–304.

10. Crook, *General George Crook*, 86–87.

11. Ibid., 88. Crook returned to the region in 1864 as one of Sheridan's subordinates. In February 1865, he was kidnapped from his headquarters at Cumberland, Maryland, by Captain John McNeill's partisan ranger company. McNeill was attempting to duplicate Mosby's capture of Stoughton (see chap. 3) and succeeded in spiriting Crook and General Benjamin Kelley into

Confederate lines. After his exchange in March 1865, Crook returned to the Army of the Potomac as a cavalry division commander. After the war, he returned to the frontier, where he was instrumental in the subjugation of several hostile Native American tribes. He would die in service in 1890 as commander of the Division of the Missouri. Warner, *Generals in Blue*, 102–104.

12. "Report of Major General John C. Fremont," *OR*, series 1, vol. 15, 5.

13. Forsythe, *Guerrilla Warfare*, 8. After the war, the pro-Union Forsythe left Loudoun County, which was part of "Mosby's Confederacy" during the last two years of the war, becoming a Baptist minister in the Midwest.

14. Rawling, *History of the First Regiment*, 149–50. Rawling was a lieutenant in the First (West) Virginia Infantry Regiment.

15. Sergeant John H. Black to "Dear Wife," 12 August 1863, in Black, "Powder, Lead and Cold Steel," 60–61.

16. Cooling, *Symbol, Sword, and Shield*, 7–8. Cooling's work outlines the maintenance and manning of the Washington defenses during the war, noting in numerous places that the personnel assigned to the defenses numbered at least 30,000 men, excluding the Army of the Potomac when it occasionally used the defenses to retreat into after defeats, and often numbered well over 50,000 men and 1,000 guns of various caliber.

17. Summers, *Baltimore and Ohio*, 145–46.

18. Throughout the war, all Federal forces in western Virginia faced two threats—regular and irregular Confederate forces. It would be misleading to presuppose that all the listed troops existed solely for the purpose of fighting guerrillas. Instead, antiguerrilla patrols should be considered part of routine military operations instead of the single mission for the Federal army. The exception to this are the units raised expressly to hunt down irregulars, such as the Loudoun County Rangers and Captain Richard Blazer's cavalry detachment. Summers, *Baltimore and Ohio*, 145–61.

Regarding figure 2, Carl Beamer's dissertation, "Grey Ghostbusters," cites the total numbers for the period slightly differently, counting troops assigned to the Washington defenses as well as the extensive railroad organization of the Federal army into the total number of Union troops fighting against the Confederate irregulars. For the purposes of this work, only the troops actively performing antiguerrilla operations are being considered, along with those permanently assigned to the western Virginia region. Consideration must be given to the conventional operations in 1861–62, and in 1864, in the region as an additional reason for expanded troop numbers. Of special note is the fact that during the era of Mosby's greatest victories (mid-1863 to fall 1864), Federal troop numbers tended to go down. Beamer, "Grey Ghostbusters," 113–14, 133.

19. Warner, *Generals in Blue*, 260–61. Warner notes that Kelley did not venture out of northwestern Virginia during his entire career. To his chagrin, he was captured by a group of sixty partisan rangers led by Captain Jesse McNeill on February 21, 1865, along with General Crook, while visiting his future bride at Cumberland, Maryland. He was later exchanged, and rose to the rank of major general before leaving the service in July 1865.

20. Cooling, *Symbol, Sword, and Shield*, 185–87; Summers, *Baltimore and Ohio*, 157–58; "The B&O R. R.: The Base of Operations for the Federal Army in 1863–1865: Reminiscences of Maj. S. F. Shaw," *Book of the Royal Blue* 2 (October 1898): 11, cited in Summers, 157–58.

21. "Report of Brigadier General Bradley T. Johnson, C.S.A.," 10 August 1864, *OR*, series 1, vol. 37, pt. 1, 356; J. P. Willard to General Benjamin Kelley, 19 July 1864, ibid., pt. 2, 397.

22. Newhall, *Memoir*, 124.

23. Hyndman, *History of a Cavalry Company*, 181, 183–85. Hyndman was not one of the postwar writers who attempted to make Mosby even greater than he was to justify his failed attempts to catch the partisan. In fact, Hynd-man believed Mosby to be no better than the bushwhackers he had previously fought in West Virginia, stating that "he [Mosby] acted more brilliantly in this sneaking kind of warfare, than others whose names are blatant from the horn of fame. But this kind of ability is very common, and is at once associated with, and evoked by reckless and corrupt morals—the large mushroom of skilled vil-lainy which the dung-hill of destructiveness sometimes surprisingly displays in war." He added, "Fortunately for Moseby [sic] the war was a very definite plane, and circumstances thus prevented the possibility of that inevitable dénouement which would have turned the serious splendor of his record, into the joke of such locality and attachment, as might have been effected for his name, by cross beams and hemp" (184).

24. Crook, *Autobiography*, 135.

25. Other Federal units had been raised prior to this time that fought guerrillas on a constant basis, but none had been expressly formed for that purpose. The Loudon County Rangers (First Virginia Cavalry, Union), First Maryland Cavalry, and others fought irregulars on a constant basis from mid-1862 onward. See Kirkby, "Partisan and Counterpartisan Activity in North-ern Virginia," 32–37.

26. Mosby, *Memoirs*, 319–20; Crawford, *Mosby and His Men*, 254–55, 299–301.

27. Crawford, *Mosby and His Men*, 255.

28. Alexander, *Mosby's Men*, 116.

29. Captain Richard Blazer to General Philip Sheridan, 4 September 1864, *OR*, series 1, vol. 43, pt. 1, 615.

30. Scott, *Partisan Life*, 365–66.

31. Ibid., 366.

32. Blazer to Sheridan, 4 September 1864, *OR*, series 1, vol. 43, pt. 1, 615; Scott, *Partisan Life*, 368, 369; Sheridan to Major General Henry Halleck, 21 November 1864, *OR*, series 1, vol. 43, pt. 1, 653. Blazer was later exchanged, under Sheridan's directive, for a captured Confederate colonel, but never returned to the region, dying of yellow fever in 1878. See Alexander, *Mosby's Men*, 128.

33. Sheridan, *Memoirs*, 276, 339–41.

34. Ibid., 338–44.

35. Reader, *History of the Fifth West Virginia Cavalry*, 248. For details on Halleck's reaction toward irregulars, see the discussion of Halleck and

General Orders Number 100 in the introduction; grammar and spelling as in the original.

36. Rawling, *History of the First Regiment*, 149–50.

37. Beach, *First New York Cavalry*, 182.

38. Lynch, *Civil War Diary*, 33, 44, 61, 129.

39. Ibid., 64, 121. Lynch also noted that many of the wagon drivers were civilians who "will most generally obey orders, whether from friends or foes, when they see a gun pointed at their heads."

40. Rhodes, *All for the Union*, 173.

41. Theodore Lang, an Unionist West Virginian officer, later wrote that he and his men believed that such a campaign of destruction could only damage the Union cause. Citing the actions of General Benjamin S. Roberts, who had been General Pope's chief of cavalry at Second Manassas, in western Virginia in 1863, Lang said "he [Roberts] began his military operations by making war upon the resident Secessionists, both men and women, forcing all who held Southern sentiments to leave their homes." While Lang agreed that some pro-Confederates should be forced south, he felt that "there was, nevertheless, in this method of ridding the community of disloyalty a question of just where to draw the line." Lang criticized General Roberts for depopulating entire regions of all people, both Unionists and Confederates, which in turn created greater animosity toward the Federal army and made Lang's counterinsurgency mission that much harder. Lang, *Loyal West Virginia*, 106.

42. Sheridan's 1864 Shenandoah Valley campaign and Sherman's "March to the Sea," are often cited as the most destructive campaigns of the Civil War. McPherson summarizes the campaign as both a retribution for irregular attacks and part of an overall strategy to starve the Confederacy into submission, stating that "it was a hard war and would soon become harder." Russell Weigley supports McPherson, seeing the destructive campaigns in the Valley and in Georgia as part of an overall strategy to destroy the ability of the South to logistically support an army. Robert Leckie, in *None Died in Vain*, and Herman Hattaway and Archer Jones in *How The North Won*, argue that the Shenandoah campaign was a natural outgrowth of an increasingly frustrating and long war, and the destruction of guerrilla bands was merely a side benefit to the overall strategy of eliminating the Confederacy's ability to make war. Michael G. Mahon, in *The Shenandoah Valley, 1861–1865*, presents a thesis that questions the effectiveness of Sheridan's campaign. Mahon demonstrates that Sheridan overestimated the destruction caused by his men, inflating divisional reports and sending the inaccurate summaries to Grant. He also believes that Mosby's activities had little to do with the launching of the campaign. See McPherson, *Battle Cry*, 777–78; Weigley, *American Way of War*, 143, 148, 205–206; Leckie, *None Died in Vain*, 611–12; Hattaway and Jones, *How the North Won*, 615–20; and Mahon, *Shenandoah Valley*, 110, 119–20, 124–26. These are but a few examples of the body of work that presents the burning of the Valley as part of an increasingly total war by 1864. A good brief summary of the historical consensus of the 1864 Valley campaign's impact on the Confederacy is in Richard N. Current, ed., *Encyclopedia of the Confederacy*, 3:1412–13, 1417–19.

43. Historians focusing on Mosby's Rangers are divided on the influence Confederate irregular warfare had on Grant's decision to send Sheridan to devastate the Valley. Virgil C. Jones, in *Gray Ghosts and Rebel Raiders*, contends that the Federals were already planning to burn the Valley and that the death of Union officers and men to guerrillas gave them additional reasons to conduct the incendiary campaign. James Ramage, in *Gray Ghost*, believes that Mosby's actions were the primary reason for the Valley campaign, and the destruction of the Confederate food supply was a secondary benefit. In *Mosby's Rangers*, Jeffry D. Wert divides the Valley campaign into several stages, all of which were focused on the destruction of Mosby and other irregulars in northwestern Virginia. In contrast, most historians of the war see the campaign as part of a scheme to destroy the logistics structure of the Confederacy, much like Sherman's 1864–65 March to the Sea (see note 42, above). Jones, *Gray Ghosts*, 309–10; Ramage, *Gray Ghost*, 216–42; Wert, *Mosby's Rangers*, 194–95, 236–38, 260–61.

44. One specific event, the death of Lieutenant John R. Meigs, son of Union Quartermaster General Montgomery C. Meigs, on October 3, 1864, provides an example of retributive burning in the 1864 Valley Campaign. Historian John L. Heatwole, in his excellent work, *The Burning: Sheridan's Devastation of the Shenandoah Valley*, details the death of Lieutenant Meigs during a chance encounter with Confederate scouts from the 1st and 4th Virginia Cavalry. Meigs encountered the Confederate patrol, which demanded his surrender. The headstrong lieutenant refused and attempted to draw his revolver; unluckily for the 1862 West Point graduate, the Confederates were slightly faster. Meigs's escorting soldiers, a private and a sergeant, were wounded and later reported that guerrillas had killed him from ambush. When another of Sheridan's aides, Major George A. Forsyth, recovered the lieutenant's body, he surmised that either Mosby or another guerrilla band had done the work. Meigs was Sheridan's aide-de-camp and one of the "Sheridan entourage" that included General Wesley Merritt, General George Crook, and General George A. Custer. According to Heatwole, Sheridan flew into a rage and ordered a five-mile swath around the area—including barns, homes and towns—burned to the ground. Contending views of the death of Lieutenant Meigs and Sheridan's burning of the area between Harrisonburg and Bridgewater, Virginia (afterwards referred to as "the Burnt District") came to light as early as 1881. In several editorials in the *Southern Historical Society Papers* of that year, the fact emerged that Meigs had not been killed by bushwackers, but by regular Confererate cavalry in a fair fight. Consequently, Sheridan's order for retributive burning was neither justified due to guerrilla attacks nor legal under the Articles of War. See Heatwole, *The Burning*, 89–93, "The Killing of Lieutenant Meigs," in *Southern Historical Society Papers (1881)*, 77–78, and "Was Lieutenant Meigs Killed in Fair Combat?" ibid, 190.

45. Newhall, *Memoir*, 124–25. Newhall considered the taking of loyalty oaths, administered by the provost marshal general, as worthless tools to stop irregular warfare, a feeling shared by Federal troops in Arkansas, Tennessee, and Kentucky. What especially frustrated him were the numerous unorganized irregulars operating in eastern Virginia. Calling them "wretches," "a scourge," "felons," and "debased," Newhall considered them worse than spies and the lowest form of humanity (123).

46. Rhodes, *All for the Union*, 87.

47. Duncan, ed., *Alexander Neil*, 70.

48. Sheridan, *Personal Memoirs*, 338; see also *OR*, series 1, vol. 43, pt. 2, 351.

49. Martin, *Boy of Old Shenandoah*, 34–37, 47. Not all Federal commanders took part in the destruction. Lieutenant Lewis Luckenbill, Ninety-sixth Pennsylvania Volunteer Infantry, wrote in his diary regarding the destruction of the Valley. He related that during a seven-mile patrol ahead of his regiment, a detachment of his men "arrested 20 men [Federal stragglers out looking for plunder]" and protected the property of a local citizen, a Mr. Hoffman, from destruction. This is odd behavior for an army bent on plunder and destruction. Lewis Luckenbill diary, 30 September 1864, NW CWRT Collection, USAMHI.

50. Merritt, "Sheridan in the Shenandoah Valley," 4:512–13. Emphasis added.

51. Hyndman, *History of a Cavalry Company*, 203.

52. Ibid., 204; Duncan, ed., *Alexander Neil*, 78. In a letter dated October 13, 1864, Surgeon Neil wrote: "I am informed that they [Mosby's men] kill all the prisoners they take and they have raised the black flag. But there are two sides that can play this game and our boys remember every one they catch, but 'tis best to tell no tales." In this case, the editor of Neil's papers believes that the surgeon was speaking of the retributive hanging of six of Mosby's men by Union troops in early October. Ibid., 71.

53. Hyndman, *History of a Cavalry Company*, 229–30.

54. Lieutenant H. H. Chipman to Captain C. H. Safford, 26 October 1864, *OR*, series 1, vol. 43, pt. 2, 470–72.

55. General George Crook to Colonel J. H. Oley, 30 October 1864, *OR*, series 1, vol. 43, pt. 2, 496–97.

56. General Orders Number 23, 17 November 1864, *OR*, series 1, vol. 43, pt. 1, 639.

57. Major General Henry W. Halleck to Brigadier General D. C. McCallum, 12 October 1864, *OR*, series 1, vol. 43, pt. 2, 348–49.

58. Mosby was able to find sufficient subsistence for his battalion, plus local troops he raised, in the Valley until the end of the war. Despite the wholesale destruction created by Sheridan's campaign in the fall, many farms, mills, and villages escaped destruction. Edward R. Phillips's *The Lower Shenandoah Valley in the Civil War* postulates that location was the key factor for Federals deciding what to destroy. Phillips contends, with ample evidence, that the closer a farm, home, or town was to the main thoroughfare along which Sheridan's army moved; the more likely it was to be destroyed. Consequently, foodstuffs stored in barn and granaries in the hinterland were relatively untouched. See 150–51, 167–69.

59. Kidd, *Personal Recollections*, 445.

CHAPTER 5

1. Clausewitz, *On War*, 491, 512. Clausewitz uses as his example the operations of Frederick the Great prior to the 1759 campaign of the Seven Years' War. Frederick's Prussians launched a series of large raids meant as

spoiling attacks, to prevent the buildup of enemy forces in Poland, Bohemia, and Franconia. According to Clausewitz, Frederick's goal was to weaken the ability of the enemy to launch a sustained offensive and to gain psychological ascendancy over his enemies. See 512–13. The offensive raid, which Morgan's and Forrest's 1862 summer raids could be considered examples of, were aimed at isolating an enemy army prior to bringing it to a decisive battle. See 541. Jomini, also studying the campaigns of Frederick the Great, wrote that the "use of light [raiding] troops" was perfect for "disquiet[ing] our adversary on several important points of his communications," adding "he will oppose [the raiders with] numerous divisions, and will scatter out his masses." To some extent, this is exactly what happened to the Federal Army of the Ohio in August 1862, as entire infantry divisions attempted to catch Morgan's and Forrest's raiders. See Jomini, *Grand Military Operations*, 2:336, 452–53.

2. Ramage, *Rebel Raider*, 8–14.

3. Ibid., 16, 18–20.

4. Edison Thomas, *Morgan and His Raiders*, 7–11. The state government of Kentucky had stopped funding, manning, or maintaining the militia in the early 1850s, believing that with the westward expansion of the frontier, an organized militia was an unnecessary drain on the state budget. Units raised in the 1850s tended to be wholly volunteer organizations, who would apply for state recognition as militia. One such unit was Morgan's Lexington Rifles. See Cecil Holland, "The Lexington Rifles, 1857–1861," Cecil Holland Papers, Special Collections and Archives, University of Kentucky, Lexington, Kentucky (hereafter UKY).

5. Ramage, *Rebel Raider*, 25, 28–29, 32, 35, 44–45; Evans, ed., *Confederate Military History*, 9:92–93; Brown, *Bold Cavaliers*, 16–25; Musgrove, *Kentucky Cavaliers in Dixie*, 129.

6. Ramage, *Rebel Raider*, 49–51, 63.

7. Keller, *Morgan's Raid*, 21.

8. Ibid. Keller describes one of Morgan's men who joined the command in late 1862 as a farmer who enlisted to escape the "terror being committed by 'Tinker Dave' Beattie, who attacked Federals, Confederates and civilians with equal fervor." Beattie was a well-known Unionist bushwhacker operating near Sparta, Tennessee. Beattie later became famous for his one-man war against his Confederate nemesis, Champ Ferguson. See ibid., 29; Brown, *Bold Cavaliers*, 70–72. Bell I. Wiley's classic *Johnny Reb, The Life of a Confederate Soldier* strongly reinforces the common belief that the Confederate soldier was a hard fighter but almost completely undisciplined. Brown quotes Grenfell in stating that "I [Grenfell] never encountered such men who would fight like the devil, but would do what they pleased, like these damned Rebel cavalrymen." According to Starr and Evans, St. Leger Grenfell was denied parole at the end of the war and imprisoned at the U.S. Military Stockade at Dry Tortugas, Florida. He later attempted to escape by boat, but an unexpected storm swept his craft out to sea and he was never heard from again. See Evans, ed., *Confederate Military History*, 9:105; Seymour, *Divided Loyalties*, 58; Logan, *Kelion Franklin Peddicord*, 61–62; Starr, *Colonel Grenfell's Wars*, 308–26.

9. Young, *Confederate Wizards of the Saddle*, 424. Young served as the commander in chief of the United Confederate Veterans in the first decade of the twentieth century and was influential in keeping the memory of Morgan alive. See also Evans, ed., *Confederate Military History*, 11:92.

10. Brown, *Bold Cavaliers*, 158–59.

11. Brian Steel Wills contends that Forrest was a member of the planter class by the late 1850s. Basing his evidence on solid sources, Wills demonstrates that Forrest was not a stereotypical slave trader, but a "businessman-planter," who was accepted by the Memphis society as one of their top entrepreneurs. Although Forrest came from humble beginnings, and lacked the pedigree of his fellow cavalry commanders Joseph Wheeler and John Hunt Morgan, his adroit business sense, wealth, and personality led him to be fully accepted as one of the leaders of the community in 1860. It is worth noting, however, that Memphis was also one of the largest slave-trading cities of the South by 1860, and the profession was looked down on in other areas, such as Charleston and Richmond. See Wills, *Battle from the Start*, 27, 29, 31–33, 35, 39.

12. Mathes, *General Forrest*, 21–22.

13. Ibid., 24–25; Company A, 90 men, was from Brandenburg, Kentucky; Company B, 80 men, southern Alabama; Company C, 90 men, Memphis; Company D, 90 men, from Texas; Company E, 80 men, Gadsden, Alabama; Company F, 90 men, Huntsville, Alabama; Company G, 45 men, Harrodsburg, Kentucky; and Company H, 85 men, Marshall County, Alabama. All numbers are estimates of company strength. See Wyeth, *Life of General Forrest*, 25–26. C. M. Stacy to "Dear Son," 9 November 1862, Hamner-Stacy Papers, Mississippi Valley Collection, University of Memphis, Memphis, Tennessee (hereafter UM-MVC).

14. Colonel Samuel Tate to General Albert S. Johnston, 4 November 1861, *OR*, series 1, vol. 4, 513; Wyeth, *Life of General Forrest*, 27.

15. General Albert S. Johnston was killed at Shiloh in April 1862, and was replaced by General P. G. T. Beauregard. General Braxton Bragg assumed command of the Army of Tennessee in late April, holding it until early 1864. Current, ed., *Encyclopedia of the Confederacy*, 1:83–89, 204.

16. Evans, ed., *Confederate Military History*, 11:98–99; Edison Thomas, *Morgan and His Raiders*, 32–33; Current, ed., *Encyclopedia of the Confederacy*, 1:204–206.

17. "Report of Colonel John H. Morgan, Second Kentucky Cavalry," 30 July 1862, *OR*, series 1, vol. 16, pt. 1, 767–68.

18. Evans, ed., *Confederate Military History*, 11:116–18, 122–23.

19. Ibid., 125–26.

20. Cooling, *Fort Donelson's Legacy*, 132–34. Cooling's outstanding study of both the war in the region and its impact on the civilian populace is perhaps the best single work on the subject. In addition to examining the entire conflict in the region from the fall of Fort Donelson in 1862 to the aftermath of Chickamauga in 1863, he also addresses the role played by Morgan and Forrest. Cooling agrees that their military effectiveness should not be underestimated, but places a greater emphasis on their roles as propaganda weapons for the Confederate cause, especially after the retreat from Perryville.

21. James Ramage concludes that Morgan's use of cavalry as mounted infantry was neither revolutionary nor unexpected. Others before 1862 had done so extensively, including Forrest and John Bell Hood in 1861. Ramage also adds that Morgan's experience in the Mexican War may have played a role, since he served as a mounted infantryman at the Battle of Buena Vista. See Ramage, *Rebel Raider*, 92.

22. In a journal entry for August 19, 1862, Major Edward O. Guerrant had one simple entry, which said "Eternal Jack Morgan blown up the tunnel—burned up the cars (40) & burned down the bridges on the Nashville & Louisville R.R. Hurrah for Morgan," a sentiment felt by many other Confederate soldiers and civilians at the time. Guerrant's attitude toward Morgan changed greatly after the failed "Great Raid" of 1863. Guerrant, *Bluegrass Confederate*, 132.

23. Musgrove, *Kentucky Cavaliers in Dixie*, 61–62.

24. Ramage, *Rebel Raider*, 94–98; Boatner, *Civil War Dictionary*, 567; Connelly, *Army of the Heartland*, 200–203; "Buell's Statement," *OR*, series 1, vol. 16, pt. 1, 34–35; "Kentuckians!" 15 July 1862, Crandell and Harwell, eds., *Confederate Imprints*, 82:2530. Buell was not surprised with Morgan's success, noting that he could not defend every town and hamlet in Kentucky with the troops on hand. Buell stated, "Is it astonishing that 1,000 cavalry, familiar with every path, should be able to penetrate this vast extent of country and escape without capture?" See "Buell's Statement," 35. Another factor in the success of Morgan's raids was the use of George Ellsworth, a highly talented telegrapher, who always accompanied the Confederate cavalryman. Ellsworth, according to all accounts, possessed exceptional skill at his job, and could duplicate the individualized "touch" of another telegrapher having heard it only once. Once in Kentucky, Morgan ordered Ellsworth to reroute trains carrying reinforcements and to gather information on pursuing enemy forces; Morgan even used the Federal telegraph system to send personal messages to friends in Louisville, and one to the Federal commander in the city, recommending the telegraph as "a great institution," and inquiring if the Federals wished to have copies of all their dispatches since July 10, since "my friend Ellsworth has them all on file." See "Report of George Ellsworth, Telegraph Operator, Morgan's Command," 30 July 1862, *OR*, series 1, vol. 16, pt. 1, 774–77.

25. Connelly, *Army of the Heartland*, 201–202; Evans, ed., *Confederate Military History*, 8:217–18; Morgan, *How It Was*, 71. The author of *How It Was*, Mrs. Irby Morgan, was distantly related to John Hunt Morgan, and was a staunch Confederate and talented observer of events during the war.

26. The Eighth Texas Cavalry is also known as "Terry's Texas Rangers," after their first commander, Colonel B. F. Terry. He was killed in a skirmish at Green River, Kentucky, in 1861, and during Forrest's first Tennessee raid, the regiment was commanded by Colonel John A. Wharton. See Wyeth, *Life of Forrest*, 84.

27. Wills, *Battle from the Start*, 72–78; Mathes, *General Forrest*, 63–66. "Report of Lieutenant Colonel John G. Parkhurst, Ninth Michigan Infantry," *OR*, series 1, vol. 16, pt. 1, 805; "Report of Brigadier General N. B. Forrest, C.S.

Army," ibid., 810–11; Bruce, "General Buell's Campaign," 121; Jordan and Pryor, *Campaigns of General Forrest*, 166–72. In Crittenden's defense, it must be stated that he had assumed command of Murfreesboro only the day before, and that preexistent conditions had led to the failure of the troops there. For example, the pickets were, as a matter of habit, withdrawn at night back to the camps. Consequently, only two men were on lookout when Forrest's raiders approached. Neither factor prevented the ending of Crittenden's career. Despite the clearing of his reputation by a court of inquiry in January 1863, Crittenden was blamed by Buell for the incident. The army commander went as far as to say: "Take it in all its features, few more disgraceful examples of neglect of duty and lack of good conduct can be found in the history of wars. It fully merits the extreme penalty which the law provides for such misconduct." After his release from captivity in October 1862, he was not given another assignment, and resigned on May 5, 1863. In many ways, his fate parallels that of Brigadier General Stoughton, who was captured by Mosby's Rangers in 1863. See chapter 3 for details on Stoughton's capture. Warner, *Generals in Blue*, 101–102; "Report of Brigadier General Crittenden," *OR*, series 1, vol. 16, pt. 1, 794–96; "General Orders No. 32," 21 July 1862, ibid., 793–94. Despite the failure to destroy the rail bridge, damage to the rails did preclude use of the Nashville and Chattanooga line until July 28. "Report of Major General Buell," ibid., 33.

    28. "Findings of the Buell Commission," 29 May 1863, *OR*, series 1, vol. 16, pt. 1, 13; "Statement of MG Buell in Front of the Military Commission," ibid., 33–35.

    29. Crook, *Autobiography*, 101–104.

    30. The Unionist units were especially disliked by the Confederate troops. Adolphus Montague, a private in the Seventh Tennessee Cavalry, wrote that these "'Home-Made Yankees' [were] composed of the roughest most good-for-nothing men who would not join the Confederates but waited for an opportunity to join the Federals that they might stay near home and pilfer the houses in the community as well as settle their grudges by attacking their personal enemies." Adolphus Wiley Montague memoir, UM-MVC, 4. See also Current, *Lincoln's Loyalists*, 29–62.

    31. Buell to General J. T. Boyle, 11 July 1862, *OR*, series 1, vol. 16, pt. 1, 733; Morse, "Relief of Chattanooga," 73, 79; Adolphus Wiley Montague memoir, UM-MVC, 11.

    32. "Buell's Report," *OR*, series 1, vol. 16, pt. 1, 34; Bruce, "General Buell's Campaign," 119–20.

    33. "Findings of the Buell Commission," *OR*, series 1, vol. 16, pt. 1, 35–36. Buell attempted to do the best he could to deal with the raiders, but was completely caught by surprise in July 1862. Forrest's attack on Murfreesboro was especially harmful, leading Buell to say that the "consequence of this disaster was serious" and the destruction of the stockpiles and rails at the town "set back two weeks" the planned advance on Chattanooga. Morgan's actions in Kentucky resulted in Buell being bombarded with requests from Unionist leaders and military officials for troops, further weakening his offensive. See ibid., 34–37.

34. Ramage, *Rebel Raider*, 111–12; "Report of Major General Buell," 36–37; Fisk, *Mississippi Valley in the Civil War*, 149; Granger, *Life of Major General Grenville M. Dodge*, 8–10, USMA-SC. Dodge recalled "every mile of railroad line had to be watched and every stream and bridge guarded from guerrillas" (10).

35. Ramage notes that the Louisville and Nashville provided over 12 million rations from June to August 1862 through the tunnels. After August 10, because of a drop in the water level, as is common in the South in late summer, the rivers became useless as an alternative means of transporting supplies. See Ramage, *Rebel Raider*, 112–13. Bruce, "General Buell's Campaign," 119.

36. Buell to Major General Henry W. Halleck, 23 July 1862, *OR*, series 1, vol. 16, pt. 2, 202.

37. Nelson's division numbered nearly 7,200 officers and men, of which approximately 6,000 were infantry and artillery, and 1,200 were cavalry. See "Monthly Return for Army of the Ohio," 1 August 1862, *OR*, series 1, vol. 16, pt. 2, 246.

38. Brigadier General Nelson to Buell, 26 July 1862, *OR*, series 1, vol. 16, pt. 2, 213.

39. Nelson to Buell, 30 July 1862, ibid., 233.

40. Wills, *Battle from the Start*, 79–81.

41. Morgan to Logan Railey, 14 September 1862, Box 16, Folder 2, Hunt-Morgan Family Papers, UKY-SC; Ramage, *Rebel Raider*, 114–16. Ramage notes that the Federal seizure of all the men at Gallatin, and their killing of three men during the arrests, infuriated Morgan. During the pursuit of the Federals back to Nashville, Morgan ordered that no quarter be given to the Union troops; Ramage states that Morgan himself took part in shooting prisoners. Citing a diary entry, Ramage quotes Morgan as saying, "There were so many of them [captured Federals] that when they threw down their arms we couldn't shoot them all" (116). Actions such as this did much to harden the war between the Federal army and Morgan's raiders, and perhaps have much to do with the view of Morgan as a guerrilla instead of a conventional cavalry commander. The quotation is originally from the L. Virginia Smith French diary, 22 March 1863, Tennessee State Library and Archives, Nashville, Tennessee.

42. Ramage, *Rebel Raider*, 116–17; "Reports of Raid on Louisville and Nashville Railroad, 19–21 August 1862," *OR*, series 1, vol. 16, pt. 1, 872, 875–76, 878, 881; Connelly, *Army of the Heartland*, 202–203; Mathes, *General Forrest*, 63–66.

43. Unorganized bushwhackers were a continual problem, in addition to the raiders, throughout the war. Colonel Robert H. Carnahan's infantry regiment, on a late July 1864 march through northwestern Kentucky, wrote that "[we] scout the country, cleaning out the bushwhackers or get cleaned out ourselves." His 200-man patrol was common duty for many Federal units in the region throughout the war. Colonel Robert H. Carnahan to "Dear Wife," 30 July 1864, Robert H. Carnahan Papers, USAMHI.

44. "Transcript from Phonographic Notes of the Buell Court of Inquiry," 25 December 1862, *OR*, series 1, vol. 16, pt. 1, 271.

45. Ibid.

46. Smith's forces had begun movement from Knoxville on August 14. Bragg's army is generally estimated at 30,000 men and Smith's at 10,000 in most maps and general accounts of the campaign. This may include the recruits picked up in Tennessee and Kentucky as the forces moved north and may include the total strength, versus the available strength, of the two armies. The only constant number is the 48,776 Confederates reported by Bragg prior to the Battle of Perryville on October 8. See Connelly, *Army of the Heartland*, 205–15; E. Kirby Smith to Adjutant General Cooper, 24 August 1862, *OR*, series 1, vol. 16, pt. 2, 777–78; Griess, ed., *West Point Atlas*, plate 16; Current, ed., *Encyclopedia of the Confederacy*, 2:889–91; Seitz, *Braxton Bragg*, 138.

47. The poor relationship between Bragg and E. Kirby Smith was not abnormal. Few officers worked well with Braxton Bragg; he had a reputation as a martinet, was rigid and aloof, and firmly believed that any non-West Point trained officer was incompetent. Such behavior led to numerous conflicts between Bragg and his subordinates, including Morgan, Forrest, Kirby Smith, James Longstreet, and others. See Seitz, *Braxton Bragg*, and McWhiney, *Braxton Bragg and Confederate Defeat*.

48. Proportionally, the Federal defeat at Richmond was the most total defeat of the war. Smith's 6,000 veterans smashed into Nelson's 6,500 green recruits, killing 206, wounding 844, and capturing over 4,000, compared with Confederate losses of 78 killed and 372 wounded. Smith proudly boasted that his men had taken over 10,000 stands of arms from the field, as well as a dozen artillery pieces abandoned by their untrained crews. See "Reports of Major General E. Kirby Smith, C.S.A.," 30 August 1862, *OR*, series 1, vol. 16, pt. 1, 931–37, and Current, ed., *Encyclopedia of the Confederacy*, 2:890.

49. Current, ed., *Encyclopedia of the Confederacy*, 2:890–91, 3:1196–98; Archer Jones, *Confederate Strategy*, 104–105, 108; Wheeler, "Bragg's Invasion of Kentucky." Confederate leaders, encouraged by the reports of Morgan and others of the undying loyalty to the Confederacy in Kentucky, expected a wave of new recruits in the state during the Kentucky campaign. It never happened, and Bragg carried nearly 10,000 muskets brought with him from Tennessee back with his army in October. General Smith wrote Bragg on September 18, 1862, and summarized the attitudes of Kentuckians toward the Confederacy, saying "their hearts are evidently with us but their blue grass and fat cattle are against us." Cooling contends that the failure to win recruits was directly related to the lack of a permanent Confederate presence in eastern Kentucky. In this respect, the raids of Morgan, while militarily effective in hindering the Federal advance, failed to keep the flame of rebellion alive in Kentucky. The failure of irregulars to promote the pro-Confederate cause was never more evident than in the surprising lack of desire on most Kentuckians to join Bragg's army. Cooling, *Fort Donelson's Legacy*, 141–44; Horn, *Army of Tennessee*, 174–75. For Morgan's role in the Kentucky invasion, see Basil W. Duke, "Morgan's Cavalry during the Bragg Invasion," 26–28; Hafendorfer, *They Died by Twos and Tens*.

50. Sheppard, *Bedford Forrest*, 76. This action permanently soured relations between Wheeler and Forrest, and was considered a personal affront by

some of Morgan's men. Thomas Connelly believes Bragg preferred Wheeler over Forrest, whom he still considered "a mere partisan," because of his penchant for drill, his West Point background, and his service in the antebellum army. Additionally, Wheeler had served under Bragg in 1861, and was noted for his loyalty and personal friendship for him. This later would lead to a conflict of Wheeler and Bragg against Forrest following the Battle of Chickamauga in September 1863. See Connelly, *Autumn of Glory*, 27; Mathes, *General Forrest*, 33, 106, 171; Young, *Wizards of the Saddle*, 133–34.

51. For Morgan, the increase in his brigade by additional regiments was welcome. According to Kelion F. Peddicord, only 80 of the original 300 Kentucky troopers who came to Tennessee with Morgan in 1861 remained by fall 1862. Logan, *Quirk's Scouts*, 49.

52. Buell was relieved of command on October 24, 1862, for failing to aggressively pursue and destroy Bragg's army, closely resembling the relief of his personal friend Major General George McClellan following the Antietam campaign. Buell was never returned to active command during the war and resigned in 1864, returning to private life. See Warner, *Generals in Blue*, 51–52. Bragg to Jefferson Davis, 24 November 1862, *OR*, series 1, vol. 20, pt. 2, 421; Henry, *"First with the Most" Forrest*, 102, 107.

53. General Joseph E. Johnston was placed in overall command of the forces of John C. Pemberton in Mississippi, Bragg in central Tennessee, and E. Kirby Smith in eastern Tennessee in November. Johnston immediately ordered Bragg to transfer 10,000 men to Pemberton, who was vainly attempting to slow Grant's advance on Vicksburg. Although damaging to Bragg's plans, the move made strategic sense—Pemberton was facing an estimated 100,000 men in Arkansas and Mississippi with only 25,000, while Rosecrans was estimated at having 60,000 to Bragg's 40,000. Like most intelligence reports in the war, the numbers were greatly overblown, but were enough to justify the transfer. Bragg continually pushed for reinforcements, contending that if the bulk of the Confederate forces in the West were given to him, he could defeat Rosecrans's army and recapture Nashville, forcing the end of the Federal attempt to take Vicksburg. Johnston disagreed and ordered the transfer; Bragg sent the troops, but began writing directly to President Davis for orders, bypassing Johnston entirely. The result was chaos and confusion for the Confederate high command on the eve of the Battle of Stones River. Connelly, *Autumn of Glory*, 32–33; Horn, *Army of Tennessee*, 194–95.

54. Horn, *Army of Tennessee*, 193–94; Connelly, *Autumn of Glory*, 35–43; Bragg to E. Kirby Smith, 30 October 1862, Braxton Bragg Papers, USMA-SC.

55. Connelly, *Autumn of Glory*, 44–45; Ramage, *Rebel Raider*, 136–37; Wills, *Battle from the Start*, 85–88; Brewer, *Raiders of 1862*, 134.

56. Rosecrans was concerned with the impact of the raiders for several reasons. The middle Tennessee region was the only one in which the Confederates still held their gains from the previous summer. Consequently, Lincoln pushed for an advance on Chattanooga as soon as possible; attacks by raiders on the vulnerable supply line to Rosecrans's army would further delay the advance. See Kenneth Williams, *Lincoln Finds a General*, 4:242–53.

57. Major General Horatio Wright to Rosecrans, 14 November 1862, *OR*, series 1, vol. 20, pt. 2, 50; Morse, "Relief of Chattanooga," 68. Wright would later command a division of the VI Corps at Gettysburg, and rise to corps command following the death of Major General John Sedgwick at Spotsylvania in 1864. He would also take part in Sheridan's Shenandoah Valley campaign. See Warner, *Generals in Blue*, 575–76. Numbers of troops on duty are from Ramage, *Rebel Raider*, 136, compiled from the *Official Records*.

58. "Report of Major General Rosecrans," 12 February 1863, *OR*, series 1, vol. 20, pt. 1, 189; Rosecrans to Secretary of War Edwin M. Stanton, 9 November 1862, *OR*, series 1, vol. 20, pt. 2, 31. The dispersal of Federal cavalry on antiguerrilla duty was common in late 1862, as pro-Union politicians and others attempted to build up support in Kentucky. See Cooling, *Fort Donelson's Legacy*, 154–61.

59. The order of battle of Morgan's command included the Second, Third, Eighth, Ninth, Tenth, and Eleventh Kentucky Cavalry regiments, the Fourteenth Tennessee Cavalry, and two artillery batteries consisting of a ten-pound rifled Parrot, two six-pound mountain howitzers, and two pairs of six- and twelve-pound smoothbores. The First Brigade, commanded by Colonel Duke and Colonel Breckinridge's Second Brigade was supplemented by an independent scout company led by Captain Tom Quirk and a guerrilla detachment led by the notorious Champ Ferguson. See Brewer, *Raiders of 1862*, 135; Sensing, *Champ Ferguson*, 131–41; Morse, "Relief of Chattanooga," 62–63; and Lighthall, "John Hunt Morgan," 86–87. Ferguson was a true guerrilla, a bushwhacker of the trans-Mississippi variety, who preyed on Unionist sympathizers in eastern Kentucky and Tennessee. Morgan brought Ferguson's band along as guides; after the fight at Rolling Fork, the guerrillas went their own way, burning a few houses and killing several Unionists. Such actions did much to cloud the image of Morgan as a guerrilla and not a conventional cavalry commander. Ferguson was executed by Federal military authorities for fifty-three counts of murder in October 1865.

60. Duke, *Morgan's Cavalry*, 17.

61. "Report of Brigadier General John H. Morgan," 8 January 1863, *OR*, series 1, vol. 20, pt. 1, 154–57; Hockersmith, *Morgan's Escape*, 12, Rare Book Collection, Special Collections, Eastern Kentucky University, Richmond, Kentucky (hereafter EKU); "Morgan's Christmas Raid," John A. Lewis Papers, UKY.

62. "Report of Brigadier General John H. Morgan," 8 January 1863, *OR*, series 1, vol. 20, pt. 1, 156; Brewer, *Raiders of 1862*, 150–55, 159–62; Ramage, *Rebel Raider*, 140–41; Logan, *Quirk's Scouts*, 70–76; Hockersmith, *Morgan's Escape*, 12–13; Butler, *John Morgan and His Men*, 193–201.

63. Brigadier General Reynolds later commanded the Army of Arkansas in 1864–65. See chapter 2 for details.

64. "Reports of Colonel John M. Harlan," *OR*, series 1, vol. 20, pt. 1, 134–41; "Report of Colonel William A. Hoskins," 6 January 1863, ibid., 141–47; Wright to Halleck, 31 December 1862, ibid., 133.; Brewer, *Raiders of 1862*, 147–50.

65. "Summary of Principal Events, Morgan's Second Kentucky Raid," *OR*, series 1, vol. 20, pt. 1, 132; Ramage, *Rebel Raider*, 104–42, 144; Duke, *Morgan's Cavalry*, 240.

66. The numbers often vary on exactly how many men accompanied For-rest on the "West Tennessee Raid," but the general consensus is approximately 2,000. Young estimates the count at 1,800 men of the Fourth, Eighth, and Ninth Tennessee Cavalry, the Fourth Alabama Cavalry, and a four-gun artillery bat-tery, all of which were poorly equipped. Young, *Wizards of the Saddle*, 134–35, 137. Wills estimates the number at 2,100, upping the count to 2,500 after For-rest was joined by another 430 troopers on Christmas Day. Wills, *Battle from the Start*, 87.

67. Wills, *Battle from the Start*, 85.

68. Brigadier General Jeremiah Sullivan to Major General U. S. Grant, 18 December 1862, *OR*, series 1, vol. 17, pt. 1, 551. Wills, *Battle from the Start*, 85–87; Mathes, *General Forrest*, 82, 85; Evans, ed., *Confederate Military His-tory*, 7:219. Many of the commands in western Tennessee were still scattered on antiguerrilla duty when Forrest's raid struck. Brigadier General Mason Bray-man, later the governor of Idaho in the late 1870s, commanded the post of Boli-var, Tennessee during Forrest's December raid. Despite the widespread alarm raised by Forrest, Brayman still focused on destroying several "band[s] of rob-bers" in the region over massing his troops to delay or defeat the raiders. See Brayman Papers, Folder 1, Items 11, 28, 59 and 81, UM-MVC.

69. "Report of Brigadier General Nathan B. Forrest, C.S.A.," *OR*, series 1, vol. 18, pt. 1, 593; Wills, *Battle from the Start*, 87–89; Young, *Wizards of the Saddle*, 442; Evans, ed., *Confederate Military History*, 8:219–20.

70. "Report of Colonel Jacob Fry," *OR*, series 1, vol. 17, pt. 1, 560–62; "Forrest's Report," ibid., 593–94; Wills, *Battle from the Start*, 89; Beard, "With Forrest in West Tennessee," 304–305.

71. "Report of Brigadier General Thomas A. Davies," *OR*, series 1, vol. 18, pt. 1, 548–49.

72. "Forrest's Report," *OR*, series 1, vol. 17, pt. 1, 595–97; Wills, *Battle from the Start*, 92–97; Young, *Wizards of the Saddle*, 146–49. Federal mili-tary forces at Parker's Crossroads consisted of two companies of the 80th Illi-nois Infantry, the 50th Indiana Infantry, the 122nd Illinois Infantry, the 3rd Iowa Infantry, and three guns of the 7th Wisconsin Battery. It is worth know-ing that Forrest outnumbered the Federals by nearly a thousand men and had more artillery. The battle cost Forrest 160 casualties and effectively ended the raid; the Federal losses were nearly 250. See Evans, ed., *Confederate Military History*, 8:220–21.

73. The Richmond newspapers, for example, ran headlines proclaiming "Morgan Again Victorious," and "Brilliant Success," in counterpoint to the casu-alty lists of Stones River and Bragg's retreat to Tullahoma. A similar response in the newspapers was printed after Forrest's western Tennessee raid. See Ramage, *Rebel Raider*, 145–46, and Wills, *Battle from the Start*, 96–97.

74. Not all historians agree with this assessment. Ramage contends that the Christmas Raid paid for itself by drawing off 7,300 Federal troops from Rose-crans's army at Stones River. This agrees with the opinion of Colonel Duke and other Confederate veterans of the raid, who believed that the raid denied large numbers of Federal troops to Rosecrans and saved Bragg's army. Brewer agrees with Ramage's assessment, claiming that the loss of the Muldraugh's Hill

trestles prevented Rosecrans from advancing after Stone's River. In neither case do the historians note that the departure of Morgan's 3,100 elite cavalrymen on the eve of the largest battle since Shiloh hampered the Confederate army. "Report of Major General Rosecrans," 12 February 1863, *OR*, series 1, vol. 20, pt. 1, 189; Ramage, *Rebel Raider*, 145–47; Duke, *Morgan's Cavalry*, 248; Brewer, *Raiders of 1862*, 170–74.

75. Sullivan to Grant, 2 January 1863, *OR*, series 1, vol. 17, pt. 1, 552; Henry, *First with the Most*, 113; Young, *Wizards of the Saddle*, 153–54. Young relates that Forrest killed or captured 2,500 Federal troops, burned fifty bridges and trestles, destroyed well over one million dollars in government property, filled fifty wagons with foodstuffs, and managed to rearm his entire command with modern weapons.

76. Morgan, *How It Was*, 71; Jordan and Pryor, *Campaigns of General Forrest*, 173. For an excellent discussion of morale on the Confederate home front, see Bell I. Wiley's *The Road to Appomattox* and Gary Gallagher's *The Confederate War.*

77. "Fry's Report," *OR*, series 1, vol. 17, pt. 1, 560–62; Colonel George Ihrie to Lieutenant Colonel John H. Rawlins, 31 December 1862, ibid., 566–67; Logan, *Quirk's Scouts*, 52.

78. The relative experience of the Federal units involved, when compared with the one and a half years of combat experience for the troopers under Forrest and Morgan, is perhaps most evident in the numerical designations of some of the units involved. During the Civil War, units were raised in numerical order in most cases; the lower a unit's number, the longer it had been in service. A perfect example to compare the relative experience of Federal and Confederate units is the battle at Parker's Crossroads on December 31. Infantry units such as the 50th and 122nd Indiana and 63rd Ohio faced Forrest's 2nd and 10th Tennessee and 4th Alabama Cavalry. Likewise, the majority of Morgan's Kentuckians had unit numerical designations in the single digits.

79. "Rosecrans's Report," *OR*, series 1, vol. 20, pt. 1, 189.

CHAPTER 6

Private Young was captured along with General Morgan during the "Great Raid" on July 26, 1863. See Horwitz, *Longest Raid*, 336.

1. Lincoln had long treasured the idea of liberating the Unionists of eastern Tennessee from the Confederacy. The area was so pro-Union that the Confederate army spent most of its time in the region on counterinsurgency duty that spread from eastern Tennessee into western North Carolina. Consequently, Federal commanders from Buell in 1862 to Rosecrans and Burnside in 1863 were constantly pressured to push troops into the region by Lincoln and other political leaders. See chapter 1, "Tennessee Troops," in Current, *Lincoln's Loyalists*; Fisher, *War at Every Door*; O'Brien, *Mountain Partisans*; and Paludan, *Victims*. The Unionists in eastern Tennessee continued their irregular warfare against the Confederates until the end of the war. Francis W. Dawson, a Confederate soldier who saw service in the region in late 1863 and early 1864, wrote: "We were very uneasy, as the woods were the favorite lurking

place for bushwhackers. As one of my men explained, 'there was a whacker in every bush.'" See Dawson, *Reminiscences of Confederate Service*, 10. George Dallas Musgrove, a private in the Fourth Kentucky Cavalry, agreed with the assessment of Unionist irregulars, calling them "skulking land-pirates" and noting that "many . . . we captured and then shot, or in army phrase, we 'lost' them." Musgrove, *Kentucky Cavaliers in Dixie*, 43.

2. Rosecrans to Halleck, 26 January 1863, *OR*, series 1, vol. 23, pt. 2, 14.

3. Major General Horatio G. Wright to Rosecrans, 11 February 1863, ibid., 58.

4. Rosecrans to Halleck, 30 January 1863, ibid., 22–23; Halleck to Rosecrans, 1 February 1863, ibid., 31; Rosecrans to Halleck, 2 February 1863, ibid., 33–34; Rosecrans to Secretary of War Edwin M. Stanton, 2 February 1863, ibid., 34; Halleck to Rosecrans, 3 February 1863, ibid., 37–38; Assistant Secretary of War P. H. Watson to Rosecrans, 5 February 1863, ibid., 45; Rosecrans to Watson, 1 March 1863, ibid., 95.

5. Kentucky had two governments, a Union and a Confederate. Other border and upper South states also had the same dual government situation, most notably Missouri, Arkansas, Tennessee, and Virginia.

6. At one point, Federal quartermasters from different departments were competing with each other for the limited number of horses, driving the price even higher. See Major T. Swords to Meigs, 29 April 1863, *OR*, series 1, vol. 23, pt. 2, 289–90.

7. Lieutenant Colonel J. W. Taylor to Brigadier General Montgomery C. Meigs, 27 April 1863, ibid., 282.

8. Halleck to Rosecrans, 28 April 1863, ibid., 284–85.

9. Meigs to Rosecrans, 1 May 1863, ibid., 300–304; Rosecrans to Montgomery C. Meigs, 10 May 1863, ibid., 321. Historian Stephen Z. Starr notes that on January 31, 1863, the total number of Federal cavalry in the region was 4,549, versus 7,980 Confederate troopers. Through Rosecrans's constant requests, the Union army entered the summer campaigning season with 10,883 cavalrymen, against the Confederates' 8,265. Morgan's defeat lowered the total number of cavalry by an additional 2,500. It is worth noting that Rosecrans, prior to Halleck and Meigs agreeing to pay for more horses, had again telegraphed Secretary Stanton directly and stated that much of his cavalry did not have mounts. Interestingly, Meigs telegraphed Rosecrans late that evening and arranged to provide additional horses. See Rosecrans to Stanton, 24 April 1863, *OR*, series 1, vol. 23, pt. 2, 270–71; Rosecrans to Meigs, 24 April 1863, ibid., 271; Meigs to Rosecrans, 24 April 1863, ibid., 271–72; and Starr, *Union Cavalry in the Civil War*, 3:225–26.

10. Major General Horatio G. Wright to Rosecrans, 11 February 1863, *OR*, series 1, vol. 23, pt. 2, 58. In central Kentucky alone, by February 1863 nearly 6,000 Federal soldiers guarded the route of the Louisville and Nashville Railroad between Louisville and the Tennessee border. This number also includes detachments patrolling the region on antiguerrilla duty, as well as men in stockades and blockhouses. See ibid.

11. "Special Orders No. 155," 20 May 1863, ibid., 347–351; Major J. H. Simpson to Brigadier General Joseph G. Totten, 20 May 1863, ibid., 347–350;

Circular, Headquarters, Department of the Cumberland, 5 September 1863, *OR*, series 1, vol. 30, pt. 3, 362–63; Morse, "Relief of Chattanooga," 68, 73. The work on the fortifications continued throughout 1863 and into 1864, never truly halting until the end of the war. For an example of the continual improvement of the fortifications, and Burnside's guidance to his engineers, see Simpson to Totten, 11 August 1863, *OR*, series 1, vol. 23, pt. 2, 607–12.

12. Rosecrans to Brigadier General Robert B. Mitchell, 17 January 1863, *OR*, series 1, vol. 20, pt. 2, 336; Rosecrans to Colonel A. Stager, 21 January 1863, ibid., 345; Rosecrans to Halleck, 22 January 1863, *OR*, series 1, vol. 23, pt. 2, 4; Rosecrans to Captain A. M. Pennock, U.S.N., 22 January 1863, ibid.; Secretary of the Navy Gideon Welles to Pennock, 23 January 1863, ibid., 5; Rosecrans to Halleck, 24 January 1863, ibid., 8–9.

13. "Report of Lieutenant Commander Leroy Fitch, U.S. Navy, regarding naval operations in the Ohio, Cumberland and Tennessee Rivers, August 23, 1862–October 21, 1863," *ORN*, series 1, vol. 23, 309–18.

14. Rosecrans, desperate for the gunboats, actually bypassed both Halleck and Stanton, writing directly to President Lincoln in February. Rosecrans's main point was that the gunboats should be commanded by the Army commander in the region, not the Navy. Lincoln wisely forwarded the issue back to the War and Navy Departments, adding "I cannot take it into my own hands without producing inextricable confusion." Rosecrans to President Abraham Lincoln, 11 February 1863, *OR*, series 1, vol. 23, pt. 2, 57; Lincoln to Rosecrans, 12 February 1863, ibid., 58.

15. Lieutenant Conger led an interesting career, starting out as a company officer in the 115th Ohio, and serving in a variety of staff duties, including assistant adjutant general on the staff of General Jacob Ammen, provost marshal of Newport, Kentucky, and railroad defense inspector. He also took part in the pursuit of Morgan's raiders during the Great Raid. See "Diary of Lieutenant Arthur L. Conger, Co. G, 115th O.V.I.," 15 June 1864–3 October 1864, 54–62, USAMHI.

16. "General Orders No. 5," 27 January 1863, *OR*, series 1, vol. 23, pt. 2, 17.

17. Lieutenant Henry Stone to Brigadier General Joseph J. Reynolds, 22 January 1863, ibid., 3; "Special Field Orders No. 26," 29 January 1863, ibid., 21–22. So serious had the punishments become that subordinate officers who committed "a grave error and neglect of duty" for not warning senior officers of tactical errors made in the guarding of wagon trains were punished as well. In such one incident, several company officers of the 6th Kentucky and 110th Illinois Infantry were "publicly reprimanded at the head of their respective regiments" and barely escaped dismissal. See "Special Field Orders No. 42," 14 February 1863, ibid., 68.

18. Rosecrans's plans for the "Roll of Honor" included the development of an elite cadre in each infantry and cavalry brigade, a "light" battalion of mounted Honor Roll members. According to his plan, they would have been armed with the newest weapons, Colt revolving rifles or Spencer repeaters, and "be excused from picket duty" so that they would be ready at a moment's notice. The general's long-term goals for these elite battalions are unclear; it

is interesting to note that the first members were those who had experience in dealing with irregulars. With their proven combat record against raiders and guerrillas, and equipped with technologically superior weapons, these elite battalions could have proven to be a workable solution to the Confederate raiding war. Halleck and Secretary Stanton resisted Rosecrans's reorganization plans and rejected the project. See Rosecrans to Halleck, 14 February 1863, *OR*, series 1, vol. 23, pt. 2, 66–68; Rosecrans to Stanton, 27 February 1863, ibid., 90–91; "General Orders No. 90," 24 April 1863, ibid., 273.

19. "Special Field Orders No. 33," 5 February 1863, ibid., 48.

20. Connelly, *Autumn of Glory*, 69–79. The upcoming summer campaign was not a surprise to the Federals. When Burnside assumed command of the Department of Ohio in March, Halleck informed him that it was probable that the Confederates would begin raiding Kentucky in force "as soon as the season is sufficiently advanced to make the roads practicable." In mid-May, Burnside's command began keeping a much closer watch on the expected raiders and began closely cooperating with each other to counter the raids. Halleck to Burnside, 23 March 1863, *OR*, series 1, vol. 23, pt. 2, 162–64; General Orlando B. Wilcox to Burnside, 18 May 1863, ibid., 339–40; Brigadier General J. T. Boyle to Burnside, 18 May 1863, 339.

21. "Report of Major General Wheeler," February 1863, *OR*, series 1, vol. 23, pt. 1, 39–41; Wyeth, *Life of General Forrest*, 145–52; Wills, *Battle from the Start*, 99–102; Evans, ed., *Confederate Military History*, 8:223–24; Jordan and Pryor, *Campaigns of General Forrest*, 226–31.

22. "Report of Major General Rosecrans," 6 March 1863, *OR*, series 1, vol. 23, pt. 1, 73–74; "Report of Major General Van Dorn," ibid., 116–18; "Report of General Forrest," ibid., 120–21; Wills, *Battle from the Start*, 104–105; Jordan and Pryor, *Campaigns of General Forrest*, 231–38.

23. "Report of Major General Rosecrans," 26 March 1863, *OR*, series 1, vol. 23, pt. 1, 176–77; "Report of General Forrest," 1 April 1863, ibid., 187–89; Starnes, *Forrest's Forgotten Horse Brigadier*, 49–59.

24. "Report of Colonel Abel Streight," 10 December 1864, *OR*, series 1, vol. 23, pt. 1, 284–93; "Report of General Braxton Bragg," 5 May 1863, ibid., 294–95; "Thanks of the Confederate Congress to General Nathan B. Forrest and the officers and men of his command," 17 February 1864, ibid., 295; Starnes, *Forrest's Forgotten Horse Brigadier*, 71–82; Fisher, *They Rode with Forrest and Wheeler*, 37–44; Maness, *Untutored Genius*, 129–46.

25. Jordan and Pryor, *Campaigns of General Forrest*, 279–80.

26. This concept is not the conventional assessment of Forrest. Biographers, historians, and contemporaries consistently fail to credit Forrest as one of the great conventional commanders of the Civil War, instead labeling all of his later campaigns as "raids," including divisional and corps-sized operations. There are several reasons for this view, including the fact that Forrest did conduct a few successful raids later in the war. Another is suggested by the attitude that the Confederate high command had toward Forrest from the beginning of the conflict. Harvey J. Matthes, in his 1902 biography, asserted what many of Forrest's supporters had long felt, that Forrest's lack of proper education, especially when compared to the West Point clique that ran the

Confederacy, prevented many of the leaders of the Confederate States from seeing him as other than a raider. Consequently, Forrest was never really accepted as a conventional military commander until the closing year of the war. Matthes, *General Forrest*, 33, 106, 177; Chalmers, "Forrest and His Campaigns," 451–86; Wolseley, "Lieutenant-General N. B. Forrest."

27. "Full Sketch of Organization and Service of the 9th Regiment, Kentucky Cavalry, C.S.A.," Doriss Collection, John A. Lewis Papers, UKY.

28. Sydney Smith, *Life*, 53.

29. Duke, *Morgan's Cavalry*, 344.

30. Boatner, "Tullahoma Campaign," 850–51.

31. *OR*, series 1, vol. 23, pt. 1, 399; DuBose, *General Joseph Wheeler*, 180–81.

32. Horn, *Army of Tennessee*, 233; Horwitz, *Longest Raid*, 3–4, 11.

33. "Report of Major General Joseph Wheeler," 7 November 1863, *OR*, series 1, vol. 23, pt. 1, 817; Duke, *Morgan's Cavalry*, 297.

34. Ibid., 818–19; Sydney K. Smith, *Life, Army Record, and Public Service*, 57; Seitz, *Braxton Bragg*, 313; Longacre, *Mounted Raids of the Civil War*, 175–77; Brown, *Bold Cavaliers*, 177.

35. Taylor, *Bowie Knives and Pistols*, 29; Brown, *Bold Cavaliers*, 179; Keller, *Morgan's Raid*, 22–23.

36. "Report of Colonel Felix W. Graham, Fifth Indiana Cavalry," 12 June 1863, *OR*, series 1, vol. 23, pt. 1, 367–69.

37. "Sanders' Raid in East Tennessee," 14–24 June 1863, ibid., 384–93; Horwitz, *Longest Raid*, 14–15.

38. Horwitz, *Longest Raid*, 4–5; Smith, *Life*, 57; "Account of Raids Made into Kentucky, Indiana and Ohio by General Morgan and Captain Hines, 1864," 22–24, James Blanton Papers, UKY. Captain Hines was another of the antebellum leaders of Kentucky, having raised a pro-Confederate company in Bowling Green in early 1861. A native of the region, Hines's skills as a scout proved invaluable. After his capture with Morgan on July 26, Hines played a pivotal role in planning and executing the escape from the Ohio State Penitentiary. In 1864, he led an abortive attempt from Canada to start a Copperhead-led revolt in Chicago. See "Account of Raids," 3–5; Catton, *Army of the Potomac: A Stillness at Appomattox*, 291–94; and *Full Account of the Capture*, 3.

39. "Account of Raids," 22–24.

40. "Account of Raids," 27–30; Major General Ambrose Burnside to Major General Henry W. Halleck, 22 June 1863, *OR*, series 1, vol. 23, pt. 1, 397–98.

41. Keller, *Morgan's Raid*, 55, 57; Horwitz, *Longest Raid*, 19–20; Ramage, *Rebel Raider*, 162–63.

42. Major General George Hartsuff to Burnside, 1 July 1863, *OR*, series 1, vol. 23, pt. 1, 679; Burnside to Hartsuff, 2 July 1863, ibid.

43. The order of battle for General Judah's division was as follows. All are regimental size unless otherwise noted.

3rd Division, XXII Corps, Department of the Ohio
Commander: Brigadier General Henry M. Judah

1st Brigade, 3rd Division, XXII Corps
Commander: Brigadier General Mahlon D. Manson
5th Indiana and 14th Illinois Cavalry
23rd Michigan, 107th Illinois, and 111th Ohio Infantry
Two Illinois artillery batteries
Total: 2,500 men, mostly infantry

2nd Brigade, 3rd Division, XXII Corps
Commander: Brigadier General Edward Hobson
1st, 9th, 11th, and Kentucky Cavalry and 2nd Ohio Cavalry
2nd East Tennessee and 7th Ohio Mounted Infantry
13th and 16th Kentucky and 80th Indiana Infantry
24th Indiana Battery (four mountain howitzers)
Total: 2,500 men, mostly cavalry

Attached Brigade (1st Brigade, 2nd Division, XXII Corps)
Commander: Brigadier General James M. Shackelford
3rd and 8th Kentucky Cavalry
12th Kentucky and 91st Indiana Infantry
22nd Indiana Battery, plus an attached section
Company K, 65th Indiana Mounted Infantry
Total: 1,800 men

Cavalry Brigade, 3rd Division, XXII Corps
Commander: Colonel August V. Kautz
2nd and 7th Ohio Volunteer Cavalry
Four mountain howitzers
Total: Approximately 1,200 men

Grand total of Federal pursuit forces led by General Judah is 8,000 combat troops, not including individual regiments of the above-listed brigades left behind to defend key locations and screen the Cumberland River from further Confederate activities. Information is from the following sources, in order: Manson's Brigade, "Abstract from the return of the Department of the Ohio," 30 June 1863, *OR*, series 1, vol. 23, pt. 2, 490; Hobson's Brigade, ibid., 492 ; Kautz's Brigade, ibid., 489, 491; "Report of Colonel August V. Kautz," 11 August 1863, *OR*, series 1, vol. 23, pt. 1, 662; and Shackelford's Brigade, "Report of Brigadier General James M. Shackelford," ibid., 639–40. General Shackelford's brigade replaced the Third Brigade, Third Division, commanded by Colonel Joseph L. Cooper, who was defending Carthage, Tennessee, prior to Morgan's crossing of the Cumberland on July 2.

44. "Judah's Report," *OR*, series 1, vol. 23, pt. 1, 655.

45. Berry, *Four Years*, 214–16; "Report of Colonel Orlando H. Moore, 25th Michigan Infantry," 4 July 1863, *OR*, series 1, vol. 23, pt. 1, 645–47; Brown, *Bold Cavaliers*, 180–82.

46. Tarrant, *Wild Riders*, 175–76; Quisenberry, "Eleventh Kentucky Cavalry," 271–73; Woodbury, *Burnside*, 293–94; Young, *Wizards of the Saddle,*

372. For his actions that day, Moore was voted the thanks of the legislature of Kentucky and was given a Regular Army rank of major; he served his postwar career on the western frontier. Horwitz, *Longest Raid*, 24.

47. Ramage, *Rebel Raider*, 164–65; Brown, *Bold Cavaliers*, 183–85; Taylor, *Bowie Knives and Pistols*, 30–32; "Report of Colonel Charles S. Hanson, 20th Kentucky Infantry," 30 July 1863, *OR*, series 1, vol. 23, pt. 1, 647–51; Young, *Wizards of the Saddle*, 374–75. According to Horwitz in *Longest Raid*, Colonel Hanson was the brother of Confederate General Roger W. Hanson, and, being from Lexington, knew Morgan personally. In addition, the Twentieth Kentucky (Union) was a veteran unit, having seen action at Shiloh, Perryville, and Corinth. Horwitz, *Longest Raid*, 27–28.

48. Horwitz, *Longest Raid*, 29–31; Berry, *Four Years*, 216–18; "Hanson's Report," *OR*, series 1, vol. 23, pt. 1, 650–51. Horwitz also notes that one of the captured Federals was Morgan's brother-in-law from his first marriage, and that Colonel Hanson was initially accused of surrendering his command without putting up a proper fight. General Burnside quickly withdrew the charges when he discovered the true story of the battle. Burnside to Hartsuff, 5 July 1863, ibid., 691, 692; Burnside to Hartsuff, 14 July 1863, ibid., 746.

49. Keller, *Morgan's Raid*, 50. The detachment also took the opportunity to rob the passengers of both vessels of their valuables, setting a standard of individual plunder for the entire command throughout the raid. See Ramage, *Rebel Raider*, 168; Brown, *Bold Cavaliers*, 189–91; and Taylor, *Bowie Knives and Pistols*, 34–35.

50. Taylor, *Bowie Knives and Pistols*, 36–43; Horwitz, *Longest Raid*, 41–42, 48–51; Young, *Wizards of the Saddle*, 379–80; "Report of Lieutenant Commander Fitch," 9 July 1863, *ORN*, series 1, vol. 25, 239–41. The *Elk* returned later that afternoon with a second gunboat, but by that time Morgan had already crossed the river.

51. Horwitz, *Longest Raid*, 50–51; Taylor, *Bowie Knives and Pistols*, 44–45; Edison Thomas, *Morgan and His Raiders*, 78; Young, *Wizards of the Saddle*, 379; Woodbury, *Burnside*, 294–95; Captain A. M. Pennock, U.S.N. to Burnside, 8 July 1863, *OR*, series 1, vol. 23, pt. 1, 710; "Hobson's Report," September 1863, ibid., 659–60.

52. Duke, *Morgan's Cavalry*, 323–24; Taylor, *Bowie Knives and Pistols*, 47–49; Brown, *Bold Cavaliers*, 191–97.

53. Brown, *Bold Cavaliers*, 49–57; Berry, *Four Years*, 221–22; Horwitz, *Longest Raid*, 62–74; Edison Thomas, *Morgan and His Raiders*, 81. One of the reasons that Morgan took greater losses than the militia was that one unit of the Indiana militia, the Ellsworth Rifles, had armed itself with the new Henry repeating rifle, a predecessor to the famous Winchester '73 of Old West fame. Capable of holding fifteen rounds, it was one of the most technologically advanced weapons of the era, and the Ellsworth Rifles, by sheer volume of fire, managed to kill or wound a fair number of the raiders. See Horwitz, *Longest Raid*, 63–64.

54. "Judah's Report," 30 July 1863, *OR*, series 1, vol. 23, pt. 1, 656–57; "Shackelford's Report," ibid., 640–41; Duke, *Morgan's Cavalry*, 324; Brown, *Bold Cavaliers*, 211–12.

55. Berry, *Four Years*, 229–31; Duke, *Morgan's Cavalry*, 32–30; Horwitz, *Longest Raid*, 201–20; Brown, *Bold Cavaliers*, 217–19; "Shackelford's Report," 30 July 1863, *OR*, series 1, vol. 23, pt. 1, 640–42; "Judah's Report," ibid., 656–57; "Hobson's Report," ibid., 660–61; "Report of Colonel August V. Kautz," 11 August 1863, ibid., 662–63.

56. Judah to Burnside, 19 July 1863, ibid., 776–77; Burnside to Judah, 19 July 1863, ibid., 777; Horwitz, *Longest Raid*, 244–46; Brown, *Bold Cavaliers*, 220–21.

57. Sydney Smith, *Life*, 67–68; Brown, *Bold Cavaliers*, 222–25; Horwitz, *Longest Raid*, 327–39; "Report of Major George W. Rue," *OR*, series 1, vol. 23, pt. 1, 667–68; "Shackelford's Report," ibid., 642–45.

58. The estimated amount of damage caused by the raid came from Confederate sources, including newspapers, that tried to present the disaster in the best light possible. According to Robert S. Vore, in *Morgan's Raid Losers*, many of the postraid claims were used by Northern farmers to make up for a wide variety of questionable losses. Vore's work is based on the exhaustive "Report of Morgan Raid Commissioners to the Governor of Indiana," printed in 1869, and the 1864 "Report of the Commissioners of Morgan Raid Claims to the Governor of the State of Ohio." Likewise, Paul G. Scarborough, in his 1955 thesis, "The Impact of the John Morgan Raid in Indiana and Ohio," depends much on the official state reports. In both cases, the total cost of the nearly 2,300 claims in Indiana, and the 4,375 claims in Ohio, totaled only $989,824.48. Whitelaw Reid's semiofficial work *Ohio in the War* states that $576,225.00 was claimed by citizens in the state; approximately $495,000 due to the Confederates, $152,000 to the Federals. Pay for the militia was also noted, and it totaled $212,318.97 for the almost 50,000 men organized into 587 companies. At the most, the raid cost the Union approximately $1.5 million in claims and associated costs, well short of the postraid boasts of the Confederate press. See Vore, *Morgan's Raid Losers*; Scarborough, "Impact of the John Morgan Raid," 218–20, 244–47; Reid, *Ohio in the War*, 2:150, 152.

59. "Report of Major General Burnside," 13 November 1865, *OR*, series 1, vol. 30, pt. 2, 547–52.

60. Morgan's capture and escape made him a celebrity on the Confederate home front. His incarceration in the Ohio Penitentiary, and treatment as a common criminal instead of a prisoner of war, infuriated many Southerners. Federal leaders held him and his officers in the civilian facility instead of a camp for practical reasons; they believed the prison to be more secure than a POW camp and were hoping to quickly exchange the raiders for Colonel Streight and his troopers captured in June. The Confederates refused to exchange Morgan for Streight, and the raider stayed in the Ohio State Penitentiary. His escape in late 1863 made headlines around the South, and Morgan visited Richmond and several other major cities in triumph. His disobedience of Bragg, however, resulted in his not being given a command for nearly six months following his release. His death in September 1864 plunged much of the South into mourning. For examples of the Confederate propaganda campaign to build Morgan into a national hero during his incarceration and after his escape, see Charleston *Mercury*, 8 September 1863, 26 October 1863, 14 December 1863, 9 January

1864, 17 September 1864; Richmond *Enquirer*, 5 January 1864, 8 January 1864, 13 September 1864.

61. Mrs. James B. Clay to James Clay, 9 July 1863, Hunt-Morgan Family Papers, Folder 2, Box 16, UKY.

62. It must be noted, however, that Guerrant was writing nearly a year after the failed raid.

63. Guerrant, *Bluegrass Confederate*, 492, 493.

64. Ramage, *Rebel Raider*, 180–82, 199–225. The failure of the Great Raid had the opposite effect on the Federals and Union loyalists in the Ohio River valley. Federal control over the region was reinforced by Morgan's later raids, which were seen as no more than robbery by the locals. Middleton Robertson, writing years later, recalled that the local Home Guard swelled in strength after the raid and was much more motivated than before; pro-war sentiment in Ohio had never been higher. This is also reflected in Northern writings about the raid during the war, which used the raid to motivate civilians to support the war effort. When combined with the string of Federal military successes in July 1863 (Gettysburg, the fall of Vicksburg, and the victory at Helena, Arkansas), the failure of the Great Raid could have only further encouraged the citizens of the Union. See Robertson, "Recollections of Morgan's Raid," and Simmons, *John Morgan Raid*.

CONCLUSION

1. Edward P. Alexander, *Military Memoirs*, 603–606; Alexander, *Fighting for the Confederacy*, 531–33; Foote, *Civil War: Red River to Appomattox*, 942.

2. General Robert E. Lee to President Jefferson Davis, 20 April 1865, in Lee, *Wartime Papers*, 938–39.

3. Judah P. Benjamin to President Jefferson Davis, 22 April 1865, *OR*, vol. 47, pt. 3, 822–83.

4. See chapter 4. Lee called the entire Partisan Ranger program an "injury instead of a benefit to the service" and believed most of the partisans, with the exception of Mosby, to be little more than organized brigands. See Lee to General Samuel Cooper, 1 April 1864, Lee, *Wartime Papers*, 688–89.

5. Even at the very end of the war, when President Davis was contemplating a larger guerrilla war, others were more concerned about anarchy than carrying on the fight against the United States. Confederate Secretary of the Navy S. R. Mallory wrote Davis, warning him that the "pacification of the country should be as speedy as practicable, to the end that the authorities of the States may enter upon the establishment and maintenance of law and order." It is clear that some Confederate leaders feared chaos over the return to the Union. S.R. Mallory to President Davis, 24 April 1865, *OR*, vol. 43, pt. 3, 833–34.

6. Beginning in the early 1970s, Civil War historians began to examine the reasons why a widespread guerrilla war did not take place after 1865, or why the Confederacy did not turn to irregular warfare from the start. Robert L. Kerby's essay "Why the Confederacy Lost" presented one of the first detailed scholarly debates on the plausibility of Confederate guerrilla war. Albert Castel's special issue of *Civil War Times Illustrated* in 1974 elaborated on the

actual irregular war that was fought, but did not examine the overall Rebel strategy for such a conflict. The issue of guerrilla warfare after 1865 continued to emerge in Civil War historiography in the last two decades of the twentieth century. Gary Gallagher discusses and dismisses the concept in his 1997 *The Confederate War*, while Richard Beringer, Herman Hattaway, Archer Jones, and William Still present the possibility of a guerrilla strategy in *Why the South Lost the Civil War* (1986). See Kerby, "Why the Confederacy Lost," 342–43; Castel, "Guerrilla War," 1–50; Gallagher, *Confederate War*, 120–21, 123–25; and Beringer et al., *Why the South Lost*, 170–73, 432, 437–40.

7. Southern nationalism, or the lack thereof, has been presented as a concordant issue with that of guerrilla warfare. The topic of Southern nationalism plays such a great role in their work, that the authors of *Why the South Lost* devote an entire chapter to it. They boldly state that "the Confederacy succumbed to internal rather than external causes. Insufficient nationalism failed to survive the strains imposed by the lengthy hostilities." Gary Gallagher disagrees with Beringer's assessment of Confederate nationalism. According to Gallagher, the Confederates, especially in the Army of Northern Virginia, possessed a high degree of nationalism. See Beringer et al., *Why the South Lost*, 64–81, 439; Gallagher, *Confederate War*, 63–111.

8. In the summer of 1865, the United States came very close to intervening in Mexico to drive out the French, who had taken advantage of the Civil War to place a puppet government in that nation. Faced with 50,000 veteran troops under General Phil Sheridan, Emperor Napoleon III abandoned the adventure in Mexico. As for Britain, there were substantial fears that the United States would turn the Grand Army of the Republic north and overrun the outposts in Canada. See Mahin, *One War at a Time*, 239–56, 269–85.

9. J. E. Johnston to Joseph E. Brown, 30 April 1865, *OR*, vol. 47, pt. 3, 855.

10. Gallagher contends, rightfully so, that a Maoist guerrilla war was an impossibility for the Confederates, based on social issues (the defense of a slave-owning aristocracy) and the Southern leadership's preference for conventional warfare. He does not recognize the impact of the Federal army, or that the Confederacy conducted an irregular war, albeit based on nineteenth-century, not twentieth-century, concepts. John Shy surmises that the Confederates were more concerned with social and racial order than with independence, and that Lee's surrender gave an honorable excuse to end the war while still maintaining the antebellum racial balance. Emory Thomas's approach is somewhat different. He contends that the issue of race is important, but secondary in any discussion of guerrilla warfare during the Civil War. According to him, the South rejected widespread irregular warfare because such a conflict did not fit into their ideas of how a revolutionary war should be fought and presented a danger to the Southern way of life. See Gallagher, *Confederate War*, 127; Mitchell, "Perseverance of the Soldiers," 124–25; Shy, *A People Numerous and Armed*, 244–45, and Emory Thomas, *Confederacy as a Revolutionary Experience*, xi, 43–57. An excellent overview and analysis of much of this argument is covered in Daniel E. Sutherland's "Sideshow No Longer."

11. The argument that the U.S. Army was a huge, but unsophisticated, war machine is strongly argued in Russell Weigley's *American Way of War* and *Eisenhower's Lieutenants*. Although the latter is a discussion of American military leadership in World War II, it presents the thesis that the American Civil War played a major role in developing how the U.S. Army fought in the 1940s. Weigley's "mobility and power" concept draws its inspiration directly from the strategies of Grant in 1864–65, claiming that "General Grant and his lieutenants defeated the Confederacy by drowning its armies in a flood of overwhelming power," and that this idea shaped how the United States would fight its wars in the twentieth century. In his *American Way of War*, Weigley goes into much greater detail about Grant's strategy in the Civil War. See Weigley's *Eisenhower's Lieutenants*, 3, and *American Way of War*, 128–52.

BIBLIOGRAPHY

NATIONAL ARCHIVES AND RECORDS ADMINISTRATION,
WASHINGTON, D.C.

Record Group 94: Office of the Adjutant General, U.S. Army, 1780–1917
    Returns from United States Volunteer Regiments, 1861–65
        State Organization Records: Arkansas, Kentucky, Tennessee, Virginia,
        and West Virginia

Record Group 107: Office of the Secretary of War, 1781–1947
    Miscellaneous Records: Intercepted Letters of Confederate Sympathizers

Record Group 109: War Department Collection of Confederate Records,
1825–1900
    Confederate Military Records
        Headquarters, Trans-Mississippi Division, 1862–65
        Records of Confederate Mobile Units: Tennessee, Arkansas, Missouri,
        and Kentucky
        Records of the Command of General John H. Morgan
    Papers of Confederate States Army Commanders
        Major General Thomas C. Hindman Papers
        Major General Theophilus Holmes Papers
        Major General Sterling C. Price Papers

Record Group 110: Provost Marshal General's Bureau, 1861–69
    Records of the Assistant Acting Provost Marshal General, Arkansas,
        1862–66
    Records of the District Provost Marshal General, Arkansas, 1863–66
    General Register of Prisoners, New Orleans, 1862–66

Record Group 153: Office of the Judge Advocate General (Army), 1692–1981
    Records of the Judge Advocate General, Department of Arkansas,
    1862–70

Record Group 393: United States Army Continental Commands, 1821–1920
    VII Corps, Army of Arkansas, 1863–64
    XXIII Corps, Army of the Ohio, 1863
    Army of the Ohio, 1862–63
    Army of the Potomac, 1861–65
    Defenses (Military District) of Washington, D.C., 1861–65
    Department and Army of Arkansas, 1862–70
    Department and Army of the Cumberland, 1861–65
    Department of Kentucky, 1862–65
    Department and Army of the Mississippi, 1862
    Department and Army of the Ohio, 1862–65
    Department of the Tennessee, 1862–65
    Records of the Provost Marshal General, Department of Arkansas

FEDERAL PUBLICATIONS AND MONOGRAPHS

U.S. Census Bureau. *Population of the United States in 1860: Compiled from
    the Original Returns of the Eighth Census.* 2 vols. Washington, D.C.: Gov-
    ernment Printing Office, 1864.
U.S. Congress. House of Representatives. *Journal of the Congress of the Con-
    federate States of America.* Washington, D.C.: Government Printing Office,
    1904.
———. Committee on War Claims, "Fourth Mounted Infantry Claims." 55th
    Cong., 2nd sess., 1898, vol. 6, H. Rept. 9219.
U.S. Congress. Senate. "Administration of the Department of Arkansas." 38th
    Cong., 2nd sess., 1864, S. Rept. 142.
———. *Journal of the Congress of the Confederate States of America.* Wash-
    ington, D.C.: Government Printing Office, 1905.
———. "Report of the Adjutant General of Arkansas for the Period of the Late
    Rebellion, and to November 1, 1866." 39th Cong., 2nd sess., 1867, S. Doc. 53.
U. S. Department of Agriculture. *Report of the Commissioner of Agriculture
    for the Year 1860.* Washington, D.C.: Government Printing Office, 1861.
———. *Report of the Commissioner of Agriculture for the Year 1866.* Wash-
    ington, D.C.: Government Printing Office, 1867.
U.S. Department of the Army. *Field Manual 31-16: Counter-Guerrilla Oper-
    ations.* Washington, D.C.: Government Printing Office, 1967.
———. *Field Manual 90-8: Counter-Guerrilla Operations.* Washington, D.C.:
    Government Printing Office, 1986.
U.S. Navy Department. *The War of the Rebellion: A Compilation of the Offi-
    cial Records of the Union and Confederate Navies.* 31 vols. Washington,
    D.C.: Government Printing Office, 1884–1922.
U.S. War Department. *Atlas to Accompany the Official Records of the War of
    the Rebellion.* 3 vols. Washington, D.C.: Government Printing Office,
    1891–95.

———. *Military Laws of the United States*. Baltimore: J. Murphy and Co., 1858.

———. Office of the Adjutant General of Arkansas. *Report of the Adjutant General of Arkansas for the Period of the Late Rebellion, 1861–1866*. Washington, D.C.: Government Printing Office, 1867.

———. *The War of the Rebellion: A Compilation of the Official Records of the Union and Confederate Armies*. 128 vols. Washington, D.C.: Government Printing Office, 1880–1902.

CONFEDERATE PUBLICATIONS AND MONOGRAPHS

Arkansas. Office of the Military Board. *Rules and Articles for the Government of the Army of Arkansas*. Little Rock, Ark.: Johnson and Yerkes, 1861.

Confederate States of America. War Department. *Army Regulations*. Atlanta: Gaulding and Whitaker, 1861.

———. *Book of Reference for Regular and Volunteer Officers and Soldiers of the Confederate Army*. New Orleans: William Bloomfield Co., 1861.

———. *Laws of the Provisional Congress of the Confederate States in Relation to the War Department*. Richmond: Tyler, Wise & Allege, 1861.

———. *Report of Major General Thomas C. Hindman*. Richmond: Printing Office, 1863.

Crandell, Marjorie L., and Richard B. Harwell, eds. *Confederate Imprints, 1861–1865*. New Haven, Conn.: Research Publications, 1974.

Matthews, James M., ed. *Public Laws of the Confederate States of America, First Congress, Sessions 1–4, and Second Congress, First Session*. Richmond: R. M. Smith, 1864.

SPECIAL COLLECTIONS AND ARCHIVES

Civil War Collection, University of Arkansas, Little Rock
    James A. Campbell Diaries, 1862–65, Item H-16
    Pamphlet 113, Gantt, E. W. "Address of Brigadier General E. W. Gantt, C.S.A., Given on October 7, 1863 at Little Rock, Arkansas"
    Pamphlet 1720. Sawyer, William E. "Marvin Hart—Civil War Guerrilla"
    Box II-1-1, Confederate States General Orders
    Item A5, Series 1, Box 1/6 (3rd Arkansas Cavalry Volunteers)
    Item A5, Series 1, Box 14/12 (Headquarters, Cavalry Division)
    Item A5, Series 1, Box 15/1 (25th Ohio Battery)
    Item A5, Series 2, Box 1/6 (Headquarters, Army of Arkansas)

Civil War Military Collection, Arkansas Historical Commission, Little Rock
    Arkansas State Tax Assessors Records, Box 18, File 8
    Circular, "To Arms! To Arms!" Headquarters, 1st Division, Arkansas Militia Records of the Mississippi Squadron, 1861–65

Library of Congress, Washington, D.C.
    Civil War Photographs Collection
    WPA Life Histories Collection, Miss Nancy Stewart Interview, 1938

Ohio Historical Society Collection, Columbus, Ohio
   Robert H. Kellogg Papers

Special Collections, Duke University, Durham, North Carolina
   Circular issued at Washington, Arkansas, August 15, 1862, entitled
      "Attention Partizan Rancers!"
   Alice Williamson Diary

Special Collections, East Tennessee State University, Knoxville
   Franklin P. Baxter Papers
   Mary Louise Pearre Hamilton Papers

Special Collections, Mississippi Valley Collection, University of Memphis,
   Memphis, Tennessee
   Brigadier General Mason Brayman Papers
   Hamner-Stacy Papers
   Adolphus Wiley Montague Memoir

Special Collections, Ruhr University, Bochum, Germany
   Bochum Immigrant Letter Collection, Hermann Family Collection

Special Collections, University of Arkansas, Fayetteville
   Haney Family Papers
   Sidney L. Jackman Memoir
   Governor Henry M. Rector Papers
   Colonel John C. Wright Memoir

Special Collections, University of California, Santa Cruz
   Newton Robert Scott Papers

Special Collections, University of Kentucky, Lexington
   James Blanton Papers
   Cecil Holland Papers
   Hunt-Morgan Family Papers
   John A. Lewis Papers

Special Collections, U.S. Army Military History Institute, Carlisle Barracks,
   Pennsylvania
   George L. Andrews Papers
   Milton A. Bailey Papers
   John W. Boucher Papers
   John P. Brownlow Papers
   Curtis R. Burke Papers
   Robert H. Carnahan Papers
   Lieutenant Arthur L. Conger Diary
   Henry Curtis Papers
   George W. Daughtery Papers
   Forman Family Papers
   Hall-Mechling Papers
   Eli P. Long Papers
   Adam C. McJunkin Papers

Addison W. McPheeters Papers
Rankin Pogue McPheeters Papers
Nathan B. Middlebrook Papers
John S. Mosby Papers
William Woodard Papers

Special Collections and Archives, U.S. Military Academy, West Point, New York
Braxton Bragg Papers
Captain James M. Crozier Diary
Rare Book Collection, various works listed below in Published Letters, Papers, Diaries, and Books

NEWSPAPERS

Arkansas
Arkadelphia, *The War Times*, April 1863
Cane Hill, *The Arkansas Traveler*, January 1863
Fort Smith, *Fort Smith Tri-Weekly Bulletin*, February 1862
———. *New Era*, December 1863 to September 1864
———. *Union*, September 1863
Little Rock, *Arkansas Gazette*, 6 April 1861 to 18 June 1863
———. *Arkansas Patriot*, 11 April 1863 to 21 July 1863
———. *Daily State Journal*, November 1861 to February 1862
Washington, *The Telegraph*, January 1862 to December, 1865

South Carolina
Charleston *Mercury*, July 1863 to September 1864

Virginia
Richmond *Enquirer*, January 1863 to September 1864

PUBLISHED LETTERS, PAPERS, DIARIES, AND MEMOIRS

Alexander, Edward P. *Fighting for the Confederacy: The Personal Recollections of General Edward Porter Alexander*. Edited by Gary W. Gallagher. Chapel Hill: University of North Carolina Press, 1989.
———. *Military Memoirs of a Confederate: A Critical Narrative*. New York: Charles Scribner's Sons, 1907.
Allen, Desmond Walls, ed. *Turnbo's Tales of the Ozarks: Biographical Stories*. Conway, Ark.: Arkansas Research Inc., 1989.
———. *Turnbo's Tales of the Ozarks: War and Guerrilla Stories*. Conway, Ark.: Arkansas Research Inc., 1987.
Allen, Theodore F. "In Pursuit of John Morgan." In *Sketches of War History: Papers Read before the Ohio Commandery of the Military Order of the Loyal Legion of the United States*. Vol. 5. Cincinnati: R. Clarke, 1903.
Baxter, William. *Pea Ridge and Prairie Grove; or Scenes and Incidents of the War in Arkansas*. Cincinnati: Poe and Hitchcock, 1864.
Beard, Dan W. "With Forrest in West Tennessee." *Southern Historical Society Papers* 37 (1909): 304–308.

Berry, Thomas Franklin. *Four Years with Morgan and Forrest*. Oklahoma City, Okla.: The Harlow-Ratliff Co., 1914.

Bishop, Albert Webb. *Loyalty on the Frontier, or Sketches of Union Men of the Southwest*. St. Louis: R. F. Stadley and Co., 1863.

————. *An Oration Delivered at Fayetteville, Arkansas on July 4, 1864*. New York: Baker and Godwin, 1865.

Britton, Wiley. *The Civil War on the Border*. 2 vols. New York: G. P. Putnam and Sons, 1904.

Bruce, George A. "General Buell's Campaign Against Chattanooga." In *Papers of the Military Historical Society of Massachusetts*. Vol. 7. Boston: Military Historical Society of Massachusetts, 1910.

Conolly, Thomas. *An Irishman in Dixie: Thomas Conolly's Diary of the Fall of the Confederacy*. Edited by Nelson Lankford. Columbia: University of South Carolina Press, 1988.

Crawford, J. Marshall. *Mosby and His Men: A Record of the Adventures of That Renowned Partisan Ranger*. New York: G. W. Carleton and Co., 1867.

Crook, George. *General George Crook: His Autobiography*. Edited by Martin F. Schmitt. Norman: University of Oklahoma Press, 1946.

Daniel, Harriet Bailey Bullock. *Remembrances of Eden: Harriet Bailey Bullock Daniel's Memories of a Frontier Plantation in Arkansas*. Edited by Margaret J. Bolsterli. Fayetteville: University of Arkansas Press, 1993.

Davis, Jefferson. *The Papers of Jefferson Davis*. 9 vols. Edited by Lynda L. Crist. Baton Rouge: Louisiana State University Press, 1989–96.

————. *A Short History of the Confederate States of America*. New York: Belford Co., 1890.

Dawson, Francis W. *Reminiscences of Confederate Service, 1861–1865*. Edited by Bell I. Wiley. Baton Rouge: Louisiana State University Press, 1980.

Denby, J. William. *The War in Arkansas, or, A Treatise on the Great Rebellion of 1861*. Little Rock, Ark.: Egis Printing Co., 1864.

Duke, Basil W. *Morgan's Cavalry*. New York: Neale Publishing Co., 1906.

————. "Morgan's Cavalry during the Bragg Invasion." In *Battles and Leaders of the Civil War*, 3:26–28. New York: The Century Co., 1886.

Ellis, Daniel. *Thrilling Adventures of Daniel Ellis, The Great Union Guide of East Tennessee*. New York: Harper and Brothers, 1867.

Estes, Thomas J. *Early Days and War Times in Northern Arkansas*. Lubbock, Tex.: Dow Printing Co., 1908.

Ewald, Johann von. *Treatise on Partisan Warfare*. Translated by Robert A. Selig and David Curtis Skaggs. New York: Greenwood Press, 1991.

Forsythe, John W. *Guerrilla Warfare and Life in Libby Prison*. Algona, Iowa: Republican Steam Plant, 1892. Reprint, Annandale, Va.: Turnpike Press, 1967, edited by Melvin Lee Steadman.

Foster, John W. *War Stories for My Grandchildren*. Washington, D.C.: Riverside Press, 1918.

A Full Account of the Capture and Wonderful Escape of General John H. Morgan with Captain T. Henry Hines. Atlanta: Intelligencer Steam Power Press, 1864.

Gantz, Jacob. *Such Are the Trials: The Civil War Diaries of Jacob Gantz.* Edited by Kathleen Davis. Ames: Iowa State University Press, 1991.

Grant, Ulysses S. *Personal Memoirs of U. S. Grant.* 2 vols. New York: C. L. Webster and Co., 1885–86. Reprint (2 vols. in 1), New York: Penguin Books, 1999.

Guerrant, Edward O. *Bluegrass Confederate: The Headquarters Diary of Edward O. Guerrant.* Edited by William C. Davis and Meredith L. Swintor. Baton Rouge: Louisiana State University Press, 1999.

Heartsill, W. W. *Fourteen Hundred and 91 Days in the Confederate Army: A Journal Kept by W. W. Heartsill of the W. P. Lane Rangers.* Edited by Bell I. Wiley. 1876. Reprint, Jackson, Tenn.: McCowat-Mercer Press, 1954.

Hyndman, William. *History of a Cavalry Company: A Complete Record of Company A, 4th Pennsylvania Cavalry.* Philadelphia: Rodgers Co., 1870.

Jordan, Thomas, and J. P. Pryor. *The Campaigns of General Nathan Bedford Forrest and of Forrest's Cavalry.* New York: 1868. Reprint, New York: DaCapo Press, 1996.

Kidd, James Harvey. *Personal Recollections of a Cavalryman: With Custer's Michigan Cavalry Brigade in the Civil War.* Ionia, Mich.: Sentinel Printing Co., 1908.

Lang, Theodore. *Loyal West Virginia, 1861–1865.* Baltimore, Md.: Deutsch Publishing Co., 1895. Reprint, Huntington, W.Va.: Blue Acorn Press, 1998.

Lee, Robert E. *The Wartime Papers of Robert E. Lee.* Edited by Clifford Dowdey and Louis H. Manarin. New York: Little Brown, 1961. Reprint, New York: DaCapo Press, 1988.

Logan, Indiana W. P. *Kelion Franklin Peddicord of Quirk's Scouts, Morgan's Kentucky Cavalry, C. S. A.* New York: Neale Publishing Co., 1908.

Lynch, Charles H. *The Civil War Diary of Charles H. Lynch of 18th Connecticut Volunteers, 1862–1865.* Hartford, Conn.: Case, Lockwood, and Brainard Co., 1915.

Mattson, Hans. *Early Days of Reconstruction in Northeast Arkansas: An Address Delivered by Colonel Hans Mattson before the Loyal Legion at St. Paul, Minnesota, March 6, 1889.* St. Paul, Minn.: The Pioneer Press Co., 1889.

McIntyre, Benjamin F. *Federals on the Frontier: The Diary of Benjamin F. McIntyre, 1862–1864.* Edited by Nannie M. Tilley. Austin: University of Texas Press, 1963.

Merrell, Henry. *The Autobiography of Henry Merrell: Industrial Missionary to the South.* Edited by James L. Skinner III. Athens, Ga.: University of Georgia Press, 1991.

Monks, William. *A History of Southern Missouri and Northern Arkansas: Being an Account of the Early Settlements, the Civil War, the Ku-Klux, and Times of Peace.* West Plains, Mo.: West Plains Journal Co., 1907.

Moore, Frank, ed. *The Rebellion Record: A Diary of American Events, with Documents, Narrative, Illustrative Incidents, Poetry, Etc.* 11 vols. New York: G. P. Putnam, 1861–63.

Morgan, Irby. *How It Was: Four Years among the Rebels.* Nashville: Barbee and Smith, 1892.

Morse, Bliss. *Civil War Diaries.* Edited by Loren J. Morse. Pittsburg, Kan.: Pittcraft, 1964.

Morse, Charles F. "The Relief of Chattanooga, October 1863, and Guerrilla Operations in Tennessee." In *Papers of the Military Historical Society of Massachusetts.* Vol. 14. Boston: Military Historical Society of Massachusetts, 1918.

Mosby, John Singleton. *The Letters of John S. Mosby.* Edited by Adele Mitchell. Richmond, Va.: The Stuart-Mosby Historical Society, 1986.

———. *The Memoirs of Colonel John S. Mosby.* Boston: Little, Brown and Co., 1917.

Musgrove, George D. *Kentucky Cavaliers in Dixie: Reminiscences of a Confederate Cavalryman.* Edited by Bell I. Wiley. Jackson, Tenn.: McCowat-Mercer Press, 1957. Reprint, Lincoln: University of Nebraska Press, 1999.

———. "Last Raid of Morgan through Indiana and Ohio." *Southern Historical Society Papers* 35 (1907): 110–21.

Musser, Charles O. *Soldier Boy: The Civil War Letters of Charles O. Musser.* Edited by Barry Popchock. Iowa City: University of Iowa Press, 1995.

Nash, Charles E. *Biographical Sketches of General Pat Cleburne and General T. C. Hindman.* Dayton, Ohio: Morningside Press, 1898.

———. *Bottom Rail on Top, Or, Thirty Years Ago.* Little Rock: Arkansas Democrat Co., 1895.

Porter, David D. *The Naval History of the Civil War.* New York: Sherman Publishing, 1886.

Quisenberry, Anderson C. "The Eleventh Kentucky Cavalry (Chenault's Regiment)." *Southern Historical Society Papers* 35 (1907): 258–89.

Rawling, C. J. *History of the First Regiment, Virginia Infantry.* Philadelphia: J. B. Lippincott, 1887.

Reid, Whitelaw. *Ohio in the War: Her Statesmen, Her Generals and Soldiers.* 2 vols. New York: Moore, Wilstach and Baldwin, 1868.

Rhodes, Elisha Hunt. *All for the Union: A History of the 2nd Rhode Island Volunteer Infantry in the War of the Great Rebellion, As Told in the Diary and Letters of Elisha Hunt Rhodes.* Edited by Robert H. Rhodes. Lincoln, R.I.: Andrew Mobray Publishers, 1985.

Robertson, Middleton. "Recollections of Morgan's Raid." *Indiana Magazine of History* 34, no. 2 (June 1938): 188–94.

Scott, John. *Partisan Life with Colonel John S. Mosby.* New York: Harper and Brothers, 1867. Reprint, Gaithersburg, Md.: Old Soldier Books, 1990.

Simmons, Flora E. *A Complete Account of the John Morgan Raid through Kentucky, Indiana, and Ohio.* Cincinnati: n.p., 1863.

Tarrant, Edward. *The Wild Riders of the First Kentucky Cavalry: A History of the Regiment in the Great War of the Rebellion, 1861–1865.* Louisville: R. H. Carothers, 1894.

Thomas, Horace H. "Personal Reminiscence of the East Tennessee Campaign." In *Papers of the Military Order of the Loyal Legion of the United States, Illinois Commandery.* Vol. 4. Chicago: A. G. McGlurg, 1891.

Vore, Robert S. *Morgan's Raid Losers.* Lima, Ohio: n.p., 1977.

Weaver, H. C. "Morgan's Raid in Kentucky, Indiana, and Ohio, July 1863." In *Sketches of War History: Papers Read before the Ohio Commandery of the Military Order of the Loyal Legion of the United States*. Vol. 4. Cincinnati: R. Clark, 1888.

Wheeler, Joseph. "Bragg's Invasion of Kentucky." In *Battles and Leaders of the Civil War*, 3:1–25. New York: The Century Co., 1886.

Williamson, James J. *Mosby's Rangers: A Record of the Operations of the Forty-third Battalion, Virginia Cavalry*. New York: Ralph B. Kenyon Publishers, 1896.

Witherspoon, William. *Reminiscences of a Scout, Spy, and Soldier of Forrest's Cavalry*. Jackson, Miss.: McCowat-Mercer Printing Co., 1910.

Woodbury, Augustus. *Major General Ambrose E. Burnside and the Ninth Army Corps*. Providence, R.I.: Sidney S. Rider and Brother, 1867.

Wyeth, John A. *Life of General Forrest*. New York: Harper and Brothers, 1899.

Young, Bennett H. *Confederate Wizards of the Saddle, Being Reminiscences and Observations of One Who Rode with Morgan*. Boston: Chapple Publishing Co., 1914.

BOOKS

Allerdice, Bruce S. *More Generals in Grey*. Baton Rouge: Louisiana State University Press, 1995.

Ash, Stephen V. *Middle Tennessee Society Transformed, 1860–1870: War and Peace in the Upper South*. Baton Rouge: Louisiana State University Press, 1988.

———. *When the Yankees Came: Conflict and Chaos in the Occupied South, 1861–1865*. Chapel Hill: University of North Carolina Press, 1995.

Ashmore, Harry S. *Arkansas: A Bicentennial History*. New York: W. W. Norton and Co., 1978.

Asprey, Robert B. *The War in the Shadows: The Guerrilla in History, Two Thousand Years of the Guerrilla at War from Ancient Persia to the Present*. 2 vols. New York: William Morrow and Co., 1975. Reprint (2 vols. in 1), 1994.

Bailey, Anne J., and Daniel Sutherland, eds. *Civil War Arkansas: Beyond Battles and Leaders*. Fayetteville: University of Arkansas Press, 2000.

Bassford, Christopher. *Clausewitz in English: The Reception of Clausewitz in Britain and America, 1815–1945*. New York: Oxford University Press, 1994.

Bauer, Jack A. *The Mexican War: 1846–1848*. New York: Macmillan, 1974. Reprint, Lincoln: University of Nebraska Press, 1992.

Beach, William H. *The First New York (Lincoln) Cavalry*. New York: The Lincoln Cavalry Association, 1902.

Bedwell, Randall, ed. *May I Quote You General Forrest? Observations and Utterances from the South's Greatest Generals*. Nashville: Cumberland House, 1997.

Beers, Henry P. *The Confederacy: A Guide to the Archives of the Government of the Confederate States of America.* Washington, D.C.: National Archives and Records Administration, 1985.

Beller, Susan P. *Mosby and His Rangers: Adventures of the Grey Ghost.* Cincinnati: Betterway Books, 1992.

Beringer, Richard E., Herman Hattaway, Archer Jones, and William N. Still, Jr. *Why the South Lost the Civil War.* Athens, Ga.: University of Georgia Press, 1986.

Birtle, Andrew J. *U.S. Army Counterinsurgency and Contingency Operations Doctrine: 1860–1941.* Washington, D.C.: Government Printing Office, 1998.

Boatner, Mark. *The Civil War Dictionary.* New York: David McKay Co., 1959.

Boritt, Gabor S., ed. *The Gettysburg Nobody Knows.* New York: Oxford University Press, 1997.

———, ed. *Why the Confederacy Lost.* New York: Oxford University Press, 1997.

Brewer, James D. *The Raiders of 1862.* Westport, Conn.: Praeger, 1997.

Brown, Dee A. *The Bold Cavaliers: Morgan's 2nd Kentucky Cavalry Raiders.* Philadelphia: J. B. Lippincott Co., 1959.

Brownlee, Richard S. *Grey Ghosts of the Confederacy: Guerilla Warfare in the West.* Baton Rouge: Louisiana State University Press, 1958.

Butler, Lorine. *John Morgan and His Men.* Philadelphia: Dorrance and Co., 1960.

Callwell, C. E. *Small Wars: Their Principles and Practice.* 1899. Reprint, West Yorkshire, England: E. P. Ltd., 1976.

Castel, Albert. *General Sterling Price and the Civil War in the West.* Baton Rouge: Louisiana State University Press, 1968.

———. *William Clarke Quantrill: His Life and Times.* New York: F. Fell, 1962.

Catalfano-Serio, Chris. *The Effect of the Civil War on Ozark Culture.* Little Rock: Arkansas Endowment for the Humanities, 1979.

Catton, Bruce. *The Army of the Potomac.* 3 vols. Garden City, N.J.: Doubleday and Co., 1952–58.

Chambers, John W., ed. *The Oxford Companion to American Military History.* New York: Oxford University Press, 1999.

Christ, Mark K., ed. *Rugged and Sublime: The Civil War in Arkansas.* Fayetteville: University of Arkansas Press, 1994.

Clausewitz, Carl von. *On War.* Translated by J. J. Graham. London: N. Trubner and Co., 1873.

———. *On War.* Translated by Michael Howard and Peter Paret. Princeton, N.J.: Princeton University Press, 1976.

Cohen, Stan. *The Civil War in West Virginia: A Pictorial History.* Charleston, W.Va.: Pictorial Histories Publishing, 1976.

Cole, Garold L. *Civil War Eyewitnesses: An Annotated Bibliography of Books and Articles, 1955–1986.* Columbia: University of South Carolina Press, 1988.

Connelly, Thomas L. *The Army of the Heartland: The Army of Tennessee, 1861–1862.* Baton Rouge: Louisiana State University Press, 1967.

———. *Autumn of Glory: The Army of Tennessee, 1862–1865*. Baton Rouge: Louisiana State University Press, 1971.

———. *Civil War Tennessee: Battles and Leaders*. Knoxville: University of Tennessee Press, 1979.

Connelly, Thomas L., and Archer Jones. *The Politics of Command: Factions and Ideas in Confederate Strategy*. Baton Rouge: Louisiana State University Press, 1973.

Connelly, William E. *Quantrill and the Border Wars*. Cedar Rapids, Iowa: Torch Press, 1910.

Cooling, Benjamin F. *Fort Donelson's Legacy: War and Society in Kentucky and Tennessee, 1862–1863*. Knoxville: University of Tennessee Press, 1997.

———. *Symbol, Sword and Shield: Defending Washington during the Civil War*. Hamden, Conn.: Archon Books, 1975.

Coombe, Jack D. *Thunder along the Mississippi: The River Battles That Split the Confederacy*. New York: Sarpedon Publishers, 1996.

Cross, James E. *Conflict in the Shadows: The Nature and Politics of Guerrilla War*. Berkeley: University of California Press, 1982.

Cunliffe, Marcus. *Soldiers and Civilians: The Martial Spirit in America, 1775–1865*. Boston: Little, Brown and Co., 1968.

Current, Richard L. *Lincoln's Loyalists: Union Soldiers from the Confederacy*. Boston: Northeastern University Press, 1992.

———, ed. *Encyclopedia of the Confederacy*. 4 vols. New York: Simon and Schuster, 1993.

Davis, Edwin A. *Fallen Guidon: The Saga of Confederate General Jo Shelby's March to Mexico*. College Station: Texas A&M University Press, 1995.

Donald, David, ed. *Why the North Won the Civil War*. New York: Macmillan, 1971.

Donovan, Timothy P., Willard B. Gatewood, and Jeannie M. Whayne, eds. *The Governors of Arkansas: Essays in Political Biography*. Fayetteville: University of Arkansas Press, 1975.

Dornbusch, C. E., ed. *Military Bibliography of the Civil War*. New York: The New York Public Library, 1967.

Dougan, Michael B., ed. *Confederate Women of Arkansas*. Fayetteville, Ark.: M and M Press, 1973.

———. *Confederate Arkansas*. University: University of Alabama Press, 1976.

DuBose, John W. *General Joseph Wheeler and the Army of Tennessee*. New York: Neale Publishing Co., 1912.

Duncan, Richard R., ed. *Alexander Neil and the Last Shenandoah Valley Campaign*. Shippensburg, Pa.: White Mane Publishing Co., 1996.

Dupuy, R. Ernest. *Men of West Point: The First 150 Years of the United States Military Academy*. New York: William Sloane, 1951.

Dupuy, R. Ernest, and Trevor N. Dupuy. *Military Heritage of America*. New York: McGraw-Hill, 1956.

———, eds. *The Harper Encyclopedia of Military History*. New York: HarperCollins, 1993.

Dupuy, Trevor N., Curt Johnson, and David L. Bongard, eds. *The Harper Encyclopedia of Military Biography*. New York: HarperCollins, 1992.

Dyer, Frederick H. *A Compendium of the War of the Rebellion.* Des Moines, Iowa: Dyer Publishing Co., 1908.

Edwards, John N. *Noted Guerillas.* St. Louis: Bryan, Brand & Company, 1877.

———. *Shelby and His Men.* Cincinnati: Miami Printing and Publishing Company, 1867.

Evans, Clement A., ed. *Confederate Military History.* 12 vols. Atlanta: Confederate Publishing Co., 1899.

Everly, Elaine. P*reliminary Inventory of the Records of United States Army Commands, 1821–1920.* Washington, D.C.: National Archives and Records Service, 1973.

Faust, Patricia L., ed. *Historical Times Illustrated Encyclopedia of the Civil War.* New York: Harper Perennial, 1991.

Fellman, Michael. *Inside War: The Guerrilla Conflict in Missouri during the Civil War.* New York: Oxford University Press, 1989.

Ferguson, John L., ed. *Arkansas and the Civil War.* Little Rock: Arkansas Historical Commission, 1962.

Fishel, Edwin C. *The Secret War for the Union.* Boston: Houghton Mifflin, 1996.

Fisher, John F. *They Rode with Forrest and Wheeler: A Chronicle of Five Tennessee Brothers' Service in the Confederate Western Cavalry.* Jefferson, N.C.: McFarland and Co., 1995.

Fisher, Noel C. *War at Every Door: Partisan Politics and Guerrilla Violence in East Tennessee.* Chapel Hill: University of North Carolina Press, 1997.

Fisk, John. *The Mississippi Valley in the Civil War.* Cambridge, Mass.: Riverside Press, 1980.

Foote, Shelby. *The Civil War: A Narrative.* 3 vols. New York: Random House, 1958–74.

Fuller, J. F. C. *British Light Infantry in the Eighteenth Century.* London: Hutchinson and Co., 1925.

Gallagher, Gary W. *The Confederate War.* Cambridge, Mass.: Harvard University Press, 1997.

Gallaway, B. P. *The Ragged Rebel: A Common Soldier in W. H. Parson's Texas Cavalry.* Austin: University of Texas Press, 1988.

Gann, Lewis H. *Guerrillas in History.* Stanford, Calif.: Hoover Institute Press, 1971.

Goodrich, Thomas. *Black Flag: Guerrilla Warfare on the Western Border, 1861–1865.* Bloomington: Indiana University Press, 1995.

———. *Bloody Dawn: The Story of the Lawrence Massacre.* Kent, Ohio: Kent State University Press, 1991.

Granger, John T. *A Brief Biographical Sketch of the Life of Major General Grenville M. Dodge.* New York: Styles and Cash, 1893.

Griess, Thomas E., ed. *West Point Atlas for the American Civil War.* Wayne, N.J.: Avery Publishing Group, 1986.

Griffith, Paddy. *Military Thought in the French Army, 1815–51.* New York: Manchester University Press, 1989.

Grimsley, Mark. *The Hard Hand of War: Union Military Policy toward Southern Civilians.* New York: Cambridge University Press, 1995.

Hafendorfer, Kenneth A. *They Died by Twos and Tens: The Confederate Cavalry in the Kentucky Campaign of 1862.* Louisville, Ky.: K. H. Press, 1995.

Hanson, Gerald T. *The Historical Atlas of Arkansas.* Norman: University of Oklahoma Press, 1989.

Harrison, Lowell H. *The Civil War in Kentucky.* Lexington: University Press of Kentucky, 1975.

Hartigan, Richard Shelly. *Lieber's Code and the Law of War.* Chicago: Precedent Press, 1983.

Hartjie, Robert G. *Van Dorn: Life and Times of a Confederate General.* Nashville: Vanderbilt University Press, 1967.

Hattaway, Herman, and Archer Jones. *How the North Won: A Military History of the Civil War.* Chicago: University of Illinois Press, 1991.

Hearn, Chester G. *Ellet's Brigade: The Strangest Outfit of All.* Baton Rouge: Louisiana State University Press, 2000.

Heatwole, John L. *The Burning: Sheridan in the Shenandoah Valley.* Charlottesville, Va.: Rockville Publishing, 1998.

Henry, Robert S. *"First with the Most" Forrest.* New York: Bobbs-Merrill Co., 1944.

Higginbotham, Don. *The War of American Independence: Military Attitudes, Policies, and Practice, 1763–1789.* New York: Macmillan, 1971.

Hockersmith, Lorenzo D. *Morgan's Escape: A Thrilling Story of War Times.* Madisonville, Ky.: Glenn's Graphic Print, 1903.

Horn, Stanley F. *The Army of Tennessee: A Military History.* New York: Bobbs-Merrill Co., 1941.

———, ed. *Tennessee's War: 1861–1865.* Nashville: Tennessee Civil War Centennial Commission, 1965.

Horwitz, Lester V. *The Longest Raid of the War: Little Known and Untold Stories of Morgan's Raid into Kentucky, Indiana, and Ohio.* Cincinnati: Farmcourt Publishing, 1999.

Hubbell, John T., and James W. Geary, eds. *Biographical Dictionary of the Union: Northern Leaders of the Civil War.* Westport, Conn.: Greenwood Press, 1995.

Ingenthron, Elmo. *Borderland Rebellion: A History of the Civil War on the Arkansas-Missouri Border.* Branson, Mo.: The Ozarks Mountaineer, 1980.

Inscoe, John, and Gordon McKinney. *The Heart of Confederate Appalachia: Western North Carolina in the Civil War.* Chapel Hill: University of North Carolina Press, 2000.

Joes, Anthony James. *Modern Guerilla Insurgency.* Westport, Conn.: Praeger, 1992.

Johnson, J. Ambler. *The Civil War in Arkansas and Missouri.* Richmond: Virginia State Penitentiary, 1967.

Johnson, Ludwell H. *Red River Campaign: Politics and Cotton in the Civil War.* Baltimore: The Johns Hopkins Press, 1958. Reprint, Kent, Ohio: Kent State University Press, 1993.

Jomini, Antoine Henri. *The Art of War.* Translated by G. H. Mendell and W. P. Craighill. Philadelphia: J. B. Lippincott and Co., 1862. Reprint, Greenwood Press, 1985.

———. *Treatise on Grand Military Operations*. Translated by S. B. Holabird. 2 vols. New York: D. Van Nostrand, 1865.

Jones, Archer. *Confederate Strategy: From Shiloh to Vicksburg*. Baton Rouge: Louisiana State University Press, 1961.

Jones, Virgil C. *Gray Ghosts and Rebel Raiders*. New York: Holt, 1956.

———. *Ranger Mosby*. Chapel Hill: University of North Carolina Press, 1944.

Josephy, Alvin M., Jr. *The Civil War in the American West*. New York: Alfred A. Knopf, 1991.

Keen, Hugh C., and Horace Mewborn. *43rd Battalion Virginia Cavalry: Mosby's Command*. Lynchburg, Va.: H. E. Howard, 1993.

Keller, Allan. *Morgan's Raid*. Indianapolis: Bobbs-Merrill Co., 1961.

Kerby, Robert L. *Kirby Smith's Confederacy: The Trans-Mississippi South, 1863–1865*. New York: Columbia University Press, 1972.

Lackey, Walter F. *History of Newton County, Arkansas*. Point Lookout, Mo.: S of O Press, 1950.

Leach, Douglas E. *Arms for Empire: A Military History of the British Colonies in America, 1607–1763*. New York: Macmillan, 1973.

Leckie, Robert. *George Washington's War: The Saga of the American Revolution*. New York: HarperCollins, 1992.

Leckie, Robert. *None Died in Vain: The Saga of the American Civil War*. New York: HarperCollins, 1990.

Leslie, Edward E. *The Devil Knows How to Ride: The True Story of William Clark Quantrill and His Confederate Raiders*. New York: Random House, 1976.

Lieber, Francis. *Guerrilla Parties Considered with Reference to the Laws and Usages of War*. New York: D. Van Nostrand, 1862.

Liddell Hart, B. H. *Sherman: Soldier, Realist, American*. New York: Dodd, Meade and Co., 1929.

Livermore, Thomas L. *Numbers and Losses in the Civil War in America*. Boston: Houghton, 1901. Reprint, Bloomington: Indiana University Press, 1959.

Longacre, Edward G. *Mounted Raids of the Civil War*. New York: A. S. Barnes and Co., 1975.

Mahin, Dean B. *One War at a Time: The International Dimensions of the American Civil War*. Washington, D.C.: Brassey's, 1999.

Mahon, Michael G. *Shenandoah Valley, 1861–1865: The Destruction of the Granary of the Confederacy*. Mechanicsburg, Pa.: Stackpole Books, 1999.

Maness, Lonnie E. *An Untutored Genius: The Military Career of General Nathan Bedford Forrest*. Oxford, Miss.: Guild Bindery Press, 1990.

Martin, Robert Hugh. *A Boy of Old Shenandoah*. Edited by Carolyn Martin Rutherford. Parsons, W.Va.: McClain Printing Co., 1977.

Matheny, H. E. *Wood County, West Virginia in Civil War Times: With an Account of Guerrilla Warfare in the Little Kanawha Valley*. Parkersburg, W. Va.: Trans-Allegheny Books, 1987.

Mathes, Harvey J. *General Forrest*. New York: D. Appleton and Co., 1902.

McKenzie, Robert T. *One South or Many? Plantation Belt and Upcountry in Civil War-Era Tennessee*. New York: Cambridge University Press, 1994.

McMurry, Richard M. *Two Great Rebel Armies*. Chapel Hill: University of North Carolina Press, 1989.

McPherson, James. *The Battle Cry of Freedom: The Civil War Era*. New York: Oxford University Press, 1988.

McWhiney, Grady. *Braxton Bragg and Confederate Defeat*. New York: Columbia University Press, 1969.

McWhiney, Grady, and Perry D. Jameson. *Attack and Die: Civil War Military Tactics and the Southern Heritage*. University: University of Alabama Press, 1982.

Millis, Walter. *Arms and Men: A Study in American Military History*. New York: G. P. Putnam's Sons, 1956.

Monaghan, Jay. *Civil War on the Western Border*. Boston: Little, Brown Co., 1955.

Moneyhon, Carl H. *Arkansas and the New South, 1847–1929*. Fayetteville: University of Arkansas Press, 1997.

———. *Impact of the Civil War and Reconstruction on Arkansas: Persistence in the Midst of Ruin*. Baton Rouge: Louisiana State University Press, 1994.

Morrison, James L. *"The Best School in the World": West Point, the Pre-Civil War Years, 1833–1866*. Kent, Ohio: Kent State University Press, 1986.

Munden, Kenneth W., and Henry P. Beers. *The Union: A Guide to Federal Archives Relating to the Civil War*. Washington, D.C.: National Archives and Records Administration, 1986.

Neagles, James C. *Confederate Research Sources: A Guide to Archive Collections*. Salt Lake City: Ancestry Publishing, 1986.

Neal, Diane, and Thomas W. Kremm. *Lion of the South: General Thomas C. Hindman*. Macon, Ga.: Mercer University Press, 1993.

Oates, Stephen B. *Confederate Cavalry West of the River*. Austin: University of Texas Press, 1961.

O'Brien, Sean M. *Mountain Partisans: Guerrilla Warfare in the Southern Appalachians, 1861–1865*. Westport, Conn.: Praeger, 1999.

Paludan, Philip S. *A People's Contest: The Union and the Civil War, 1861–1865*. Lawrence: University of Kansas Press, 1996.

———. *Victims: A True Story of the Civil War*. Knoxville: University of Tennessee Press, 1981.

Patton, James W. *Unionism and Reconstruction in Tennessee, 1860–1869*. Gloucester, Mass.: P. Smith, 1934.

Perrett, Geoffrey. *A Country Made by War: From the Revolution to Vietnam, the Story of America's Rise to Power*. New York: Random House, 1989.

Phillips, Edward R. *The Lower Shenandoah Valley in the Civil War: The Impact of War Upon the Civilian Population and Civilian Institutions*. Lynchburg, Va.: H. E. Howard, 1993.

Quimby, Robert S. *The Background of Napoleonic War: The Theory of Military Tactics in Eighteenth-Century France*. New York: Columbia University Press, 1957.

Ramage, James. *Gray Ghost: The Life of John Singleton Mosby*. Lexington: University Press of Kentucky, 1999.

———. *Rebel Raider: The Life of General John Hunt Morgan*. Lexington: University Press of Kentucky, 1986.

Reader, Frank. *History of the Fifth West Virginia Cavalry*. New Brighton, Pa.: Daily News, 1890.

Roberts, Bobby, and Carl Moneyhon. *Portraits of Conflict: A Photographic History of Arkansas in the Civil War*. Fayetteville: University of Arkansas Press, 1987.

Rodenbough, Theo F., ed. *The Photographic History of the Civil War*. 10 vols. New York: Review of Reviews, 1911.

Rubin, Louis D. *Virginia, A Bicentennial History*. New York: W. W. Norton and Co., 1977.

Schultz, Diane. *Quantrill's War: The Life and Times of William Clarke Quantrill*. New York: St. Martin's Press, 1996.

Seitz, Don C. *Braxton Bragg: General of the Confederacy*. Columbia, S.C.: The State Co., 1924.

Sensing, Thurman. *Champ Ferguson: Confederate Guerrilla*. Nashville: Vanderbilt University Press, 1942.

Seymour, Digby G. *Divided Loyalties: Fort Sanders and the Civil War in East Tennessee*. Knoxville: University of Tennessee, 1963.

Shalhope, Robert E. *Sterling Price: Portrait of a Southerner*. Columbia, Mo.: University of Missouri Press, 1971.

Shanks, Henry T. *The Secession Movement in Virginia, 1847–1861*. Richmond, Va.: Garrett and Massie, 1934.

Shea, William L., and Earl J. Hess. *Pea Ridge: Civil War Campaign in the West*. Chapel Hill: University of North Carolina Press, 1992.

———. *War in the West: Pea Ridge and Prairie Grove*. Fort Worth, Tex.: Ryan Place Publishers, 1996.

Sheppard, Eric W. *Bedford Forrest: The Confederacy's Greatest Cavalryman*. New York: Dial Press, 1930.

Shy, John. *A People Numerous and Armed: Reflections on the Military Struggle for American Independence*. New York: Oxford University Press, 1976.

Siepel, Kevin H. *Rebel: The Life and Times of John Singleton Mosby*. New York: St. Martin's Press, 1983.

Smith, Sydney K. *Life, Army Record, and Public Service of Dr. Howard Smith*. Louisville, Ky.: Bradley and Gilbert Co., 1890.

Starnes, Gerald. *Forrest's Forgotten Horse Brigadier*. Bowie, Md.: Heritage Books, 1995.

Starr, Stephen. *Colonel Grenfell's Wars: The Life of a Soldier of Fortune*. Baton Rouge: Louisiana State University Press, 1971.

———. *The Union Cavalry in the Civil War*. 3 vols. Baton Rouge: Louisiana State University Press, 1979–85.

State Historical Society of Missouri. *A Guide to Civil War Collections, Western Historical Manuscript Collection*. Kansas City: State Historical Society of Missouri, 1990.

Steele, Philip W., and Steve Cottrell. *Civil War in the Ozarks*. Gretna, La.: Pelican Publishing Co., 1994.

Summers, Festus P. *The Baltimore and Ohio in the Civil War.* New York: G. P. Putnam, 1939.

Sutherland, Daniel. *Guerrillas, Unionists, and Violence on the Confederate Homefront.* Fayetteville: University of Arkansas Press, 1999.

Sutton, Bob E. *Early Days in the Ozarks.* Eureka Springs, Ark.: Echo Press, 1950.

Swiggett, Howard. *The Rebel Raider: A Life of John Hunt Morgan.* Indianapolis: Bobbs-Merrill Co., 1934.

Taylor, David L. *With Bowie Knives and Pistols: Morgan's Raid in Indiana.* Lexington, Ind.: TaylorMade Write, 1993.

Thomas, David Y. *Arkansas in War and Reconstruction, 1861–1874.* Little Rock: United Daughters of the Confederacy, Arkansas Division, 1926.

———. *The Confederate State Government in Arkansas.* Dallas: Southwestern Political and Social Science Association, 1925.

Thomas, Edison H. *John Hunt Morgan and His Raiders.* Lexington: University Press of Kentucky, 1975.

Thomas, Emory M. *Bold Dragoon: The Life of J. E. B. Stuart.* New York: Harper and Row, 1986.

———. *The Confederacy as a Revolutionary Experience.* Englewood Cliffs, N.J.: Prentice-Hall, 1971.

———. *The Confederate Nation: 1861–1865.* New York: Harper and Row, 1979.

Thompson, George H. *Arkansas and Reconstruction: The Influence of Geography, Economics, and Personality.* Port Washington, N.Y.: Kennikat Press, 1976.

Townsend, William H. *Lincoln and the Bluegrass: Slavery and Civil War in Kentucky.* Lexington: University of Kentucky Press, 1955.

Trotter, William R. *Bushwhackers: The Civil War in North Carolina, The Mountains.* Winston-Salem, N.C.: John F. Blair Publishers, 1988.

Tse-tung, Mao. *Mao Tse-tung on Guerrilla Warfare.* Translated by Samuel B. Griffith. New York: Praeger Publishers, 1961.

Urwin, Gregory J. W. *Custer Victorious: The Civil War Battles of General George Armstrong Custer.* London: Associated University Presses, 1983.

Urwin, Gregory J. W., and Roberta Fagan, eds. *Custer and His Times: Book Three.* Conway: University of Central Arkansas Press, 1987.

Vandiver, Frank E. *Their Tattered Flags: The Epic of the Confederacy.* New York: Harper and Row, 1970.

Warner, Ezra. *Generals in Blue: Lives of Union Commanders.* Baton Rouge: Louisiana State University Press, 1964.

———. *Generals in Gray: Lives of Confederate Commanders.* Baton Rouge: Louisiana State University Press, 1959.

Weigley, Russell F. *The American Way of War: A History of United States Military Strategy and Policy.* New York: Macmillan Publishing Co., 1973.

———. *Eisenhower's Lieutenants: The Campaigns of France and Germany, 1944–1945.* Bloomington: Indiana University Press, 1981.

Wiley, Bell I. *The Life of Billy Yank, the Common Soldier of the Union.* New York: Bobbs-Merrill, 1952.

———. *The Life of Johnny Reb, the Common Soldier of the Confederacy.* New York: Bobbs-Merrill, 1943.

———. *The Plain People of the Confederacy.* Baton Rouge: Louisiana State University Press, 1943.

———. *The Road to Appomattox.* Memphis: Memphis State College, 1956.

Wertz, Jay, and Edwin C. Bearss. *Smithsonian's Great Battles and Battlefields of the Civil War.* New York: William Morrow and Co., 1997.

Williams, Kenneth P. *Lincoln Finds a General: A Military Study of the Civil War.* 5 vols. New York: Macmillan, 1949–59.

Williams, T. Harry. *Lincoln and His Generals.* New York: Knopf, 1952.

Wills, Brian S. *A Battle from the Start: The Life of Nathan Bedford Forrest.* New York: HarperCollins, 1992.

Woods, James M. *Rebellion and Realignment: Arkansas' Road to Secession.* Fayetteville: University of Arkansas Press, 1987.

Wyeth, John A. *Life of General Forrest.* New York: Harper and Brothers, 1899.

ARTICLES AND CHAPTERS

Bailey, Anne J. "The Mississippi Marine Brigade: Fighting Rebel Guerrillas on Western Waters." *Military History of the Southwest* 22, no. 1 (spring 1992): 34–41.

Barnes, Kenneth C. "The Williams Clan: Mountain Farmers and Union Fighters in North Central Arkansas." In *Civil War Arkansas: Beyond Battles and Leaders,* edited by Daniel Sutherland and Anne Bailey, 155–76. Fayetteville: University of Arkansas Press, 2000. First published in *Arkansas Historical Quarterly* 52, no. 3 (autumn 1993): 286–317.

Bearss, Edwin C. "The Federal Struggle to Hold Fort Smith." *Arkansas Historical Quarterly* 24, no. 1 (spring 1965): 149–79.

———. "General William Steele Fights to Hold Out Northwest Arkansas." *Arkansas Historical Quarterly* 25, no. 1 (spring 1966): 36–93.

Black, John H. "Powder, Lead and Cold Steel: Campaigning in the Lower Shenandoah Valley with the Twelfth Pennsylvania Cavalry—The Civil War Letters of John H. Black," edited by David J. Coles and Stephen D. Engle. *Magazine of the Jefferson County Historical Society* 55 (December 1989): 17–114.

Boatner, Mark. "Tullahoma Campaign." In *The Civil War Dictionary,* edited by Mark Boatner, 850–51. New York: David McKay Co., 1959.

Bowen, Don R. "Guerrilla War in Western Missouri, 1862–1865: Historical Extensions of the Relative Deprivation Hypothesis." *Comparative Studies in Society and History* 19 (January 1977): 30–51.

———. "Quantrill, James, Younger, et al.: Leadership in a Guerilla Movement, Missouri, 1861–1865." *Military Affairs* 41 (February 1977): 42–48.

Castel, Albert. "The Guerrilla War." *Civil War Times Illustrated* 34 (October 1974): 1–50.

Chalmers, James R. "Forrest and His Campaigns." *Southern Historical Society Papers* 7 (1879): 451–86.

DeBlack, Thomas. "1863: 'We Must Stand or Fight Alone.'" In *Rugged and Sublime: The Civil War in Arkansas*, edited by Mark K. Christ, 59–104. Fayetteville: University of Arkansas Press, 1994.

Delmuth, David O. "Federal Military Activities in Northwest Arkansas." *Arkansas Historical Quarterly* 38, no. 2 (summer 1979): 131–45

Dougan, Michael. "Life in Confederate Arkansas." *Arkansas Historical Quarterly* 31, no. 1 (spring 1972): 15–35.

Eno, Clara B. "Activities of Women of Arkansas during the War between the States." *Arkansas Historical Quarterly* 3, no. 1 (spring 1944): 4–27.

Fagan, Roberta E. "Custer at Front Royal: 'A Horror of the War'?" In *Custer and His Times: Book Three*, edited by Gregory J. W. Urwin and Roberta E. Fagan, 17–81. Conway: University of Central Arkansas Press, 1987.

Gates, John N. "Indians and Insurrectos: The U.S. Army's Experience with Insurgency." In *In Defense of the Republic: Readings in American Military History*, edited by David C. Skaggs and Robert S. Browning, 177–83. Belmont, Calif.: Wadsworth Publishing Company, 1991. First published in *Parameters: The Journal of the U.S. Army War College* 13, no. 1 (March 1983): 59–68.

Holladay, Florence E. "The Powers of the Confederate Trans-Mississippi Department, 1863–1865." *Southwestern Historical Quarterly* 21 (July 1917–April 1918): 229–98, 333–59.

Huff, Leo E. "Guerillas, Jayhawkers, and Bushwhackers in Northern Arkansas during the Civil War, 1861–1865." *Arkansas Historical Quarterly* 24, no. 1 (spring 1965): 127–48.

Hughes, Michael A. "Wartime Gristmill Destruction in Northwest Arkansas and Military Farm Colonies." In *Civil War Arkansas: Beyond Battles and Leaders*, edited by Anne J. Bailey and Daniel Sutherland, 31–46. Fayetteville: University of Arkansas Press, 2000. First published in *Arkansas Historical Quarterly* 46, no. 2 (summer 1987): 167–86.

Ingenthron, Elmo. "Silas Claborn Turnbo, An Early Historian of the Upper White River Valley." *White River Valley Historical Quarterly* 4, no. 1 (fall 1970): 1–4.

Kerby, Robert L. "Why the Confederacy Lost." *The Review of Politics* 35 (July 1973): 326–43.

"The Killing of Lieutenant Meigs of General Sheridan's Staff—Proof That It Was Done in Fair Combat." *Southern Historical Society Papers* 9 (1881): 77–78.

Mackey, Robert R. "Bushwhackers, Provosts and Tories: The Guerrilla War in Arkansas." In *Guerrillas, Unionists, and Violence on the Confederate Homefront*, edited by Daniel E. Sutherland, 171–86. Fayetteville: University of Arkansas Press, 1999.

Merritt, Wesley. "Sheridan in the Shenandoah Valley." In *Battles and Leaders of the Civil War*, edited by Robert Johnson and Clarence Buel, 4:535–48. New York: Century Co., 1884–88. Reprint, New York: Random House, 2001.

Mitchell, Reid. "The Perseverance of the Soldiers." In *Why the Confederacy Lost*, edited by Gabor S. Boritt, 109–32. New York: Oxford University Press, 1992.

Moneyhon, Carl H. "Disloyalty and Class Consciousness in Southwestern Arkansas, 1862–1865." *Arkansas Historical Quarterly* 52, no. 3 (autumn 1993): 223–43.

Neal, Diane, and Thomas W. Kremm. "An Experiment in Collective Security: The Union Army's Use of Armed Colonies in Arkansas." *Military History of the Southwest* 20, no. 2 (fall 1990): 169–82.

Richter, Wendy. "The Impact of the Civil War on Hot Springs, Arkansas." *Arkansas Historical Quarterly* 43, no. 2 (summer 1984): 125–42.

Roberts, Bobby L. "General T. C. Hindman and the Trans-Mississippi District." *Arkansas Historical Quarterly* 32, no. 4 (winter 1973): 297–311.

Sharp, Arthur G. "War on the River: The Mississippi Marine Brigade at the Battle of Lake Chicot." *Civil War Times Illustrated* 21, no. 6 (October 1982): 18–23.

Shea, William L. "1862: A Continual Thunder." In *Rugged and Sublime: The Civil War in Arkansas*, edited by Mark K. Christ, 21–58. Fayetteville: University of Arkansas Press, 1994.

———. "A Semi-Savage State: The Image of Arkansas in the Civil War." In *Civil War Arkansas: Beyond Battles and Leaders*, edited by Anne J. Bailey and Daniel E. Sutherland, 85–100. Fayetteville: University of Arkansas Press, 2000. First published in *Arkansas Historical Quarterly* 48 (winter 1989): 309–28.

Stone, Jayme Milsap. "Brother against Brother: The Winter Skirmishes along the Arkansas River: 1864–1865." In *Civil War Arkansas*, edited by Anne J. Bailey and Daniel E. Sutherland, 195–212. Fayetteville: University of Arkansas Press, 2000.

Sutherland, Daniel E. "Guerrillas: The Real War in Arkansas." In *Civil War Arkansas: Beyond Battles and Leaders*, edited by Anne J. Bailey and Daniel E. Sutherland, 133–54. Fayetteville: University of Arkansas Press, 2000. First published in *Arkansas Historical Quarterly* 52, no. 3 (autumn 1993): 257–85.

———. "Sideshow No Longer: A Historiographical Review of the Guerrilla War." *Civil War History* 46, no. 1 (March 2000): 5–18

"Was Lieutenant Meigs Killed in Fair Combat?" *Southern Historical Society Papers* 9 (1881): 190.

Wert, Jeffry D. "Western Virginia, Union Department of." In *Historical Times Illustrated Encyclopedia of the Civil War*, edited by Patricia L. Faust, 815. New York: Harper Perennial, 1986.

Williams, Burton J. "Missouri State Depredations in Arkansas: A Case of Restitution." *Arkansas Historical Quarterly* 23, no. 2 (summer 1964): 343–52.

Williams, T. Harry. "The Military Leadership of North and South." In *Why the North Won the Civil War*, edited by David Donald, 16–54. New York: Macmillan, 1971.

Wolseley, Viscount. "Lieutenant General N. B. Forrest, Lord Wolseley's Estimate of the Man and the Soldier." *Southern Historical Society Papers* 20 (1892): 325–33.

UNPUBLISHED THESES AND DISSERTATIONS

Barksdale, Ethelbert. "Semi-Regular and Irregular Warfare in the Civil War." Ph.D. diss., University of Texas, Austin, Texas, 1941.

Beamer, Carl. "Grey Ghostbusters: Eastern Theater Union Counter-Guerrilla Operations in the Civil War." Ph.D. diss., Ohio State University, 1988.

Bolden, Benjamin. "So Long as Strangers Are the Rulers: General Frederick Steele and the Politics of Wartime Reconstruction in Arkansas." Master's thesis, University of Arkansas, Fayetteville, 1992.

Chapman, Jesse L. "The Ellet Family and Riverine Warfare in the West, 1861–1865." Master's thesis, Old Dominion University, 1985.

Fisher, Noel C. "The Other War: Guerrilla Warfare and Pacification in East Tennessee, 1861–1865." Master's thesis, Ohio State University, 1987.

Kirkby, Michael Ross. "Partisan and Counterpartisan Activity in Northern Virginia." Master's thesis, University of Georgia, 1977.

Lighthall, Laurence J. "John Hunt Morgan: A Confederate Asset or Liability?" Master's thesis, Georgia State University, 1996.

Mackey, Robert R. "A Self-Inflicted Wound: The Confederacy's Guerrilla War in Arkansas, 1862–1865." Master's thesis, Texas A&M University, 1997.

Martin, James B. "'Have Them Shot at Once': Guerrilla Warfare in Kentucky, 1863–1865." Master's thesis, University of Texas, Austin, 1986.

Matheny, Michael. "The Impact of the Frontier on American Military Methods from 1755 to 1783." Master's thesis, University of Dayton, 1972.

Royston, A. Kendall. "The Legal Mind Fights the Illegal War: An Examination and Evaluation of Colonel John Singleton Mosby's Partisan Strategy and Tactics while in Command of the Forty-Third Battalion, Virginia Cavalry, 1863–1865." Master's thesis, George Mason University, 1980.

Scarborough, Paul G. "The Impact of the John Morgan Raid in Indiana and Ohio." Master's thesis, Miami University, 1955.

Smith, Robert F. "Confederate Attempts to Influence Public Opinion in Arkansas, 1861–1865." Master's thesis, University of Arkansas, Fayetteville, 1953.

Tripp, Richard L. "Cavalry Reconnaissance in the Army of Northern Virginia: J. E. B. Stuart's Cavalry, 1861–1864." Master's thesis, Duke University, 1967.

INDEX